Managing
IT Professionals in
the Internet Age

Pak Yoong
Victoria University of Wellington, New Zealand

Sid Huff
Victoria University of Wellington, New Zealand

IDEA GROUP PUBLISHING

Hershey • London • Melbourne • Singapore

Acquisitions Editor:	Michelle Potter
Development Editor:	Kristin Roth
Senior Managing Editor:	Jennifer Neidig
Managing Editor:	Sara Reed
Copy Editor:	Larissa Vinci
Typesetter:	Cindy Consonery
Cover Design:	Lisa Tosheff
Printed at:	Yurchak Printing Inc.

Published in the United States of America by
    Idea Group Publishing (an imprint of Idea Group Inc.)
    701 E. Chocolate Avenue
    Hershey PA 17033
    Tel: 717-533-8845
    Fax: 717-533-8661
    E-mail: cust@idea-group.com
    Web site: http://www.idea-group.com

and in the United Kingdom by
    Idea Group Publishing (an imprint of Idea Group Inc.)
    3 Henrietta Street
    Covent Garden
    London WC2E 8LU
    Tel: 44 20 7240 0856
    Fax: 44 20 7379 0609
    Web site: http://www.eurospanonline.com

Library of Congress Cataloging-in-Publication Data

Managing IT professionals in the Internet age / Pak Yoong and Sid Huff, editors.
     p. cm.
    Summary: "This book explores the ways in which the work life of IT professionals - from the perspectives of both the individual IT worker, and managers of such workers - has had to change and adapt to the Internet Age"--Provided by publisher.
    ISBN 1-59140-917-9 -- ISBN 1-59140-918-7 (softcover) -- ISBN 1-59140-919-5 (ebook)
 1. Information technology--Management. 2. Personnel management. I. Yoong, Pak, 1945- II. Huff, Sidney Laurence.
  HD30.2.M3643 2006
  004.068'3--dc22
                              2006010097

British Cataloguing in Publication Data
A Cataloguing in Publication record for this book is available from the British Library.

Managing IT Professionals in the Internet Age

Table of Contents

Section II: Professional Development of IT Professionals

Section III: Management of IT Professionals

Preface

The history of computing in organizations began in the early 1950s, with the first commercialization of computing technology. Over the past 50-plus years, we have witnessed amazing growth and change. Huge and very expensive mainframe computers gave way to minicomputers in the 1970s, then to personal computers in the 1980s, to networks of computers, and most recently to a world where computer chips exist inside nearly all everyday appliances, and networked devices are *de rigueur*.

In parallel with the changes in computing technology, the professionals who develop, implement, and maintain the technology in our organizations have also experienced many changes–in the tools they use, in the nature of the work they do, in expectations others have of them, and so forth. The prototypical early computer professionals were either engineers or were self-trained; they wore white lab coats and carried clipboards, and worked mainly in "machine rooms." Those were the wild west days, when it seemed that computers made anything possible. The IT professionals of the day were viewed as exceptional individuals, able to understand the inner mysteries of the "electronic brains," and to coax those complex machines into performing useful work. If they were programmers (most were), they probably wrote code in assembly language. They were often seen as a priesthood, functioning with few rules or principles of good practice; they were making it up as they went along.

During the 1960s, it started to become clear that the role of computers in organizations was becoming more and more important, and that formal training in computing was needed. This first led to the rise of computer science programmes in universities and in polytechs and colleges. Some time later, starting in the 1970s, information systems (originally called data processing or MIS), as a subject of study in business schools, also began to emerge. The emergence of the academic fields of computer science, and information systems, began to inject a greater degree of codification and standardization into the practice of computing. Slowly but surely, this changed the nature of the IT profession, reducing the extent of independence and freedom to do things however one wished, and increasing the necessity of following "best practice," of teamwork, of following someone else's rules.

As computer science and information systems academic programmes grew and prospered in the 1960s and 1970s, research into computing *per se*, and into the application of computers in organizations burgeoned as well. Nearly all of this research was directed toward the computing artefact and its application. However beginning in the early 1970s, a few researchers began to formally study the IT profession itself. One of the first people to apply serious research to what was then referred to as "computer personnel" was professor Daniel Couger at the University of Colorado. Couger observed that many IT professionals seemed to march to a different drummer, and he was curious about what it was that motivated these individuals—what made them tick? His early studies of programmer motivation, conducted jointly with his colleague Robert Zawacki, applied the Hackman-Oldham job diagnostic survey tool, and soundly confirmed certain commonly held suspicions. They showed that the computer personnel (programmers and systems analysts) exhibited an astoundingly high levels of *need for growth*, and equally astounding low levels of *need for social interaction*. These studies achieved two important results. First, they confirmed some of the widely held stereotypes regarding "computer people" of the day—socially challenged nerds more comfortable writing programmes than interacting with other people. But more importantly, their work helped to legitimize and popularize the study of computer personnel as important and worthwhile, and interesting! Their early findings that IT professionals, as a group, were strikingly different in certain ways from other professional groups signalled the importance of developing a better understanding of all aspects of the profession. If, for example, companies had a better understanding of what motivated their programmers and analysts, they could put in place HR systems designed specifically to keep such people happy and fulfilled in their work. This would presumably lead to more productive employees, and lower turnover (high levels of job turnover among IT professionals has long been recognized as a serious problem).

More recently, the rise of the Internet has seen a new wave of changes inflicted upon the IT profession. Following the advent of the worldwide web in the early 1990s, the importance of the Web and the Internet to organizations of all types and sizes has grown remarkably. New communication channels including e-mail, instant messaging, VoIP, electronic commerce, supply chain integration, e-learning, e-government…the ways in which the Internet is impacting organizations continues to grow. From the perspective of IT professionals today, the worldwide Web has become *the* platform upon which new information systems are developed. This requires a strong understanding of new technologies: programming for the Web is different in many ways from "old fashioned" programming. But equally important is the impact the Internet and the Web have had upon the relevance and role of IT professionals in organizations today. Once a company begins to engage in e-business, the computing stakes rise dramatically. It's one thing if an internal system fails, and quite another if a system which connects a company to its customers or suppliers fails. For example, in June 2004, the Royal Bank of Canada, Canada's largest bank, experienced a massive system failure, which impacted its ability to process payrolls–not its own payroll, but the payrolls of many of its customers, including the Ontario government! Millions of transactions, from direct pay deposits to bill payments, were affected during the outage. RBC had to deploy over 200 staff to work round-the-clock shifts over a period of days to fix the problem. For the bank's brand-new CIO, this was truly a trial by fire. A new term has been coined, only semi-facetiously, to reflect the importance of such events: MTCA, or "Mean Time to CEO Awareness." The shorter the time it takes for the problem to elbow its way onto the CEO's radar screen, the more serious it is, and the more likely that some IT professional's head is going to be on the block.

The presence of the Internet has also resulted in new non-technical demands being placed on IT professionals. Because Web-based e-business systems *become* the business—as seen by the firm's customers, suppliers or partners— the people who design, build, and implement those systems need to have a much stronger understanding of the business itself than was the case in the past. No longer can an IT professional "hide" from developing a broad and deep understanding of the nature of the business he or she works in. On top of the need for IT workers to understand their businesses better comes an ever-increasing rate of technological change. IT staff in years past revelled in the fact that change in the IT profession was rapid: they enjoyed the challenge of keeping up with new technologies in particular. However today the rate of change is even greater, to the point that even the keenest IT professional finds it impossible to stay current across the breadth of technologies that populate the leading edge. That, and the greater degree of exposure that firms have to their IT systems, mentioned earlier, has seen stress levels among IT workers skyrocket in recent years.

Another factor which is exerting a major impact on the IT profession is outsourcing, and especially offshoring (shifting some IT work to firms based in places such as India or eastern Europe). Again, the Internet has made this economically viable. While some of the early prognostications were gloomy, in fact the impacts of IT outsourcing are by no means all negative for IT professionals. Concentrating more IT development work in the service-providing firms rather than user firms results in a higher degree of professionalism and overall quality, which is good for the user firms and also good for the IT professionals. Offshoring low-level IT work such as mundane programming to a low-wage country means that the work that remains is the more challenging, and more interesting and creative conceptual work that cannot be done offshore. Nevertheless, outsourcing and offshoring is not going away, and IT professionals in developed countries need to adapt to the new world left in its wake.

Because so many seismic shifts have occurred in the world of the IT professional during the past decade–since the rise of the Internet–we felt it was timely for a book that would, drawing upon rigorous and careful research, explore these shifts. We have organized the material in this book into three sections: gender and work-life balances, professional development of IT professional, and management of IT professionals.

Section I, *Gender and Work-Life Balance Issues*, includes three chapters, two of which address the issue of women in the IT profession, and the third the issue of work-life balance of IT professionals. In *Managing New Zealand Women in IT*, Keri Logan and Barbara Crump (Massey University, New Zealand) explore the reasons behind the low participation rate of women in IT professions. Drawing on data from two recent studies, they examine barriers such as the glass ceiling, salaries, and work-life balance issues, which affect women's participation rate and advancement opportunities in IT. In Chapter II, *Gender and the Information Technology Workforce: Issues of Theory and Practice,*" Eileen Trauth and Jeria Quesenberry (The Pennsylvania State University, USA) argue that managers would benefit from the availability of an appropriate theory as a basis for better understanding the data regarding women in the IT profession. Such a theory would provide a firmer foundation for taking appropriate action than that provided by speculation and guesswork. They present and elaborate one such theory in this chapter. Chapter III, by Helen Richardson and Darrell Bennetts (The Open Polytechnic of New Zealand), explores the issue of work-life balance within the IT profession. The chapter is divided into two sections. In the first section, the authors present a top-down examination of the sociology of a typical IT worker. In the second section the authors explore the concept of emotional intelligence, its interpretation in the case of IT professionals, and the implications for "emotional self-management" by IT workers.

Section II, *Professional Development of IT Professionals*, includes four chapters. In Chapter IV, Eugene Cash (New Zealand Food Safety Authority), Pak Yoong, and Sid Huff (Victoria University of Wellington, New Zealand) focus on the changes that have taken place in the competencies required of IT professionals, in light of the economic and organizational changes wrought by the Internet. They present a three-level cascading model involving business changes, project changes, and finally competency changes. In Chapter V, *Staffing Electronic Commerce Projects: Framework for Developing Appropriate Skill Sets*, Fred Niederman and Xiaorui Hu (Saint Louis University, USA) develop and illustrate a conceptual framework as an extension and reformulation of several of the current "fit" theories of human resource management. Chapter VI includes a case study by Bernd Carsten Stahl and Chris Wood (De Montfort University, UK) in which they look at the challenge of teaching ethical issues in an undergraduate IT programme. Stahl and Wood describe an approach they developed in the context of their case study. The final chapter in this section, Chapter VII, by Ani Patke and Tony Hooper (Victoria University of Wellington, New Zealand), considers skills needed by IT professionals, in this case by studying the perceptions of undergraduate IT students as well as recent graduates of tertiary IT programmes.

Finally, Section III of the book, *Management of IT Professionals*, includes five chapters. Chapter VIII, by Jerry Luftman and Rajkumar Kempaiah (Stevens Institute of Technology, USA) is titled *Managing IT Professionals: Human Resource Considerations*. In it the authors draw on data from a variety of recent surveys to paint a broad picture of the current situation and future challenges within the IT profession. It particularly addresses the question of retaining IT talent, and also the issue of stress in the IT workplace. Chapter IX, by Eugene Kaluzniacky (University of Winnipeg, Canada), titled *Increasing the Effectiveness of IT Management through Psychological Awareness*," again raises the issue of stress in the IT workplace, and, drawing on them Myers-Briggs type indicator (MBTI) framework, proposes "multidimensional psychological awareness" as a way of addressing that problem. Chapter X, *The Impact of Agile Methods on Managing IT Professionals*, is contributed by Mark Tolman, Fiona Darroch, and Mustafa Ally (University of Southern Queensland, Australia). Here the authors sketch the development of "agile programming" methodology, and explore its impact on organizational culture, project management, and the management of IT professionals. Chapter XI, *Cultural Diversity Challenges: Issues for Managing Globally Distributed Knowledge Workers in Software Development*, comes from Haiyan Huang and Eileen Trauth (The Pennsylvania State University, USA). The focus of this chapter is on the cultural diversity challenges of managing globally distributed knowledge workers engaging in software development work. The ubiquity of the Internet has made global distribution of software development work commonplace. However, this has led to a number of unanticipated challenges, many of which relate to cultural differences. The authors propose a framework within which cross-cultural aspects globally distributed IT personnel may be fruitfully examined. Finally, Chapter XII is titled *The Journey to New Lands: Utilizing the Global IT Workforce through Offshore-Insourcing*, by Subrata Chakrabarty (Texas A&M University, USA). Offshore insourcing of IT work refers to the idea of a company setting up its own IT department or subsidiary in another country, and then channelling the company's IT work to it. In this chapter, the authors explore this phenomenon in the greater context of an economic analysis of IT work.

Acknowledgments

We would like to acknowledge the help of all involved in the collation and review process of the book, without whose support the project could not have been satisfactorily completed.

Most of the authors of the chapters included in this book also served as referees for articles written by other authors. Thanks go to all those who provided constructive and comprehensive reviews.

Special thanks also go to the publishing team at Idea Group Inc. In particular to Kristin Roth and Jan Travers, who continuously prodded via e-mail to keep the project on schedule. Their contributions throughout the whole process from inception of the initial idea to final publication have been invaluable.

In closing, we wish to thank all of the authors for their insights and excellent contributions to this book.

Drs. Pak Yoong and Sid Huff
School of Information Management
Victoria University of Wellington
New Zealand
December 2005

Section I:

Gender and Work-Life Balance Issues

Chapter I

Managing New Zealand Women in IT

Keri A. Logan, Massey University, New Zealand

Barbara Crump, Massey University, New Zealand

Abstract

This chapter discusses workplace attitudes and policies that continue to affect women's participation, retention, and promotion in the information technology (IT) workforce. It draws on data collected from two qualitative studies of New Zealand women working in the industry. The findings reveal that there are some distinct differences in the way in which males and females operate in the workplace, and that women's values and different work practices are often not taken into account by management. Managers of IT professionals who recognise the subtleties of the gendered culture of the IT work environment and who develop and implement equitable policies and strategies will be rewarded by a creative, innovative, and productive workforce.

Introduction

The information rich, technology-driven economies of developed and developing countries require a highly skilled, adaptable, and innovative information technology (IT) workforce. A diverse workforce, constituted of people of different ethnicities, abilities and gender, is recognised as contributing to a more creative, innovative organisation with "business case" benefits that include reducing the costs of labour turnover, improving the understanding of the needs of current customers and enhancing the organisation's reputation and image (European Union, n.d.; Yasbek, 2004).

Unfortunately, the technology sector of many Western industrialised countries is male dominated with women forming a minority in the skilled and highly skilled computing workforce, especially at the senior level. Males hold the majority of the highest paying, leading-edge jobs and females are concentrated in the lowest areas in terms of skill, status, mobility, and pay (Bernstein, 1999; Edwards, 1994; Panteli, Stack, & Ramsay, 2001). According to figures published by the University of Cambridge in 2004, the number of women in the IT industry in England declined. Between 1999 and 2003, female participation had halved—from 109,900 to 53,700 (Nash, 2005). There is a similar low participation rate in New Zealand. Moreover, salaries for female IT workers are reported as being less than their male counterparts working at the same level with equivalent skills, qualifications, and experience.

The industry is noted for its above-average turnover (Bort, 2003; Gartner Group, 2000) and attracting and retaining women, in particular, is a problem. Some progressive managers, concerned about the IT labour shortage and low female participation rate, have implemented policies and strategies aimed at promoting women and other minorities within the organisation. The initiatives include formal mentoring schemes, targeted training, as well as a variety of work/life balance initiatives. These policies have been found to positively affect business performance in improving staff retention rates, thus saving businesses money on recruitment costs, attracting better recruits, and minimising stress (Yasbek, 2004).

The question of why there is such a low female participation rate in the IT industry in Western countries has been addressed by a number of researchers in recent decades. Explanations include the glass ceiling that restricts advancement to top executive positions, the more subtle gender differences in work experiences such as receiving supervisory career support, being included in the informal communication network and fitting into an established male-dominated computing culture (Panteli et al., 2001; Peters, Lane, Rees, & Samuels, 2002). Harvard University's President, Larry Summers, called for "rigorous and careful" thinking to explain the gender gap and said the most likely explanations are that "(1) women are just not so interested as men in making the sacrifices required by high-powered jobs, (2) men may have more 'intrinsic aptitude' for high-level science, and (3) women may be victims of old-fashioned discrimination." He said that "In my view, their importance probably ranks in exactly the order that I just described" (Ripley, 2005, p. 45).

Larry Summer's belief that women "are just not so interested" may have some validity given that the majority work in a male-dominated industry where policies and the dominant cultural norms cater to male interests and needs. The reasons why they may appear "just not so interested," however, are because they are faced with dichotomous imperatives. While the notion of working mothers is accepted and endorsed in some countries, the care of children is still the prime responsibility of women (Palermo, 2004). Women still undertake the majority (if not all) of the unpaid household duties and are the main caregivers of elderly parents. They juggle the work/home nexus and they bring to their jobs a different set of values, priorities and goals as well as a different approach to work. IT management need to recognise, when implementing work/life balance, development and incentive policies, that there are differences in the criteria women deem critical to taking, and continuing, a job as compared with men (Desmond, 2002).

The research findings that this chapter presents focuses on workplace attributes and policies that have been found in studies to be consistently rated higher by women than by men at statistically significant levels (Desmond, 2002). These relate to barriers associated with the glass ceiling, salaries and work/life balance issues and they have implications for managing and retaining IT professional women in this Internet age. The results are based on two recent studies that aimed to evaluate current New Zealand IT employment practices that affect women's participation and advancement opportunities.

The New Zealand Research

Ninety-five women working in middle to senior computing positions in New Zealand participated in the two studies. Their computing jobs were across occupational sectors that include businesses focused on software development as well as IT occupations in non-computing industries such as a programmer in an insurance company and their salaries ranged from $30,000 to $100,000 plus.

The first study was completed in 2000 where 20 Wellington women described their entry to the industry and their perceptions and experiences of learning and working in their different environments (Crump & Logan, 2000). The results from this qualitative research, together with the IT literature, guided the objectives and development of the semi-structured interview questions for the second, and more recent, 2004 national study. The interpretive analysis was informed by Trauth's (2002) Theory of Individual Differences. The larger national study was funded by a grant from the Society for Research on Women and supported by the New Zealand Computer Society and the Women in Technology organisation. They advertised details of the study on their Web sites that resulted in 75 women from the four main cities participating in the audio taped, semi-structured interviews that lasted between 45-80 minutes. All women worked in skilled to highly skilled computing positions in 67 public and private organisations. The women's ages ranged from 23 to 61 years with an average age of 39. The verbatim transcripts were content analysed into categories and sub-categories defined according to themes and/or repetitive concepts. The qualitative software program N6 (QSR, 1991-2002) was used to assist data management and to explore the data by searching the coded text.

Barriers relating to the glass ceiling and that were viewed as impacting on women's advancement to more senior levels were key themes in the interviews. They are: disparate pay, women don't ask, networking, and work/life balance. The following section presents an analysis of the IT literature addressing these themes, followed by results of the two studies.

The Glass Ceiling

This term refers to invisible, artificial, and often impenetrable barriers, which prevent a person from rising up the corporate ladder despite the suitability of their qualifications, experience, and aptitude. The literature identifies women, in particular, as being at an impasse once they rise to a certain occupational level. Very often the ceiling is apparent to the women, but not to the executives who hold the power to support and select them for promotion (Greene, 2004; Wernick, 1994). Selection processes are often based on informal practices and procedures where personal contacts and knowledge play a major role (Guido, 2003). Moreover, in the male-dominated IT industry where there are few women there is a natural human tendency for senior males to prefer others like them to join their ranks (Hemenway, 1995). This tendency to "flock together" with people who are similar in interests and attitudes has been identified in social psychological research (Baron & Byrne, 1977).

The importance of visibility in order to achieve advancement has been identified by Wernick (1994). It is suggested that the low numbers of women in the IT workforce not only contribute to them being overlooked for promotion but has resulted in the issue of gendered jobs within the IT workforce. In Panteli et al's (2001) report on gender-based patterns of employment and work experience in computing in the United Kingdom, women were found to be increasingly assigned projects and roles which were considered to use their feminine skills (that is, collaborative team working and effective communications skills). Their roles were seen as lower status and having less value than the more technical projects offered to their male counterparts. These researchers believe this is a type of task segregation that prevents women gaining the knowledge, experience, and visibility considered necessary by their mainly male superiors that will lead them to the top jobs and, of course, higher pay.

Disparate Pay

Studies in the United Kingdom and America reveal that IT women not only report barriers to promotion but are often faced with receiving lower salaries than men even when age, education, organisational tenure, job tenure, and number of years in the IT field are controlled for (Baroudi & Igbaria, 1995; Peters et al., 2002). Sumner and Niederman's (2003-2004) research on the impact of gender differences on IT professionals in the United States found that the mean salaries of male IT professionals were greater than those of female IT professionals.

Statistics New Zealand 2001 census figures show that there is a large majority of female data entry operators (on the lower salaries) and a minority of females in the skilled IT occupations. It is interesting that in spite of approximately a quarter of New Zealand's total IT workforce being women they hold only about 8% of senior management roles in IT compared with 31% of women in senior roles nationwide (High Tech's High Heelers, 2005). Figure 1 presents salaries of the skilled and highly skilled IT occupations that include systems analyst, computer application engineer, computer programmers, operators and support

Figure 1. Salaries for male and female skilled and highly skilled IT workers (Based on Statistics New Zealand 2001 census data)

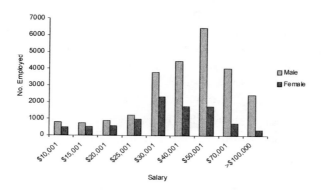

technician and IT management (Statistics New Zealand categories). Female participation up to the $40,001 salary band is between 38% and 44%. This includes part-time and full-time employment (Statistics New Zealand). The average full-time annual earnings of New Zealand's employed labour force is $40,924 (New Zealand Immigration Service, 2003). From $50,001 female participation decreases noticeably, trending from 21% to 12% for salaries $100,001 and over.

Varying reasons for the disparity in male/female IT salaries have been posited, with Sumner et al. (2003-2004, p. 29) suggesting that "factors influencing these outcomes are complex" and referring to Maupin's (1993) contention that gender discrimination is built into a plethora of work practices, cultural norms, and images that appear unbiased.

Women Don't Ask

Apart from organisational practices and influences, Babcock and Laschever (2003) believe that reasons for women earning less than their male colleagues is because women do not ask or negotiate for higher pay and promotions and better job opportunities. Women are urged to "learn to demand more, negotiate better and tougher, and walk away when the money's not right" (Advancing Women, n.d., final para). These "human nature" barriers also contribute to the glass ceiling, thus blocking the advancement of IT women (Hemenway, 1995). Another avenue that facilitates advancement and that has often been used by men is networking.

Networking

Critical to advancement is access to information, and this is often gained through networking. Traditionally networking provides employees with the opportunity to socialise on an informal or formal basis with senior executives. Such interaction serves a multiplicity of purposes from simply "getting to know the right people," to gaining support and obtaining the organisational information relevant to promotion and career progression (Wernick, 1994). Historically, many clubs had a male only membership that only changed in recent decades to include women. As well, many of the prestigious schools were single sex and strong networking affiliations were activated through attendance (Redwood, 2003).

Unfortunately, research shows that women have not had the same access to these networks as men within or outside their organisation (Ahuja, 2002; Igbaria & Chidambaram, 1995). They frequently choose not to participate in work-organised social events because of disinterest in the type of activities offered and home management obligations. Ragins and Cotton (1991) suggest that this lack of access to, and participation in, informal networks impacts on women in two ways. First, organisations often rely on such networks for recruitment. Second, advancement in the field is often a direct result of relationships formed through these networks.

Work/Life Balance

While there have been recent changes in the roles played by men and women with respect to family life, many women engaged in the workforce still undertake the major role in sustaining the support systems which keep things running smoothly in the home (Center for Ethical Business Cultures, 1997). Women in IT have greater difficulties with affecting a balance between work and home because of two factors inherent in the industry. First, there is a culture of working long, unsociable hours. The long hours, together with care giving and home management responsibilities often result in conflict with trying to balance personal and work responsibilities. Second, because the IT workplace is male dominated there is less consideration of work/life balance policies of particular concern to women who have to juggle work, family and home. Yasbek (2004) states that the culture of the workplace impacts strongly on the implementation and uptake of work/life policies and where an organisation has a larger proportion of women, particularly at executive level, there is usually greater emphasis placed on policies such as job sharing, flexi-time, childcare and part-time work. These two factors become critical influences contributing to the glass ceiling. Palermo (2004) suggests women may be reluctant to apply for more senior positions as they seek some level of personal achievement and satisfaction in both career and home and therefore look for roles that will accommodate both. She proposes "the recruitment and retention of smart women may require the reconfiguration of senior positions into 'smarter' positions" (p. 18).

The next section examines the findings from the two New Zealand studies, being cognizant of the factors that impact on the glass ceiling previously discussed.

New Zealand Results and Discussion

What Glass Ceiling?

The results of the New Zealand research confirmed the dearth of women working in IT. Despite the IT gender literature identifying the negative consequences of the dominant IT male culture (Sumner et al., 2003-2004) the majority of these women did not perceive any overt instances of the glass ceiling. In most organisations, the women were invariably a small minority in their section, no matter whether they were in the softer side, such as business analysis, or the harder side, such as programming. Some of them held the top IT positions in their organisation and few perceived any overt inequality in opportunities for promotion. Many of the women who were in middle-ranking positions believed there were no barriers preventing them from promotion to the senior positions. The main problem as they saw it was simply that women were not entering the industry and so were not there to be promoted. The "'pipeline problem'–namely, there just aren't enough young women with technical skills coming out of universities and into the industry" (DeBare, 2003) is identified as contributing to this.

The Importance of Soft Skills

Nearly two thirds of the women interviewed in this study worked in the soft aspects of IT, that is, in positions such as business analysis or project management where effective communication, collaboration, and teamwork are valued. Contrary to Panteli et al.'s (2001) assertion that women are often channelled into less mission critical work because "'hard' development or technology or work in the field are seen as the key areas" (p. 13) they felt that their softer skills were highly valued by management and clients and key to their organisation. They did not report the perception that male colleagues were advantaged in training opportunities that Panteli et al. reported. The New Zealand women believed that there was pressure on many of their male colleagues to develop and improve their communication and presentation skills, reflecting this decade's greater emphasis on a user/client-focused IT environment.

Personal Agendas

Although the women did not identify organisational glass ceiling barriers, they referred to issues relating to their own personal agendas that impacted on promotion, thus revealing the glass ceiling as complex. Several women had been offered opportunities for advancement but had turned them down because they felt they did not have the skills. Others said they were simply not ambitious and were satisfied with the work they were doing and the salaries they were earning. Still others did not wish to be promoted as it meant a move away from IT work into a more managerial style job. A further concern for some of the women was to decide whether to have children, how they would cope, what support systems were in place, etc. This was a personal dilemma, which acted as a "handbrake" on their career aspirations.

Confidence

Reflection on these personal agenda comments reveals the covert and opaque nature of barriers influencing the glass ceiling. The lack of confidence (shown by the women who had been offered promotion to more senior positions but declined them because they felt inadequate for the job) became a recurring theme in the interviews. Many women (21) discussed the difference in the appearance of confidence between male and female IT workers. The comment by one woman who said "... all these guys I work with they seem to be so confident and so sure and I feel like I don't know what I am doing" summed up the majority opinion of the interviewees. Others felt that men overestimate their abilities with two women relating instances where their male colleagues applied for jobs with a lower skill set than their own. These women said they did not feel competent enough to apply and were amazed at the temerity of their male colleagues. Several women recognised the danger of generalisation when categorising all males as confident, thus rejecting the essentialist argument that suggests there is a "masculine" technological style. However, they still thought that men appeared innately confident.

A senior IT manager believed that confidence "is definitely an issue" and is a critical factor for women wishing to return to the workforce after time out for children. She believed that "a woman wants to be assured that she can do something before she has to sort of do it." In a Thought Leadership Debate, it was noted that "women typically feel they are doing a bad job unless someone tells them they are doing a great job." It was noted that this "tends to be the opposite for men" (Kavanagh, 2005, p. 40).

There was general agreement that men have the confidence to be "risk-takers" whereas women like to take the safer approach and "want to be sure of things from the outset." This character trait has implications for breaking through the glass ceiling. Without the confident attitude that men present, women are more likely to not be considered for advancement and negotiating their salaries will likely not be as effective as their male colleagues.

Salaries and Negotiation

Most of the women were satisfied with their salary and believed it to be equivalent to their male colleagues, and in some cases better. However, most did not know what salaries their co-workers earned. This contradicts the studies discussed earlier and could be a reflection of New Zealand's legislative steps towards narrowing the gender gap (Herd, 2005), the establishment of a Commission for Equal Employment Opportunities together with the small IT industry in a country of just over four million people. However, it was noticeable that the women, both managers and employees, perceived males as being much more aggressive in their negotiations for higher salary and promotion. One manager commented, "some men push hard and you do pay them more than you want to." The main perception was that men projected themselves much more strongly and that women were often reluctant to praise themselves and tended to accept what was offered to them rather than negotiate for more. The following quotes indicate how the issue of confidence impacted self-perception of competencies and the ability to negotiate to higher salaries: "One of my star performers is a woman but she rated herself lower than I did" and "Women tend to feel embarrassed about saying 'I want more, I am worth more.'"

Networking

The women reported that the days of taking time out to play golf or attend long lunches appear to have all but disappeared. Instead, there was a variety of mainly informal opportunities for socialisation. These included Christmas parties, lunches and in one case, a "funky whanau [family] day" in a large stadium and free entertainment provided for employees and their families. The most common form of socialising was Friday night drinks. The majority of the interviewees said they enjoyed meeting with their colleagues in this way, but did not always attend (including male employees) because parental and other responsibilities were prioritised.

The socialisation was not only viewed as a "means of relaxing with people I would not otherwise get to know" and celebrate the week's successes but provided context for one manager's employees. She believed she gained a more holistic view of the employee when socialising away from stressful work situations thus enhancing her managerial job. By talking to "the family and the partners…from my point of view I have got that history of what is going on in their home life to be more understanding and maybe reach a compromise."

Discussing and sharing problems and developing confidence and new skills were given as benefits arising from networking. Many of the women belonged to the Women in Technology organisation and found this to be an excellent way of networking with other women. Some also belonged to the New Zealand Computer Society and used their functions as a forum for keeping in contact with colleagues and networking in general. This was important for one consultant who said she had always "gone to lots of Computer Society things" and when asked how she gets her jobs replied: "Through networking; absolutely, completely through networking."

Women who belonged to e-mail lists found electronic networking especially useful for making contacts and solving problems. One woman found the e-mail lists on the e-government site a "great way to contact people" and others mentioned The Wise Women, Dreamweaver and Web Grrls lists as being useful. One woman said: "the Dreamweaver list is mainly men but the women are the most knowledgeable. It is good because you can ask dumb questions but the nerds quite enjoy taking the time to answer."

Work/Life Balance

It was obvious that the gender specific division of labour which results in the working woman taking the main responsibility for family and home management (Oechtering & Behnke, 1995) was still expected, and being undertaken, by most of the women. This was a prime reason for all of the women, whether or not they had families, to view flexible working hours as very important. Only two of the organisations did not allow flexible work hours a finding congruent with results of a survey by TMP/Hudson (West & Burroughs, 2002) indicating that flexi-time is the most common work/life policy offered to workers. Organisations implemented flexible time in a variety of ways. In some cases, core hours were set and flexibility was allowed around those set hours. In other situations the women could start early in the morning to enable them to be home by 3 P.M. for their children. In one situation where there was joint custody, the woman was allowed to work less hours on the weeks when she looked after the child and make up those hours on the alternate weeks. Managers who were interviewed all stated that they were sympathetic to the needs of women with families. One said she understood that "a lack of flexibility affects women in a way it doesn't affect men because the burden [of child care responsibility] remains on them."

Telecommuting, or working from home was another option offered by some organisations and used by some participants. One woman said, "I can choose to log in from home and have the morning at home and suit myself, leave late, work late, whatever. Telecommunications has made the difference—if you are thinking of children, then the ability to work from home is stronger than ever." However not all women who had this option chose to take it, and one said she "could not stand working at home with her children around her."

Part-time work painted a different picture. Very few of the women worked part-time, and most of the organisations did not allow it. Nor was part-time work considered by the women to be appropriate in many situations because there is a customer expectation of 24/7 availability. One woman with four children believed that "having the flexibility and being able to work from home is probably actually more important than being able to do part-time."

Many women commented that long hours were expected in the IT work place and some participants said that long working hours impacted their work-life balance. A number of the women in managerial positions believed that it was important to provide time off in lieu of working extended hours as they considered anyone who was consistently working long hours became unproductive. While the women accepted the often long and unusual hours as being a part of, and often necessary, in their IT environment they then expected to have some freedom and flexibility at other times.

Very few organisations provided childcare facilities, but this appeared to be of little concern to most. Those with pre-school children preferred to find childcare close to their homes. The greatest concern came from women with school age children who worried about after school facilities and holidays. One woman said: "School holidays are a nightmare. I just worry and worry and worry until I have got every day covered."

Conclusion and Implications for Managing IT Personnel

The issue of why women are not visible in the higher-salaried IT positions is complex. Some make a conscious decision to opt out of seniority in terms of status and salary, not because they are "just not so interested as men in making the sacrifices required by high-powered jobs" (Ripley, 2005) but to prioritise family and to have the time to pursue and enjoy other interests. Women are the ones who commonly accept responsibility for managing both home and work. Some lack positive self-perception and confidence in their ability to cope with the challenges of top positions. The subtle and covert influence of decades of gendered socialization where women were not in top positions, together with the lack of critical mass of women in similar positions, reinforces their belief that they are not capable of appointment to these jobs. Organizational culture is influenced by the assumptions, values, beliefs, meanings, and expectations that employees of a particular organization, work unit, group or team hold in common (Hodge & Anthony, 1988; Schein, 1992). When the majority of that group are male, the IT workplace culture will suit and reflect males and their interests. However, IT managers with a female workplace minority who recognise that the male IT culture can contribute, in subtle and covert ways, to the glass ceiling are better able to respond and ensure an equitable workplace. The challenge for managers of IT women in today's Internet age is their ability to recognise the subtleties of the gendered culture of the IT working environment, how these impact on women and to implement strategies and policies which will counter them.

These findings have implications for managers of IT professionals wishing to foster an equitable and diverse workplace. The Internet age has provided the technology to work in more flexible ways, as discussed earlier, such as e-networking, mentoring and aspects of teleworking. Management and policies that are responsive to their workers' needs and that provide flexibility in work location (physical and virtual) and in work times will be rewarded with loyal and high-performing employees. They will also more likely retain skilled IT women and be attractive to those women re-entering the IT industry after child care. Workers react positively to opportunities and incentives in their environments, resulting in high performance (Smits, McLean, & Tanner, 1993) and after weighing up the costs and benefits the business case for adopting work/life balance policies has been shown to yield a positive net impact (Comfort, Johnson, & Wallace, 2003; Yasbek, 2004).

The different negotiation styles between men and women will influence mana-gerial decisions on promotion and salary. Women are much more likely than men to think that simply working hard and doing a good job will result in recognition in salary increases and promotion. Managers who are sensitised to the differ-ences in negotiation styles between men and women will ensure equitable salaries based on merit thereby deflecting the influence of gendered subtleties.

This study revealed the difference in confidence between men and women. Managers could foster confidence in women female IT workers not only through the above initiatives but by encouraging them (through subscription) to join networking groups such as the New Zealand Computer Society, Women in Technology, and Te Waka Wahine Wa-Hangarau (TWWW) (see www.twww.org.nz).

With IT an essential component of a global market the need for a diverse IT workforce that includes higher representation of women will improve an organization's productivity. As the first woman to head IBM says, "diversity in itself is a critical success factor in making teams work and organizations successful" (High Tech's High Heelers, 2005, p. 11).

This study has the usual limitations associated with qualitative research. The possibility of method bias in interpreting the data was mitigated by at least two researchers being present at all interviews and the verbatim transcripts read and coded by three researchers independently. The sample is believed to be broadly representative of age and occupations of New Zealand's IT women working in 67 organisations. However, care needs to be taken in drawing extensive conclusions because of the self reporting nature of the data collection.

The research reported here focused on women only and further insights into managing IT professionals would be gained through analyzing results of a quantitative survey that included male and female IT workers. Future research could investigate exemplary organizations with a culture that is inclusive of both genders and that have implemented innovative policies around the issues raised by the women in this study.

Acknowledgments

We wish to thank all the women who gave their time to this project, Associate Professor Andrea McIlroy for her continued enthusiasm and support for this project and Lana Wang, Research Assistant, for her valuable input.

References

Advancing Women. (n.d.). *Women and workplace strategies.* Retrieved April 12, 2005, from http://www.advancingwomen.com/wk_glassceiling2.htm

Ahuja, M. K. (2002). Women in the information technology profession: A literature review, synthesis and research agenda. *European Journal of Information Systems, 11*(1), 20-34.

Babcock, L., & Laschever, S. (2003). *Women don't ask: Negotiation and the gender divide.* Princeton: Princeton University Press.

Baron, R. A., & Byrne, D. (1977). *Social psychology: Understanding human interaction* (2nd ed.). Boston: Allyn and Bacon.

Baroudi, J. J., & Igbaria, M. (1995). An examination of gender effects on career success of information systems employees. *Journal of Management Information Systems, 11*(3), 181-201.

Bernstein, D. R. (1999). Java, women, and the culture of computing. *Proceedings of the 12th Annual Conference of the National Advisory Committee on Computing Qualifications: The new learning environment* (pp. 21-28). Dunedin, New Zealand.

Bort, J. (2003). *Come payday, it's good to be you.* Retrieved January 17, 2005, from http://www.nwfusion.com/you/2003/0721salary.html

Center for Ethical Business Cultures. (1997). *Creating high performance organisations: The bottom line value of work/life strategies.* Retrieved March 5, 2005, from www.cebcglobal.org/Publications/WorkLife/WL_Report.htm

Comfort, D., Johnson, K., & Wallace, D. (2003). *The evolving workplace series: Part-time work and family-friendly practices in Canadian workplaces*. Human Resources Development, Statistics Canada. Retrieved March 16, 2005, from www.statcan.ca/english/freepub/71-584-MIE/free.htm

Crump, B., & Logan, K. (2000). Women in an alien environment. *New Zealand Journal of Applied Computing and Information Technology, 4*(1), 28-35.

DeBare, I. (2003). *High-tech industry zipping along, but women often are left behind*. Retrieved March 7, 2005, from www.sacbee.com/static/archive/news/projects/women/wcmain.html

Desmond, P. (2002). *Defining the gender gap*. Network World, July 7. Retrieved January 17, 2005 from http://www.nwfusion.com/you/2002/salary_side2.html

Edwards, P. N. (1994). From "impact" to social process: Computers in society and culture. In S. Jasanoff (Ed.), *Handbook of science and technology studies*. Beverly Hills, CA: Sage Publications.

European Union. (n.d.) *Managing diversity — What's in it for business?* Retrieved June 14, 2005, from http://www.stop-discrimination.info/fileadmin/pdfs/Fact_Sheets/Managing_Diversity.pdf

Frenkel, K. A. (1990). Women and computing. *Communications of the ACM, 33*(11), 34-47.

Gartner Group. People 2000 Annual Compensation Survey. Retrieved March 11, 2003, from http://www.itaa.org

Greene, K. (2004, November 8). Women at the top: A smart move. *The Dominion Post*, p. C4.

Guido, M. (2003). *Study: Tech has glass ceiling. Barriers belie industry's ceiling*. Mercury News. Retrieved December 14, 2003, from http://siliconvalley.com/mld/siliconvalley/news/local

Hemenway, K. (1995). Human nature and the glass ceiling in industry. *Communications of the ACM, 39*(1), 55-61.

Herd, J. (2005). *Cracks in a glass ceiling: New Zealand women 1975-2004*. Dunedin, NZ Federation of Graduate Women (Otago Branch).

High Tech's High Heelers. (2005, April). *Management Women, 2*(1), 10-12.

Hodge, B. J., & Anthony, W. P. (1988). *Organizational theory*. Boston: Allyn & Bacon.

Igbaria, M., & Chidambaram, L. (1995). Examination of gender effects on intention to stay among information systems employees. Special Interest

Group on Computer Personnel Research Annual Conference. *Proceedings Of The 1995 ACM SIGCPR Conference on Supporting Teams, Groups, and Learning Inside and Outside the IS Function Reinventing IS*. ACM Press: New York.

Kavanagh, J. (2005, February 15). Thought leadership debate reveals gender bias holding back female IT professionals. *Computer Weekly*, 40. Retrieved March 31, 2004, from the Business Source Premier database.

Millar, M. (1998). *Cracking the gender code: Who rules the wired world?* Toronto: Second Story Press.

Nash, E. (2005, March 31). *Outdated attitudes are reinforcing IT's gender imbalance*. Computing. Retrieved June 13, 2005, from http://www.computing.co.uk/articles/print/2071839

New Zealand Immigration Service. (2003). *Rates of pay*. Retrieved February 3, 2005, from http://www.immigration.govt.nz/migrant/settlementpack/Work/ConditionsOfEmployment/RatesOfPay.htm

Oechtering, V., & Behnke, R. (1995). Situations and advancement measures in Germany. *Communications of the ACM, 38*(1), 75-87.

Palermo, J. (2004). *Breaking the cultural mould: The key to women's career success*. Hudson Global Resources and Capital Solutions. Retrieved November 30, 2004, from http://nz.hudson.com/documents/au 2020Series Women Whitepaper 03112004.pdf

Panteli, N., Stack, J., & Ramsay, H. (2001). Gendered patterns in computing work in the late 1990s. *New Technology, Work, and Employment, 16*(1), 3-17.

Peters, J., Lane, N., Rees, T., & Samuels, G. (2002). *SET Fair, A report on women in science, engineering, and technology*. Retrieved October 22, 2003, from http://huminf.uib.no/~hilde/blog/archives/000763.html

QRS International Pty Ltd. (1991-2002). N6 [Computer software], Melbourne, Australia.

Ragins, B. R., & Cotton, J. L. (1991). Easier said than done: Gender differences in perceived barriers to gaining a mentor. *Academy of Management Journal, 34*(4), 939-951

Redwood, J. (2003). *Men, women, and networking*. Retrieved February 3, from http://xtramsn.c.nz/business/0,,5008-225480,00.html

Ripley, A. (2005, March 7). Who says a woman can't be Einstein? *Time, 9*, 44-54.

Schein, E. (1992). *Organizational culture and leadership* (2nd ed.) San Francisco: Jossey Bass.

Smits, S. J., McLean, E. R., & Tanner, J. R. (1993, Spring). Managing high-achieving information systems professionals. *Journal of Management Information Systems, 9*(4), 103-120.

Statistics New Zealand (2004). Requested commissioned statistical tables based on 2001 Census data. Retrieved from http://www.stats.govt.nz/census/

Sumner, M., & Niederman, F. (2003-2004, Winter). The impact of gender differences on job satisfaction, job turnover, and career experiences of information systems professionals. *Journal of Computer Information Systems, 44*(2), 29-39.

Trauth, E. M. (2002). Odd girl out: An individual differences perspective on women in the IT profession. *Information Technology & People, 15*(2), 98-118.

Wernick, E. (1994, May). *Preparedness, career advancement, and the glass ceiling.* Draft Report for the United States Glass Ceiling Commission. Retrieved January 27, 2005, from http://www.ilr.cornell.edu/library/downloads/keyWorkplaceDocuments/GlassCeilingBackground15 Preparedness.pdf

West, J., & Burroughs, D. (2002). *New Zealand Job Index Survey July 2002-December 2002.* Retrieved November 24, 2003, from http://www.hudsonresourcing.co.nz/node.asp?SID=1434

Yasbek, P. (2004, January). *The business case for firm-level work-life balance policies: a review of the literature.* Wellington, NZ: Labour Market Policy Group, Department of Labour. Retrieved February 9, 2004, from http://www.dol.govt.nz/publication-view.asp?ID=191

Chapter II

Gender and the Information Technology Workforce:
Issues of Theory and Practice[1]

Eileen M. Trauth, The Pennsylvania State University, USA

Jeria L. Quesenberry, The Pennsylvania State University, USA

Abstract

Despite increases of women in the labor force, females are largely under-represented in the American IT workforce. Among the challenges that managers face in addressing the under representation of women in the IT workforce is the identification of an appropriate theory as a basis for understanding data about gender and IT in order to reverse the gender imbalance. Hence, the purpose of this chapter is to demonstrate the managerial implications of theory choice when addressing the under representation of women in the IT workforce. We provide an overview of the three main theoretical perspectives, the essentialist theory, the social construction theory, and the individual differences theory of gender and IT, which are used to understand and investigate the IT gender gap. We then make the argument that the essentialist and social construction theories do not provide the analytical robustness required to pay attention to more nuanced managerial recommendations. Finally, we demonstrate how the individual differences theory of gender and IT can significantly contribute to the reconfiguration of analytical knowledge of the IT gender gap and spur innovative management policies.

Introduction

The explosion of the Internet has transformed and revolutionized the information technology (IT) workforce. The IT workforce has also become a large component of the world's economy and researching the composition and predicting the direction of the industry is an important matter for discussion. In addition, organizations and managers strive to identify ways to foster a business climate that encourages successful participation in the information economy. Therefore, researching, measuring, and evaluating the IT workforce are of growing importance.

Unfortunately, women are largely under represented in the American IT workforce, a phenomenon typically termed the IT gender gap. This female under representation in technical careers has gained the attention of researchers who have concluded that women are alarmingly under represented in the IT workforce, despite the recent growth of female workers in the American labor force. Thus, those concerned with managing IT professionals are faced with the task of recruiting, motivating, and retaining the necessary personnel to meet the current and future demands of the information age while promoting greater diversity and equality within the field.

Among the challenges that managers face in addressing the under representation of women in the IT workforce is the identification of an appropriate theory as a basis for understanding data about gender and IT, so as to reverse the gender imbalance. Hence, the purpose of this chapter is to demonstrate the managerial implications of theory choice when addressing the under representation of women in the IT workforce. We begin with a brief background on the under representation of women in the IT workforce. Next, we provide an overview of three theories used to understand and explain the IT gender gap: (1) the essentialist theory; (2) the social construction theory; and (3) the individual differences theory of gender and IT. In this discussion, we demonstrate how these theoretical foundations serve as a lens for interpretation and recommendations to address the IT gender gap. We then make the argument that the essentialist and social construction theories do not provide the analytical robustness required to pay attention to more nuanced managerial recommendations. Next, we demonstrate how the individual differences theory of gender and IT can significantly contribute to the reconfiguration of analytical knowledge of the IT gender gap and spur innovative management policies. Evidence of these contributions are drawn from research projects conducted in Australia and New Zealand (Trauth, 2002; Trauth, Nielsen, & von Hellens, 2000; Trauth, Nielsen, & von Hellens, 2003), Ireland (Trauth, 1995, 2000, 2004) and the United States (Morgan, Quesenberry, & Trauth, 2004; Quesenberry & Trauth, 2005; Quesenberry, Morgan, & Trauth, 2004; Quesenberry, Trauth, & Morgan, 2006; Trauth & Quesenberry, 2005; Trauth, Huang, Morgan, & Quesenberry, 2006; Trauth, Quesenberry, & Morgan, 2004; Trauth, Quesenberry, & Yeo, 2005).

Background

The historical under representation of women in IT disciplines has been an area of study for many years and researchers have concluded that women are alarmingly under represented in the IT workforce (Arnold & Niederman, 2001; Crawford, 2001; Nielsen, von Hellens, Greenhill, & Pringle, 1997; Sumner & Werner, 2001; von Hellens & Nielsen, 2001). The Information Technology Association of America (ITAA) shows that over time there has also been a decline in the participation rates of women in the US IT workforce. For example, in 1996, women represented 41% of the American IT workforce, in 2002, they represented 34.9%, and in 2004, they represented only 32.4% (ITAA, 2003, 2005). Yet, during the same periods, the percentage of women in all U.S. occupations was approximately half of the labor force (Bureau of Labor Statistics, 2005). The amount of women in the IT workforce has also declined in Canada over the last decade from 28% in 2001 to 25% in 2003 (Downie, Dryburgh, McMullin, & Ranson, 2004). In Europe, the Workforce Aging in the New Economy project (2004) found that the IT downturn in the late 1990s led to more sustained job losses for women than men. For example, in the UK and Germany, men outnumber women five to one in IT professions; in the Netherlands it is seven to one. Furthermore, in 2001, only 22% of the Australia IT workforce was comprised of women (Trauth et al., 2006).

The reason for the under representation of women in the IT workforce is a complex and challenging area of study because no single factor can be identified as the root cause. In addition, Adam, Howcroft, and Richardson (2002) explain that the topic of gender and IT is just beginning to surface and it is thus important to understand the gender dimensions being considered in current research. Therefore, selecting a robust theoretical perspective is critical in order to understand and formulate recommendations that address the IT gender gap.

Main Thrust of This Chapter

Currently, the gender and IT workforce literature is dominated by three main theories and includes: the *essentialist* theory, the *social construction* theory, and the *individual differences theory of gender and IT*. The remainder of this section provides an overview of each theory and demonstrates how each perspective influences managerial recommendations.

The Essentialist Theory

The essentialist theory is based on the assertion of fixed, unified, and opposed female and male natures (Trauth, 2002; Trauth et al., 2004; Wajcman, 1991). The explicit biological difference between the sexes has led to a typical assumption that other observed differences between men and women are also due to biological determinates (Marini, 1990). Thus, biological influences precede cultural influences and set predetermined limits to the effect of culture (De Cecco & Elia, 1993). With regard to IT gender gap research, the essentialist theory uses biological differences between men and women to explain differences in their relationship to technology. Any difference in male or female behavior is believed to be inherent, fixed, group-level and based upon bio-psychological characteristics.[2] These studies conclude that men, as a group, make decisions about technology based upon different criteria than women do as a group (Trauth, 2002; Trauth et al., 2004).

Gender and IT research with an essentialist theoretical foundation views gender as a fixed variable that is typically manipulated within a positivist epistemology[3] (e.g., Dennis, Kiney, & Hung, 1999; Gefen & Straub, 1997; Venkatesh & Morris, 2000). In this research, people are divided into the two separate groups of male and female who have different or opposing inherent psychological characteristics. Furthermore, these psychological characteristics affect their relationship to or their adoption of technology. Adam, Howcroft, and Richardson (2001) argue that the essentialist theory places too much focus on psychology at the cost of examining individual gender characteristics. Thus, this perspective does not account for the influence of context because it adopts a determinist stance of gender traits and preferences (Trauth, 2002; Trauth et al., 2004).

The essentialist theory also influences subsequent managerial recommendations by suggesting that men and women should be treated differently with regard to IT. An extrapolation of this notion to IT workforce considerations is that there should to be two different workforces: a female IT workforce and a male IT workforce. Thus, as Trauth has said elsewhere "policies for addressing the gender imbalance would focus on assumed inherent differences between women and men and the equality issue would focus on 'separate but equal'" (Trauth, 2002, p. 101). The following briefly describes three examples of such research:

- Gefen and Straub (1997) argue that men and women inherently differ in their perceptions of email usage. In doing so, the authors extend the technology acceptance model (TAM) to account for differences in technology acceptance and usage by gender. The authors recommend that new communications environments should be created that account for gender differences by employing different media and training for men and women.

- Venkatesh and Morris (2000) utilize TAM to demonstrate how gender can be used as a moderator of technology. Their research examines mean differences between women and men in terms of abilities, traits, and psychological constructs. Venkatesh, Morris, and Ackerman conclude that women and men process information and make decisions about technology usage in very different ways. Therefore, managers implementing new technologies must consider acceptance and usage needs as applicable by gender.

- Venkatesh, Morris, and Ackerman (2000) investigate how gender differences influence technology adoption and sustainability and recommend that marketing and training should account for these differences. Specifically, productivity-enhancement factors (i.e., usage) should be emphasized for men and balanced factors (i.e., support and claims by peers) for women.

It can be argued that one of the most important outcomes that have arisen from the essentialist stream of gender and IT research is the attention the topic has received in the information system (IS) discourse. For instance, *MIS Quarterly,* a top IS journal, typically did not publish research on gender issues of IT prior to the late 1990s. Yet, two major articles appeared in the journal: Gefen and Straub (1997) and Venkatesh and Morris (2000). Although, these studies dichotomize people by gender, they begin to demonstrate the need for robust investigations of human characteristics in order to provide more nuanced findings and recommendations for interventions and/or policy changes.

The Social Construction Theory

Marini (1990) explains that the existence of historical and cross-cultural variation in gender role differentiation and stratification provides strong evidence that biological differences do not fully account for differences between the sexes. For instance, employment segregation, or division of labor by sex, differs by culture and society and changes over time. Marini highlights the labor force differences between communist and democratic societies and the changes in the gender segregation in U.S. labor force during World War II. These changes in cultural and temporal views about women working demonstrate that their absence or presence in male-dominated careers is due to social constraints rather than biological forces. Hence, as an alternative to the essentialist perspective, the social construction theory argues that human outcomes cannot be fully understood by biological factors. Rather, these outcomes must be explained from a socio-cultural formation perspective (Berger & Luckmann, 1966). According to this theory, societal factors, instead of biological forces, are the primary constructs that shape individuals and their relationship to IT (Marini, 1990). Hence, IT has been socially shaped as "men's work" something that, places IT careers outside the female domain (Trauth, 2002; Trauth et al., 2004).

In gender and IT literature, the social construction theory tends to reflect an interpretive epistemology as a lens to investigate the IT gender gap phenomenon. In this sense, gender is broadly viewed as two separate groups of men and women who are affected by different sets of sociological influences. Hence, men and women are viewed as having different or opposing socio-cultural characteristics, which subsequently affect their relationship to and adoption of technology. As Trauth (2002) has argued, the social construction theory can be problematic because "the message is that women in the IT profession, as a group, are different from men, as a group, in the profession, albeit for sociological rather than biological or psychological reasons" (p. 102). In this sense, the social construction theory is a robust perspective as it accounts for a range of social influences and messages women receive in a given context. Yet, the focus on monolithic societal messages makes it challenging to investigate the diversity of people. Men and women as groups do not receive or respond to societal messages in the same way.

The majority of gender and technology research (e.g., Cockburn, 1983, 1985, 1988; Cockburn & Ormrod, 1993; Wajcman, 1991) and gender and IT research (e.g., Adam, Emms, Green, & Owen, 1994; Balka & Smith, 2000; Eriksson, Kitchenham, & Tijdens, 1991; Lovegrove & Segal, 1991; Slyke, Comunale, & Belanger, 2002; Spender, 1995; Star, 1995; Webster, 1996) utilize the social construction theory, rather than a biological or psychological theory (Trauth, 2002; Trauth et al., 2004). These studies typically result in two types of managerial recommendations for addressing the IT gender gap. One recommendation is to assimilate women into IT education and professions by helping them to fit into a male domain (e.g., Nielsen, von Hellens, Greenhill, & Pringle, 1997; Nielsen, von Hellens, Greenhill, & Pringle, 1998; Nielsen, von Hellens, Pringle, & Greenhill, 1999; Nielsen, von Hellens, & Wong, 2000; Pringle, Nielsen, von Hellens, Greenhill, & Parfitt, 2000; von Hellens & Nielsen, 2001; von Hellens, Pringle, Nielsen, & Greenhill, 2000; von Hellens, Nielsen, & Trauth 2001). The second recommendation focuses on the call to reconstruct the world of computing to become more of a "female domain" (e.g., Spender, 1995; Webster, 1996). The following briefly describes three examples of such research:

- Joshi, Schmidt, and Kuhn (2003) found that negative stereotypes of the IT workforce permeate images and conceptions held by both men and women. Specifically, the authors found that the IT workforce is plagued with stereotypical images of IT employees who only sit in front of a computer all day, workers who are nerds or geeks, and other stereotypes including that all IT employees wear glasses. Unfortunately, the stereotypic images of the IT field do not fade away once students are informed about IT careers. These influences can be subtle, but create a difference in how women see IT and imagine their roles within it. As a result, the authors recommend that actions be taken to remove or reduce the pervasiveness of negative stereotypes of the IT workforce.

- Nielsen et al. (2000) conducted an interpretive investigation of learning organizations and found that the learning environment influences subsequent skills development. The authors recommend that masculine values of learning organization be expanded, so that female students can negotiate the environment.

- Balcita, Carver, and Soffa (2002) found that the under representation of women in the IT workforce creates a lack of female mentors and role models. As women look for support through mentoring, role models or social support they are typically disappointed. Without the much needed encouragement and guidance of co-workers of their own gender, women are left in search of support. As a result, the authors recommend efforts be taken to produce additional female mentors and role models.

A number of important findings have come from social construction research primarily by understanding and recommending ways to achieve greater social inclusion. A number of findings have recommended ways in which women can more easily fit into the IT workforce. For instance, research has suggested that support structures, such as mentors (e.g., Townsend, 2002), support groups (e.g., Ahuja, Robinson, Herring, & Ogan, 2004) and role models (e.g., Cohoon, 2001, 2002), are of extreme importance. In addition, positive societal message about women working and women working in technical careers are important in closing the IT gender gap (e.g., Joshi et al., 2003; von Hellens et al., 2001, 2000). A number of other findings have suggested that the domain of IT work should be adapted to more easily accommodate diverse employees including women. In this sense, Webster (1996) and Wajcman (2000) focus on the social shaping of female gender identity and the implication for women's relationship to workplace technologies. Furthermore, Spender (1995) offers another perspective based on the analysis of women as a social group in cyberspace and predicts that an influx of female values into the cyberspace virtual world will accompany an increased female presence (Trauth et al., 2004).

The Individual Differences Theory of Gender and IT

The notion that individual differences causes differences in human behavior is not new to IT research (Couger, Zawicki, & Oppermann, 1979; Jago & Scammel, 1982; Jiang, Klein, & Pick, 1996; Zmud, 1979), however researchers have only recently begun to examine individual differences with respect to gender and IT. At the forefront of this research are Trauth's studies of the individual difference theory of gender and IT (Trauth, 2002; Trauth et al., 2004) which rejects essentialism and offers refinement of various under-explored areas of the social construction theory. This refinement is accomplished by focusing on an individual level of analysis while understanding that the skills needed to enter or to be successful in IT workforce span the gender continuum. More specifically, the theory examines the individual variations across genders as a result of both personal characteristics and environmental influences in order to understand the participation of women in the IT profession. Hence, the focus is on differences *within* rather than *between* genders. The theory also examines women as individuals who possess different technical talents and inclinations and respond to social shaping in unique and particular ways.

According to this theory, the individual differences believed most relevant to gender and IT are grouped into three classes: personal data, shaping and influencing factors and environmental context (Trauth et al., 2004) (see Table 1). Personal data includes: demographic data (such as age, race and ethnicity), lifestyle data (such as socio-economic class and parenting status), and work-place data (such as job title and technical level). Shaping and influencing factors include personal characteristics (such as educational background, personality traits, and abilities) and personal influences (such as mentors, role models, experiences with computing, and other significant life experiences). Environmental context includes cultural attitudes and values (such as attitudes about IT and/or women), geographic data (about the location of work) and economic and policy data (about the region in which a woman works). Collectively these constructs contribute to the differences among women in the ways they experience and respond to characteristics of IT work, the IT workplace, and societal messages about women and IT.

To date, the individual differences theory of gender and IT has reflected an interpretive epistemology as a lens to investigate the IT gender gap phenomena.

Table 1. Constructs of the individual differences theory of gender and IT (Trauth et al., 2004)

High Level Construct	Sub Category Construct
Personal data	Demographics Lifestyle Workplace
Shaping and influencing factors	Personal characteristics Personal influences
Environmental context	Cultural attitudes and values Geographic data Economic data Policy data

Individual characteristics cross genders and combine with sociological influences to affect an individual's particular relationship to IT. As Trauth (Trauth, 2002; Trauth et al., 2004) explains, gender-based characteristics are not assigned to a group level; rather they are applied or challenged at an individual level when appropriate. Thus, not all women react in similar ways to technology. According to this theory, women, as individuals, experience a range of different socio-cultural influences, which shape their inclinations to participate in the IT profession in a variety of ways.

As previously mentioned, to date the individual difference theory of gender and IT is being developed through qualitative studies conducted in Australia/New Zealand, Ireland, and the United States. Data collection methods employed in these research projects include: in-depth, face-to-face interviews with female practitioners and academics, behavioral observations of the participants, and document analysis of the regions in which they live and work. The interview length ranges from 60 and 120 minutes, although the majority of interviews are approximately 90 minutes in length. Interviews are held in private meeting spaces with the interviewer and the interviewee. Generally, the interviews are held in the interviewee's place of employment, but upon request, the interviews are occasionally held in alternative locations such as interviewee's home or off-site meeting facilities.

In terms of managerial recommendations, the individual differences theory of gender and IT has been applied to a number of themes. The following briefly describes three examples of such research:

- Morgan et al. (2004) investigated how women in the IT profession are affected by and relate to predominately male informal social networks. These social networks are important for information sharing in a less formal setting, and to establish and build trust in personal relationships. The research presented a conceptual framework to explain the reactions and strategies with respect to the network that women employ for continued participation in the IT profession. The framework illustrated the experiences of both "insiders" and "outsiders" to the network. The analysis demonstrated that women respond to exclusion from the network in a variety of ways, depending upon environments, personalities, and responsibilities. The findings recommend that organizational social networking barriers be examined and removed and programs be implemented to increase the number of female role models and mentors.

- Quesenberry et al. (2004, 2006) investigated the role of balancing work-family issues in the IT profession and the connection between these issues and the under representation of women in technical careers. This research presented a framework for analyzing work-family balance to show the range of ways in which work-family considerations influence women's IT career decisions. The findings illustrated an identifiable theme that crosses geographical regions and timeframes: societal messages are complex and difficult to digest, and are processed in different ways by different women. Yet, these messages contribute to the decisions women make about their professional and personal lives. Consequently, more innovative work-life programs should be introduced such as flexible work arrangements, part-time employment, and return to work training programs that take into account the variety of work-family issues that women confront.

- Trauth et al. (2005) analyzed the role of environmental context in the under representation of women in the IT workforce in order to strengthen the environmental construct of the individual differences theory of gender and IT. The results suggested that economic factors (e.g., size of the information economy, household income, and cost of living) and cultural factors (e.g., attitudes and values regarding women, women working and women working in IT) exert an influence on the experience of women in the IT profession. These findings bolster an argument in favor of looking beyond the data at hand, to the women *in context* and recommend considering regional influences in organizational decision making.

To date, these empirical studies have focused on an improved understanding of the under representation of women in the IT workforce by supporting the individual differences theory of gender and IT. A major contribution of this research is the recognition that not all women are the same and hence, experience different influences and react to the same influences differently. Thus, management practices toward women should not stereotype or generalize to a holistic group of women. Another contribution of the individual differences theory of gender and IT is that it offers an alternative viewpoint on gender and

IT by allowing for the examination of individual variation among women. In this sense, this research is investigating the IT gender gap from a fresh theoretical perspective.

Implications for Research

The essentialist and social construction theories have several shortcomings with regard to the robustness of the perspective. The essentialist theory has been roundly criticized and rejected in the burgeoning literature on gender and technology (Cockburn, 1983, 1985; Wajcman, 1991, 2000). Adam et al. (2002) argue that an essentialist perspective dichotomize males and females by relying on stereotypical characteristics. Whereas, the social construction theory has been criticized as it tends to depict individuals as empty organisms that are filled and shaped by society and consequently under emphasizes the role of consciousness or intention (De Cecco & Elia, 1993). In this sense, the shaping of people's beliefs about gender operates at a group level and as a result, influences the choices of all men or women in the same ways.

It can also be argued that the essentialist and social construction theories view gender and technology as fixed. Both theories assume that women in the IT profession, as a group, are different from men, as a group, either for biological, psychological, or sociological reasons. This suggests a gap in the theoretical options available for analyzing gender and IT (Trauth et al., 2004) with regard to postmodernist thoughts of Haraway and Butler and the argument that there is no "universal woman." Women do not constitute a tightly knit group with common interests, backgrounds, values, behaviors, and mannerisms, but rather have come from a range of classes, races, sexual orientations, geographic locations, and generations. As a result, women as a group have experienced a range of challenges in their history, needs, and aspirations. Therefore, more cross-cultural comparisons are needed that examine a range of diverse factors such as social, economic, institutional, cultural, and political aspects and their role in encouraging or discouraging women from participating in science (Schiebinger, 1999).

The individual differences theory of gender and IT promises to contribute to the reconfiguration of analytical knowledge of the IT gender gap and spur innovative management policies for several reasons. First, researchers have stressed the need to think about issues of gender in conjunction with, and not in isolation from, issues of class, race, ethnicity, and sexual orientation, and have forcefully illustrated that differences among women must be understood and theorized in order to avoid essentialist generalizations about "women's problems" (Kvasny, 2003; Naryayan, 1998). The individual difference theory accounts for this diverse perspective of people and does not generalize individuals by demographic group. Secondly, Adam and Richardson (2001) explain that gender research should emphasize the making of knowledge through the lived experiences of women's lives. This is particularly important because the power structures at play in organizational settings require more detailed analysis than is available in typical approaches. Furthermore, Adam et al. (2002) argue the theoretical need to recognize the role of women's agency (or the ability of women to exert power over themselves) in shaping their position and resisting stereotypical assumptions about their behavior. The individual difference theory of gender and IT is directed at the study of women as individuals including their personal agency and influences in order to gain an in-depth understanding of their experiences.

Implications for Practice

With regard to practice, the under representation of women in the IT workforce limits the diversity of IT products and services (Joshi & Kuhn, 2001; Trauth et al., 2006; Wardle, 2003). Elmuti (2001) argues that being sensitive to a variety of people and having a diverse workforce is beneficial in gaining a competitive edge in the marketplace. Hartenian and Gundmundson (2000) found evidence that diverse workgroups make higher quality decisions, are more creatively motivated and have higher productivity potentials than less diverse groups. In addition, Florida (2002) reports a strong correlation between the most successful high tech economies and diversity indices in a demographic study of the population characteristics of US high tech sectors. Thus, one aspect of developing the IT innovation capacity of an organization is developing the diversity of the local population (Trauth et al., 2006). Addressing the under representation of women in the IT workforce would contribute to a more diverse workforce and thus, more diverse goods and services.

The individual differences theory of gender and IT is centered on a deep understanding of personal and social shaping constructs that influence gender and IT, which subsequently allows for innovative and robust managerial recommendations. Hence, implications for practice include several awareness factors and intervention recommendations. In terms of awareness, it is important that organizations, managers and employees be aware of diversity issues facing the IT workforce. The individual difference theory of gender and IT has been used to explain diversity in the global IT workforce and recommends that managers expand their definition of diversity (Trauth et al., 2006). Furthermore, the individual difference theory of gender and IT demonstrates that there is a range of differences within women as a gender group. Personal factors such as race, age, geographical location, influences, and characteristics shape women at an individual level and thus, make gender generalizations insufficient.

Conclusion

The nature of the IT workforce is diverse due to its integration of concepts from a wide variety of disciplines, such as management information systems, computer science, and engineering. Yet, the actual demographic makeup of the IT workforce does not reflect a diversity of people. The reason for this lack of female diversity is a complex and challenging area of study because no single factor can be identified as the root cause. Therefore, selecting a robust theoretical perspective is critical to understand and formulate recommendations that address the IT gender gap. For these reasons, the goal of this chapter is twofold. First, is to demonstrate how theory choice impacts managerial recommendations that are given to address the IT gender gap. The second is to demonstrate how the individual differences theory of gender and IT, in particular, can significantly contribute to the reconfiguration of analytical knowledge of the IT gender gap and spur innovative management policies. Professionals and academics faced with the task of addressing the IT gender gap must understand the relationship between theoretical perspectives, epistemological assumptions and managerial recommendations, particularly in order to recognize how holistic perspectives, such as the individual differences theory of gender and IT, offers actionable and innovative managerial recommendations.

References

Adam, A., Emms, J., Green, E., & Owen, J. (1994). *Women, work and computerization: Breaking old boundaries: Building new forms.* Amsterdam, The Netherlands: North-Holland.

Adam, A., Howcroft, D., & Richardson, H. (2001, July 27-29). *Stormy weather: The gender dimension of research debates in IS.* International Federation for Information Processing, Working Group 8.2 Conference, Boise, Idaho.

Adam, A., Howcroft, D., & Richardson, H. (2002). Guest editorial. *Information Technology and People, 15*(2), 94-97.

Adam, A., & Richardson, H. (2001). Feminist philosophy and information systems. *Information Systems Frontiers, 3*(2), 143-154.

Ahuja, M., Robinson, J., Herring, S., & Ogan, C. (2004). Gender issues in IT organizations: exploring antecedents of gender equitable outcomes in higher education. *Proceedings of the 2004 SIGMIS Conference on Computer Personnel Research* (pp. 120-123). Tucson, Arizona. ACM Press.

Anita Borg Institute. (2005). *Chronicle of controversy*. Press Room. Retrieved from http://www.anitaborg.org/pressroom/pressreleases_05/responses all.htm

Arnold, D., & Niederman, F. (2001). The global workforce. *Communications of the ACM, 44*(7), 31-33.

Balcita, A. M., Carver, D. L. & Soffa M. L. (2002). Shortchanging the future of information technology: The untapped resource. *ACM SIGCSE Bulletin, 34*(2), 32-35.

Balka, E., & Smith, R. (2000). *Women, work and computerization: Charting a course to the future*. Boston: Kluwer Academic Publishers.

Berger, P. L., & Luckmann, T. (1966). *The social construction of reality: A treatise in the sociology of knowledge*. New York: Doubleday.

Bureau of Labor Statistics. (2005). *Women in the labor force: A databook*. U.S. Department of Labor, Division of Labor Force Statistics, retrieved on April 26, 2006 from http://www.bls.gov/cps/wlf-databook2005.htm

Caws, P. (1967). Scientific method. In P. Edwards (Ed.), *The encyclopedia of philosophy* (p. 339). New York: Macmillan.

Cockburn, C. (1983). *Brothers: Male dominance and technological change*. London: Pluto Press.

Cockburn, C. (1985). *Machinery of dominance: Women, men and technical know-how*. London: Pluto Press.

Cockburn, C. (1988). *Machinery of dominance: Women, men, and technical know-how*. Boston: Northeastern University Press.

Cockburn, C., & Ormrod, S. (1993). *Gender and technology in the making*. London: Sage.

Cohoon, J. M. (2001). Toward improving female retention in the computer science major. *Communications of the ACM, 44*(5), 108-114.

Cohoon, J. M. (2002). Recruiting and retaining women in undergraduate computing majors. *ACM SIGCSE Bulletin, 34*(2), 48-52.

Couger, D. J., Zawicki, R. A., & Oppermann, E. B. (1979). Motivation levels of MIS managers versus those of their employees. *MIS Quarterly, 3*(3), 47-56.

Crawford, D. (2001). Editorial pointers. *Communications of the ACM, 44*(7), 5.

De Cecco, J. P., & Elia, J. P. (1993). A critique and synthesis of biological essentialism and social constructionist views of sexuality and gender. *Journal of Homosexuality, 24*(1), 1-26.

Dennis, A. R., Kiney, S. T. & Hung, Y. (1999). Gender differences in the effects of media richness. *Small Group Research, 30*(4), 405-437.

Downie, R., Dryburgh, H., McMullin, J., & Ranson, G. (2004). *A profile of information technology in Canada.* Workforce Aging in the New Economy International Report, Number One. Retrieved from http://www.wane.ca/PDF/IR1.pdf

Elmuti, D. (2001). Preliminary analysis of the relationship between cultural diversity and technology in corporate America. Equal Opportunities International, *20*(8), 1-16.

Eriksson, I. V., Kitchenham, B. A., & Tijdens, K. G. (1991). *Women, work, and computerization: Understanding and overcoming bias in work and education.* Amsterdam, The Netherlands: North-Holland.

Florida, R. (2002). *The rise of the creative class.* New York: Basic Books.

Gefen, D., & Straub, D. W. (1997, December). Gender differences in the perception and use of e-mail: An extension to the technology acceptance model. *MIS Quarterly, 21*(4), 389-400.

Harding, S. (1991). *Whose science? Whose knowledge?: Thinking from women's lives.* Milton Keynes: Open University Press.

Hartenian, L., & Gundmundson, D. E. (2000). Cultural diversity in small firms: Implications for company performance. *Journal of Developmental Entrepreneurship, 5*(3), 209-219.

Information Technology Association of America (ITAA). (2003). ITAA blue ribbon panel on IT diversity. Retrieved from http://www.itaa.org/workforce/docs/03divreport.pdf

Information Technology Association of America (ITAA). (2005). *Untapped talent: Diversity, competition, and America's high tech future.* Executive summary. Retrieved from http://www.itaa.org/eweb/upload/execsummdr05.pdf

Jago, A. G., & Scammel, R. W. (1982). Decision-making styles of managers: A comparative evaluation. *Information and Management, 5*(1), 19-29.

Jiang, J. J., Klein, G. S., & Pick, R. A. (1996, July). Individual differences and systems development. *ACM SIGCPR Computer Personnel, 17*(3), 3-12.

Joshi, K. D., & Kuhn, K. (2001). Gender differences in IS career choice: Examine the role of attitudes and social norms in selecting IS profession. *Proceedings of the ACM SIGCPR Conference* (pp. 121-124). San Diego, California.

Joshi, K. D., Schmidt, N. L., & Kuhn, K. M. (2003, April). Is the information systems profession gendered?: Characterization of is professionals and IS careers. *Proceedings of the ACM SIGMIS CPR Conference* (pp. 1-9). Philadelphia.

Kvasny, L. (2003, April). Triple jeopardy: Race, gender and class politics of women in technology. *Proceedings of the ACM SIGMIS CPR Conference* (pp. 10-12). Philadelphia.

Lovegrove, G., & Segal, B. (1991). *Women into computing: Selected papers 1988-1990.* London: Springer-Verlag.

Marini, M. M. (1990). Sex and gender: What do we know? *Sociological Forum, 5*(1), 95-120.

Morgan, A. J., Quesenberry, J. L., & Trauth, E. M. (2004). Exploring the importance of social networks in the IT workforce: Experiences with the "boy's club." In E. Stohr & C. Bullen (Eds.), *Proceedings of the 10th Americas Conference on Information Systems* (pp. 1313-1320). New York.

Naryayan, U. (1998). Essence of culture and a sense of history: a feminist critique of cultural essentialism. *Hypatia: A Journal of Feminist Philosophy, 13*(2), 86-106.

Nielsen, S. H., von Hellens, L. A., Greenhill, A., & Pringle, R. (1997). Collectivism and connectivity: culture and gender in information technology education. *Proceedings of the ACM SIGCPR Conference* (pp. 9-13). San Francisco.

Nielsen, S., von Hellens, L., Greenhill, A., & Pringle, R. (1998). Conceptualising the influence of cultural and gender factors on students' perceptions of it studies and careers. *Proceedings of the 1998 ACM SIGCPR Computer Personnel Research Conference.*

Nielsen, S., von Hellens, L., Pringle, R., & Greenhill, A. (1999). Students' perceptions of information technology careers: conceptualising the influence of cultural and gender factors for IT education. *GATES, 5*(1), 30-38.

Nielsen, S., von Hellens, L., & Wong, S. (2000). The women in IT project: Uncovering the pride and prejudices. In *Proceedings of the 6th Australasian Women and Computing Workshop* (pp. 45-55). Griffith University, Brisbane.

Orlikowski, W. & Baroudi, J. (1991). Studying information technology in organizations: research approaches and assumptions. *Information Systems Research, 2*(1), 1-28.

Pringle, R., Nielsen, S., von Hellens, L., Greenhill, A., & Parfitt, L. (2000). Net gains: Success strategies of professional women in IT. In E. Balka & R. Smith (Eds.), *Women, work and computerization: Charting a course to the future.* Boston: Kluwer Academic Publishers.

Quesenberry, J. L., & Trauth, E. M. (2005). The role of ubiquitous computing in maintaining work-life balance: Perspectives from women in the IT workforce. In C. SØrensen, Y. Yoo, K. Lyytinen, & J. I. DeGross (Eds.), *Designing ubiquitous information environments: Socio-technical issues and challenges* (pp. 43-55). Springer: New York.

Quesenberry, J. L., Morgan, A. J., & Trauth, E. M. (2004). Understanding the "Mommy tracks": A framework for analyzing work-family issues in the IT workforce. In M. Khosrow-Pour (Ed.), *Proceedings of the Information Resources Management Association Conference,* New Orleans, Louisiana (pp. 135-138). Hershey, PA: Idea Group Publishing.

Quesenberry, J. L., Trauth, E. M., & Morgan, A. J. (2006). Understanding the "Mommy tracks": A framework for analyzing work-family balance in the IT workforce." *Information Resource Management Journal, 19*(2), 37-53.

Schiebinger, L. (1999). *Has feminism changed science?* Cambridge, MA: Harvard University Press.

Slyke, C. V., Comunale, C. L. & Belanger, F. (2002). Gender differences in perceptions of Web-based shopping. *Communications of the ACM, 45*(7), 82-86.

Spender, D. (1995). *Nattering on the net: Women, power, and cybespace.* North Melbourne, Victoria: Spinifex Press Pty Ltd.

Star, S. L. (1995). *The cultures of computing.* Oxford: Blackwell Publishers.

Sumner, M., & Werner, K. (2001). The impact of gender differences on the career experiences of information systems professionals. *Proceedings of the ACM SIGCPR Conference* (pp. 125-131). San Diego, California.

Townsend, G. C. (2002). People who make a difference: Mentors and role models. *ACM SIGCSE Bulletin, 34*(2), 57-61.

Trauth, E. M. (1995). Women in Ireland's information industry: Voices from inside. *Eire-Ireland, 30*(3), 133-150.

Trauth, E. M. (2000). *The culture of an information economy: Influences and impacts in the republic of Ireland.* Dordrecht: Kluwer Academic Publishers.

Trauth, E. M. (2002). Odd girl out: An individual differences perspective on women in the IT profession. *Information Technology and People, 15*(2), 98-118.

Trauth, E. M. (2004, March). Women and Ireland's knowledge economy: Snapshots of change. Keynote Presentation, *International Women's Day Celebration,* University of Limerick, Limerick, Ireland.

Trauth, E. M., & Quesenberry, J. L. (2005, June 23-24). Individual inequality: Women's responses in the IT profession. In G. Whitehouse (Ed.), *Pro-*

ceedings of the Women, Work and IT Forum, Brisbane, Queensland, Australia.

Trauth, E. M., Huang, H., Morgan, A. J., Quesenberry, J. L., & Yeo, B. (2006). Investigating the existence and value of diversity in the global IT workforce: An analytical framework. In F. Niederman & T. Ferratt (Eds.), *Managing information technology human resources,* Information Age Publishing: Greenwich, Connecticut (pp. 333-362).

Trauth, E. M., Nielsen, S. H., & von Hellens, L. A. (2003). Explaining the IT gender gap: Australian stories for the new millennium. *Journal of Research and Practice in IT, 35*(1), 7-20.

Trauth, E. M., Nielsen, S., & von Hellens, S. (2000). Explaining the IT gender gap: Australian stories. *Proceedings of the 10th Australasian Conference on Information Systems.*

Trauth, E. M., Quesenberry, J. L. & Yeo, B. (2005). The influence of environmental context on women in the IT workforce. In M. Gallivan, J. E. Moore, & S. Yager (Eds.), *Proceedings of the 2005 ACM SIGMIS CPR Conference on Computer Personnel Research,* Atlanta, Georgia (pp. 24-31). ACM Press: New York.

Trauth, E. M., Quesenberry, J. L., & Morgan, A. J. (2004). Understanding the under representation of women in IT: Toward a theory of individual differences. *Proceedings of the ACM SIGMIS Computer Personnel Research Conference,* Tucson, AZ.

Venkatesh, V., & Morris, M. G. (2000). Why don't men ever stop to ask for directions? Gender, social influence, and their role in technology acceptance and user behavior. *MIS Quarterly, 24*(1), 115-139.

Venkatesh, V., Morris, M., & Ackerman, P. (2000). A longitudinal field investigation of gender differences in individual technology adoption decision making processes. *Organizational Behavior and Human Decision Processes, 83*(1), 33-60.

von Hellens, L., & Nielsen, S. (2001). Australian women in IT." *Communications of the ACM, 44*(7), 46-52.

von Hellens, L., Nielsen, S., & Trauth, E. M. (2001). Breaking and entering the male domain: Women in the IT industry. *Proceedings of the 2001 ACM SIGCPR Computer Personnel Research Conference.*

von Hellens, L., Pringle, R., Nielsen, S., & Greenhill, A. (2000). People, business, and IT skills: The perspective of women in the IT industry. *Proceedings of the 2000 ACM SIGCPR Computer Personnel Research Conference.*

Wajcman, J. (1991). *Feminism confronts technology.* University Park: The Pennsylvania University Press.

Wajcman, J. (2000). Reflections on gender and technology studies: In what state is the art?" *Social Studies of Science, 30*(3), 447-464.

Wardle, C. (2003, April 22-24). Luncheon panel: Fostering diversity in the IT workforce. *Proceedings of the 2003 SIGMIS Conference on Computer Personnel Research*. Philadelphia.

Webster, J. (1996). *Shaping women's work: Gender, employment, and information technology*. London: Longman.

Workforce Aging in the New Economy (WANE). (2004). *Europe, phase one: A selection of initial findings on employment diversity*. Retrieved from http://www.wane.ca/PDF/EUBriefing.pdf

Zmud, R. (1979). Individual differences and MIS success: A review of the empirical literature. *Management Science, 25*(10), 966-979.

Endnotes

[1]   This research has been funded by grants from the National Science Foundation (grant number EIA-0204246) the Science Foundation Ireland, and the Australian Research Council.

[2]   The essentialist perspective is reflected in the recent remarks of Dr. Lawrence Summers, former President of Harvard, at an academic conference, when he suggested the innate differences between men and women may be the reason why few women succeed in math and science careers (Anita Borg Institute, 2005).

[3]   Epistemology is a theory of knowledge, which specifically delineates how beliefs can be legitimized as knowledge (Caws, 1967; Harding, 1997; Orlikowski and Baroudi, 1991).

Chapter III

Work-Life Imbalance of IT Workers in the Internet Age

Helen Richardson, The Open Polytechnic of New Zealand, New Zealand

Darrell Bennetts, The Open Polytechnic of New Zealand, New Zealand

Abstract

These days, no information technology (IT) manager or worker will have escaped the expectation from a client that a job needed to be completed "yesterday." The field of information systems (IS) research is only beginning to develop models for understanding the emerging issue of workload pressures upon IT workers, and their consequent need to maintain a balance between work and home. IT organisations need to consider how they manage their IT workers, departing from the traditional efficiency approach to staff management, and moving towards one better suited to the globalised environment within which businesses now operate. In its two parts, this chapter will consider the challenges of work-life balance that IT workers increasingly face. These days, IT workers are more vulnerable than other work employment groups to the pressure of contemporary workload expectations and deadlines. Research in the fields of sociology and psychology can help fill in detail on this emerging issue, otherwise absent from contemporary IS research. Sociology and Psychology can help IT practitioners better understand the increasing human cost of the currently increasing commercial pressures. In its first part, this chapter utilises some straightforward sociological concepts to background how "top down" or strategic management of IT workers could be improved within the IT sector. Sociologists have long had a strong interest in social change, in the ways in which both work and non-work ("leisure") activities are changing within an increasingly globalised world. Many IT workers are now suffering both physical and mental symptoms due to commonplace business management approaches, which ultimately forgo long-term business profitability for short-term bottom lines. The second part of this chapter utilises the understanding of emotional intelligence within psychology and applies it as a bottom up strategy to illustrate how IT workers can cope with work-life imbalance. Here, a case study illustrates how the emotional qualities of resilience and adaptability that some IT workers possess can enable them to overcome work-life imbalances within the pressured context of globalised IT production. Leading on from the case study, the chapter will provide guidance on how IT workers might foster these qualities using HR techniques from the recently developed field of emotional intelligence. By utilising what have so far been interrelated, yet also independent, discussions within sociology and psychology on the effects of the Internet Age upon IT workers, this chapter aims to provide a balanced approach to the intellectual and emotional management of IT workers.

Part I: The Sociology of a Typical IT Worker: A "Top-Down" Analysis

Introduction

The Internet Age began in the 1990s. It was characterised by increased connectivity and constant change. All workers, most notably the typical IT worker, were presented with new challenges by this Age, in both their professional and in their personal lives. Many analysts predicted that the Internet Age would provide businesses with increasingly cheaper electronic connections between employees, which would consequently develop flexible work environments. The anticipated benefits included more exciting employment opportunities and the potential to work from home (Rowe, 1990). This new age also produced many challenges for the typical IT worker. Longer work hours, the potential threat of redundancy, and the constant requirement to be on call, now dominate the daily lives of the IT workers who heralded the arrival of the Internet Age (de Bruin & Dupuis, 2004).

Definition

What we mean by a "typical IT worker," is an employee of a company that is involved in computer education, research, design, manufacture or sales of computer hardware or software, including telecommunications and microelectronics (Costigan & Ó hÉigeartaigh, 2003; Keen, 1980). In both their domestic and working lives, IT workers are increasingly finding themselves in social contexts that are underpinned by a phenomenon of broad social change, wrought by the development of the Internet Age. This chapter considers what are now demonstrably *interrelated* spaces or spheres of a typical IT worker's life: professional and private, rational and emotional domains.

Historical Background

The story of the Internet Age begins in sleepy Silicon Valley of the 1970s. The events that would unfold here at this time and continue through to the present day have deep historical origins.

The most significant driving force in the IT industry's relatively short history has been a business ethos of capitalism, and—for the most part—*American* capitalism. Traditionally, the "Age of Science" has driven Wall Street's rational approach to business. The ethos of this age is dominated by a drive towards the financial benefits of pursuing rational ends. Here, *efficient*, rational, methods of production have become more esteemed and sought after (Weber, 1975a, b, c). The *processes* we use to create goods or services (in sociological terms, the *means* of production) became more important to every company's bottom line, than the end products or services. This was seen in the move from small cottage industries, where the craftsman created a specialised product for the customer to the mass production of the industrial age. Consider the car makers of old, each a craftsman, who hand built each car to the specifications of each of the perspective owners needs, to the mass production under Ford, where as Ford himself said "you could have any colour car you wanted as long it was black" (Sennett, 1998). Here the process of manufacture was enhanced to increase the number and speed of production under the new slogan of "efficiency." Industrial machinery was often brought in the name of efficiency and eliminated the less productive human workers. Industrial machinery, which would later include information technology, advanced the dominance of this model of "Wall Street" rationality in business management and practice. This approach was not the sole intellectual framework within which American business operated across the 19th and 20th centuries. Nor was it exclusively the domain of American companies. Nevertheless, it was—and remains today—arguably the most significant intellectual approach to business development and planning worldwide.

As more efficient machinery was developed and more efficient processes of factory production arose in most industrialised countries, rural workers were drawn to cities to take up work in these industries for the promise of better wages, higher living conditions and, perhaps, an improvement in social standing (Castells, 2000a). The social structures of the industrialised societies that pursued the rational ideal of efficiency were significantly affected by the patterns of rural-urban drift that followed. In more recent times, a series of advances in information technology has encouraged the development of new types of social practices in these now modernised, urban-centred, cosmopolitan, societies.

In the 1970s in Silicon Valley, California, professional military and scientific communities, and the young academics specialising in electronics that belonged to these communities, began to develop the first personal computers and the telecommunication technology necessary for the Internet Age. Although other countries worked with similar ideas and added to the pool of knowledge, as seen in the French "Minitel," it was American capitalism that would ensure the dominance of Silicon Valley in the time to come. Since this time, information technology has come to be viewed as means to *enable freedom*: the subsequent development of the Internet out of this environment embodies this ideal of "free spirit" within enterprise. With the support of some of these talented students and their professors, (for example, Mr. Hewlett and Mr. Packard), businesses were established and these emerging IT products became rapidly commercial enterprises. Over the subsequent decades through to the present day, the uptake of these new technologies by the business world was phenomenal (Castells, 2000a; Mackun, 2005), for it was quickly realised that this new technology was able to rapidly change the efficiency and hence the profitability of businesses (Agarwal & Ferratt, 1998; Robinson, 1999).

So too, it is in sunny Silicon Valley that the "identity" of the IT worker we know today first appeared. They were a new kind of employee, often-bright young university graduates with a talent for electronics, who enjoyed the workings of a logical computer and could absorb themselves for hours in the development of new applications (Rogers & Larson, 1984). Due to many "start up" businesses being high risk, employment was transient as workers jumped from project to project, rather than remaining in one company for a long time (Saxenian, 1994). Contract employment became the norm, and staying in any job for more than two years was considered detrimental to a professional career (Sennett, 1998; Swart, Kinnie, & Purcell 2003). Furthermore, to support the drive for innovation, traditional work practices were dismissed in favour of ones that allowed a spirit of creativity to prevail. The image of the "geek" or "nerd" began to take hold in this burgeoning industry, with jeans, T-shirts, and long hair being part of the informal uniform (Kearney, 2002; Ramsay, 1999). Also, the practice of working from home and providing creative office furnishings originated from these workers.

As a result, a new work environment was developed within the highly sophisticated technology cluster of Silicon Valley IT companies which, in turn, resulted in a new labour market with its own distinctive skill levels, workforce expectations, and management ideology (Dunlop, 1988; Ziehl, 2003). This new labour market was not protected by union regulations. The protection of employee rights through unionism has a much weaker tradition in America than in other first world societies. Along with the positive work practices already mentioned, others also then arose such as long work hours and high-pressure environments, driven by the need to develop the next product before your competitor did.

These untroubled days of curiosity-driven research and technological advancement would turn out to be relatively short lived. Venture capitalists were quickly attracted to the resultant advances in information technology, as they realised the hefty financial gains to be achieved from these innovations. The creation of the PC, networking technology for LANs, WANs, the Internet and its hypertext interface, the World Wide Web, and the current mobile and wireless revolution, would soon become all-important developments in the formation of the Internet Age. Moreover, these modern technologies have enabled businesses to advance their enterprise globally by taking advantage of the new flexibility resulting from these technological advances.

There were further sweeping changes in the 1990s in the wider commercial world, where "booms and busts" became commonplace. Oil crises led to a sharp decline in the world economy and businesses needed to restructure to survive (Castells, 2000a). New management practices were introduced that replaced layers of middle management with a new type of inventive, adaptable, and hard working IT worker. Information technology had by this time become indispensable to the efficiency and profitability of business. IT workers became much sought after, and as a consequence were highly paid.

This boom in IT business would not outlast the decade, and IT workers became victims of their own revolution. Information technology often did not yield the profitability predicted, and businesses soon wanted to rid themselves of, what at times could be, difficult to manage and costly IT sections. The tide turned on IT work and workers, and IT came to be perceived as not a core function of in-house business, and was subsequently outsourced to private contractors (Lacity & Willcocks, 1998). In successive years over the 1990s, the worldwide IT labour market changed, and what was once a shortage of talented IT workers became a glut. The IT industry and its workers suffered a "boom and bust cycle" long synonymous with capitalist enterprise. The most infamous example of this phenomenon was the boom that the Internet brought, with wealthy Americans investing in *dot.com* start-ups. The cycle began again when investors did not get the returns they envisioned and the so-called "dot.com crash" of the late 1990s began (Weber, 2004). IT workers were discarded and left jobless as a result. Although in relative time the job loss was often seen to be short lived, even six months can have devastating impact on IT workers and their families, as one worker discusses (Koeber, 2002; Richardson, 2005):

So many of my friends lost their job and had to pack up their family and head overseas. It took them two or three contract jobs to find stability and the impact on relocating a family put huge strains on their families. I did not want to do this, so I stayed jobless for six months, we almost lost our house….

More recently, recognisable trends have started to become identifiable among affected IT workers. They have begun to demonstrate a number of unemployment-related problems, as both mental and physical illnesses; family and relationship breakdowns, and a general feeling of being burnt by the industry they once loved increasingly becomes commonplace (Kaluzniacky, 2004). It is in light of this historical context and understanding, that HR and IT managers, and IT workers themselves, are still able to choose how to implement this technology, in business, in employment and in their personal lives. Furthermore the, now worn-out, practices of management may need to be revisited to better aid IT workers who are at the coalface of this change (Scholarios & Marks, 2004). It now seems that all is not so rosy in the little sunny valley in California.

Sociological Concepts Identified

Over the 1990s to the present day, the evolutionary drive of the Internet Age has been determined by a series of significant advances in information technology. These advances have been shaped by underlying social structures which have, in turn, informed the business practices and social environments that IT workers live and work within (Castells, 2000a). To better comprehend the social experience of the typical IT worker's life, the following key areas of current sociological thinking are useful to our discussion:

- Identity
- Work
- Globalisation

Identity

In current sociological terms, personal identity is understood to be how individuals *form* and then *maintain* a sense of self-identity in order to *understand themselves* within personal and business relationships, families, communities, and wider social organisations. It is through this formation and maintenance of self-identity that we can each find our way through the world that we live within (Johnston, 2003). Different from personality traits, self-identity involves choice; that as members of wider social groups (families, communities, etc.), people choose the groups with which they want to be identified. Individuals continually negotiate their self-identity by negotiating between these groups. For example, a man may choose to take on and maintain the self-identity of *worker* and place this in high status over other social roles that are expected of him, such as that of *husband*, or *father* or of a social sports *team member*. In this scenario, effort is directed to the maintenance of the "worker" aspects of his self-identity, more so than the other social roles that he has. When the management of this becomes too extreme, as seen in "workaholism" or "job loss" (Woodward, 2000) identity can become "corroded" and social individuals can experience vulnerability (Sennett, 1998). Later on in the chapter, we will explore this further.

Work

Within sociology, "work" is defined as a state that is within a social context and has been discussed in terms of peoples' working lives or paid employment (Marshall, 1998). Here, work is defined as the physical, mental, and emotional effort exerted to produce a consumable good or service. Technology has increasingly been introduced to the intellectual frameworks of this analysis, and with it has in recent years come the recognition of the *transformative power* that work has over the social lives of employees, and of IT workers in particular.

By contrast, within information systems research, "non-work" social spaces, such as the home, have often been an under-explored phenomenon. For many sociologists, unpaid work requires an equally important consideration as paid employment. Unpaid work provides the "glue" that binds together many social situations. Housework has traditionally been viewed as the realm of women, within Western societies, and includes cooking, cleaning, childcare and looking after the elderly and sick (Abercrombie, Hill, & Turner, 2000). But, the domestic sphere of "home" can also provide a social context for both domestic labour *and* leisure time. Leisure time is sociologically categorised as the time left over from paid work. Both leisure and unpaid work have seen increasing use of technology to either take over or be involved in these activities (Abercrombie, Hill, & Turner, 2000). Recently there has also been a significant crossover or "spill-over" between the areas of work and non-work, as "work" at home (whether paid or unpaid) has become more computerised.

Globalisation

Globalisation has become a much-discussed idea in sociology. Held, McGrew, Goldblatt, and Perraton (1999, p. 2) have defined globalisation as "the widening, deepening, and speeding up of world-wide interconnectedness in all aspects of contemporary social life, from cultural to criminal, the financial to spiritual". Globalisation has come to epitomise the Internet Age, as vast spans of fibre optics and satellite links have allowed new forms of social representation in terms of time and space. Initially, it was thought that globalisation would create a global village. However, sociologists have recently shown that globalisation has instead disconnected the world from the national, geographically formed "political spheres" that we commonly call countries, which have traditionally been reinforced by the physical separation of land, sea, and mountains. The forming of this electronic network has given rise to the traditional financial global centres of London, Tokyo and New York, turning the world into a "global financial casino" of these capitalist elites or hubs, that run twenty-four hours a day, seven days a week, and can now seamlessly cut across the traditional restrictions of time and space. Those not in the hub or the support network of the hub of this vast network can become marginalised in virtual ghettos (Abercrombie, Hill, & Turner, 2000; Castells, 2000a). Thus, globalisation is not so much a "world-wide" phenomenon, as it is an acceleration and concentration of the already-established international twentieth century economic networks. The increasing tempo of work (both paid and unpaid) that results from the structural processes of globalisation affects IT workers in new and profound ways, in particular the very environment they and their families live in increasingly experiencing significant upheaval and disruption. In the following discussion, it is this disruption of the traditional work and home in which we will be especially concerned.

Changes of Self-Identity
Among IT Workers

The quality of life experienced by workers in Western societies has been significantly affected by the increasingly commonplace role of computer technology. Since the 1990s, white-collar workers' patterns of work have significantly changed since the introduction of networking and the Internet-connected technology that has integrated workplaces and homes (Castells, 2000b). As we have seen, the IT industry has been at the heart of Western society's change over the past thirty years and IT workers have been both the beneficiaries and victims of this exciting and ever changing field of work (Scholarios & Marks, 2004).

The computer technology that we all experience today first emerged as a commonplace business tool in the 1970s. Then, IT workers routinely used punch card systems in their daily work. The keyboards of dumb terminal mainframes would in turn replace this system, and likewise would become superseded by the networked PCs. This was an exciting time for those who entered the IT profession, as they were at the hub of the thrilling escalation of new computing technologies that large businesses rapidly adopted. Information technology machines became a core system for the execution of business. Corporations came to rely on their information systems twenty-four hours a day. This required IT workers to increasingly move to shift work as a standard business practice. IT workers spent long hours working at keyboards, looking at screens, and in general just working long hours; the compensation was high pay (Barrett, 2001). Nevertheless this was not to last, as mainframe technology was superseded by client server systems.

The in-house, highly paid IT worker consequently found him/herself superseded too. This was to be the beginning of a long trend in IT employment, with each revolution in technology the IT workers were faced with potential "obsolescence." There were two avenues to pursue to resolve this issue: retrain to the new technology or change sectors (*Computer World*, 2004). This trend has continued, with the advent of outsourcing the IT function, to the dot.com crash of the Internet era; all following on from the boom and bust cycle of business transactions. This is not fuelled by the innocent invention of new technology but *by the capitalist efficiency-led application of IT within globalised organisations' business practices.*

Currently this trend has reached a new height with the Internet Age. Many IT jobs are now sent offshore, leaving numerous middle class white collar workers unemployed in America and subsequently in European countries, as they have had to replicate this system in order to compete with the "bottom line" profitability that American parent companies dictate (Castells, 2000a). Though the initial statistics have been drawn into question as new data *surfaced,* the shock to white middle class IT workers cannot be underestimated. In America calls for unionisation were made, an unprecedented response to an industry that has traditionally had no such desire. Two IT workers illustrate the impact this had to their psyche (Richardson, 2005):

I have been made redundant three times, so now I only contract, then I know when I will be without a job. I am lucky I do not have children, I can do this, other friends cannot.

I was made redundant two years ago, at last I have a permanent job but it is the same long hours and lack of family time, now the market is buoyant again I am looking for another job, I want to get the maximum pay before it goes under again.

Analysis of these recent trends has shown that the typical IT worker of the future will need to be creative, or even be *artistic,* as only highly innovative workers will be employed in Western countries. All routine IT work is increasingly being undertaken off-shore in China, India, the Philippines and Russia (Pink, 2005; Prusak, 2004; Saunders, 2004). Nevertheless the paradox mentioned in the previous section remains: many IT workers, despite the professional hardships they encounter, cannot imagine working in any other industry. As one IT manager shows the range of emotions about working in the IT industry (Richardson, 2005):

I would like to see a survey to see how many are stuck in the IT industry because they cannot get paid this much anywhere else...

At a later time the same worker stated:

I work in the industry as I like the excitement, it is always changing. I was working in England when virtual reality first appeared, I set up a business in this area but it failed as I did not quite get the business model right, there was a lot of competition in London, but I am still interested in virtual reality, now I am looking at e-storage, there is always something new.

Being mindful of these last comments, we will soon look at the benefits—and disadvantages—that technology has brought IT workers, in particular in the areas of exciting job opportunities and job flexibility.

To better understand the impact of the Internet Age on IT workers, the sociological theories of the formation and maintenance of self-identity; the impact of technology on work and home; and the impact of globalisation require individual consideration. Although our discussion will begin by looking at self-identity, these different areas of analysis do not stand alone. There are inter-relationships between them. Correspondingly, our discussion of self-identity will provide poignant examples of the impact that each of these areas of everyday life: self-identity, home, work, and globalisation, can have upon each other. In sum, the interrelatedness of these social phenomena ultimately shapes and directs the performance capabilities of the typical IT worker.

Self-Identity in an Increasingly Technological World

The formation and maintenance of self-identity in IT work is just beginning to be researched. As the world is constantly changing, traditional social structures are altered, people's concepts of whom they are will necessarily change too. In this context, IT workers face questions of self-identity that are quite identical to those of other types of workers. All must reconcile the fundamental changes in society that have cumulated into what we now call the Internet Age, for along-side the social changes to family and work, technology has also been used to reshape the wider world (de Bruin & Dupuis, 2004). What makes IT workers distinctive here is that they are at the very coal face of this change, being not only the instigators of new forms of technology which are changing the Western world, they are also all too often the first to be shaped by new management practices, and new forms of living and working, that the advancements in technology bring.

Within Information Systems research, studies show that because of the new nature of the work, identity is hard to form. This has been further blurred by the constant change of work skills, so that what it means to be an IT worker constantly changes too. Added to this, due to the blurring of work and leisure-time activities, the idea of what it is to be an IT worker in fact extends beyond simply being what the sociologists consider a **role**, but is instead a **true identity**, in that it is not just a task they perform, but it becomes part of their *internalised sense of self* (Castells, 2000b; Scholarios & Marks, 2004).

The IT industry has been one of the first to feature flexibility of employment as a commonplace mode of work. Contract, part-time and project-based employment are the usual employment arrangements within this sector. For some workers this provides exciting and constant changing employment. It also potentially allows a healthy balance between work and life. However, in many cases IT sector employees fix the primary basis of their self-identity on their role as a worker. They self-identify as an "IT worker," and can as a result forgo an attachment to (for example) their identity as a parent or partner. In turn, the basis of these workers' self-identities often proves itself to be of limited substance during times of crisis. Where these IT workers might (as commonly occurs) become redundant in a boom and bust cycle, they in a sense become "lost" in this new employment pattern (*de Bruin & Dupuis,* 2004). A feeling of misplacement arises. What were highly skilled workers become victims of the prevailing dynamics of the globalised economic system.

This sense of disconnection arises not only through (un)employment in the IT sector. More than the employees of other business sectors, typical IT workers today experience a blurring of the boundaries between their sense of self-identity as workers, lovers, parents, or individuals. This is because—in all these separate areas of social life—*a connection to information technology is central* to the primary formation and maintenance of the typical IT worker's primary self-identity.

IT Workers as Parents

The traditional stereotyped image of the IT worker as a young white male is being broken down, partly because these "young" men have now aged and have families of their own. But, more to the point, there have always been families in the background of each IT worker's personal life. Acknowledgment of family life and IT career has often been forgone in an industry where long and irregular hours are the norm. The need to be constantly on call, which makes planning family activities difficult at the best of times, conflicts strongly with the requirements of IT business needs. As we will see later, this problem is compounded by this group demonstrating specific genetic traits that cause syndromes in their children and make those who are parents more vulnerable to stress.

Gender, Race, and the Technology of Confusion

The dilution of the hitherto stable institution of the traditional family unit is at the heart of many individual's confusion about their personal role in society (Castells, 2000a). Recent years have seen more women taking additional paid employment in order to maintain their family's standard of living, continue their access to education, or otherwise maintain a household economy following the dissolution of a relationship. Further still, some women have chosen to forgo traditional family and relationships to focus instead on their careers (Castleman, Coulthard, & Reed, 2004; Giddens, 2002). Consequentially, clear distinctions between male and female forms of self-identity are in many cases now eroding. The IT workplace has been slow to represent this change. Traditionally cast as a "boys club" it is often a hard world for a woman to enter and sustain (*Igbaria, & Lak,* 1997; Margolis & Fisher, 2002; Queensberry, Morgan, & Trauth, 2004). Those who sustain this bifurcation or division of gender roles in the IT sector would argue that men have "more logical" minds than women, which makes the male gender better suited to computer programming. Recent research has shown, nevertheless, that the skills traditionally seen as more feminine, such as empathy, are desperately needed by this sector (Kaluzniacky, 2004).

Other changes in sexual identity have occurred such as the opening up of attitudes to sexuality in modern society (Castells, 2000b; Giddens, 2002). Information Systems research is now coming to address the identity of gay IT workers. As some of the preliminary findings have discovered, when talking to an IT worker who identifies as gay (Richardson, 2005):

Many gay men choose to work in IT as they find it a less judgmental place to work, the logical computer does not discriminate. I have met more gay IT men in the gay network than I have met hairdressers, we are swarming in them. Gay men don't want to be hairdressers any more, I guess IT workers are the new hairdressers (laugh).

Reflecting on this statement he continues:

Though they are often gay men who identify with masculinity so you would not know many of them are gay, this may be part of the attraction too, by doing IT work they can be gay but feel like a regular "man" too.

Recent studies have shown that many gay workers and other minorities are drawn to IT as this industry is considered to be accepting of social diversity (Florida, 2002). In the United Kingdom many Indian or coloured women take up a career in IT for these very reasons. This further still breaks away from the traditional stereotype of IT workers at "white young European males" (Igbaria, & Wormley, 1992).

Domestication of IT Technologies

The most significant non-work phenomenon that affects the formation and maintenance of the typical IT worker's self-identity is the *domestication* of information technology. For many IT workers, the outer boundaries of self-identity commonly become blurred when they overlap the private and personal with the professional. Here, an individual's work role develops personal meaning beyond merely that of a "job." It becomes an all-encompassing definition for his or her social life.

IT systems are increasingly ever present within IT worker's homes. This enables a corresponding increase of IT modes of work at home (Castells, 2000a). Although this has initially been highlighted as something that would improve the working conditions of IT specialists, the reality has been a very mixed experience. For many it has meant bringing more work home. This can reduce the distinction of work and leisure separation, resulting in increased burn out for workers (Castells, 2000b; Wright & Cropanzano, 1998).

Another significant issue for the domestication of IT systems is the increasingly commonplace addiction to online gaming among IT workers. For some online-gamers, an online community provides a network of friends. For others it isolates them from friends and family (Castells, 2000b). Some IT workers find it hard to escape the technology they use at work and truly relax. In one interview an IT Manager talked of one his young programmers (Richardson, 2005):

He worked long hours on the computer at work and for relaxation would stay up all night playing "Everquest", I asked him when he slept, he said he only got four hours sleep a night.

Globalisation and Social Interaction

The emergent phenomenon of globalisation has had a deep-seated impact on the formation and maintenance of self-identity in modern society (Giddens, 2001, p. 61):

Globalization is fundamentally changing the nature of our everyday experiences...forcing a redefinition of intimate and personal aspects of our lives, such as the family, gender roles, sexuality, personal identity.... We are faced with a move towards a new individualism (before which) the weight of tradition and established values is retreating...traditional frameworks of identity are dissolving and new patterns of identity emerging.

Never has this statement been truer than in recent times for the typical IT worker, who commonly experiences a destabilization of the bases of his or her self-identity, such as from the mass job losses in America due to the historically unprecedented outsourcing of recent years. This trend has begun to spread through the rest of the Western world. The universal effect of this trend has been highly skilled, highly paid individuals being reduced to unskilled, unemployed masses. As one IT Project Manager comments (King, 2004, p. 2):

IT was a career, but now it's a job.... The way the job is now, we might as well ask people if they'd like fries with that project.

A primary effect of globalisation upon IT workers has been the breakdown of working conditions. This has produced a significant paradox in the IT industry, now being reflected in other job categories, of professional workers being subject to longer working hours, more limited job security and shrinking employee benefits (Castells, 2000a; de Bruin & Dupuis, 2004). This can lead to a feeling of personal helplessness (King 2004, p. 2):

Outsourcing is euphemistically called 'global sourcing'...Memos [about outsourcing] are self-congratulatory about how it will benefit employees, totally ignoring how many fewer domestic employees we have year to year.

In these current patterns, a result of globalisation upon the formation and maintenance of self-identity among IT workers is increasingly being identified as the *corrosion* of what had hitherto been formed in robust and concrete social circumstances (Sennett, 1998). So, the lack of certainty of IT workers' (increasingly global) *social sphere* corrodes the bases of their self-identity with the increasingly common prospect of redundancy due to outsourcing of IT work to more profitable economies. This can leave the typical IT worker feeling vulnerable, alienated and powerless. In sum, the contemporary, globalised, technology-driven, efficiency driven model of practice that is currently favoured by international business eats away at the trust an IT worker has for his or her employing organisation, and can contribute significantly to a reduction in his/her sense of self-identity. On this corrosion of an IT worker's self-identity, one outspoken IT worker discusses how off-shoring affected his identity (Pardon, 2004):

One year ago, I resigned my IT job with...a Fortune 500 international corporation.... I resigned because I was too disgusted and demoralized to continue working in the profession I enjoyed because my employer had made it evident that American workers are expendable, replaceable and disposable no matter how loyal, productive, competent, or well educated. I concluded there was no future for me with [company name] or in IT.

Globalised work patterns are *consuming* workers' understanding of the world, and of themselves (Giddens, 1991). No longer is mere geographical distance the primary determinant of social isolation. Today, the rapid change that a global context perpetuates upon IT workers, through networked and/or global organisations forming and disbanding across countries and continents, also significantly creates experiences of isolation and dissociation. For many IT workers, globalisation has taken away their ability to have mastery over their lives. Although this feeling of powerlessness at work is less damaging than the breakdown of personal relationships, the impact can flow into the personal sphere. As a result, the typical IT worker's self-identity is now in constant flux.

Maintenance of Work-Life Balance

From the personal benefits and costs of working in a sector that emphasises the constant need for a successful business to stay ahead of the competition, we will next turn our attention to how the domestication of information technology has affected this group of workers. New electronic technology is increasingly being used by IT workers not just for work but for recreation at home. It is important to consider how technology not only impacts IT workers at the office but how it impacts on their domestic lives, as the breaking down of boundaries in technology use between home and work can increase the levels of stress for these workers (Kanter, 1977).

The ability to work from home has usually been considered to provide workers a better balance of work-life commitments. But this belief is not necessarily manifested in the lives of IT workers (Finegold, Mohrman, & Spreitzer 2002; Goodwin, 2004). New research has shown that, in the context of working from home, the separation of work and leisure time cannot be managed properly in all cases, which in turn can lead to confusion and blurring of work and leisure time for IT workers, leaving them little time to mentally or physically free themselves of information technology. This results in increased levels of stress (*Scholarios & Marks, 2004;* Stewart, 2001). In particular, if IT workers are not trained properly, this stress can result in low commitment to his or her employer, with a consequential high turnover of employees in this sector (Wright & Cropanzano, 1998). Proper consideration of the need for IT workers to be constantly on call, the commonplace practice of working from home, and—in both cases—the attendant result of longer working hours therefore requires thoughtful consideration. The use of information technology as a means of relaxation in an IT worker's home, as means to tune out from "life" can cause further separation from family and their wider face-to-face networks (Yee, 2005, in press) and traditional leisure pursuits (de Bruin & Dupuis, 2004). These are significant concerns and deserve closer consideration.

In the last two decades there has been significant change in the types of technology that have entered the home environment. Initially technology such as the television and videocassette recorders (VCRs) were primarily for leisure and group activities (Stewart, 2001). The entry of technology in recent times has followed a new trend, it is based around individualistic rather than group based use, examples are, the personal computer (PC) and cell phones. Furthermore, these technologies are also used in the work environment and this has created a blur between work and leisure time.

The first change in the blurring of work and home life has been referred to as the *third space* or *life-space* (Dholakia, Mundorf, & Dholakia, 1996; Stewart, 2000). This type of space—where public and private life blurs—has to date been unexplored in Information Systems research, but sociology has begun to unravel this dilemma. Research has begun to show that, *how* workers negotiate the boundaries of these traditional spaces—work and home—is important in determining work-life balance. What must be considered is that in its consistently developing evolution, IT is not just crossing physical boundaries, but is now also transgressing workers private "values, ideas, experiences and expectations" (Stewart, 2001, p. 5).

The Impact of Technology upon the Boundaries between Home and Work

For decades, the ability to work from home has been considered one of the key benefits that will come from an information society. Indeed many employers have allowed workers to take computers and mobile technology home not only to work from home, but also to learn from home, and to allow others in their households also to develop IT skills. Regardless, other trends have begun to emerge, where technology has a negative impact on workers. This is especially true for the high demand and fast pace world of IT workers.

Sociologists have identified that successful integration of work and home, with the aid of technology is largely dependent on how an organisation manages this. Nippert-Eng (1995), details three types of workplace: one with *fixed boundaries*, one described as *the greedy employee* and, thirdly, one that lets *employees determine their own boundaries*. While these are three discrete types, organisations tend to drift between extreme occurrences of these types. This "drifting" can vary depending on both the organisation in question, and the circumstances of its employees at a given point in time. Especially contingent in this matrix is the matter of recent pressures on the declining product sales in the IT industry. As one study describes this inconsistency displayed in a high-tech organisation which had a reputation for flexible employment:

Engineers seem to agree that if there is a deadline that involves their work, it is their responsibility to stay late. As one engineer put it, 'When it is crunch time, no one refuses. You know you just have to do it.' (Perlow, 1998, p. 4)

This is often for short-term gain. Across a long-term period however it may prove counter productive. For an employee the need to work from home may be due to family commitments whether it is care for a child or an elderly relative, as such it can be a "time of life" issue rather than a permanent requirement. The failure to manage the spillover of work into one's home life can result in a strained personal relationship. All adults learn from experience, but what may seem to be a defining point for others, is often a lesson that the typical IT workers learns too late.

Another example of this dilemma was where one employee who had been working from home changed, after observing that physical presence at work made a good impression in the eyes of management rather than any results that were have been achieved (Perlow, 1998, p. 21):

...[He–her manager] was really impressed when he ran into me at 2 A.M. one morning.... I used to just go to the kitchen table and use my PC, but after the reaction I got from my manager I decided it was important to do that early morning work in the office.... It is better to be seen here if you are going to work in the middle of the night.

Conversely, other IT workers have used information technologies to establish boundaries between the spaces they occupy at work, and at home (Stewart, 2001, p. 2):

People use ICTs to make and maintain barriers, given that many technologies are linked symbolically to work. Some people identify ICTs closely with work, particularly the telephone and the computer, and often when they refuse to bring work home they actively resist using these technologies at home too.

For some employees learning how to use both these techniques is not intuitive even if company policy and culture support such actions. For instance, it can be beneficial for employees to turn cell phones off when at home, if this is the company policy. But for many this is not a given, as the cell phone also is used for social interaction in their home life. Equally, e-mail is frequently used for social correspondence. IT workers are often very driven people. They may not find it easy to intellectually determine how to best control their use of technology and install boundaries around its use in the home environment.

The Benefits of Current IT Sector Business Practices

Irrespective of the remuneration rates of the IT sector, IT workers find some of the most important benefits of working in their industry to be the excitement that comes from working with cutting edge technologies, and working from home. For many this is the rapid change and exciting use and development of programmes and gadgetry. Many IT workers opt later in their careers to become consultants so they can move from exciting new projects to project as they love the taste of something new. As one consultant explains (Richardson, 2005):

I was working as a programmer for a [government scientific agency] and I saw the consultants come in and get the best jobs, so I decided to become one too [...] I hate maintaining a system, I like to design them and consultancy lets me do this [...] Later I took a job for a mobile phone in Africa it was great while it lasted, my wife got to go on lots of Safaris, but the company went under later, so it was back to finding another contract.

With the advent of multimedia the field is drawing not just on the technical skills but also allowing workers now to express their artistic abilities in industries such as film and gaming (Kaluzniacky, 2004). As one IT worker explained who had recently worked in the film industry (Richardson, 2005):

One of the great things in this industry is that everyone gets recognition in the credits, you know at the end of a movie, there everyone's name is, no other industry does this. It's there forever, to show the grandchildren.

Virtual Work

Although the previous benefits that this technology brings IT workers are important, the most fundamental change technology can bring is flexibility (Bently & Yoong, 1998; Castells, 2000b). IT work like many occupations has benefited from the IT revolution in this aspect. This is due to the creation of the networks both within companies and external to them. In particular, the Internet has allowed people's homes to be connected to their work, effectively creating "e-homes" (Castells, 2000a). This, in combination with mobile technology, has enabled employees to work from home.

Research has identified four patterns this can take (Qvortup, 1992): the substitutor, the self-employed, the supplementer and the telecommuter. The substitutor is the most common form of working from home, this is the employee who takes work home to do extra work after hours. The self-employed means working for yourself from your own home. The supplementer is the traditional view of telework, whereby a worker is employed solely from home, this has had much lower uptake rates than expected and lastly the telecommuter sees workers going to satellite offices in their suburb and connecting into their regular work through networks.

The benefits these various forms of teleworking can bring are the ability to meet life commitments such as childcare and care of the elderly, avoiding traffic jams and even saving costs on office clothing. Also, being able to work from home can be more relaxing and have fewer interruptions, letting work time become more productive.

When managed well this form of flexible working can increase company commitment, trust, and job satisfaction, resulting in more productive and creative work by IT employees (Finegold et al., 2002). Research has determined that IT software workers can be bonded to their work through flexible work arrangements, making them feel that for the ability to have a balanced life style that they in turn will "gift" their employers "hard work." This is said to create in the worker a *socio-emotional* response towards work (Whitener, 1997). The reason for this is that such management practices form part of the psychological employment package (Scholarios & Marks, 2004).

However, some of these benefits are double-edged and what at first can seem like a benefit can also have side effects. When workers aren't able to maintain a work-life balance, research has shown there is increased turnover, absenteeism, a decline in commitment and emotional exhaustion, in this industry sector (Dex & Scheibl, 1999; Scandura & Lankau, 1997). We will next discuss some of the main negative effects that technology brings to IT workers. These are, being tied 24 hours a day to one's work, increased responsibility, redundancy and outsourcing threats and technology related health hazards (Kaluzniacky, 2004).

The Domestic Disadvantages of Current IT Sector Business Practices

Although the flexibility that technology can bring to the workplace has been part of orthodox management practice for the past two decades, often a different picture emerges on how this flexibility has been enacted. In many industries flexible work practices have not been adopted, for instance, many female IT employees are still not allowed to work from home or when they do their career progression is affected. However in the IT industry this could be seen as an extreme example of how technology can be used in a way that is failing employees. Many IT workers would say it is this day-to-day intrusion and spillover into their personal sphere that affects their successful maintenance of a work-life balance.

The reason that many businesses might treat IT workers this way is that IT has become fundamental for most commerce. It is now hard to identify any industry that does not rely on IT for its basic services needs. With this comes the demand that these services never have down time. This sees technical support workers at all levels tied to their work twenty-four hours a day (Castells, 2000a). In past years, this had taken form in the standard use of electronic pagers, which these days has rapidly moved to the recurrent use of cell phones. As one IT worker talks of their binding to technology (Richardson, 2005):

I have become much better at balancing technology and home, I do not check e-mail as soon as I get home, but unfortunately I cannot do away with this [he looks down at his cell phone]. At 41 I have learned to separate out technology from home.

Another female worker also discusses how she manages her boundaries between work and home life:

Company name" is very helpful about if you want to work from home, they keep asking me if I want a lap top or a note book, but I've made a decision not to work from home, my company is very keen, no I don't want a laptop or a note book [...] I think it would get in the way of my home life[...] I think it is okay if you have kids but otherwise it just means working longer hours.

Rather than most businesses enabling the productivity of telework, research has shown that the most frequent use of teleworkers are those who work from home is in the supplementor mode (Castells, 2000a). In this mode workers end up taking increasing amounts of work home. In the case of the story of a parent working at home with a sick child, the balance is doubled edged, for the flexibility is at a price, for the child does not get the care of a parent, frequently they are popped in front of the TV while the parent continues to work (Sennett, 1998). Or, when a spouse comes home instead of helping with household chores they have to finish an urgent report (Perlow, 1998). Here is an interesting example where the spouse at home is a male who faces this very challenge. He, picks up his daughter from the baby-sitter, brings her home, makes dinner, feeds her, bathes her, plays with her, and puts her to bed, while his wife works. He is a loving and committed father, however he raised the following concerns:

It gets hard having to be a single parent every night of the week.... I love her [his daughter] and spending time with her, but sometimes it just gets to be too much. Sometimes I want some time to myself, time in the yard, time to finish all the projects that I want to do. . . Sometimes I just feel cheated that I don't have a wife who has dinner on the table when I get home. . . I don't really understand what she [his wife] is doing, but I always give her the benefit of the doubt. (Perlow, 1998, p. 8)

One reason for this constant contact is the high level of importance that IT has for business management and practice (Ross, Beath, & Fiedler, 1996). This, not just their contracts, is what drives employees to be in constant demand. Related to the importance of technology in the business world, is the fact that for many companies IT does not only provide them with the competitive edge but they need it simply to remain in business (Andrews & Niederman, 1998). For IT workers this means that the latest technology needs to be adopted, as this is not an industry of complacency. Both in terms of employers driving workers to keep upskilled but also with the threat of redundancy looming in this industry, no IT worker can sit on their laurels.

With requirements to do work after hours, this further extends the potential for IT workers to suffer, both physically mentally. Mental stress in this industry was initially found to be due to the noise of printers and machines, but as technology has improved these issues have reduced and been replaced by others such as the stress that a constant noise of a cell phone ringing can bring. As one chief information officer (CIO) exclaimed about taking his mobile technology on holiday,

It's just not possible for most CIOs to completely disconnect; they take along their Blackberrys or laptops and at least periodically check their e-mail. (Blodgett, 2003, p. 1)

Physical stress results from the increasing hours spent on computers and mobile devices, where repetitive strain injuries compound in the form of headaches, backaches, carpal tunnel syndrome, and eyestrain. This stress is compounded by the looming threat of redundancy and temporary employment rather than the traditional salaried workforce. Members, they feel they cannot complain about health and safety issues (King, 2004).

So we see that IT workers are not only the creators of technology but also at the mercy of its implementation in their work environments. Management policies are fundamental to how IT is used whether to the detriment or betterment of the worker's professional development *and* quality of life.

Leisure and the Domestication of Information Technology

Some key personality traits that research has identified in the typical IT worker, places him or her at higher risk from addiction to the use of information technologies than other workers. The typical IT worker can have a workaholic attitude to work, and also a "playaholic" attitude to computer games. The domestication of technology therefore has an impact on IT workers, as it enables the overflow of work responsibilities into the domestic sphere. This "overflow" effect has especially been seen in the rise in popularity of PC online gaming among IT workers. Of course, the phenomenon of employees who use a networked PC between 9 A.M. and 5 P.M. at work, and then proceed to spend many more hours in front of another computer "gaming" at home, is not unique to the IT sector. However, this is an especially pertinent issue in the IT industry. For many IT workers, the love of working with computers began with playing computer games. An online discussion run by the BBC (2003) on computer games addiction, saw one IT worker describe his time spent playing computer games:

I grew up working in the computer industry starting in 1977. I have always had a fascination for games. This has grown with me and now I spend the majority of my sitting down leisure time playing them—10-20 hrs per week at a guess. I may watch no TV at all for weeks. In fact the TV has become a kind of console itself, purely used for watching DVDs and videos.

And another comment by a games programmer:

The best games are always extremely addictive. Until recently I worked as a games programmer and was reminded more than once, cycling home after a night spent in the office playing BF1942, of the old line from Scarface, advising drug dealers never to touch their own product.

The main dangers with these and other technologies such as television, are that if a person becomes addicted it can remove them from socially interacting with friends and family. In addition, healthier life style can suffer in terms of exercise and diet. Other workers find sense of community with online gaming and meeting up in face-to-face groups (Yee, 2005). Again, the first IT worker in the BBC discussion explains the social benefits he finds with gaming:

Recently I have discovered online gaming in the form of Sony's Everquest, and this has opened up a whole new playing environment and experience for me. I like this game especially for the social interaction and the challenging environment, without all of the unnecessary violence of some games. I have teenage kids and they have grown up knowing about games through me. They both play, but neither have gotten to the stage where it takes over their lives, they still socialise more with their friends outside of the home. (BBC, 2003)

Moreover, they may provide a place to escape from the stress of constant change in their daily lives. The British sociologist Anthony Giddens (1991) has analysed how "media consumers" usually form their self-identity in a place of stability. In a classic case, Giddens analysed the formation of self-identity among a group of television soap opera fans. His conclusions are especially analogous to the sense of stability that an online gamer can get from regular and constant interactivity with a personal computer.

Ironically, the compulsive qualities of computer games can often carry harmful effects. Employers need to be aware of these issues and the HR Managers similarly need to universally consider the IT worker as a whole person in this regard. The issues that IT workers may have at home can flow directly into their performance as an employee (Robbins, 1984). HR managers should also be aware that constant computer game play can result in occupational overuse syndrome, which can compound with damage from constant keyboard use when at work. In addition, the greater social cost of IT workers frequently taking work home produces a corresponding increase in "electronic babysitting" (Castells, 2000a). In addition, such babysitting is moving from the use of television as an artificial pacifier to now increasingly centre on domestic gaming consoles.

Video game playing is only one example of technology issues that HR and IT managers need to beware of in employees with regard to the domestic impact of technology in the Internet Age. Other documented addictions that need to be considered are online pornography, chat rooms and other Internet related addictions (Suler, 2002), all of which can seep into the work environment.

Globalisation, Self-Identity, and IT Profitability

Before we can move on to consider the representative case study of a selected IT worker and the question of emotional intelligence in IT workers, we must next consider the foremost issue to impact on the social lives of IT workers: globalisation.

Although information technology has been seen as being able to bring the world together, what many have witnessed in recent years has been the transformation of the world into an IT network that, for the most part, serves the privileged elite of Western societies. While the world's unconnected countries remain excluded, and consequently become the poorer for it, culturally and financially, the "digital divide" creates IT "ghettos" within first world societies. The principal capitalist businesses that dominated world business before the IT revolution remain as those who benefit the most from advances in the IT sector (Castells, 2000a; Held et al., 1999). The continuing dominance of these elites has been attributed to their ability to control social space and chronological time through the accelerated advances that IT has provided their business models.

Within Sociology, a robust consideration of the consequences of globalisation usually features first-order analyses of socially experienced *space* and *time*. It is particularly common for those of us who live in modern societies to take for granted the "spaces" we occupy in each day, or the ways that clocks and watches seem to rule how we utilise our time everyday. Much recent sociological analysis has been interested in the ways in which social life is constituted within chronological time and physical space. More than we realise, the "free will" we assume we exercise in our daily activities may in fact be constrained and determined by the unseen social conventions within social time and space.

For example, this new thinking of both time and space as being socially constructed, has a pivotal role in the formation and maintenance of individual self-identity, and of the roles we can take on when at work or at home. It is commonplace that we all present different aspect of our personalities to the other people in our lives, depending on the nature of each relationship that we have. We are "different people" to, for example, our significant other, our blood relatives, and our employers. All these differing relationships are bound by distinct space and time contexts. We usually behave differently towards our work colleagues when in a morning meeting at work, than we would when socialising with them at an evening drink at the pub. It is the social context–the *space*–within which we are sharing their company that makes us instinctively change our behaviour. Similarly, social construction of time has also changed. When drinking at the pub, we are "off the clock," and therefore behave in more sociable ways towards our colleagues.

On a global scale, the world's elite businesses control social space by the maintenance of their "localised" business nodes—New York, London, and Tokyo—as the global centres of capital and international financial transactions (Castells, 2000a; Held et al., 1999). Service networks have arisen to support the ongoing maintenance of these centres. The escalating circuit of global financial transactions has had a significant impact upon the IT industry. The social location of IT jobs has become left vulnerable by the very networks the sector has invented and put in place. Through the now globalised nature of these networks, alternative, cheaper, labour sources can be accessed and utilized. Furthermore, it has become a common saying, that an IT job can be done anyplace in the world that you can connect a keyboard to. Worldwide, following the *efficiency* driven *rationality* of first Wall Street, and now London and Tokyo, many IT jobs are increasingly being outsourced to cheaper countries. Forrester Research has forecast that one in nine jobs in the American information technology industry will be "off-shored" by 2010 (Pink, 2005). However several alternative responses to this global management of space are developing. Outsourcing has been achieved by employing bright young computer enthusiasts or elderly retired workers in rural areas of America rather than off-shoring jobs (Kaluzniacky, 2004).

Correspondingly, modern time has become compressed through the continuing dominance of these business nodes over world finance. Through the *efficiency* driven use of information technology within these centres, business transactions now commonly occur in "real time." The everyday electronic transactions of globally connected businesses keep the core hubs of the global financial elite in operation twenty-four hours a day worldwide. As a consequence, we now live in an era of "timeless time." This pushes business into faster cycles of competition and transaction, as everything needs to be done yesterday - today is too late.

The impact of this "timeless time," this *timelessness*, has been a continual push of the capabilities of networking services. The push is now to link up key global business nodes into spaceless and timeless connectivity twenty-four hours a day (Castells, 2000a). This means that more than ever before, IT workers will have to *incessantly* provide technical support for the networks they created without down time. This international timelessness raises the already existing pressure upon IT workers to increasingly find new ways of working, so that such timelessness can be enhanced; so that the globally-networked financial entrepreneurs and brokers can conduct speculation at an ever growing pace. As the dependence on IT increases in this way, so does the need to have systems continually up and going, to help speculators make *instantaneous* multi-million— even multi-billion—dollar decisions.

Crossing Borders: Global Outsourcing

For centuries, migrant workers have left the localised social sphere of "home" and have crossed borders either towards the promise of a better life, or in order to escape an impoverished one. However, a special tension, hitherto unprecedented in other domains of skilled and unskilled employment, arises for modern IT workers in the contemporary equivalent of this phenomenon. As noted in our earlier discussion of the formation and maintenance of self-identity by IT workers, globalised business practices have produced an increase in the "cross-cultural traffic" of migrating IT workers. Not just across geographical borders, this traffic also migrates virtually, as IT support is often conducted remotely, with the need for IT workers to either travel trans-nationally as part of their work, or to emigrate in order to remain employed. The increasingly obligatory mobility across both virtual and physical "local" boundaries into hitherto unknown space increases the work-related stress experienced by the typical IT worker.

The outsourcing of core IT employment by many firms over the 1990s and in recent years has had an irrevocable impact on the tenor of IT employment worldwide. Outsourcing has turned highly skilled and highly paid employees into unemployed itinerants, with little chance of reemployment in their country of origin. In human terms, this is the ultimate risk that the privileging of the "localised" global business nodes of New York, London, and Tokyo has effected the workers who do not occupy those global business centres or their service networks.

Globalised business practice carries with it the need to operate in consideration of different local time zones. As we have already established, IT workers have a tradition in working in different time, as they have always had to be "night dwellers," to bring back crashed networks or do critical system upgrades at the weekend. However operating in different time zones extends this intrusion on family and other outside relationships and in general spills-over into IT worker's private sphere, further straining at home relationships where family time is often at a minimum. The resultant tension from this ubiquitously trans-national, migratory mode of employment can result in the splitting up of families or the breakdown of traditional support networks that family and friends could provide in times of crisis (Ziehl, 2003).

Rather than lead directly to the growth of efficiency—and in turn profitability—the instrumental logic of conflated space and timeless time only estranges further the typical IT worker's already destabilized self-identity.

Conclusion

It is both important and *relevant* for IT and HR managers to consider the argument developed across part one of this chapter. This being that the traditional model of business, based on rational principles and processes that privilege efficiency and profitability over human responsiveness to rapid social change, may not be best suited to an Internet Age, which is constantly driven by the "timeless time" of globalised competition. Without forsaking the necessities of fostering creativity and ensuring profitability, more than ever before new ways now are needed to manage IT workers with a long-term rather than short-term focus. We hope that this discussion will encourage chief executives, IT, and HR managers to identify the full range of issues that their employees are potentially facing and begin to build new approaches that acknowledge and work with the issues above for sustainable and socially responsible business practices in the Internet Age (Goleman, Boyatzis, & McKee, 2001).

Part II: The Emotional Intelligence of IT Workers: A "Bottom-Up" Analysis

Introduction

Recently, IT and HR Managers have come to recognise the role that IT workers' emotional intelligence increasingly plays in those workers' day-to-day management of their workload pressures. In organisational psychology, emotional intelligence (EQ) is related to IQ, which may determine how people succeed in life. However, unlike traditional measurement and management of intelligence, EQ can be enhanced, so that even when people naturally do not possess a rich level of EQ, they can learn and become more emotionally competent (Goleman, 1998).

In this second part of the chapter, we are especially interested in the role that EQ plays in the daily work and domestic routines of the typical IT worker. We look at how we can psychologically understand the individual IT worker, why compared to over workers they are more vulnerable, what their strengths and how they can be helped to reinforce these skills by their IT and HR managers.

The Vulnerability of IT Workers

This section recounts both past and current research, which uniformly shows that IT workers are more vulnerable to occupational stress than other types of employees. In some cases, this stress results in the physical manifestation of health problems such as heart attack, headaches, ulcers (Kaluzniacky, 2004), as well as mental illness, as seen in mental breakdowns, relationship break ups, depression, job disinterest and in some cases, work sabotage. Included in our discussion is an important point that the very skills that draw IT workers to the logical structure of computers, and make them exceptionally talented with these machines, leave them less capable in the **emotional areas** of both work and their personal lives (Kaluzniacky, 2004).

Vulnerability Identified

The emotional vulnerability of IT workers is already well established in academic literature. Early studies have identified a commonplace occurrence for IT workers to not score in the feeling categories of Myers-Briggs personality testing. More recent studies have confirmed these findings, despite the changing nature of IT work and the greater requirement in the IT industry for its workers to have more "people" skills (Kaluzniacky, 2004). Further research has shown that they exhibit higher levels of stress than other industry sector counterparts (Fujigaki & Mori, 1997).

Research at Cambridge University Psychology Research Centre has identified a link between Autism and Asperges Syndrome for the employment category of engineers, which IT workers fall under (Baron-Cohen, et al. 1998). This has been referred to as the "male brain" or "geek syndrome" (Baron-Cohen, 2002; Pink, 2005; Silverman 2001). This research identifies a genetic predisposition to *phenotypically* acquiring Asperges Syndrome, that is, the typical IT worker may not carry the complete complement of traits to have fully developed Asperges Syndrome, but will exhibit a more limited set of qualities of this syndrome. Affiliated with this are traits such as poor social skills, addictive personality, and talent with logic problem solving. The phenotypical Asperges in IT workers is enacted both at work and home by these workers finding it hard to separate their self-identity from their work, and by these workers having limited life experience and a stunted degree of human understanding (Rogers and Larson, 1984). Often marital relationships are strained by the limited levels of communication and quality of time spent with partners (Hollands, 1985). This, compounded with alienation and long work hours, cause distances to develop between IT workers and family and friends (Hayes, 1989).

For the children of IT workers this has been nicknamed "Silicon Valley Syndrome". As these children have a higher rate of these syndromes, as the parents who live and work in computer clusters are much more likely to meet and pass on the full syndrome to their children (Baron-Cohen, 2002; Baron-Cohen, et al. 1998; Silverman, 2001). This makes a job, which by nature strains family relationships, by not allowing good separation of home and family life, even more strained as IT workers who are parents have a higher frequency of children with special needs. Further, birth defects have been attributed to the pollution in these industrial hubs. Microsoft Corporation already is aware of this situation and provides special funding for families that have children with Asperges Syndrome (Silverman, 2001).

The very skills that make IT workers talented with computers: having a highly developed capacity for rational thought; being able to make decisions upon rational, rather than emotional bases, make them more vulnerable to workplace stress. These workers are unable to articulate how they feel. Also, the inability to deal with co-workers, managers, customers and family, creates new levels of anxiety as bad situations turn worse because of inept emotional responses to social situations. The attributes of phenotypical autism such as high concentration on one task are important to solving urgent business problems but the cost is often the neglect of family and friends at home.

Nevertheless IT workers also exhibit some other traits which early research results (Richardson, 2005) are beginning to show, these are emotional strengths of adaptability and resilience, which many IT workers have or have developed. The following case study illustrates these strengths.

Case Study

This case study takes a look at the life history of an IT worker as he progresses with his career in the last fifteen years of the emergence of the Internet Age. It highlights the issues that this IT worker faced and how he strove to maintain a balance between his work responsibilities and his home life. Issues dealt with will range from long work hours, unpredictable hours, redundancy, being tied electronically by mobile devices, responsibility, and the neglect of family time.

Networking, Redundancy, Early Retirement

Marc, a happy and enthusiastic young man, moved to the bank. With his first child on the way, the relaxed help desk job he had at a government department was not going to make ends meet. It was a huge step up, he now had to be much more diligent about how he worked. He was dealing with millions of dollars in losses if systems went down. The pay was good, but the hours were long and chaotic, and he always had to have a pager (and later a mobile phone) wherever he went. Every time the microwave would go off at home it would make him for years later, jump. Some days the pager would be thrown across the room. He heard stories of other workers who had thrown it down the toilet, but of course, there was always a replacement. It was the disruption to family and leisure time that this beeping and ringing brought. He says, "you could not settle down for a nice drink if you were on call as you had to be sober to respond" "and even when you weren't on call I would often be contacted as I knew something that someone else did not."

[…]

Then with a new baby, life took another turn. Firstly, the phone ringing in the middle of the night would wake the baby and father alike. But later as the little boy grew up there were days when he would not see his father. One story is of how the child crawling along, discovered the answer phone, like all good children of IT workers they hit the button… "hello, this is Marc, I am not here at the moment, but if you leave your name and number I will get back to you"… The child thought his daddy was in the machine. The child hit the memo button, crying "daddy, daddy where are you, come home, daddy I want you"…. When Marc got home he replayed his voicemail messages, only to hear his desperate child's recorded cry. Marc commented that this was one of the worst moments of his life, as he had not seen his child for three days in a row.

[…]

Marc moved on from the bank, to become a consultant, he carefully chose the firm for their culture of employee development. Life was great here, lots of office drinks and parties and presents from the company, like a Hawaiian shirt for Christmas. However, after a merger, the overseas parent company wanted to restructure and consolidate. Despite Marc's excellent track record he was considered surplus to requirements, this left him with a large mortgage and now two children to support. This was a tough time in his life. Luckily, he had redundancy insurance and his wife worked part-time. He kept himself busy applying for jobs in the morning and gardening in the afternoon. He enjoyed the change of lifestyle and the whole family benefited from the slowdown in pace of life. Six months later Marc was working again and in an exciting job, but the work had started coming home again. Marc says "when you get paid this much you are expected to put in the extra hours."

[…]

Ten years later from when Marc began in IT he is still in the industry. He has at last overcome the disrupted sleep patterns and the fear of the phone ringing. Now he has a job that is exciting, though like any IT job there is always the latest project, but he will go home and help with the family, the housework, before settling down to work again. He says his work/family balance comes from the beautiful garden he has. When he walks through it at the end of the day, "this is where work ends and family begins." Now Marc is busy planning to buy investment properties, like so many of his friends in IT he is looking to retire early. They realise it is a tough industry and they are planning for a time when they can reap the rewards of their hard work.

As we can see in this case study, despite the tremendous obstacles that have arisen in this IT workers life, Marc has still managed to fine a way through the chaos and find balance in an industry that is willing to consume all of its workers' lives. His experience of the IT sector showed that this industry can be very cruel. It can treasure you highly one minute and discard you the next. What Marc has managed to see is what the potential is with high wages he receives and that with proper investment he can look forward to early retirement.

This worker demonstrated the incredible adaptability and resilience of typical IT workers. They do not give up when problems arise but look for a way to adapt to the situation. When Marc became redundant he created a plan of what he would do in his day, apply for jobs in the morning, and work in the garden in the afternoon. It could be said that the very nature of the IT industry attracts people with these qualities as it is the taste for something new and exciting that draws many in. Also they continually have to learn how to use new technology, this again parallels the skills needed in their life to cope with IT employment.

So, although some workers may have the qualities of adaptability and resilience other find it harder and need help in coping with these changing times. On the strength of the evidence detailed in this discussion, the short-term pursuit of efficiency in IT systems is no longer enough to ensure business success, as IT workers struggle with the need to manage a balance of professional and personal responsibilities in life. They need strong organisation guidance built into the very way organisations do business, and their leaders to inspire and direct them (*Castleman, Coulthard, & Reed, 2004;* Hall & Richter, 1988; *Scholarios & Marks, 2004*). Established research into emotional intelligence within the discipline of psychology can provide helpful insight and techniques to help IT workers. The next section describes what emotional intelligence is and how understanding it may help IT and HR managers better manage IT workers.

IT Workers and Emotional Intelligence

As we saw in the first part of this chapter, IT workers can have specific resource needs that deserve consideration. Some readers might consider the scenarios that have been presented in this chapter to provide bleak and predetermined outcomes for IT workers. To the contrary, our discussion should not be seen as only illustrating the purported limitations of IT workers but to provide better understanding of the talent that these workers can bring to their sector, and help IT and HR managers tailor better training to deal with workplace stress for these employees.

In recent times, a new theoretical area has emerged in the field of psychology. It is called emotional intelligence or emotional quotient (EQ). In contrast to personality testing, EQ looks not only at inherited personality traits but also at psychological qualities that give people emotional rather than intellectual intelligence. This is a significant advancement, for EQ it is not dependent solely on genetically inherited traits and can be enhanced with training (Goleman, 1998). EQ is a concept that stems from the idea that our ability to emotionally cope with the world is crucial to how we succeed in life (Cherniss, 2000). This term evolved as it was realised that cognitive ability of intelligence quotient (IQ) alone was not the sole indicator of success in life (Wechsler, 1940). The term emotional intelligence was coined in 1990 by Salovey and Mayer (Cherniss, 2000, p. 2):

...a form of social intelligence that involves the ability to monitor one's own and others' feelings and emotions, to discriminate among them, and to use this information to guide one's thinking and action.

EQ is *value free*. We can all have positive and negative emotions. Analysis of EQ considers how people use these emotions to succeed in life, that ultimately people have a choice about how they deal with these emotions. EQ is not a new concept, this notion has been debated within Psychology since 1943. However, up to 1998, the concept of EQ had remained fixed and unchanging until Daniel Goleman published *Emotional intelligence: Why it can matter more than IQ*, which brought the term into the common language of the business world. It has since been an important research topic to the professional disciplines of management and HR. Goleman's work had been significantly influenced by the field of positive psychology, for which Salovey and Mayer (1990) are the most significant analysts. For Salovey and Mayer, EQ spans two primary domains: the ability of individuals to manage their own emotions and the ability of individuals to manage the emotions of others. In his book, Goleman utilised Salovey and Mayer's ideas to extend EQ as a tool for management and business practice, and developed five concepts of "basic emotional and social competencies":

- knowing one's emotions (self-awareness)
- managing emotions (self-regulation)
- motivating oneself
- recognising emotions in others' (empathy)
- handling relationships (social skills)

As we will see the qualities of resilience and adaptability we saw in the case studies, are reflected in the EQ competencies outlined next:

Self-Awareness

Self-awareness is the ability to know your emotions, recognizing feelings as they occur, and discriminating between them. Furthermore it is the ability to connect these feelings to the way you act on those feelings and at the same time you retain confidence in your self-worth and capabilities.

The qualities of self-awareness are vitally important for migrating IT workers (whether employed or unemployed). Such workers need to be able to understand that their circumstances are not their own fault, and employ self confidence to move forward, rather than become burnt out or depressed.

Emotional self-awareness can also give an individual the confidence to speak up for him or herself as he or she is comfortable with communicating feelings.

Self-Regulation

Self-regulation is the ability to handle feelings so they're relevant to the current situation and therefore he or she can react with relative appropriateness in stressful circumstances. They can exhibit self-control and can balance the intellectual and emotional aspects of social circumstances when making decisions.

For newly outsourced IT workers, this is the biggest emotional challenge they may have yet faced to date. Their range of possible responses in such circumstances is worth considering. Might they go berserk or "go postal" as America's have termed this response and have a violent explosion of anger in reaction to the treatment they received at the hands of the organisation to which they have bonded. Alternatively, might they become numb with shock, seemingly paralysed and unable to continue with life. Or, might they manage to pick themselves up and keep going.

Self-Motivation

Self-motivation is the ability to "gather up" one's feelings and direct them towards achievement of a goal, despite self-doubt, inertia, or impulsiveness. IT workers with high EQ are highly self-directed, they can prioritize and set realistic and yet still challenging goals, and achieve these.

In IT good self-motivation is a vital skill as new projects often times arise unannounced. IT workers work under the constant pressure of performing well, or otherwise lose work. How they balance family and home life; when the project demands a 24/7 mentality, is a constant issue. Determining when to take work home, when to remain late at the office, or when to stop and take an hour off to be with the family, are all skills that often do not come readily for IT workers.

Empathy

Empathy is the ability to recognizing feelings of others and "tuning in" to both the spoken and unspoken cues in communication from others. Having empathy leads to improved ability to communicate with others. Furthermore, it is the ability to feel compassion and understand divergent viewpoints to one's own. Empathy also provides individuals with a highly developed social conscience. The empathic worker pursues his/her own goals, concerned not only for personal benefits or consequences, but also for the benefit of those with which they interact.

The skill of empathy has been shown to be the quality most lacking in IT workers, as it is akin to the Myers-Briggs category of "Feeling" which studies has shown IT workers are most notably lack (Kaluzniacky, 2004). In the IT business world the lack of this ability leads to systems that do not match users needs. In terms of dealing with the social world beyond day-to-day work activities, this often manifests as the typical IT worker "not seeing it coming" when management announces that IT positions are to be outsourced. Often such IT workers become so wrapped up in their tasks that they miss much of what could help prepare them for looming changes. In such cases, the ability to share compassion and help fellow colleagues deal with job loss is weaker among IT workers.

Social Skills

Good social skills enable us to handle interpersonal interaction, conflict resolution, and negotiations in both professional and personal settings. In short, this is the ability to manage other peoples' emotions. This also involves the ability to lead people, be a change catalyst and bond with others.

Many of the attributes of good social skills are often not associated with the typical IT worker. Many such workers do not wish to manage staff, but instead apply themselves to the more logical workings of computer technology. The lack of these "people" skills leads to many issues within IT project teams.

In times of globalisation this is even more paramount. If IT workers cannot rely on each other then it is indeed a sad time for the IT industry. One of the most effective ways for people to cope with the situations outlined in this chapter is to talk to someone who has been in a similar situation to him or herself. This is the foundation of group therapy. However, often IT workers steer away from emotional conversations, preferring to find bonding in the logical technology they create. Which does not bode well for them during times of crisis.

Emotional Self-Management for IT Workers

The underpinning theory of EQ stems from neuroscience, and looks at the two parts of the brain: the primitive amygdala, and the rational higher brain the central cortex (Golman, 1998). The amygdala is programmed to deal with the life threatening situations that our ancestors once did, such as an attack by a Sabre Toothed Tiger. We would get a surge of adrenaline and this would prepare us to "fight or flight". However this response is not suitable for modern day stresses. Often we find we are in constant stress in this modern world both at home and work. The chemicals released in stress situations are harmful to our bodies if constantly secreted, leading to the all too well documented effects such as heart attacks (Kreitner & Kinicki, 1992).

Furthermore, the brain's neural pathways can be rewired permanently in stress pathways, taking us back to into instant "fight or flight" at the slightest external trigger, a phenomena of the past seen in war and trauma victims know as post traumatic stress syndrome (PTSD). Once the brain is rewired it can never fully recover, only be retrained to cope better with the situation (Goleman, 1998).

Those with more logical brains types, as is the case for many IT workers, are more prone to succumbing to both these injuries, as the right side of the brain that controls the emotional part of the brain is less developed (Goleman, 1998). This means that less control can be exhibited on the amygdala, to override the logical pathways into a fight or flight response. This not only leaves the typical IT worker with much more limited EQ but also makes him or her susceptible to much higher levels of physical and psychological injury as a result of workplace stress. To manage the emotional well being in IT workers it is important to realise that this group is particularly susceptible and that early intervention is important to prevent the workers entering the PTSD phase, and especially before they face the possible risk of heart disease.

Optimism

Those who manage their emotions the best have been found to have high levels of optimism (Salovey & Mayer, 1990). This accommodates a combination of all five of the above-noted EQ categories. Optimism is defined as being able to see the positive side in a negative situation, in particular, knowing how to deal constructively with anger, negativity and failure. These people persist and overcome obstacles, and thus manage their emotions and succeed. Some people naturally have this trait and even within the IT population this is true, as we can see from the case study selected, that this IT worker had high levels of optimism. However the proponents of EQ will point out that optimism can be learnt.

Optimism allows us to override our biologically programmed "flight or flight" response in times of stress by employing coping strategies. In the simplest form this can involve going for a walk, counting to ten, generally slowing down and relaxing. However more fundamental approaches than these can be used to provide a deeper level of help for employees at times of heightened stress, such as during restructuring or outsourcing.

Psychology has developed a range of techniques to help people overcome stress and trauma. One of the most important lessons is to teach coping strategies (Lazarus & Folkman, 1984). What has been discovered is that when under stress we all will react in a multitude of ways. In IT an example could be when a worker ignores a project deadline as it is unreasonable. They can also choose to become isolated from work colleagues and minimize interaction in response to interpersonal pressures within the project team. Others may work through the night to finish a project, as the work will only be there in the morning, and as a consequence ignore private commitments, such as family responsibilities. Others still utilize coping strategies, such as joking about the project and how ridiculous the deadlines can be.

What we see is a multitude of coping strategies, but often someone with lower EQ will only use one strategy and become locked into it. For instance, such a worker may ignore his or her co-workers and use hostility to ensure that he or she is excluded from difficult projects. Coping in this way leads to the development of a bad reputation and possible loss of work, particularly if a round of redundancy occurs. Alternatively, the low EQ worker may exercise his or stress at home, and these circumstances therefore remain unseen at work. Such IT workers need to develop a variety of coping strategies. This means drawing on all the EQ qualities. They need to learn to know when they are stressed and take action, talk to their manager, talk to their co-workers, go out to lunch, go home early, do relaxation techniques or help a colleague who is going through the same situation.

There are many ways to strengthen the EQ of IT workers. More fundamental strengthening of an IT worker's emotional well-being can be achieved by focusing on spiritual well-being (Kaluznaiacky, 2004). Psychologists have identified that our core spiritual self is fundamental for strengthening ourselves from potential crises. Understanding the qualities each IT worker can bring to the world and to the workplace will therefore go far in enabling their positive responsiveness to workplace stress. Maybe an IT worker has good logical skills, or is good at listening to people, or likes to help others. It has been written elsewhere that we should all look to our passions, dreams or long term desires. For instance, one worker who was facing burn out at work, sought guidance to look for his passion in life, it turned out his life long goal was that he wanted to put water into his village in Africa. He managed to integrate this into his career plan and provide water to many villages and achieve business benefits for his company too (Goleman, Boyatzis, & McKee, 2001). If strengthened sufficiently, people can be resilient against most actions life can throw at them, whether at work or at home.

There are many techniques that can be used to enable employees' development of their emotional well-being. One, is for the IT worker to keep a piece of paper with them at all times and note down thoughts and feelings as they arise, what they see that they are good at, what they want to achieve in their life (Cooper & Sawaf, 1996). Encourage workers to take the paper with them to meetings, to lunches, wherever the worker goes so that when inspiration strikes they can note down and not lose these thoughts. From this, employees can build up a picture of how they can be spiritually strengthened and begin to work their life plan around this strategy. Other techniques include using a specially created deck of cards. Workers use them to analyse what their inner spiritual self is and what it needs to be strengthened. Another technique is that employees set their alarm clocks 10 minutes earlier than their usual rising time and use this time to note down their emotional state when they wake up. By being aware of your emotional state upon rising you can learn to manage this as the day progresses (Cooper & Sawaf, 1996). This can be added to by selecting two other times during the day to reassess how they are going emotionally and how they can plan how they are going to react.

An alternative approach incorporates EQ building into team meetings (Goleman, 1998). This has been successfully conducted in American schools. The meeting begins with people expressing their emotional state. This would not be compulsory but it can be a highly effective means to let emotions become part of the work force. In particular this has been found effective for males who are not used to expressing emotions. Even if they cannot articulate theirs, it gets them used to hearing emotions expressed and gaining confidence that it is okay to express emotions in the workplace.

Lastly, group therapy is the psychological technique that has been found to be the most valuable way to help individuals when they are going through a crisis (Kfir, 1989). Through talking with others who are in the same situation, healing can be achieved and a way forward found where close friends and relatives fail. Further still, to cope with changing times talking with others in the same situation can help employees build a narrative or story of what it is like to be an IT worker in today's changing world (Epson & White, 1992; Sennett, 1998). Often a metaphor can be used from these discussions and used to allow workers to build an identity and strengthen themselves in a time when, as we have seen it is difficult to achieve this by traditional means. The use of a metaphor and the building of it into a narrative allows people to share emotions and by sharing emotions they can build up their own strengths. As most IT workers are male, talking about emotions in a professional setting is often difficult (Golman, 1998; Kaluznaiacky, 2004). Sharing stories is much easier as you can form a third person or talk about a "friend" until your comfort levels are such that you are able to talk about your own stories. Group therapy can be done face-to-face, or online. The anonymity of these groups has also proven an important aspect to their success (Joinson, 2003).

Face-to-face communication in groups could be organised when significant change is happening, for instance in times of restructure or outsourcing. Also the option to have groups form to support workers and families could be done, as often networking does not happen in this work environment for how can employees families meet when they are too busy working to have a social life in the first place.

Although face-to-face contact would be preferable it may be a case that the anonymity of an online group may be a preferred medium to help a group of predominately male workers, who often have been shown to have problems expressing emotional situations (Joinson, 2003). In both cases a trained moderator or facilitator is suggested, as IT workers will probably have to be nurtured into helping them open up about these highly intimate inner workings. Also the advantage of online groups is that minority work groups could be specifically targeted as online group therapy has proven highly successful in this context (Fogel, Albert, Schnabel, Ditkoff, & Neugut, 2003). This means the specific needs of workers such as gay, lesbian, ethnic minorities, parents and married workers can be addressed. Employees can then approach a group they feel an affinity for at a given point in time. The added advantage of an online group is that for workers on the run or with tight time frames another meeting may just add to their stress levels. Being able to tune in at a time that suits them may provide them with the flexibility they need.

Further online resources can be provided via the intranet, of useful websites on stress relief and also company created digital narratives of other worker's scenarios and how they build emotional stress could be provided (Robbins, 2003). This is a growing technique that organisational behaviour is adopting to help employees deal with organisation and home stress. Another approach is to also to create a website for families of workers to help them and provide spaces for them to form online groups. This could also involve the creation of CD ROMs that easily plug into web resources but hold their own content.

Although technology holds some solutions to helping workers cope with stress, it is important to realise particularly for this work group it is fundamental to provide help that takes them away from the technology, as this is part of the cause of their stress in employees. Alternative policies companies are coming up with are e-mail free days. Options such as these need to be explored.

Future Trends

It is uncertain whether the future of the IT sector will provide its workers with stable employment conditions. What is being seen at present is the separation of high and low skill sets. Lower skilled activities are being divested off-shore, despite the optimism that this leaves space for a new era of creative IT workers. Many potential creators of new paradigms are turning away from the industry to hone other life skills. Loss of even one such worker can have a significant impact on a nation's economy (Florida, 2002). There is urgent need for more research to be conducted to help better understand the stress IT workers face and how to develop tailored techniques to help them deal with them and further still for the industry to learn not only to reduce stress but also build up the creative potential in their IT workers, for the two have shown to be intrinsically linked (Cooper & Sawaf, 1996).

Conclusion

Space and time have changed, IT workers are now in the Internet Age where IT systems have to run 24/7, employment structures are flexible with temporary and contract work is the norm and where "work time" and "home time" constantly clash. The rules of the Internet Age are new and understanding them is hard for IT workers. The confusion or pressure from career uncertainty that IT workers now increasingly face is compounded as they are not only the creators of this change but the primary victims of it too. As we have shown in this chapter, IT workers are psychologically and thus physically more vulnerable than other work categories. This industry recruits workers with logical rather than emotional strengths. As we have seen, these workers base their identity around IT performance and interaction, both professionally and socially, both at work and at home. The shock of redundancy in an industry they love leaves many burned-out. In a globalised world, these threats have accelerated to become mass job losses in what have in past years been booming employment markets. Now more than ever before, these highly skilled professionals must be nurtured to allow their talents to develop and grow. As creative producers of information technology systems, their innovations are vital to future continuance and growth of commercial business. IT and HR managers can utilise new understanding of this emerging issue, through drawing upon the knowledge of other research sectors, such as sociology and psychology. The sociological analysis of social change, self-identity, work, home, and globalisation can all help in the redevelopment of the current management philosophies that presently contribute to this issue. Equally important are the monitoring and management of emotional intelligence in IT workers. Proper support in this domain can help IT workers themselves build up greater emotional strengths. This includes learning how to develop better; self-awareness, self-regulation, self-motivation, empathy, and how to handle relationships. Management support in this area will not only help them professionally provide better products to their customers but will teach them the life skills to cope with the roller coaster ride of employment in IT.

By utilising the insights of these top-down and bottom-up approaches, IT and HR managers would be able to advance their present understanding of how to nurture IT workers. This would not only help these workers survive the increasing pressures of current deadlines, but it would also help them thrive in their present work conditions and progressively advance their creative development of the Internet commercial applications.

References

Part I

Abercrombie, N., Hill, S., & Turner, B. S. (2000). *The Penguin dictionary of Sociology* (4th ed.). London: Penguin Books.

Agarwal, R., & Ferratt, T.W. (1998). Recruiting, retaining, and developing IT professionals: An empirically derived taxonomy of human resource practices. In *Proceedings of the ACM SIGCPR Conference* (pp. 292-302). Boston.

Andrews, A., & Niederman, F. (1998). A firm-level model of IT personnel planning. *Proceedings of the ACM SIGCPR Conference* (pp. 274-285). Boston.

Ang, S., & Slaughter, S. A. (2001). Work outcomes and job design for contract versus permanent information systems professionals on software development teams. MIS Quarterly, *25*(3), 321.

Barrett, R. (2001). *Symbolic analysts or cyberserfs? Software development work and workers*. Working Paper, Monash University.

BBC. (2003). *Are we becoming video game addicts? Britain is turning into a nation of gamers, research by the UK games industry trade body suggests. Have your say*. Retrieved February 2005, from http://news.bbc.co.uk/1/hi/talking_point/3189985.stm

Bently, K., & Yoong, P. (1998). Teleworking and a knowledge worker: An exploratory analysis. *Proceedings of the 9th ACIS Conference* (pp. 26-37). Sydney

Blodgett, M. (2003). Relax: Don't do it. *CIO Magazine.* Retrieved February 2005, from http://www.cio.com/archive/010103/9.html

Bone, A. (2003). The big call. *New Zealand Listener*, 189, 3299. Retrieved February 2005, from http://www.listener.co.nz/printable,417.sm

Carayon, P., Hoonakker, P., Marchand, S., & Schwarz, J. (2003, April 10-12). Job characteristics and quality of working life in the IT workforce: The role of gender. *Proceedings of the ACM SIGMIS Conference* (pp. 58-63). Philadelphia. Retrieved February 2003, from http://cqpi2.engr.wisc.edu/itwf/docs/ACM%202003%20Carayon%20et%20al.pdf

Castells, M. (2000a). *The rise of the network society. The information age: Economy, society, and culture* (Vol. 1). Blackwell: Oxford.

Castells, M. (2000b). *The power of identity. The information age: Economy, society and culture* (Vol. 2). Blackwell: Oxford.

Castleman, T., Coulthard, D., & Reed, R. (2004). The lifecycle squeeze: Young professionals negotiating career and family in a hungry economy. *Produced for an upcoming conference, yet to be published.*

Chan, S. (2002). Getting the virtual work contract done—Practicalities and organizational dynamics. *Employment Relations Today, 28*(4), 27.

CIPD. (2003). *Trends and issues in career management.* London: CIPD.

Computer World. (2004). Sidebar: What IT workers are saying. November 8, 2004. Retrieved February 2005, form http://www.computerworld.com/printthis/2004/0,4814,97228,00.html

Costigan, L., & Ó hÉigeartaigh, M. (2003). *An evaluation of the professional and personal development of information technology workers in Ireland and the United States.* Working Paper NCIRL 2003, 3, 1-24. Retrieved February 2005, from http://www.ncirl.ie/Research/working_papers/NCIRL-003-2003.doc

de Bruin, A., & Dupuis, A. (2004). Work-life balance?: Insights from non-standard work. *New Zealand Journal of Employment Relations, 29*(1), 21-38.

Dex, S., & Scheibl, E. (1999). Business performance and family-friendly policies. *Journal of General Management, 24*(4), 3.

Dholakia, R. R., Mundorf, N., & Dholakia, N. (1996). *New infotainment technologies in the home: Demand-side perspectives.* Hillsdale, NJ: Erlbaum.

Dunlop, J. J. (1988, May). Have the 1980's changed U.S industrial relations? Economic and political policies and demographic and social trends affected labor-management practices, but have caused no fundamental changes. *Monthly Labor Review, 5*(3). Retrieved April 2006, from http://www.find articles.com/p/articles/mi_m1153/is_n5_v111/ai_6832401

Finegold, D., Mohrman, S., & Spreitzer, G. M. (2002). Age effects on the predictors of technical workers' commitment and willingness to turnover. *Journal of Organisational Behavior, 23*(1), 655-674.

Florida, R. (2002). *The rise of the creative class.* New York: Basic Books.

Foster, K. R., & Moulder, E. (2000, August). *Are mobile phones safe?* IEEE Spectrum, 23-28. Retrieved February 2005, from http://www.spectrum.ieee.org/publicfeature/aug00/prad.html

Fujigaki, Y., & Mori, K. (1997). Longitudinal study of work stress among information system professionals. *International Journal of Human-Computer Interaction, 9*(4), 369-381.

Giddens, A. (1991). *Modernity and self-identity: Self and society in the late modern age.* Cambridge: Polity.

Giddens, A. (2001). *Sociology* (4th ed.). Oxford: Polity Press.

Giddens, A. (2002). *Runaway world—How globalisation is reshaping our lives.* (2nd ed.). London: Profile Books.

Goleman, D. (1998). *Emotional intelligence: Why it can matter more than IQ.* New York: Bantam Books.

Hall, D. T. & Richter, J. (1988). Balancing work life and home life: What can organisations do to help? *Academy of Management Executive, 2*(3), 213-223.

Held, D., McGrew, A., Goldblatt, D., & Perraton, J. (1999). *Global transformations.* Oxford: Polity.

Ho, M. (2002). *Mobile phones & cancer.* ISIS miniseries, Fields of Influence. Retrieved February 2005, from http://www.isis.org.uk/FOI2.php?printing=yes

IEEE Committee on Man and Radiation. (2001, January-February). Human exposure to radio frequency and microwave radiation from portable and mobile telephones and other wireless communication devices. *IEEE Engineering and Medical Biology,* 128-131. Retrieved February 2005, http://ewh.ieee.org/soc/embs/comar/phone.htm

Igbaria, M., & Lak, C. (1997). The impact of gender on career success of information systems professionals A human-capital perspective. *Information Technology & People, 10*(1), 63-86.

Igbaria, M., & Wormley, W. (1992). Race effects on organizational experiences and career success among MIS managers and professionals. *MIS Quarterly, 16*(4), 507-529.

Johnston, B. (2003). *The sociology of cyberspace: The Internet, identity and self.* Retrieved March 2005, from http://MMU Sociology - Cyberspace - Self + identity.htm

Kaluzniacky, E. (2004). *Managing psychological factors in information systems work: An orientation to emotional Intelligence.* Hershey, PA: Idea Group.

Kanter, R. M. (1977). *Work and family in the United States: A critical review and agenda of research and policy.* New York: Russell Sage Foundation.

Kearney, A. T. (2002). *Joint venture: Silicon Valley network. "Connecting today's youth with tomorrow's technology careers.* 2002 Workforce Study, with A.T. Kearney. Retrieved March 2002, from http://www.Jointventure.org/workforce/Workforce_Final.pdf

Keen, P. (1980). MIS research: Reference disciplines and cumulative tradition. In E. McLean (Ed.), *Proceedings of the 1st Conference on Information*

Systems Research: Contemporary Approaches and Emergent Traditions. Amsterdam: North Holland.

King, J. (2004, November 8). *Going down fast: IT morale is being swamped by slashed budgets, overwork, fear of outsourcing and lousy bosses.* Computer World. Retrieved February 2005, from http://www.computerworld.com/printthis/2004/0,4814,97224,00.html

Kirkpatrick, D. (2003). The Net makes it all easier-including exporting U.S. jobs. *Fortune, 147*(10), 146.

Koeber, C. (2002). Corporate restructuring, downsizing, and the middle class: The process and meaning of worker: Displacement in the "new" economy. *Qualitative Sociology, 25*(2), 217-246.

Kreitner, R., & Kinicki, A. (1992). *Organizational behaviour* (2nd ed.). Homewood, IL: Irwin.

Lacity, M. C., & Willcocks, L. P. (1998). An empirical investigation of information technology sourcing practices: Lessons from experience. *MIS Quarterly, 22*(3), 363-408.

Lai, H. (1998, October 25-28). *Neurological effects of radiofrequency electromagnetic radiation.* Paper presented to the Workshop on possible biological and health effects of RF electromagnetic fields. Mobile Phones and Health, Symposium, University of Vienna, Austria.

Mackun, P. (2005). *Silicon Valley and Route 128: Two faces of the American technopolis.* NTEA Article. Retrieved February 2005, form http://www.ntea.net/?q=node/view/68

Margolis, J., & Fisher, A. (2002). *Unlocking the clubhouse: Women in computing.* Cambridge, MA: MIT Press.

Marshall, G. (1998). *Oxford dictionary of Sociology.* Oxford: Oxford University Press.

Moody, J. W., Beise, C. M., Woszczynski, A. B., & Myers, M. E. (2003). *Journal of Computer Information Systems, 43*(4), 63-71.

Nippert-Eng, C. E. (1995). *Home and work.* Chicago: University of Chicago Press.

Pardon, J. (2004). Lost you job yet? *Job Destruction Newsletter, 983,* 1-10. Retrieved November 2005, from http://www.zazona.com/shameh1b/JDNewsArchive/2004/2004-04-12%20Three%20Excellent%20Op-eds.txt

Perlow, L. A. (1998). Boundary control: The social ordering of work and family time in a high-tech corporation—Special Issue: Critical Perspectives on Organizational Control. *Administrative Science Quarterly.* Retieved February 2005, from http://www.findarticles.com/p/articles/mi_m4035/is_n2_v43/ai_21073408/pg_10

Pink, D. H. (2005). Revenge of the right brain: Logical and precise, left-brain thinking gave us the Information Age: Now comes the conceptual age–ruled by artistry, empathy, and emotion. *Wired, 13*(2), 1-3. Retrieved February 2005, http://www.wired.com/wired/archive/13.02/brain.html?pg=2

Prusak, L. (2004). Talk given at Victoria University of Wellington.

Queensberry, J. L., Morgan, A. J., & Trauth, E. M. (2004, May). A mommy track? A framework for analyzing work-family issues in the IT workforce. *Proceedings of the Information Resource Management Association International Conference*, New Orleans, LA. Retrieved March 2005, from http://ist.psu.edu/cis/eileentrauth/researchareasgender.htm

Qvortup, L. (1992). Telework: Visions, definitions, realities, barriers. In R. Bruce, Guile, & J. B. Quinn (Eds.), *Technologies* (pp. 77-108). Paris: OECD.

Ramsay, H. (1999). *Close encounters of the nerd kind*. Paper presented to the Worklife 2000 Programme, Sweden.

Richardson, H. (2005). *Work-life balance in IT workers*. Unpublished research findings, The Open Polytechnic of New Zealand.

Robinson, T. (1999). Reinventing the business wheel. *Informationweek, 739*, 6-10. Retrieved April 2006, from http://www.informationweek.com/739/39ssoo.htm

Roepke, R. (2000). Aligning the IT human resource with business vision: The leadership initiative at 3M. MIS Quarterly, *24*(2), 327.

Rogers, E. M. & Larson, J. K. (1984). *Silicon Valley fever: Growth of high-technology culture*. New York: Basic Books.

Ross, J. W., Beath, C. M., & Fiedler, K. D. (1996). Develop long-term competitiveness through IT assets. *Sloan Management Review, 38*(1), 31-42.

Rowe, C. (1990*). Contrasting perspectives: People and chips.* Oxford: Blackwell Scientific Publications.

Saunders, R. A. (2004, July 18-21). *A new Web of identity: The Internet, globalisation, and identity politics of post-soviet space.* Warsaw Special Convention of the ASN.

Saxenian, A. L. (1994). *Regional advantage: Culture and competition in Silicon Valley and Route* 128. Cambridge, MA: Harvard University Press.

Scandura, A., & Lankau, M. J. (1997). Relationships of gender, family responsibility and flexible work hours to organizational commitment and job satisfaction. *Journal of Organizational Behavior, 18*(4), 377-391.

Scholarios, D., & Marks, A. *(2004).* Work-life balance and the software worker. *Human Resource Management Journal, 14*(2), 54-75.

Sennett, R. (1998). *The corrosion of character: The personal consequences of work in the new capitalism.* New York: Norton.

Stewart, J. (2000). Cybermatics: The cybercafe and the community. In M. Gurstein (Ed.), *Community Informatics: Enabling Communities with Information and Communications Technologies* (pp. 320-338). Hershey, PA: Idea Group Publishing.

Stewart, J. (2001). The social consumption of information and communication technologies (ICTs): Insights from research on the appropriation and consumption of ICTs in the domestic environment. *Cogn Tech Work, 5*(1), 4-14.

Suler, J. (2002). The basic psychological features of cyberspace. In *The Psychology of Cyberspace*. Retrieved February 2005, from www.rider.edu/suler/psycyber/basicfeat.html

Swart, J., Kinnie, N., & Purcell, J. (2003). *Managing the careers if IT professionals: A competing identity perspective.* Working paper series. University of Bath, 16, 1-38.

Turner, C. (2000). *The information e-conomy: Business strategies for competing in the Digital Age.* London: Kogan Page Ltd.

Weber, M. (1975a). Religious rejections of the world and their directions. In H. Gerth & C. W. Mills (Eds.), *From Max Weber: Essays in sociology* (pp. 323-359). New York: Oxford University Press.

Weber, M. (1975b). *Roscher and Knies: The logical problems of historical economics.* New York: The Free Press.

Weber, M. (1975c). Science as a vocation. In H. Gerth & C. W. Mills (Eds.), *From Max Weber: Essays in sociology* (pp. 129-159). New York: Oxford University Press.

Weber, R. (2004). Some implications of the Year-2000 Era, Dot-com Era, and offshoring for Information Systems pedagogy. MIS Quarterly, *28*(2), 9.

Whitener, E. M. (1997). The impact of human resource activities on employee trust. *Human Resource Management Review, 7*(4), 389-404.

Woodward, K. (2000). *Questioning identity: gender, class, nation.* London: Routledge.

Wright, T. A. & Cropanzano, R. (1998). Emotional exhaustion as a predictor of job performance and voluntary turnover. *Journal of Applied Psychology, 83*(3), 486-493.

Yee, N. (2005, in press). *The* Psychology of MMORPGs: Emotional investment, motivations, relationship formation, and problematic usage. In R. Schroeder & A. Axelsson (Eds.), *Avatars at work and play: Collaboration and interaction in shared virtual environments.* London: Springer-Verlag.

Ziehl, S. C. (2003). Forging the links: Globalisation and family patterns. *Society in Transition, 34*(2), 320-337.

Part II

Ang, S., & Slaughter, S. A. (2001). Work outcomes and job design for contract versus permanent information systems professionals on software development teams. MIS Quarterly, *25*(3), 321.

Baron-Cohen, S. (2002). The extreme male brain theory of autism. *Trends in Cognitive Sciences, 6*, 248-254. Retrieved April 2006, from http://wwwautis mresearchcentre.com/research/project.asp?id=2

Baron-Cohen, S., Bolton, P., Wheelwright, S., Short, L., Mead, G., Smith, A., & Scahill, V. H. (1998). Does autism occur more often in families of physicists, engineers, and mathematicians? *Autism, 2*, 296-301. Retrieved April 2006, from http://wwwautis mresearchcentre.com/research/project. asp?id=2

Carayon, P., Hoonakker, P., Marchand, S., & Schwarz, J. (2003). Job characteristics and quality of working life in the IT workforce: The role of gender. *Proceedings of the ACM SIGMIS Conference* (pp. 58-63). Philadelphia April 10-12, 2003. Retrieved February 2003, from http://cqpi2.engr.wisc.edu/ itwf/docs/ACM%202003%20Carayon%20et%20al.pdf

Castleman, T., Coulthard, D., & Reed, R. (2004). The lifecycle squeeze: Young professionals negotiating career and family in a hungry economy. *Produced for an upcoming conference, yet to be published.*

Cherniss, C. (2000). *Emotional intelligence: What it is and why it matters.* Paper presented at *the* Annual Meeting of the Society of Industrial and Organizational Psychology, New Orleans, LA, April 15, 2000. Retrieved February 2004, from http://www.eiconsortium.org/research/ what_is_emotional_intelligence.htm

Cooper, R., & Sawaf, A. (1996). *Executive EQ: Emotional intelligence in leadership and organizations.* San Francisco: Jossey-Bass.

Ebersole, E. S. *(2000).* Current science: Cell phone hang-ups. S*tanford, 86*(6), 4. Retrieved May 2005, from http://www.findarticles.com/p/articles/ mi_m0BFU/is_6_86/ai_67326279

Epson, D., & White, M. (1992). *Experience, contradiction, narrative, and imagination.* Adelaide: Dulwich Centre Publications.

Florida, R. (2002). *The rise of the creative class.* New York: Basic Books.

Fogel, J., Albert, S. M., Schnabel, F., Ditkoff, B. A., & Neugut, A. I. (2003). Racial/ethnic differences and potential psychological benefits in use of the Internet by women with breast cancer. *Psychol-Oncology, 12*(2), 107-117.

Fujigaki, Y., & Mori, K. (1997). Longitudinal study of work stress among information system professionals. *International Journal of Human-Computer Interaction, 9*(4), 369-381.

Goleman, D. (1998). *Emotional intelligence: Why it can matter more than IQ.* New York: Bantam Books.

Goleman, D., Boyatzis, R., & McKee, A. (2001). *Primal leadership: Realizing the potential of emotional intelligence.* Cambridge: Harvard Business School Press.

Goodwin, B. (2004, February 11). A balanced workforce is a productive one. *Computer Weekly*, 55. Retrieved April 2006, from http://www.computer weekly.com/Articles/2004/10/29/206361/Abalancedworkforceisaproduct iveone.thtm

Hall, D. T., & Richter, J. (1988). Balancing work life and home life: What can organizations do to help? *Academy of Management Executive, 2*(3), 213-223.

Hayes, D. (1989). *Behind the Silicon curtain: The seductions of work in a lonely era.* Boston: South End Press.

Hollands, J. (1985). *The Silicon syndrome: How to survive a high-tech relationship.* Toronto; New York: Bantam Books.

Joinson, A. N. (2003). *Understanding the psychology of Internet behaviour: Virtual worlds, Real lives.* UK: Palgrave MacMillan.

Kaluzniacky, E. (2004). *Managing psychological factors in information systems work: An orientation to emotional intelligence.* Hershey, PA: Idea Group.

Kirkpatrick, D. (2003). The Net makes it all easier-including exporting U.S. jobs. *Fortune, 147*(10), 146.

Kfir, N. (1989). *Crisis intervention verbatim.* New York: Hemisphere Publishing Corporation.

Kreitner, R., & Kinicki, A. (1992). *Organizational behaviour* (2nd ed.). Homewood, IL: Irwin.

Lazarus, R. S., & Folkman, S. (1984). *Stress, appraisal, and coping.* New York: Springer.

Pink, D. H. (2005). Revenge of the right brain: Logical and precise, left-brain thinking gave us the Information Age: Now comes the conceptual age–ruled by artistry, empathy, and emotion. *Wired*, 13.02, 1-3. Retrieved February 2005, from http://www.wired.com/wired/archive/13.02/ brain.html?pg=2

Prusak, L. (2004). Talk given at Victoria University of Wellington, School of Information Management.

Richardson, H. (2005). *Work-life balance in IT workers*. Unpublished research findings, The Open Polytechnic of New Zealand.

Robbins, S. P. (2003). *Organizational behavior*. UpperSaddle River, NJ: Prentice Hall.

Robinson, T. (1999). Reinventing the business wheel. *Informationweek*, (739), 6-10.

Roepke, R. (2000). Aligning the IT human resource with business vision: The leadership initiative at 3M. *MIS Quarterly, 24*(2), 327.

Salovey, P., & Mayer, J. (1990). Emotional intelligence. *Imagination, cognition, and personality, 9*(3), 185-211.

Scholarios, D., & Marks, A. *(2004)*. Work-life balance and the software worker. *Human Resource Management Journal, 14*(2), 54-75.

Sennett, R. (1998). *The corrosion of character: The personal consequences of work in the new capitalism*. New York: Norton.

Silverman, S. (2001). The geek syndrome: Autism—and its milder cousin Asperser's syndrome—is surging among the children of Silicon Valley: Are math-and-tech genes to blame? *Wired*, 9-12. Retrieved February 2005, from http://www.wired.com/wired/archive/9.12/aspergers_pr.html

Wechsler, D. (1940). Nonintellective factors in general intelligence. *Psychological Bulletin, 37*, 444-445.

Section II:

Professional Development of IT Professionals

Chapter IV

Reframing, Retooling, and Reskilling:
Coping with Change in the Internet Age

Eugene Cash, New Zealand Food Safety Authority, New Zealand

Pak Yoong, Victoria University of Wellington, New Zealand

Sid Huff, Victoria University of Wellington, New Zealand

Abstract

An IS professional's ability to perform in his or her role is vital to the utilisation of information systems within an organisation. The introduction of e-commerce has opened a new set of challenges for the IS professionals who are most frequently tasked with developing e-commerce solutions. However, they often do not have the competencies required to successfully execute these e-commerce projects. This competency deficit raises an important question: to what extent have the competency requirements of IS professionals changed because of the introduction of e-commerce? Furthermore, how do IS professionals managed the changes in their work environment due to the implementation of e-commerce in their organisations?

Fifteen IS professionals, who are employed in businesses implementing or maintaining e-commerce strategies, were interviewed. The results indicate that the implementation of e-commerce in organisations has introduced three main areas of change to their internal work environment: (a) business changes – the perceptions of senior managers on their current role, (b) project changes – the realization that IS projects have to be managed differently and finally (c) competency changes – the need to acquire new skills and knowledge. As a consequence to these changes, the IS professional developed the following coping skills: (a) reframing – the changing of mental models that determine how we make sense of the world and how we take action based on these models, (b) retooling – the restructuring and reorganising of IS processes, especially around project management and (c) reskilling – the learning of new competencies in the e-commerce environment.

Introduction

Organisations face an increasingly volatile business environment driven by intensified global competition, rapid changes in technology, and the erosion of traditional boundaries within which business is conducted. It is these changes that have impacted on the competencies required by IS professionals and more significantly on the rate at which these competencies evolve. In 1970, the United States Department of Labor estimated the professional occupational half-life— an approximation of how many years it takes for 50 percent of a person's skill-set to become obsolete—to be 15 years. Today's professional half-life is around three years (Tapsell, 1999). In addition, in the near future, an IS professional's skill development may no longer be provided by their employers, requiring professionals to become responsible for their own skill development to stay employable (Salzman, 1998). In the business world of mergers, acquisitions, downsizing and business and technical transformations, IS professionals more than ever before will have to remain attuned to role and competency changes to remain competitive in their careers (McMorrow, 1999).

One technological change having dramatic effects upon the business environment and organisations is the Internet. Its advent has brought a fundamental change for organisations and people in the IS domain (Gantz, 1997). In 1993, few outside academia had heard of, let alone utilised, the Internet (Loshin, 1995); today it is widely utilised. By the year 2005, 1.2 billion people around the world will have Internet access (Computer Industry Almanac, 2002). In 1993, there were 26,000 domain names; today this number exceeds five million (U.S.

Department of Commerce, 2000). The utilisation of Internet Web sites has proven beneficial for many organisations: small businesses which use the Internet grow on average 46% faster than those that do not (American City Business Journals, 1998). The Internet has become a new business medium, with e-commerce revenues ranging from $US800 billion to in excess of US$1 trillion. In New Zealand electronic transactions are expected to reach US$11.6 billion by 2003 (Caminos, 2000).

The reason for such an impact can be found in the way the Internet broadens both the *reach* and *range* of an organisational IT platform. That is to say, information can be readily shared and distributed across the Internet (the reach) which is able to link to and communicate with practically anywhere with a phone line (the range) (Keen, 1991). E-commerce, a strategy utilising the Internet to interact between businesses and consumers, exaggerates this reach and range by specifically linking businesses to clients and customers previously ignored by similar systems, for example, electronic data interchange (EDI) (Carr, 1997; Dalton, 1999). Providing organisations with the ability to exchange information "among constantly changing sets of customers, suppliers, and research collabo-rators..." (Kalakota & Whinston, 1996. p. 31), IS professionals will now be in a flexible system where they will work more closely with both internal and external entities and will be included in major operating decisions (Kalakota & Whinston, 1996). This progression has created a new set of challenges with IS professionals now expected to wear the many hats needed to assume a leading role–becoming strategists, futurists, politicians, change agents, and integrators (Dalton, 1999; Kerr, 1990). Insuring they have the appropriate competencies to perform in these roles is nothing less than survival of the fittest.

The implications of the Internet, and specifically e-commerce, for the role of the IS professional does not stop at the individual. Organisations also have an acute interest in e-commerce competency requirements. Many organisations hold their employees to be their best source of sustainable competitive advantage in the global marketplace (Stichweh, 1993). Organisations require the best skilled employees to achieve future goals—aware that retaining talent and remaining competitive and profitable depends upon their ability to develop the knowledge and skills of employees (Garger, 1999). Retaining talent by developing the competencies of employees was highlighted in a Com Tech Educational Services study: "Close to 70% of technology professionals identified the opportunity to acquire new skills as the primary reason for remaining with their organisation, rating it higher than a competitive salary, company culture and superior technol-ogy..." (Tapsell, 1999, p. 51). That organisations remain competitive and profitable from having the right skilled employees was illustrated in a Senn and Lee study (1995), highlighting a positive relationship between spending on IT staff development and the performance of the firm.

Third parties interested in how roles and competencies are changing for IS professionals are the educational institutions charged with instructing future IS authorities. IS curriculum needs are driven by what occurs in the business world, thus educational institutions are obliged to keep abreast of industry changes and must continually adjust curricula to meet the needs of society (Nelson, 1991; Niederman, Brancheau, & Wetherbe, 1991).

Competencies are clearly attracting greater attention in today's work environment. The reason for this lies in what has been discussed in this chapter. Knowledge, skills and abilities do more than impact upon the capacity of an IS professional to perform in a role; they impact upon an IS professional's ability to shape the organisation, and to remain challenged and happy in their job. Competencies impact upon the performance of the firm, and the ability of the organisation to retain staff. It is little wonder then that this subject has received consistent and significant attention in the academic press (Brancheau & Wetherbe, 1987; Dickson, Leitheiser, Nechis, & Wetherbe, 1984; Martin, 1985; Niederman et al. 1991). The purpose of this chapter is to report part of a larger study that examined the impact of e-commerce on the role of the IS professional (Cash, Yoong, & Huff, 2004). In particular, it examines how IS professionals perceived the changes in their work environment due to the implementation of e-commerce in their organisations.

Methodology

Case research methodology was used in this research and is defined as a form of empirical enquiry that "investigates a contemporary phenomenon within its real-life context; when the boundaries between phenomenon and context are not clearly evident…" (Yin, 1989, p. 23). Case research is "preferred in examining contemporary events…when the relevant behaviours cannot be manipulated" (Yin, 1994, p. 8). For these reasons, the researchers felt that case research was the most appropriate approach to studying the phenomenon under investigation.

Research Participants

Fifteen IS professionals took part in this study. They were selected from a variety of private and public New Zealand and Australian-based organisations, including consulting firms and financial service organizations (see Table 1).

Participants within the organisations held a variety of positions, including IS project managers, IS consultant, IS manager and Web developer (see Table 2).

Table 1. Organisation type

Type of Organisation	No. of companies	No. of participants
Financial Institutions	3	7
Public Sector Organisation	1	1
Management Consulting Firms	2	3
E-commerce Consulting Firms	2	2
Other Private Sector Organisations	2	2

Table 2. Participant occupations

Occupation	1st Round	2nd Round	Total No.
Project manager	3	3	6
IS manager		3	3
IS consultant		2	2
Programmer	1	1	2
Web developer		1	1
Systems analyst	1		1
Total	5	10	15

All were currently participating, or had recently participated in e-commerce projects.

Results

Conceptualisation of Change in the E-Commerce Environment

Based on the interview data, it was found that participants were discussing, directly or indirectly, three types of change in the e-commerce environment: business, project, and competency.

Business changes—changes in what the business (senior management) was demanding and in the way in which e-commerce initiatives and the IS professionals themselves were perceived by the organisation, was the broadest set of changes discussed by the informants. It was these business changes as a result of e-commerce that were subsequently seen to lead to project changes within the organisation: the second change. To meet the demands of the business (as reflected and dictated by the external environment), traditional project management processes, timeframes, and methods were modified. Adapting traditional project management concepts to satisfy internal and external constraints and demands was perceived to lead to the last area of change: competency. Competency changes—changes in what IS professionals need to know to perform in their roles—were perceived as evolving as a result of new and salient project demands.

Looking at the previous paragraph the reader may well notice that each change is significantly different. Business change involves changing perceptions whereas project change involves changing processes. Alternatively, competency change involves changing specific knowledge, skills and abilities. The type and level of change (or coping skills) is examined in Table 3.

Given these changes are "extensions" or varying "magnifications" of an overall concept of change in the e-commerce environment, the way in which they impact and influence each other is also related. The relationship of the three changes is illustrated in Figure 1.

As Figure 1 illustrates, the relationship between the three changes is two-way. While the broadest changes lead to a change up the pyramid, it is the respective change that allows the level beneath to be realised. Thus optimal change in the e-commerce environment is cyclical, with each influencing or allowing the other

Table 3. Type and level of change in the e-commerce environment

Type of change	Change description	Level of change
Business	The business (senior management) changing expectations, perceptions and compliance (mental models) in relation to e-commerce projects, the IS department, and the IS professional	Reframing
Project	A change in traditional project processes–timeframes, deliverables, and management	Retooling
Competency	A change in the knowledge, skills and abilities of the IS professional (Grouped into the domains of technical, business, relationship, and conceptual)	Reskilling

Figure 1. The hierarchy of changes in the e-commerce environment

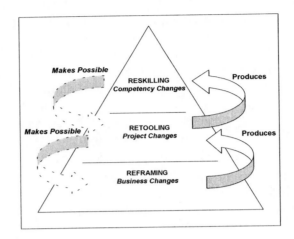

to be realised. Business changes–changes in the way the organisation perceives the e-commerce system (e-commerce, the project, and the IS professional)—places pressure and demands that can only be met by changing traditional project processes. It is these project changes that subsequently drive the IS professional to evolve their competency domains; dealing with the new challenges encountered in a different project environment.

It is the respective changes, however, that enables the previous change to be realised. Without the IS professional changing the competencies required to effectively perform, project changes cannot be successfully realised. Similarly, the business changes—reframing, cannot be fulfilled unless project changes are first achieved.

The next three sections introduce the reader to how and why the three concepts (business, project, and competency) experienced change in the e-commerce environment. It is aimed at providing some initial thought before the specific business (reframing), project (retooling) and competency (reskilling) changes are examined.

Reskilling:
Required Competency Changes

The narrowest change participants discussed related to reskilling—the IS professional learning new competencies in the e-commerce environment. To most informants, dealing with some e-commerce changes meant coming to grips with a new range of technical, business, relationship, and conceptual skills:

...There are new technologies and applications which I need to understand. As a result I have attended training programmes to help me upscale my knowledge in a particular area.

Talking with them [senior management] *a lot more has meant I've needed to learn more about how the business operates, and in what way the business sees the strategy changing in the future. It's meant having to understand the business models and I guess also having to understand current business issues...*

This change is focused on how the technical, business, relationship, and conceptual competency domains have changed for the IS professional in the e-commerce environment. As previously discussed, this competency change has occurred because the way a project is run in the e-commerce environment has changed. IS professionals are evolving their KSA domains in order to adapt to the changing project environment around them. This is explored in the next section.

Retooling: Adapting Project Processes

Participants also described change broader than the need to learn new skills in fresh areas. They also focused on how they have changed the way they work in the e-commerce environment: discussing how aspects of their current project processes have needed to adapt. Alterations to development methodologies, planning, and team structures require a different kind of learning, as the following informant explains:

I would say it's changed the way I work...now I am interacting with a lot more vendors and managers in order to get the project ticked off [completed]....

This change has been termed retooling (project change) and essentially encompasses the restructuring and reorganising of IS processes, both individually and in the wider IS environment to "bring about the changes required to support the companies business thrusts" (Rose, 1995, p. 34). Retooling is effectively a re-engineering of how IS professionals currently organise their work processes for the purpose of adapting to a rapidly changing business environment and is what informants described as occurring in the e-commerce environment:

I'm modifying a lot of the processes and methods of project management which [Company X] has traditionally used. I've found personally that the way I develop and manage a project has needed to be changed...because of the nature of the environment.

I have found it interesting because when I started working at [Company X] the makeup on how to work on and manage a project was quite well defined...but that's all changed with these projects because it just won't work, it's too formal...too structured...[and] doesn't allow you to manage in change.

To cope with the unpredictable e-commerce environment, professionals discussed retooling as a way to change the internal dynamics of the project to match the variety and complexity of the e-commerce environment.

As Figure 1 (the hierarchy of changes in the e-commerce environment) indicates, project changes are produced by business changes (reframing). The business "thinking differently" about e-commerce projects, and the role of IS professionals within these projects, is examined in the next section.

Reframing: Business Expectations, Perceptions, and Compliance Changes

The last level of change discussed by the participants, and the broadest of all, is termed reframing. The complexity of e-commerce has dictated changes not only to the project environment, but also to the way the business perceives the IS professional and the way the IS professional perceives the "system"—the e-commerce work environment. Reframing deals with the changing of mental models that determine how we make sense of the world and how we take action (Singe, 1990). Another definition sees mental models as an:

Internal representation of the system structure and function that provides explanatory and understanding power. (Bostrom, Olfman, & Sein, 1990, p. 105)

The majority of participants discussed the reframing of the e-commerce system (their role, the project and related work processes) by senior management. Participants, either directly or indirectly, noted the changes in perception those around them had gone through to understand and manage e-commerce projects:

Development timeframes are definitely being demanded faster. The business, to a certain extent, measures the success of the [e-commerce] *project on how long it takes to complete it. They want it developed and implemented faster I expect because others in the market are doing the same thing and we have to get there first.*

I think the business expects us to alter significant parts of the business, or at least impact on multiple levels of the business. They want us to offer a solution which is different and which will bring about significant results...

As the following participants explain, this change in perception has been critical in dealing with the complexity of e-commerce:

...You've got to be able to create new work for each different client, because each client has got a unique business problem they are trying to solve. It is not a standardised problem you are going to reapply like a cookie cutter at every client....

I think you're able to think a lot more out of the box simply because when you are trying to find a solution within an environment you're constrained by elements of that environment. At this stage, I feel like we've got a blank sheet of paper and we can say, 'let's forget about the best way of doing it, let's forget about everything else that surrounds us, let's just ask ourselves the question 'what does the customer want?' and then work backwards from that...

Why are organisations—or rather, those within them—reframing? Reactive and static skills-based training, founded on market demands, cannot keep pace with a dynamic business environment. The traditional skill development model, following the static (Lewin, 1951) unfreeze-change-refreeze change model, is inadequate. A new strategy has developed that allows individuals to develop dynamically and flexibly. Reframing and retooling—along with reskilling—has ensured that organisations cope with the e-commerce environment through a continuous development process. The following authors "frame" their views:

...potentially one of the most significant changes is that e-business forces a change in the mind set...This mind set change can often be the deciding factor to determine if e-business initiatives succeed. (Caminos, 2000. p. 20)

Learning is inevitable in the future. Change is coming so fast now that people must constantly retool and rethink what they're doing...In the workplaces of the future, learning will be ubiquitous, unavoidable, constantly challenging and frequently chaotic. (Argyris, Bellman, Blanchard, & Bloch, 1994, p. 36)

This chapter has introduced three concepts of change (both in terms of type and level) to the reader and has also explored some of the initial findings with respect to these changes. In the next section, we will explore the likely impact of these changes on the role of the IS professional.

Emerging Roles of IS Professionals

E-commerce has produced a fundamental shift in strategy and focus for many organisations. This has had an impact upon the role of the IS professional. The discussion and findings of the previous sections can be used to build up a holistic picture of emerging roles for the IS professional in the e-commerce environment. We proposed four such roles: *eInitiator, eEducator, eDriver,* and *eProphet.*

- **eInitiator:** In the emerging e-commerce environment the IS professional is predominantly the person responsible for in-depth thinking on the subject. They are responsible for seeking answers to questions like: What is and is not feasible with e-commerce? What are the objectives for the project? What resources will be required? and etc. Although e-commerce is becoming an established business theme, IS professionals still find they have to initiate active and achievable e-commerce discussions with senior management, working through the "buzz words"—business and technical jargon and rhetoric—towards an obtainable vision for e-commerce within the organisation. We consider the *eInitiator* role to be important as it enable the IS professional to assist the organisation in setting up and establishing the seeds of e-commerce.

- **eEducator:** In this role, the IS professional cultivates e-commerce knowledge within the organisation. As e-commerce begins to gain credibility in the eyes of senior management, the IS professional is required to proactively inform the business about the strategic potential of e-commerce, and where future trends may be heading. Whether to satisfy business demands or ensure senior management support, this role focuses upon making sure the business is sufficiently well informed to implement future e-commerce strategies. The IS professional essentially shepherd a process that, for many organisations, is considered to be a high-risk, low return option. In this process the IS professional is both teaching the business about e-commerce and learning about organisational strategies.

- **eDriver:** The IS professional drives the e-commerce initiatives within the organisation. Once the initiatives have received the necessary approval and backing, the IS professional begins to develop the e-commerce solution. Given the complexity of solutions and the lack of understanding by the organisation, the IS professional plays a coaching role, initiating new strategies achievable for the business, and organising "plays"—strategies—which may eventuate in the future. Often, the IS professional progresses from someone teaching management to someone executing e-commerce solutions. The IS professional plays a proactive consulting role, developing a solution for the organisation, while informing management as to where achievable future strategies may lie. In this role the IS professional is someone with the knowledge, skills, and abilities to guide not just the IT strategy but, in some cases, create the organisation's strategy.

- **eProphet:** The organisation has recognized the IS professional with the competency to plan and subsequently develop the e-commerce solutions with little intervention from senior management. Essentially, senior managers credit the IS professional with capable business knowledge, someone able to lead the organisation's e-commerce strategies. In this role the IS professional is recognized as being the person who actively finds, promotes and develops business strategies—not just e-commerce strategies, but strategies for the whole organisation. As an eProphet the IS professional engages in forecasting future e-strategies for the business, and for many, becoming perceptive as to possible future strategies the business may adopt in the future.

Conclusion

This chapter reports an exploratory study focusing on the impact of e-commerce on the role of an IS professional. The results suggest that the implementation of e-commerce in organisations has introduced three main areas of change to their internal work environment: (a) business changes, (b) project changes, and finally (c) competency changes. As a consequence to these changes, the IS professional developed the following coping skills: (a) reframing, (b) retooling, and (c) reskilling. We believe that understanding the impact of changes on the IS professional will remain a primary concern of IS researchers and practitioners as we continue to discover novel and more sophisticated applications of the Internet. For this reason, research into IS professional competencies is both important and constructive and should be conducted on a continuing basis.

References

American City Business Journals. (1998). Small business use of Net grows at high-speed pace. *Bizjournals.* Retrieved June 22, 2002, from http://www.bizjournals.com/sanjose/stories/1998/06/15/focus3.html

Argyris, C., Bellman, G., Blanchard, K., & Bloch, P. (1994). The future of workplace learning and performance. *Training and Development, 48*(5), 36-47.

Bostrom, R. P., Olfman, L., & Sein, M. K. (1990). The Importance of learning style in end-user training. *MIS Quarterly, 14*(1), 101-119.

Brancheau, J., & Wetherbe, J. (1987). Key issues in information systems management. *MIS Quarterly, 11*(1), 23-45.

Caminos, M. (2000). The e-business tsunami. *CIO, 6*(3), 16-21.

Carr, J. (1997). Commerce demands co-operation. *Infoworld, 19*(1), 45-46.

Cash, E., Yoong, P., & Huff, S. (2004) The impact of e-commerce on the role of a IS professional. *The DATABASE for Advances for Information Systems, 35*(3), 50-63.

Cheney, P. H. (1988). Information systems skills requirements: 1980 & 1988. *Proceedings of the 1988 ACM Special Interest Group on Computer Personnel Research* (pp. 1-7). ACM.

Computer Industry Almanac Inc. (2002). *Internet users will top 1 billion in 2005.* Computer Industry Almanac. Retrieved March 27, 2002, from http://www.c-i-a.com/pr032102.htm

Dalton, G. (1999). E-business evolution. *Informationweek, 7*(37), 50-66.

Dickson, G., Leitheiser, J., Wetherbe, J., & Nechis, M. (1984). Key information systems issues for the 1980s. *MIS Quarterly, 8*(3), 135-159.

Gantz, J. (1997). E-commerce puts IS in the fast lane. *Computerworld, 31*(5), 33.

Garger, E. (1999). Goodbye training, Hello Learning. *Workforce, 78*(11), 35-42.

Kalakota, R., & Whinston, A. B. (1996). *Frontiers of electronic commerce.* Boston: Addison-Wesley.

Keen, P. (1991). *Shaping the future, business design through information technology.* Boston, MA: Harvard Business School Press.

Kerr, J. (1990). Business gains competitive advantage through expanded IS role. *Insurance and Technology, 15*(5), 24-26.

Lewin, K. (1951). *Field theory in social science.* New York: Harper & Row.

Loshin, P. (1995). *Electronic commerce.* Boston: Charles River Media.

Martin, E. W. (1985). Critical success factors of Chief MIS/DP Executives. *MIS Quarterly, 6*(2), 1-9.

McMorrow, J. (1999). Future trends in human resources. *HR Focus, 76*(9), 7-10.

Nelson, R. (1991). Educational needs as perceived by is and end-user personnel: A survey of knowledge and skill requirements. *MIS Quarterly, 15*(4), 503-521.

Niederman, F., Brancheau, J., & Wetherbe, J. (1991). Information systems management issues for the 1990s. *MIS Quarterly, 15*(4), 474-500.

Rose, I. (1995). Retooling the information systems professional. *Journal of Systems Management, 46*(1), 6-13.

Salzman, H. (1998). Restructuring and skill needs: Will firms train? *Annals of the American Academy of Political and Social Science, 559*, 125-141. Retrieved from http://ann.sagepub.com

Senge, P. (1990, Fall) The leader's new work: Building learning organizations. *Sloan Management Review, 32*(1), 7-23.

Senn, J., & Lee, J. (1995). Investing in IT's human resource: The impact on performance of the firm. *Proceedings of the 1995 ACM SIGCPR Conference on Supporting Teams, Groups, and Learning Inside and Outside the IS Function* (p. 240). ACM.

Stichweh, R. (1993). Capturing the people advantage. *Executive Excellence, 10*(7), 18-19.

Tapsell, S. (1999). Time to retrain. *Management, 46*(7), 49-50.

U.S. Department of Commerce. (2000). *Domain Name Registration*. U.S. Department of Commerce. Retrieved August 27, 2000, from http://home.doc.gov/Science_and_Technology

Yin, R. K. (1989). *Case study research: Design and methods, revised edition*. Newbury Park: Sage Publications.

Yin, R. K. (1994). *Case study research, design and methods* (2nd ed). Newbury Park: Sage Publications.

Chapter V

Staffing Electronic Commerce Projects:
Framework for Developing Appropriate Skill Sets

Fred Niederman, Saint Louis University, USA

Xiaorui Hu, Saint Louis University, USA

Abstract

Electronic commerce (e-commerce) personnel are instrumental in developing and maintaining electronic commerce programs and projects within firms. In spite of the dot-com bust, the number of firms developing and using e-commerce for interactions with customers and suppliers is growing. Personnel competence as individuals and as a group can be a decisive force in determining the level of success of e-commerce projects. In this chapter, we present a conceptual framework as an extension and reformulation of several of the currently active fit theories of human resource management and industrial psychology. We propose consideration of five categories of skills that should be present in organizational e-commerce workforce (human computer interface, data storage and analysis, transaction/application development, infrastructure, and project management). Finally, based on the adjusted concepts of fit, we present a set of propositions showing expected relationships between organizational and fit related variables on workforce outcomes.

Introduction

Internet, since its launch in 1972, has significantly changed the world. It connects hundreds of thousands of different networks from over 200 countries around the world. Millions of people working in science, education, government, and business professions utilize the Internet to exchange information or perform business transactions around the globe. According to NUA Internet Surveys (2002), the number of Internet users has surpassed 605.6 million as of September 2002. The Internet has penetrated to people's everyday life, altered the way companies do business, created new services and jobs, and changed the way people work. Using Internet technology, companies often find new outlets for their products and services abroad (Quelch & Klein, 1996) by linking directly to suppliers, business partners, and customers. Despite the recent collapse of dot-com startups and the Wall Street re-valuation of technology stocks, the Internet has undoubtedly emerged as a crucial communications technology in the information era. This has led to penetration of Internet by "clicks and mortar" companies with both Web and traditional presence.

However, the transition from traditional to "click and mortar" firm is not always smooth and easy. We frequently observe in the trade literature that e-commerce projects have gone awry. Burke and Morrison (2001) have documented the mechanics of how this happens. Organizations have a tendency to vastly underestimate the difficulty in shifting from a static Web page that serves basically as an automated brochure to a dynamic Web program that provides online information exchange and facilitates real-time transactions. As technologies support more sophisticated Web activities, the demand for knowledge and skills of the e-commerce personnel supporting e-commerce programs expands correspondingly. It is logical to propose that a key success factor for the development and implementation of e-commerce applications is the technical and organizational competence of the e-commerce personnel to which the project is assigned. It is, therefore, of significant importance for e-commerce projects' managers to bring the greatest possible understanding of the dynamics affecting productivity to their personnel decisions.

This chapter has three objectives. First, we intend to present our conceptual framework as an extension and reformulation of several currently active fit theories in the fields of human resource management and industrial psychology.

Second we intend to take an in-depth look at the IT skills set, which should be expected to be present in the organizational e-commerce workforce. Finally, based on the adjusted concepts of fit, we present a set of propositions demonstrating expected relationships among the framework components.

Literature Review

Fit Theories

For generations, management and industrial psychology researchers have been studying issues of employee outcomes including "performance, motivation, extra-role behaviors, work attitudes, retention, group cooperation, and group performance" (Werbel & Gilliland, 1999, p. 209). One major direction of that research focuses on the validation of a belief that the fit between the work environment (in a variety of aspects) and the attributes of the individual should predict various work-related and individual outcomes. Where the match is close, the outcomes should be better than where there is a significant gap between individual and organization (e.g., Edwards, 1991, 1996; Kristof, 1996; Livingstone, Nelson, & Barr, 1997; Werbel & Gilliland, 1999). For example, a skill element of a taxi driver's job is to drive efficiently from place to place. Individuals with a high level of skill at "finding shortcuts" should be more productive than those without the skill. However, as the nature of work changes significantly in response to the growing prevalence of information technology, which helps organization reorganize, replace, and invent new work, the simple match between job requirements and individual skills could only explain part of the variance in outcomes.

A number of additional matches have been proposed to supplement the job environment, such as individual attribute match. For example one study focusing on the employee selection process proposes three fits that are important in influencing outcomes. Werbel and Gilliland (1999) propose that the person-job, person-organization, and person-workgroup fits are critical in different situations. In this formulation, person-job fit is the congruence between the "demands of the job and the needed skills, knowledge, and abilities of a job candidate (Werbel & Gilliland, 1999, p. 211 referencing Edwards, 1991)." The idea of person-organization fit would add to "technical job performance" factors, such as pro-social behavior, organizational citizenship, and organizational commitment. Person-workgroup fit "refers to the match between the new hire and the immediate workgroup (i.e., coworkers and supervisor) (Werbel & Gilliland, 1999, p. 217)."

The idea here is that the strengths of one individual may be complemented by the strengths of another individual to provide stronger overall team outcomes. Although the discussion of these types of fit are presented by Werbel and Gilliland within the context of employment selection, it stands to reason that similar issues can be addressed, though perhaps on a smaller scale, toward the selection of individuals within a firm for work on a specific project or in a particular work role. In addition, we propose a new match dimension. The new match addresses the issues that job strain and retention is the "compensation" needs of an individual and the benefits provided by the job. Together with the job need—individual skill match, these theories comprise a job demand/job supply theory.

E-Commerce Knowledge, Skills, and Abilities

There has not yet been much discussion on the topic of e-commerce knowledge, skills, and abilities in the MIS literature. Aladwani (2002) followed frameworks of Lee, Trauth, and Farwell (1995), Nelson (1991), Rada (1999), and Trauth, Farwell, and Lee (1993) to identify IT personnel skill needs and has identified 16 distinct skills (see Table 1). Table 1 replicates Aladwani, 2002. In the paper, the ranks by practitioners and academics are contrasted in terms of both usefulness and competence of new IT graduates. This valuable study should be extended by (1) including background from the substantial knowledge developed by human

Table 1. High-level skills needed by developers of e-commerce systems

Knowledge Area	High-Level Skill
Technical	1. Web programming
	2. Web networking
	3. Web databases
	4. Web security
	5. Web management
	6. Web site design
Human	7. Interpersonal communication
	8. Problem solving
	9. Conflict resolution
	10 Collaboration
	11. Dealing with change
Organizational	12. Organizational goals and objectives
	13. Organizational policies and procedures
	14. Organizational functions and processes
	15. Organizational culture
	16. Organizational constraints

resource and industrial psychologies regarding predictors of work outcomes and (2) considering a more detailed level of skill requirements recognizing the differences between traditional IT and emerging e-commerce projects.

One study has recently contrasted the perceived usefulness of job skills and the responding Web masters perceptions of her or his competencies for each skill (Wade & Parent, 2001-2002). Overall this study suggests that technical skill deficiencies lead to lower productivity, with organizational skill deficiencies also, and in a more pronounced manner, leading to lower productivity. However, this study, springing from an IT employee model, contrasts technical and organizational skills rather than IT and Web production skills.

Although the development of e-commerce Web sites has a strong technical component, Holzschlag (2000) has proposed viewing the development of a Web site as more of an artistic production. By interacting in a constant feedback loop with customer/users, the development process has some analogy to the development of films and other creative products. The term "Web publication specialist" is used to emphasize the many non-technical elements necessary for successful e-commerce development, which include interface and functionality design involving artistic, usability, policy, and functionality issues. Specialists in this area would not necessarily have or need technical IT skills. The category of Web publication specialist refers to those individuals with marketing, communications, and other backgrounds that are necessary to develop successful Web projects. Skills in this area, as applied to IS projects, have not been fully studied. Moreover, these skills may be difficult to specify since elements of innovativeness, creativity, and the ability to generate excitement are difficult to quantify.

McKee (2001) and Wenn and Sellitto (2001) evaluated necessary e-commerce skills by considering the requirements for successful e-commerce projects and the specific skills needed to accomplish these tasks. McKee (2001) presents a detailed diagram of elements needed for successfully building an e-commerce site derived from practice. His work highlights the variety of skills ranging from

Figure 1. Representation of e-commerce skill portfolio

the most technical infrastructure manipulation to sensitivity regarding business needs and marketing processes. Wenn and Sellitto (2001) focus on some of the tools, languages, and standards that are either required or recommended for more robust performance on e-commerce sites. Both sets of research suggest that the full range of skills need not be present in every team member.

Extrapolating from and extending these works, we propose five distinguishable but overlapping skill areas needed for e-commerce projects. These pertain to working with the human interface, the applications/transactions, the database, and analysis of data, the underlying technical infrastructure, and the project management where these skill areas are blended through individuals into finished products. This model is visually displayed in Figure 1.

Human Resource Influence on E-Commerce Work Outcomes

Based on the discussions of fit and e-commerce work, we propose a model of four factors projected to influence the level of work outcomes (see Figure 2). In this model, it is expected that the way an organization positions its e-commerce work will influence how an e-commerce project is organized, which will in turn influence the specification of both the group level demand and individual level supply of knowledge abilities and skills. It is further posited that the match between group level skill demand and various configurations of individual level knowledge, skills, and abilities will lead to varied work outcomes.

Figure 2. Factors influence e-commerce work outcomes

Propositions

E-Commerce Work Organization

It is recognized that there are at least three distinguishable types of e-commerce projects. First, business-to-business (B2B) projects connect two or more organizations for streamlining standard transactions. This can be a continuation of electronic data interchange (EDI) or can be shifting toward Internet oriented interconnections which include a broad array of marketplaces, auctions, industry level activities, and unique partnership arrangements. Second, business to consumer (B2C) e-commerce aims at linking an organization to its customers emphasizing on efficient shopping. For example, Amazon.com provides quick access to specific books with a few added features like reviews by prior customers and a list of similar books that are available to customers. Third, virtual communities (VC) aim primarily at meeting the peer-to-peer needs of members but may include some business transaction capability. Typically, a development project in this area will emphasize underlying structures that participants themselves can manipulate in ways that they themselves see as enhancing value.

As the nature of e-commerce program varies, so should the nature of projects and how they are organized to support the program. Ultimately, as the nature of the organizational e-commerce program varies so will the skills required to develop them. For example, B2B projects may need to emphasize absolute reliability, to institute capacity for high volumes of information flow, and to incorporate advanced auditing features. Emphasis on highly technical skills may, therefore, overshadow (but not remove the need for) Web production skills for these projects. In contrast, B2C and virtual community e-commerce programs are more likely to emphasize entertainment, news and product information, and opportunities for meaningful participation. These types of project require excellent Web production skills to attract and retain customers or participants but also require excellent IT technical skills to ensure that content is delivered effectively and efficiently.

Proposition 1: Different types of e-commerce work will produce different e-commerce projects (work arrangements).

E-Commerce Project Organization (Work Arrangements)

We expect generally that e-commerce work within organizations will be organized into a set of interconnected projects. The notion of an e-commerce project here is intended to be broad and inclusive. Some project theorists, notably Evaristo and van Fenema (1999), distinguish between programs (consisting of sets of related projects) and individual projects. However, in practice, large projects may have many interrelated aspects or "sub-projects" and, for our purposes, the specific distinction is not crucial. The discussion of e-commerce projects here is not intended toward the most micro-level project that may only use one of many skills without regard to others; nor to describing a permanent departmental structure. Rather, this paper considers e-commerce projects as activities large and small toward the creation and maintenance of organizational e-commerce capabilities. One of the complexities of research in this area comes from the probability that different industries and organizations within industries may organize their e-commerce technologies and development or maintenance programs differently. Finding common terminology and normalizing the view between organizations will be critical for achieving comparability.

E-commerce work tends to be done as a set of various types of interlocking projects within an organization. In terms of the various fit models previously discussed, we propose that the idea of blending individual worker and job characteristics could be reformulated. The e-commerce work demands for skills, abilities, and knowledge can be defined on a project level. For example, development of a Web accessed product catalogue by a retail firm will require a range of publication, technology, and marketing skills, which are most possibly beyond the capability of any one individual. At one extreme, a single manager will coordinate the ingress and egress of various specialists contributing to components of the project until it is finished. At another extreme a team of generalists, who may stress various subsets of the demanded skills individually, will work together over a period of time on the project until it is completed or abandoned. It is likely that neither extreme will be observed as frequently as various points on the continuum between them with small permanent teams adding and releasing various specialists through the course of the project. Depending, however, on where along this continuum an organization tends to operate in developing its e-commerce applications, different ratios of individuals' knowledge, skills, and abilities versus group level and organization skills will be prevalent in predicting positive work outcomes. Moreover, depending on how work is arranged, we would expect to find varying tendencies for individuals with key skills to be more highly regarded, and that all individuals should need some skill overlap to have a significant chance of making an important, even if not proportional contribution.

Proposition 2: Different types of e-commerce projects (work arrangements) will generate different patterns of group level skill requirements and different collections of individual members' skill sets.

E-Commerce Knowledge, Skills, and Ability Requirements at a Group/Project Level

What constitutes the best combination of people with various skills for an e-commerce project remains an open question. Staffing of e-commerce projects requires a parallel blending of skill sets including traditional IT skills (e.g., programming, analysis, infrastructure management) and adding skills in marketing, publication/media development, and supply chain mechanics (Niederman & Hu, 2003). Based on Niederman and Hu (2003), we classify e-commerce skills into five categories, human interface design skills, database skills, development and transaction skills, networking and infrastructure skills, and management skills. The approach taken here varies somewhat from a traditional human resource approach to defining individual level skills through job analysis then adding group dynamics skills (Klimoski & Jones, 1995). Rather than attempt to define a set of individual skills and add team level attributes, our approach is to consider the skills required for project accomplishment. In this manner, we examine whether one or more individuals contribute each requisite skill within the project context.

Human Interface Design Skills

An initial set of skills pertaining to the human interface design can be inferred from the characteristics of good interfaces. These characteristics include layout, content awareness, aesthetics, user experience, consistency, and minimal user effort (Dennis & Wixom, 2000). Human interface designers need creativity to propose interesting and innovative approaches to the interface. They also need the engineering skills to translate creative ideas into efficient and effective technical components. Finally, they need the interpersonal skills to elicit desirable characteristics from users and potential users as well as gather feedback for improvement. As Holzschlag (2000) points out, methodologies for development of artistic endeavors are moving from pre-production to post-production processes that have some resemblance to IT project management techniques, which include some prototyping and rapid application development approaches. At the minimum, an extensive e-commerce project will require the following human interface skills: (1) balancing aesthetics with functionality; (2) capturing functionality with high usability; (3) anticipating user preferences; (4) developing insights into the characteristics of present and future (potential) users; (5) recognizing and incorporating new business opportunities; (6) scanning for and incorporating knowledge of the latest multimedia tools and techniques; and (7) creating "fun," excitement, mystery, in a "virtual environment" (particularly for B2C or communities).

Proposition 3a: At an e-commerce project level, there will be demand for human interface knowledge, skills, and abilities from one or more individuals.

Application/Transaction Skills. Where static pages and assertions are not sufficient for the e-commerce application, the human interface skills must be supplemented with significant application/transaction processing analysis, design, coding, and maintenance skills. In some ways the object-oriented approach and client-server technology can lead to isolation of program elements and ease of maintenance. On the other hand, distributed objects require mechanisms for coordination, scaling, optimization, and consistency of change and update that can be quite daunting. To keep these tasks manageable, an environment needs to be created within which many of these tasks can be handled by default or by specialists in network or database management.

Proposition 3b: At an e-commerce project level there will be demand for application/transaction knowledge, skills, and abilities from one or more individuals.

Data Storage and Analysis Skills

Storing permanent data offers its own challenges. Making managerial use of stored data pertaining to products, customers, and trends requires both database and analysis skills. Customer resource management, for example, entails the development and integration of software to support numerous distinct marketing tasks largely based on the accumulation of information about customers and their purchasing and browsing tendencies. The deployment of these systems is non-trivial involving the capture of large quantities of data as they are generated, filtering data for accuracy, storing it in a retrievable manner, and retrieving the most appropriate subsets of data for immediate use with existing and potential customers as well as for generating standard trend reports and data mining for discovery of new customer relationships.

Proposition 3c: At an e-commerce project level, there will be demand for data storage and analysis knowledge, skills and abilities from one or more individuals.

Infrastructure Skills

The infrastructure presents the need for knowledge of many programming languages, sets of environment building tools, standards and common Internet courtesies and practices, hardware, network, middleware, and how all these technologies interact together. Infrastructure specialization combines knowledge in numerous arcane and demanding areas. It can be anticipated that e-commerce projects will require new Web-oriented skills blended with traditional technical IT skills. More specifically, infrastructure skills will include: (1) blending new elements into the existing infrastructure; (2) matching infrastructure resources with project requirements; (3) acquiring and creating Internet related tools; and (4) possessing abilities to operate in an Internet environment and to resolve issues in terms of access, transportation, protocols, and security.

Proposition 3d: At an e-commerce project level, there will be demand for infrastructure knowledge, skills, and abilities from one or more individuals.

Management Skills

Management is the glue that holds together the various specializations. McKee (2001) describes a new position: the e-commerce architect. In his formulation, an individual is responsible for creating the overall functional and operational vision for the e-commerce system. As described, the position requires strong managerial skills that should include: the ability to motivate employees, decompose tasks, assign tasks, resolve conflict, measure interim outcomes, and make adjustments to maximize the work outcome of a group. It is the management of projects that directs the diverse skill elements into the accomplishment of final outcomes. For programs of any size, it is management that through scheduling, allocation of resources, human interaction, and follow up to bring the relevant skills to bear where and when needed. Additionally, management skills are required for interacting with the environment external to the project. Aladwani (2002), for example, lists five "human" and another five "organization" skills pertaining to abilities to work in groups as well as to present the project within the context of organizational needs.

It can also be argued that each individual team member needs management skills including participating in collective documentation and procedure, generating new ideas and translating them to common understandings, resolving conflicts, and understanding the business context of the new systems. However, we would expect that in any but the smallest projects, designating one or more specific individuals to be responsible for project management will lead to improved outcomes. This is in addition to competencies for communication and understanding the business context among project members in general.

Proposition 3E: At an e-commerce project level, there will be demand for technical project management knowledge, skills, and abilities from one or more individuals.

An interesting aspect of e-commerce projects is that many (if not all) will have novel elements that force the project team to move into some uncertain areas. For the project personnel as a group, an ability to improvise would seem critical to successful e-commerce project management (Kanter, 2001). In spite of focus groups, surveys, and other methods for discovering the attitudes and preferences of clients, once available to the public there is a very good chance that users will find new, unintended applications while being baffled by what appeared to be straightforward designs. As a result, there is usually an element of guided experimentation involved in finding the right combination of ingredients to address the range of customer needs and preferences. This is likely the case most often in B2C and community sites, but can also be the case in B2B settings where new technology can stimulate the redesign and improvement of existing business processes. It can be expected that some self-training, organizational training, even trial and error during the course of the project will expand the skill base of the project team while performing its tasks.

It should be expected that projects can succeed even though not every skill is fully present at the beginning of the projects. On the other hand, major and even minor gaps in the team's skill set may need significant managerial attention to prevent significant errors or difficulties. Following this scenario, the ability to keep a successful group together, to expand its membership, to recombine experienced workers with newcomers in a way that transfers skills and knowledge, can be a crucial element in making best use of limited human resources.

Proposition 4a: At an e-commerce project level, there will be demand for "group dynamics" knowledge, skills, and ability from one or more individuals.

Proposition 4b: At an e-commerce project level, there will be demand for the ability to dynamically learn, acquire new skills, and accomplish tasks without formally acquiring specific skills from one or more individuals.

Just because a project may demand a range of skills, it doesn't necessarily mean that all individuals will be treated equally. Based on the individual attributes brought to the group and project, we would expect:

Proposition 5a: Individuals with "key" skills will have more influence and play a more central role in the group.

Proposition 5b: Individuals will need at least some overlap between their individual skill set and the project needs to make sufficient contribution for high levels of peer and self evaluations.

Outcomes

A variety of work related outcomes have been examined in fit theory in human resource research. Some of the frequently researched outcomes include quality and speed of performance, citizenship behaviors, job satisfaction, organizational commitment, absenteeism, retention, and work unit dynamics (Werbel & Gilliland, 1999, p. 232). Some of these, such as quality, speed of performance and absenteeism, attach clearly to assessment of particular projects. Others, such as job satisfaction, retention, and citizenship behaviors, relate to long-term success and cost-effectiveness of e-commerce programs.

Proposition 6a: Closer matching of project demand and the sum of individual knowledge, skills, and abilities in the domain of human interface will lead to better project level and program level work outcomes.

Proposition 6b: Closer matching of project demand and the sum of individual knowledge, skills, and abilities in the domain of application/ transactions will lead to better project level and program level work outcomes.

Proposition 6c: Closer matching of project demand and the sum of individual knowledge, skills, and abilities in the domain of data management and analysis will lead to better project level and program level work outcomes.

Proposition 6d: Closer matching of project demand and the sum of individual knowledge, skills, and abilities in the domain of technology infrastructure will lead to better project level and program level work outcomes.

Proposition 6e: Closer matching of project demand and the sum of individual knowledge, skills, and abilities in the domain of management will lead to better project level and program level work outcomes.

In contrast, we would expect that as group dynamics mature and as the second order skills of learning and improvising are developed, the match between e-commerce project skill demand and the sum of individual skills will have diminishing influence on work related outcomes at the project and program levels.

Proposition 6f: Closer matching of project demand and the sum of individual knowledge will have less influence on project level and program level work outcomes as group dynamics mature.

Proposition 6g: Closer matching of project demand and the sum of individual knowledge will have less influence on project level and program level work outcomes as the abilities to learn and improvise matures.

Conclusion

The purposes of this chapter have been to present our conceptual framework as an extension and reformulation of several of the currently active fit theories of human resource management and industrial psychology; to delineate the skills which should be expected to be present in organizational e-commerce work; and present a set of propositions showing expected relationships among identified variables. It is intended that these discussions will present a basis for continued study and contribution in this research area. Clearly, the major next step in such a research program would be to verify the assumptions and relationships presented. For example, such study should include ensuring that the range of possible e-commerce missions, project configurations, skill demands, and employee skill sets are adequately covered. Additionally, the existence of causal relationships among these framework components needs to be empirically tested.

Study in this area can take many forms. It would seem premature to expect precise measures on some of these dimensions when we still aren't sure that the range of values is fully known. This area would seem ripe for qualitative research with the intent of discovering the way the identified factors interact to lead to (or away from) e-commerce success.

The authors strongly propose that developing a clearer sense of the best practices in staffing e-commerce work will offer practitioners the potential for taking actions making their use of development resources both more efficient and effective. Labor is a major component in the expense of building and maintaining e-commerce programs. Not only would efficient and effective labor create savings for organizations, it would potentially lead to secondary benefits including enjoyment of the benefits offered by sites and encouragement to develop new Web services. From a research stand point, the concept of pooling skill needs at a project level and understanding more about better ways to combine individual skills into the overall project staffing presents a new way to approach a variety of human resource issues particularly as we move increasingly toward a knowledge-based economy.

Acknowledgment

Our thanks to the anonymous reviewers of an earlier and substantially different version of this paper presented at the 2003 Computer Personnel Research (SIGMIS, ACM).

References

AAUW. (2000). *Tech-savvy: Educating girls in the new computer age.* Retrieved from http://www.aauw.org/2000/techsavvy.html

Aladwani, A. M. (2002, December 13-15). *An exploratory investigation of requisite skills needed by developers of e-commerce systems.* The International Conference on Informatics Education & Research, Barcelona, Spain.

Bernstein, D. S. (2001). America's 10 Most Wanted. *Computerworld,* February 26. Retrieved March 14, 2001, from http://www.computerworld.com/cwi/story/0,1199,NAV47-81_STO57985,00.html

Booch, G. (2001). Developing the future. *Communications of the ACM, 44*(3), 119-121.

Burke, D., & Morrison, A. (2001). *Business @ the speed of stupid.* Cambridge, MA: Perseus Publishing.

Dennis, A., & Wixom, B. H. (2000). *Systems analysis and design: An applied approach.* Indianapolis, IN: John Wiley & Sons.

Edwards, J. R. (1991). Person-job fit: A conceptual integration, literature review, and methodological critique. *International Review of Industrial and Organizational Psychology* (vol.6, pp. 283-357). New York: Wiley.

Edwards, J. R. (1996). An examination of competing versions of the person-environment fit approach to stress. *Academy of Management Journal, 39*(2), 292-339.

Evaristo, R., & van Fenema, P. C. (1999). A typology of project management: emergence and evolution of new forms. *International Journal of Project Management, 17*(5), 275-281.

Gallivan, M., Truex III, D. P., & Kvasny, L. (2002, May). An analysis of the changing demand patterns for information technology professionals. In M. Mandviwalla (Ed.), *Proceedings of the 2002 ACM SIGCPR Conference* (pp. 1-13). Kristiansand, Norway.

Holzschlag, M. E. (2000). Turning chaos into order: Managing Web projects. *Web Techniques, 5*(1), 16-19.

Ives, B., & Olson, M. (1990). Manager of technician? The nature of the information systems manager's job. *MIS Quarterly, 5*(4), 49-63.

Kanter, R. M. (2001) *Evolve!: Succeeding in the digital culture of tomorrow.* Cambridge: Harvard Business School Press.

Klimoski, R. J., & Jones, R. G. (1995). Staffing for effective group decision making: Key issues in matching people and teams. In R. Guzzo & E. Salas (Eds.), *Team effectiveness and decision making in organizations* (pp. 291-332). San Francisco: Jossey-Bass.

Kristof, A. L. (1996). Person-organization fit: An integrative review of its conceptualizations, measurement, and implications. *Personnel Psychology, 49*(1), 1-49.

Lee, D. M. S., Trauth, E. M., & Farwell, D. (1995). Critical skills and knowledge requirements of is professionals: A joint academic/industry investigation. *MIS Quarterly, 19*(3), 313-340.

Livingstone, L. P., Nelson, D. L., & Barr, S. H. (1997). Person-environment fit and creativity: an examination of supply-value and demand-ability versions of fit. *Journal of Management, 23*(2), 119-146.

McKee, J. (2001). Skill sets for the e-commerce professional. *Skill Sets for the E-Commerce Professional Conference*, SSECP 2001, June 2001, Melbourne, Australia. Full paper obtained directly from author.

Nelson, H. J., Irwin, G., & Monarchi, D. E. (1997). Journeys up the mountain: different paths to learning object-oriented programming. *Accounting, Management, and Information Technology, 7*(2), 53-85.

Nelson, R. R. (1991). Educational needs as assessed by IS and end-user personnel: A survey of knowledge and skill requirements. *MIS Quarterly, 15*(4), 502-525.

Niederman, F., & Hu, X. (2002, April). Electronic commerce personnel in the age of clicks and mortar: Toward a framework of individual and project level skills. In E. Trauth (Ed.), *Proceedings of Computer Personnel Research (ACM SIGMIS) Conference*.

NUA surveys. Retrieved October, 9, 2002, from http://www.nua.ie/surveys/how_many_online/

Quelch, J. A., & Klein, L. (1996, Spring). The Internet and international marketing. *Sloan Management Review,* 60-75.

Rada, R. (1999). IT skills standards. *Communications of the ACM, 42*(4), 21-26.

Trauth, E., Farwell, D., & Lee, D. (1993, September). The IS expectations gap: Industry expectations versus academic preparation. *MIS Quarterly, 17*(3), 293-307.

Vitalari, N. P., & Dickson, G. W. (1983). Problem solving for effective systems analysis: An experimental exploration. *Communications of the ACM, 26*(11), 948-956.

Wade, M. R., & Parent, M. (2001-2002). Relationship between job skills and performance: A study of Web masters. *Journal of Management Information Systems, 18*(3), 71-93.

Wenn, A., & Sellitto, C. (2001, June). *Emerging technical standards: Towards an identification of skillsets needed by Web site developers*. Skill Sets for the E-Commerce Professional Conference, SSECP, Melbourne, Australia. Full paper obtained directly from author.

Werbel, J. D., & Gilliland, S. W. (1999). Person-environment fit in the selection process. In *Research in Personnel and Human Resources Management* (vol. 17, pp. 209-243).

Chapter VI

Forming IT Professionals in the Internet Age:
A Critical Case Study

Bernd Carsten Stahl, De Montfort University, UK

Chris Wood, De Montfort University, UK

Abstract

This chapter considers the question how professional issues can be taught in an undergraduate environment where little academic experience is to be expected. It develops a theoretical framework, which justifies the need for such teaching and indicates that codes of conduct can be a useful vehicle to address these issues. Given the constructivist teaching theory that was deemed appropriate for the subject, the chapter proceeds to discuss the realisation of the teaching of professional standards in a HND programme in a UK university. The chapter discusses the result of the module and the strengths and weaknesses of the approach as well as a follow-up investigation into student's views of professionalism.

Introduction

Moral and ethical issues can be of high importance in computing. These issues can often be framed in terms of professionalism or professional behaviour by computing professionals. The standard of professional behaviour is subject to scrutiny by professional bodies. Learning the basics of these standards is something that should happen simultaneously with the learning of other professional knowledge, which, for computing professionals, is usually done in academic institutions. This means that university education in computing should cover professional issues and that these have to include moral and ethical issues. This much is generally accepted wisdom and supported by most computer professionals as well as most professional bodies or associations.

What is much less clear than this is how professional and ethical issues can and should be taught. There are different ways of approaching the topic. Some think that it is useful to clearly tell students what their professional duties and obligations are (cf. Gotterbarn, 2004). Others try a more interactive approach in order to have students develop their own moral reasoning skills (cf. Probert, 2002). Some think that the topic is a sub-topic of professionalism whereas others see it as part of moral philosophy that pervades practical matters such as computing. Furthermore, there are many practical problems to overcome (Dawson & Newman, 2002). Computing students are frequently very interested in core computing subjects such as programming languages, databases, etc., but much less so in "soft" areas such as professionalism or ethics. Then there are questions of scarcity and resources as teaching time needs to be allocated to other subjects and teachers with the necessary specific skills are often hard to find in computing faculties.

This chapter describes the solution that the authors developed in order to address these problems. It discusses theoretical considerations as well as their practical application. Briefly, the idea was to let students develop a code of conduct specific to their own situation as computing students. This code was then to be contextualised with other professional codes and these codes were then to be applied to the major project they were working on in parallel. In order to explain this approach, the chapter will begin with a brief review of the literature on the teaching of computer ethics, professionalism, and codes of ethics. It will then detail the background of the course as well as our approach as it developed with regards to the theoretical considerations. Finally, we will review the success of the approach by looking at the authors' as well as the students' perception of the idea of professionalism and the success of the module.

Some Theoretical Considerations

As indicated in the introduction, the theoretical considerations to be taken into account when planning how to teach ethical issues to computing students are extensive and cover several areas. In order to explain why we chose to proceed the way we did, it is important to briefly review the literature in some of these areas.

Teaching of Computer Ethics

The first question to ask in this module was: why do it at all? Why should one teach ethical issues related to computing to undergraduate students? Two types of answers are given to this, the educational and the pragmatic. Given the existence of ethical issues in computing (Moor, 2000), the educational approach stresses that it should be part of the students' learning experience to be exposed to these issues and to learn how one can deal with them. This is seen as part of the enlightening experience of education and as part of the empowerment that should result from it (Dawson & Newman, 2002; Settle & Berthiaume, 2002). The pragmatic approach stresses that so-called "soft skills" are important in working environments (Noll & Wilkins, 2002), that possessing them hence increases chances of employment for graduates (Rahanu, Davies, & Allen 2002). Both of these arguments probably influenced the decisions of professional and accrediting bodies, so that the inclusion of professional and ethical issues is now a requirement for many students in America as well as in the UK (Bynum, 2000; Huff & Martin, 1995; Ross, Rogerson, & Prior, 2002).

While the usefulness or even necessity of teaching ethical issues in computing is not in question, it does raise a number of problems. First, there is the problem of content. Philosophical ethics is a vast field and a subject that most computing students have little affinity to. Second, there is the problem of a coherent morality or lack thereof. In a modern multi-cultural society, it cannot simply be assumed that the students have coherent views on moral questions. It has in fact been argued that the opposite is the case. Particularly in areas of computing and ethics, such as intellectual property or hacking, a lack of conformity to rules has been observed (Lipinski & Buchanan, 2002).

Given the lack of time and other constraints of the module that will be explained later, we decided to use an intuitionist approach where the students' moral intuitions were used as a starting point of the discussion. While we fundamentally recognise the importance of philosophical ethics in solving moral dilemmas, we refrained from discussing it in great depth in the hope that the module would raise the awareness and interest to the point that students would choose a more theory-based follow-up module in a later stage of their academic career. Furthermore, we hope that our approach of having the students construct a code of conduct for themselves would expose them to the very ethical reasoning skills that ethical theories represent.

Professions and Professionals

As the question of ethics in computing in this chapter is framed in terms of professionalism, it is useful to reflect for a moment on what a profession is. Furthermore, there is a close relationship between professionalism and codes of ethics, which are our main vehicle for addressing ethical issues. The term "profession," like most terms, is ambiguous. Etymologically the word derives from the Latin "pro," meaning "before" and "fateor" meaning "to avow" (Mason, Mason, & Culnan, 1995, p. 153). This suggests that profession stands for a declaration of faithfulness, which is presumably why the concept was originally linked to fidelity to a religious order. It has since come to mean "licensure by a governing agency that authorizes practice of defined and constrained activities in exchange for remuneration" (Gleason, 2002, p. 115).

Professions may be best characterised by the specific properties that their members, the professionals, display. One of the most frequently cited properties of professionals is the specialised training they possess and their unique access to a complex body of knowledge (Ladd, 1995; Weckert & Adeney, 1997). This privileged knowledge allows professionals to develop a higher than normal degree of autonomy (Spinello, 1997) as well as a relatively high social status. On the other hand, this special position of the professional demands certain actions or considerations from him or her. Professionals play an important role in society and they are therefore expected to conform to a high standard of conduct and to extended service to society (von Weltzien Hoivik, 2002). Being a professional can be described as a special role that a person can acquire which gives the bearer special privileges but also special responsibilities (Johnson, 2001; May, 1992). Professions are collectives of professionals which aim at preserving the status of the professionals but also at controlling access to the status and the behaviour of its members (Johnson & Mulvey, 1995).

Is the area of computing a profession? The answers to this question diverge. Some say that it is the process of becoming a profession (Forester & Morrison, 1994). Others say that, even if it is no profession yet, it should be one (Gleason, 2002). What is important for us is that computing or information systems workers usually regard themselves as professionals (Oz, 1992). We can therefore follow Weckert and Adeney (1997) and simply treat computing as a profession as long as it displays the aforementioned characteristics. Especially for questions of ethics and behaviour computing can rightly be seen as a profession because it uses the means of other professions to modify members' behaviour.

This brings us back to the topic at hand. Professionalism, as we have seen, is a potentially wide area which covers many subjects. In this chapter, we emphasise the ethical issues related to professions. This is justified by the importance that ethics has for professions. The high reputation of profession members and their specific knowledge bring with them moral responsibilities and obligations. Professionals as experts in their fields need to be more aware of ethical issues than others (Buchanan, 2001). This is also recognised for computing professionals (Rogerson, 1998).

Despite all of the advantages of professions and their beneficial ethical effects, one should be aware, however, that there is also criticism of professions and professionalism. On the one hand, there are practical considerations which render doubtful whether professions can be effective in the sense indicated. Possible questions include: What is the relationship between professions and individual professionalism (Smith & McKeen, 2003)? What happens if there is a conflict of interest between different professional or private obligations? Can professions really create higher standards of accountability (von Weltzien Hoivik, 2002)? What is the role of the public? How can situations be avoided where professionals patronise an emancipated public (Johnson & Nissenbaum, 1995)? On the other hand, there are more fundamental problems. Professions can be seen as barriers to market entry which aim mainly at sustaining their members' privileges and keeping competition out (Newton, 1998). Consequently, one can ask whether professions are really necessary (Kultgen, 1998).

The conclusion we have drawn from this review of the literature on professions is that they are useful for discussing ethical issues with computing students but that it is important to keep a critical view of them if one wants to avoid moral indoctrination. From a wider perspective, one can criticise the idea of professionalism as a means to convey ethics for its implied assumptions about ethics. Professionalism is fundamentally individual whereas many of the problems faced by professionals are of a nature that precludes individual solutions (cf. Walsham, 1996). This leads us to the next area of theory, to the realisation of professional ethics, to codes of conduct.

Codes of Conduct

A central theme of professions that emerged from the discussion of the literature is that they regulate the behaviour of their members. They often do this by developing a set of behavioural standards that are embodied in a code of conduct

(Spinello, 1997). Codes of conduct are thus the representation of the moral and ethical standards of the profession. As such, they are supposed to hold the profession accountable to the public (Anderson, Johnson, Gotterbarn, & Perrolle, 1993). The purposes of codes are thus internal and external. Internally they are part of the self-definition and the self-regulation of the profession (Johnson, 2001). Externally, codes reflect the profession's standards and thereby create expectations and trust (Jones & Bowie, 1998).

Codes can fulfil these aims in several ways. They can raise awareness of problems and they can demonstrate the complexity of issues. When a professional is faced with a moral or ethical problem, the codes can be used as examples of how problems should be addressed and which aspects have to be taken into consideration. They thus act as moral rules but also as ethical reflection of these rules. In many cases, they give specific guidance on particular problems that have been identified as important for the profession. In the case of computing one of the central problems is that of intellectual property, and codes can therefore be used to promote and enforce a specific moral attitude to intellectual property (MacDonald & Fougere, 2002). Codes can thus render moral problem manageable for professionals (Gotterbarn, 1995).

While codes thus seem like a valuable approach to moral and ethical problems they can also be problematic. It is not clear whether codes can deal with new problems, which presumably are often the most difficulty ones to solve (O'Boyle, 2002). The underlying morality of the codes may not be universal and reflect the particular worldview of the authors. Codes can thus be misused as vehicles of moral indoctrination, which in itself may be ethically problematic. Then there is the big issue of the relationship of philosophical ethics and codes. Which ethical theory should a code be based on? Is it virtue ethics, because the professional should be a virtuous (Lilley, 2002) and authentic individual (Probert, 2002)? Given the problems of virtue, should one not look to more universal ethical theories such as ideas of rights (Walsham, 1996) or the typical deontological versus teleological debate?[1] And then there is the problem of moral practice versus ethical theory. Codes may suggest that ethics is a matter of applying an ethical theory to a moral problem, what van den Hoeven (1997) called "engineering ethics," which may again be an ethical problem in itself.

Our conclusion to be drawn from this brief discussion is that codes are useful vehicles for teaching ethical issues in professionalism because they are often promoted by professions. At the same time, one must be very careful not to overestimate their value and teach students to be able to critically reflect on them and not just take them at face value.

Having now discussed the theoretical background of the content of our module, a last question to be considered from a theoretical perspective is that of the teaching approach, of the underlying pedagogical theory.

Positivist or Constructivist Teaching

A comprehensive discussion of learning theories or pedagogical approaches is far beyond the confines of this chapter. It is nevertheless imperative to orient oneself in these matters in order to be able to choose a coherent approach. This chapter will thus briefly introduce two important teaching paradigms as they are frequently discussed with regards to teaching and IT. The two paradigms are the positivist and the constructivist one.

The two paradigms originally refer to metaphysical perspectives, with positivism representing the realist idea that the world is given independent of the observer, whereas constructivism holds that the observer creates the world through perception and interaction. We believe that ontological considerations are at the bottom of the concepts of positivism and constructivism. However, they are also related to matters of epistemology, methodology, and ethics. While these are fundamental philosophical questions, which we will again not be able to address, what is important for us is that they result in two different styles of teaching. For the positivist, truth consists of correct statements about reality, which can be taught and learned. The constructivist on the other hand holds that students have to create their reality and truth is context dependent. (For a more extensive discussion of the two approaches in IS research and teaching, see cf. Alavi, 1994; Alavi, Wheeler, & Valacich, 1995; Bruckman, 2002; Leidner & Jarvenpaa, 1995; Piccoli, Ahmad, & Ives, 2001.) The choice of either of these ontologies has many consequences, which are often described by the alternative of the teacher being the "sage on the stage" or the "guide on the side" (Fodor, 2000).

We do not want to make a principal statement as to which approach is better but we believe that in the case of ethical and professional issues a positivist approach is not promising. Ethics and norms are social constructs and in order to be understood they need to be experienced. Specifically, this means that confronting students with existing professional codes of conduct does not look like a promising way of teaching professional issues.

Given all of these theoretical considerations we tried to develop a teaching module called "Professional Standards" that was theoretically sustainable despite the constraints it had to contend with.

The Case: Professional Standards for HND Computing Students

In this section, we will discuss the application of our theoretical ideas to the reality of an undergraduate HND course. In particular, we focus on the 2003/4 cohort. We will introduce the academic programme in which the module was taught, the constraints we had to contend with and give a description of the content and the specifics of the module.

The Programme

At De Montfort University the Higher National Certificate (HNC) in Computing, although a qualification in its own right, can be considered to be the early part of the Higher National Diploma (HND) in Computing. The HND itself is a sub degree level qualification that equates to approximately 2/3 of a degree. Although progression to degree level qualification is available to these students their entry profiles may be less academically robust than traditional degree level entrants. When the Professional Standards module was offered, this cohort of students was in the first semester of their second year of study.

Under the curriculum model, all modules occupied 15 weeks of the academic year, with typically a 12 week teaching and learning stage followed by a revision and formal examination period. Not all modules involved formal written exams and the Professional Standards module was entirely coursework assessed; involving two written assignments and a computer based test. Timetabled activities were lectures (large group activities involving the whole cohort of 130 students), tutorials, typically maximum 24 students, and computer laboratory sessions with similar numbers to tutorials. This module was supported by a virtual learning environment (VLE) Web site, Blackboard; this medium was used to support the face-to-face contact sessions.

Constraints

The Professional Standards module was required to shadow an associated Software Development project activity that students were engaging with and to deliver the theoretical project skills required for this project module. Thus the primary focus for much of the early part of the module was on this aspect of the students' activities; although we recognised the need for this essential work within the module, potentially, it could distract attention from the ethical thinking we were wishing to introduce. Our approach to addressing this dilemma is described next.

The Module

We wanted to encourage the students to reflect on their own perceptions of ethical conduct and to see if this could lead towards the formulation of a code of conduct (COC) that may be particularly relevant to their particular situation as students on a university undergraduate course. Our primary aim was to promote discussion between students and encourage the evolution of a student code of conduct.

Lectures were used to link materials to core texts and also to signpost appropriate materials made available on the module VLE Web site.

The first assignment asked students to reflect on a chosen organisation to which they belonged and in particular to consider the societal impact of the organisation from the viewpoint of the individual member, the organisation itself, and society at large. This was an attempt to move student's thinking away from the technical facets of the organisation towards thinking about the effect of the organisation within the three contexts described. This assignment was submitted in week six of the semester.

The second assignment, entitled "A professional review of your HNC project," asked the students to consider the theme of the HNC Project module they were pursuing and, again, to consider not the technical development of the topic but to reflect on the potential impact of a fully implemented version of their project and to consider where a COC may be appropriately applied. This assignment was submitted in week 12, at the end of the term and after tutorial activity that focussed around development of an appropriate COC.

Materials from the various tutorial sessions was collected and collated. The comments were incorporated into an online document, displayed within the VLE, that was continuously updated to show to all students how their collective thinking was developing.

Our approach to teaching professional and ethical issues in computing was thus centred around the attempt to have students develop their own code of conduct. In order to guide them toward this, we tried to introduce them to successively complex ethical issues. Initially we asked them which rules they were supposed to follow in companies or organisations. This was meant to raise their awareness that they are always part of a set of more or less explicit rules they are meant to follow. We then discussed brief case studies of ethical and professional issues with them which centred on the usual problems, including intellectual property, privacy, relationships within organisations, etc. Given the time constraints we were under, we were not able to cover all relevant issues of computer ethics. For example, we neglected issues of gender even though they are arguably of central importance with regards to professional issues (cf. Adam, 2002; Wheeler, 2001). The students were asked to name the rules they thought the protagonists in the case studies should follow. These rules were collected, classified, and generalised in the hope of developing a code of conduct accessible to our students. During these steps, we also introduced a brief version of ten ethical principles and we tried to get the students to identify the ethical assumptions behind the professional rules they were developing.

This approach seemed to adequately reflect the theoretical bases laid out previously. We addressed ethical issues within computing working primarily with the students' ethical intuitions. However, the ethical principles which can be used to justify such intuitions were discussed and further readings were indicated to those students who developed an interest. The design of the module also allowed the students to reflect on what it means to be professional and how professional duties and rules resemble general rules and where the differences are. Since almost all of our student work part time, we could draw on a wealth of experience and given expectations. For most of the students this was the first time that they considered their chosen academic subject, namely computing, as a profession. By asking the students to develop their own code of conduct, we managed to force them to consider the strengths and weaknesses of this approach without forcing an overly theoretical debate on them. Finally, by using their ethical intuitions and collecting these to form a code of conduct we were able to use a constructivist teaching method, which we believed to be appropriate for ethical issues. Students had to engage with ethical dilemmas, they had to produce their own solution and critically discuss it with other students in order to find a consensual code. From a theoretical point of view, this Professional Standards module thus lived up to the theoretical considerations we wanted to base it on.

Discussion of the Module

We believe that the structure of our module was well designed to meet the theoretical expectations discussed earlier. It allowed the students to create their own approach to professional matters and to engage critically with the expectations they were likely to face. At the same time, it was not a moral indoctrination but an attempt to help them develop their abilities to be critical and autonomous members of a profession whose help they could use but whose weaknesses they could also see. Such theoretical considerations are of little value, however, if they are not supported by practical success in teaching the material. We will therefore discuss in this section how the students interacted with the module and how the tutors evaluated it.

Student Interaction with the Module

Over a period of four weeks, weeks 8 to 12 of the term, students collectively began to outline a COC that might be relevant to their current situation—undergraduate computing students. The VLE was used as both a means of making materials available (BCS COC, Student Lab COC, Student regulations) and also a central location where the Students COC was incrementally developed as feedback from F2F discussions in tutorial sessions (maximum 24 students) was incorporated into a Word document which was regularly updated to reflect the developing awareness of related issues.

Some concepts that emerged as significant and relevant are briefly presented here under five headings:

1. **Attendance:** The importance of regularly attending timetabled activities featured prominently among students' expectation of professionalism, with a requirement of 75% as an absolute minimum acceptable without mitigating circumstances. Attendance should be prompt and equally assignment work for assessment should be submitted on time.

2. **General behaviour:** Much emphasis was placed on mutual respect, student to student and student to staff. This was extended to respect for property owned by others, this also extended to general polite demeanour and general good comportment. There was an acknowledgment that behaviour off-campus was also important and that students should not engage in activities that might bring the University into disrepute. There should be minimal disruption of other people's workspace (e.g., controlled use of mobile phones).

3. **Use of computers:** There was discussion of issues that are very much to the fore in the lives of computing students such as plagiarism, appropriate usage of computers and networks in a socially acceptable way—no gambling, no offensive material. No 'unpleasant' emails should be sent.

4. **Legal issues:** There was recognition of externally imposed constraints such as the Data Protection Act, Computer Misuse Act, and intellectual property rights (MP3 files). Privacy and theft of electronic materials was also mentioned.

5. **Implementation issues:** It was felt that a COC must be fair and reasonable; it should embed accepted social/legal/moral/religious norms in

so far as they exist in a pluralist and multicultural setting (Gert, 1999). A COC should be enforceable but any sanctions imposed should also be seen to be acceptable and fairly applied to all. Any COC should be brief and to the point, must be understandable and should be valued by the group.

Summarising these issues, one can say that the students engaged with ethical issues in computing and their impact on what it means to be a professional. However, they engaged on a rather pre-reflective level. The typical reaction to our case studies and ethical dilemmas was the citation of a rule that the students had been confronted with before. The previous examples show that the students were typically concerned with those issues that the university is trying to impress upon them. The same pattern occurred in the final assignment where students were asked to critically apply a code of conduct to their major systems development project. Many of them developed a grid of rules reflecting the previous issues but only very few of them were able to reflect critically on these rules. The ethical foundations and justifications of the rules were generally not understood and not deemed important. Also, legal considerations played an important role in their codes. Matters of data protection and intellectual property were generally framed in terms of the law without any thought of the limits of this approach or questions regarding the ethical basis of legal regulations.

A fundamental problem was the willingness of students to engage with the material. Attendance of the tutorials was often very poor and sketchy and only a very small minority managed to follow the tutorials regularly. This means that the didactical steps used to support students' engagement with the material generally did not work as most students who did turn up lacked some of the prior information.

Tutor Evaluation of the Module

The overall aim of the module, to engage students in reflective thinking about ethical issues relating to their studies, was achieved to some degree but some issues emerged that we would address differently. Due to the constraints, the actual discussion of ethical and professional issues only started in the second half of the semester. This meant that many of the students may have misunderstood the purpose of the module and ceased to engage with it before the actual heart of the matter started to be discussed. We would thus start the process of developing a COC at the beginning of the term and defer other matters to a later time or move them to another module. We felt it would be helpful to reduce, or eliminate, the project skills component of this module. Furthermore, the late start of the actual delivery process of the professional issues, also left us little time to engage more deeply in the process of critical evaluation of professional matters and COCs.

A possible improvement of teaching might be realised by increasing the online interactivity between students. It might further support discussion and increase the active reflective participation that we were seeking to encourage. On this same theme of active involvement, we would propose less emphasis on formal lectures in favour of a more seminar oriented approach. The introduction of a particular formal ethical appraisal technique might allow further appreciation of issues relating to nascent computing professionals

Did students really develop their ——but we do not offer here evidence of added value. This may be beyond the scope of this module. Perhaps it should be awareness raising that is the main objective here. If so, then there is evidence to support a statement that some students are becoming aware of the contextual impact of the technical systems they are developing.

There is still an impression that ethical and moral issues are considered remote from the reality of what students consider themselves to be engaged in. Although there is evidence that, with encouragement, students can be motivated to positive reflection on more general issues of comportment they have yet to develop any real appreciation of their personal ethical responsibility for technical computer based systems development.

Perceptions of Professionalism

Having undertaking the previous research and finding out that the students had a very different understanding of the meaning of professionalism from the one that we found in the literature, we wanted to extend the scope of our investigation. We believed that it would be useful to establish the students' starting point when considering issues of profession/professionalism.

A Preliminary Survey

To establish the context within which we were working an attempt to capture initial student perceptions of what might constitute professionalism was made with the following year's cohort (September 2004). In the first lecture, the audience was invited to note down on a piece of paper any words, phrases or ideas that they associated with the concept of professional or professionalism; this was carried out right at the beginning of the activity so no suggestions had yet been formally introduced to the students. Essentially the responses can be regarded as a starting benchmark against which developing awareness of the concept of professionalism could be measured.

The cohort was broadly similar in number (approximately 130) and background experience to the previous year's group so we assume that the responses made can be regarded as typical of this sort of student set. The submissions were collected and the responses were grouped under headings which represented similar ideas to identify key themes.

The most frequently occurring concept was "high standards" identified by 39 (30%) students as a feature of professionalism. Other significant groupings, in descending order of frequency were: "knowledge" 23 (17.7%) responses, "expert" 21 (16.2%) responses, "organised, efficient, goal oriented, meets deadlines" 20 responses (15.38%), "smart, formal, neat, tidy, well presented" 18 (13.9%) responses. A further 29 key words were identified but each scored less than 10% frequency. For the purposes of referencing our particular interest in Codes of Conduct this was explicitly mentioned by 6 (4.6%) respondents with 'ethical' identified by 4 (3%) respondents.

Interpretation of Students' Perceptions

These perceptions voiced by the students were of interest because in some way the contravened our expectations and thus our prior research approach. When we devised the idea of having students produce a code of conduct in order to understand what it means to be a professional, we assumed that they would have shared ideas that at least partly refer to questions of ethics and morality and to the question how one should behave. Only on this assumption does it actually make sense for the students to consider the rules of behaviour for professionals and to construct their own expectations of professionalism accordingly.

This approach is fundamentally jeopardised when students do not share the perception that normative questions are at the heart of what it means to be a professional. As the results show, our students had a completely different view of professionalism that is mainly concerned with static achievements instead of procedural solution of problems. Their idea of professionals is characterised by attributes that professionals have and can acquire and which can be ascertained in a simple manner. These include a body of knowledge, external appearances, or integration into given structures. While we concede that these can be seen as relevant for professionals it strikes us that they are in fact derived characteristics which must be based on the ethical underpinning in order to be professionally useful. Otherwise they can be put to highly unprofessional use, such as the concentration camp guard who also needs to be punctual, immaculately dressed and aware of regulations, but whom we would be loath to call a professional.

Since the students' perceptions put our whole approach in jeopardy, it might be worth considering where it comes from. Part of the reason is certainly their upbringing which stresses the positively given and measurable attributes of individuals to the detriment of their wider capacities. This is one aspect of a culture and society which believes in the quantification of reality and the measuring of everything of importance. We are thus faced with a serious impediment to developing professionalism which is part of a set of wider and societal questions. One can thus say that there seems to be an intrinsic contradiction between a society which calls out for professional behaviour but at the same time seems to have little interest in socialising potential professionals in such a way that it would allow them to be professionals.

Conclusion

Concluding, one can say that our approach was a mixed success. We still believe that the theoretical set-up of the module was good and that it addressed the most important theoretical considerations. Some students enjoyed it and seemed to develop their ethical reasoning skills and successfully reflected on the importance of professionalism and codes of conduct. For the majority of the students, however, one can safely say that they did not engage with the subject and only regarded it as a minor obstacle on their way to the HND award.

We believe that there are two groups of reasons for this. On the one hand, there are institutional problems and external constraints that precluded the module from being completely successful. We were forced to include professional skills parts that were not necessarily conducive to critical thinking skills. These aspects may have turned students' attention from the module before they had a chance to engage with the important matters.

On the other hand, there was the problem with the students' perception of the module and with their willingness to even consider it relevant. This was somewhat surprising, given that they all had experience of expectations toward professionals. They were all expected to conform to norms in other areas of their lives but generally did not seem to reflect on this. Students adhere to norms or break them, if they can get away with it, but rarely seem to challenge them or reflect on their justification. The very idea of analysing the strengths and weaknesses of codes of conduct seemed to be alien to most of them. One might argue that we stretched the students too far by asking them to develop a COC without prior introduction to philosophical ethics. However, the module was designed to help the students develop thoughts about norms and rules with regards to situations they were familiar with. We therefore do not believe that the intellectual effort involved in the module precluded a successful conclusion.

Another problem may be that during their first year in the HND course they seem to have been exposed mainly to a completely different style of teaching, which followed the positivist paradigm and was thus contrary to our teaching philosophy. In the positivist paradigm, students are supposed to learn the truth and reproduce it in tests. They thus had an expectation of something similar to come and were confused when they were promptly asked to construct their own answers and to be critical. A typical reaction was that the subject was "waffly" and that nothing concrete and useful could be gained by attending it. If this perception is correct, then it indicates that there is a major problem. On the one hand, professional issues and their ethical reflection can rightly be argued to be of high importance. On the other hand, students do not seem to share that perception and expect to be taught subjects that do not include the ambiguities intrinsic to ethical matters. Universities and other teaching institutions will have to countenance this contradiction and our guess is that addressing it will mean modifying students' expectations of what university studies are about. This, of course, is a major change that goes far beyond questions of ethics and professionalism and requires a wide-ranging discourse including not only students and teachers but other societal stakeholders such as politicians, employers, and primary and secondary educators.

Limitations

The limitations of this research are manifold. We only looked at one particular student population for a short duration. It is impossible to know whether the results are generalisable and, if so, whether this only refers to HND students or to the student population in general. Then there is the problem of attitudinal research which includes all sorts of biases and can never claim scientific correctness. Also, we decided to take the results of students' work to evaluate the success and perception of the module rather than doing direct research by interviewing or surveying them. We nevertheless believe that the argument provided in this chapter is a relevant contribution to the discussion of how to address professional and ethical issues in computing.

Acknowledgments

Earlier versions of this chapter were presented at ETHICOMP 2004: *Challenges for the Citizen in the Information Society*, Syros, Greece, 14 to 16 April 2004 and the UK Academy for Information Systems Annual Conference: *Information Systems 'Unplugged', Developing Relevant Research.*

Newcastle, UK, 22-24. March 2005. The authors would like to thank the reviewers and the audience for valuable contributions to the chapter.

References

Adam, A. (2002). Cyberstalking and Internet pornography: Gender and the gaze. *Ethics and Information Technology, 4*(2), 133-142.

Alavi, M. (1994). Computer-mediated collaborative learning: An empirical evaluation. *MIS Quarterly, 18*(2), 159-174.

Alavi, M., Wheeler, B. C., & Valacich, J. S. (1995). Using IT to reengineer business education: An exploratory investigation of collaborative telelearning. *MIS Quarterly, 19*(3), 293-312.

Anderson, R. E., Johnson, D. G., Gotterbarn, D., & Perrolle, J. (1993). Using the new ACM code of ethics in decision making. *Communications of the ACM, 36*(2), 98-106.

Bruckman, A. (2002). The future of e-learning communities. *Communications of the ACM, 45*(4), 60-63.

Buchanan, E. A. (2001). Ethical considerations for the information professions. In R. A. Spinello & H. T. Tavani (Eds.), *Readings in cyberethics* (pp. 523-534). Sudbury, MA: Jones and Bartlett.

Bynum, T. W. (2000). Global information ethics and the information revolution. In R. M. Baird, R. Ramsower, & S. E. Rosenbaum (Eds.), *Cyberethics: Social and moral issues in the computer age* (pp. 274-291). New York: Prometheus Books.

Dawson, R. J., & Newman, I. A. (2002). Empowerment in IT education. *Journal of Information Technology Education, 1*(2), 125-141.

Fodor, J. L. (2000). Teaching philosophy with multimedia. In: R. M. Baird, R. Ramsower, & S. E. Rosenbaum (Eds.), *Cyberethics: Social and moral issues in the computer age* (pp. 354-358). New York: Prometheus Books.

Forester, T., & Morrison, P. (1994). *Computer ethics: Cautionary tales and ethical dilemmas in computing* (2nd ed.). Cambridge, MA; London: MIT Press.

Gert, B. (1999). Common morality and computing. *Ethics and Information Technology, 1*(1), 57-64.

Gleason, D. H. (2002, November 13-15). ICT professionalism. In I. Alvarez, T. Bynum, J. Alvaro De Assis Lopes, & S. Rogerson (Eds.), *The Transformation of Organisations in the Information Age: Social and Ethical*

Implications. Proceedings of the 6ᵗʰ ETHICOMP Conference, Lisbon, Portugal (pp. 113-124). Lisbon: Universidade Lusiada.

Gotterbarn, D. (1995). Computer ethics—Responsibility regained. In D. G. Johnson & H. Nissenbaum (Eds.), *Computers, ethics, & social values* (pp. 18-24). Upper Saddle River, NJ: Prentice Hall.

Gotterbarn, D. (2004). On licensing computer professionals. In T. W. Bynum & S. Rogerson (Eds.), *Computer ethics and professional responsibility* (pp. 156-164). Oxford: Blackwell Publishing.

Huff, C., & Martin, D. C. (1995). Computing consequences: A framework for teaching ethical computing. *Communications of the ACM, 38*(12), 75-84.

Johnson, D. G. (2001). *Computer ethics* (3ʳᵈ ed.). Upper Saddle River, NJ: Prentice Hall.

Johnson, D. G., & Mulvey, J. M. (1995). Accountability and computer decision systems. *Communications of the ACM, 38*(12), 58-64.

Johnson, D. G., & Nissenbaum, H. (1995). *What is computer ethics?* In D. G. Johnson & H. Nissenbaum (Eds.), *Computers, ethics, & social values* (pp. 1-15). Upper Saddle River, NJ: Prentice Hall.

Jones, T. M., & Bowie, N. E. (1998). Moral hazards on the road to the "virtual" corporation. *Business Ethics Quarterly, 8*(2), 273-292.

Kultgen, J. (1998). The ideological use of professional codes. In R. N. Stichler & R. Hauptman (Eds.), *Ethics, information, and technology: Readings* (pp. 273-290). Jefferson, NC: MacFarland & Company.

Ladd, J. (1995). The quest for a code of professional ethics: an intellectual and moral confusion. In D. G. Johnson & H. Nissenbaum (Eds.), *Computers, ethics, & social values* (pp. 580-585). Upper Saddle River, NJ: Prentice Hall.

Leidner, D. E., & Jarvenapaa, S. L. (1995). The use of information technology to enhance management school education: A theoretical view. *MIS Quarterly, 19*(3), 265-291.

Lilley, S. (2002, November 13-15). Bringing oversight review inline with online research. In I. Alvarez, T. Bynum, J. Alvaro De Assis Lopes, & S. Rogerson (Eds.), *The Transformation of Organisations in the Information Age: Social and Ethical Implications. Proceedings of the 6ᵗʰ ETHICOMP Conference,* Lisbon, Portugal (pp. 619-629). Lisbon: Universidade Lusiada.

Lipinski, T. A., & Buchanan, E. A. (2002, November 13-15). There's a place for us(e): Incorporating the responsible application of new technologies into the K-12 curriculum. In I. Alvarez, T. Bynum, J. Alvaro De Assis Lopes, & S. Rogerson (Ed.), *The Transformation of Organisations in the Informa-*

tion Age: Social and Ethical Implications. Proceedings of the 6th ETHICOMP Conference, Lisbon, Portugal (pp. 631-642). Lisbon: Universidade Lusiada.

MacDonald, L. E., & Fougere, K. T. (2002). Software piracy: A study of the extent of coverage in introductory MIS textbooks. *Journal of Information Systems Education, 13*(4), 325-330.

Mason, R. O., Mason, F., & Culnan, M. J. (1995). *Ethics of information management.* Thousand Oaks; London; New Delhi: SAGE.

May, L. (1992). *Sharing responsibility.* Chicago: University of Chicago Press.

Moor, J. H. (2000). If Aristotle were a computing professional. In R. M. Baird, R. Ramsower, & S. E. Rosenbaum (Eds.), *Cyberethics: Social and moral issues in the computer age* (pp. 34-40). New York: Prometheus Books.

Newton, L. (1998). The origin of professionalism: Sociological conclusions and ethical implications. In R. N. Stichler & R. Hauptman (Eds.), *Ethics, information, and technology: Readings* (pp. 261-272). Jefferson, NC: MacFarland & Company.

Noll, C. L., & Wilkins, M. (2002). Critical skills of IS professionals: A model for curriculum development. *Journal of Information Technology Education, 1*(3), 143-154.

O'Boyle, E. J. (2002). An ethical decision-making process for computing professionals. *Ethics and Information Technology, 4*(4), 267-277.

Oz, E. (1992). Ethical standards for information systems professionals: A case for a unified code. *MIS Quarterly, 16*(4), 423-433.

Piccoli, G., Ahmad, R., & Ives, B. (2001). Web-based virtual learning environments: A research framework and a preliminary assessment of effectiveness in basic it skills training. *MIS Quarterly, 25*(4), 401-426.

Probert, S. K. (2002). Ethics, authenticity, and emancipation in information systems development. In A. Salehnia (Ed.), *Ethical issues of information systems* (pp. 249-254). Hershey, PA: IRM Press.

Rahanu, H., Davies, J., & Allen, M. (2002, November 13-15). To evaluate a computer-based learning environment against traditional means of delivery. In I. Alvarez, T. Bynum, J. Alvaro De Assis Lopes, & S. Rogerson (Eds.), *The Transformation of Organisations in the Information Age: Social and Ethical Implications. Proceedings of the 6th ETHICOMP Conference*, Lisbon, Portugal (pp. 661-670). Lisbon: Universidade Lusiada.

Rogerson, S. (1998). *Ethical aspects of information technology: Issues for senior executives.* London: Institute of Business Ethics.

Ross, M., Rogerson, S., & Prior, M. (2002, March 15-17). Professional issues: Views of students versus computer professionals. In G. King, M. Ross, G.

Staples, & T. Twomey (Ed.), *Proceedings of INSPIRE VII, Quality in Learning and Delivery Techniques* (pp. 149-163). Limerick, Ireland: The British Computer Society.

Settle, A., & Berthiaume, A. (2002). Debating e-commerce: Engaging students in current events. *Journal of Information Systems Education, 13*(4), 279-285.

Smith, H. A., & McKeen, J. D. (2003). Developments in practice XI: Developing IT professionalism. *Communications of the Association for Information Systems, 12*(4), 312-325.

Spinello, R. (1997). *Case studies in information and computer ethics.* Upper Saddle River, NJ: Prentice Hall.

van den Hoeven, J. (1997). Computer ethics and moral methodology. *Metaphilosophy, 28*(3), 234-248.

von Weltzien Hoivik, H. (2002). Professional ethics: A managerial opportunity in emerging organizations. *Journal of Business Ethics, 39*(1-2), 3-11.

Walsham, G. (1996). Ethical theory, codes of ethics and IS practice. *Information Systems Journal, 6*(1), 69-81.

Weckert, J., & Adeney, D. (1997). *Computer and information ethics.* Westport, CT; London: Greenwood Press.

Wheeler, D. (2001). New technologies, old culture: A look at women, gender, and the Internet in Kuwait. In C. Ess & F. Sudweeks (Ed.), *Culture, technology, communication: Towards and intercultural global village* (pp. 187-212). Albany: SUNY Press.

Endnote

[1] The deontological and teleological approaches are two of the main types of ethical theories in philosophical ethics. Deontological ethics is based on the idea that the most important aspect of ethics is that of duty. It is closely linked with the German philosopher Immanuel Kant. Teleological approaches, on the other hand, believe that the aim or outcome of actions are the most important aspect for their ethical evaluation. One example of a teleological ethics is utilitarianism whose ethical criterion is the greatest good for the greatest number of people. Utilitarianism is linked to James and John Stuart Mill and Jeremy Bentham. This dichotomy is an important part of philosophical debate but it is rather complex and abstract and we wanted to avoid confusing students with too much ethical theory.

Chapter VII

Professional Skills Acquisition in the Internet Age:
Exploring the Perceptions of Undergraduates and Recent Graduates

Ani Patke, Victoria University of Wellington, New Zealand

Tony Hooper, Victoria University of Wellington, New Zealand

Abstract

If academic institutions are to be responsive to changing student and industry requirements, they need to continually match their academic offerings with both market and student requirements. In recent years, universities throughout the world have experienced a serious decline in student enrolments in information systems and electronic commerce programmes. From existing literature as well as from empirical studies, this chapter explores the skills acquisition process of information systems students in order to match undergraduate and graduate perceptions of "hard" and "soft" skills requirements in the Internet Age.

Introduction

The arrival of the Internet and its consequences for business and industry saw a rapid increase in the number of students seeking to qualify in information systems. The technology—and its business potential—clearly captured the imagination of people of all ages. The resulting rapid increase in student numbers left academic institutions hard-pressed to cope–and to find suitably qualified professionals fit for the task. To cope with the flood of interest, and to help future proof their technological offerings in the marketplace, many large companies established their own "industry qualifications" to help meet the demand for IT/IS skills.

Since the "DotCom crash" that ushered in the 21st century economy, universities throughout the world have experienced a serious decline in student enrolments in Information Systems and Electronic Commerce programmes. Was this a reflection of the "commoditisation" of IT as claimed by Nicholas Carr (2004) or was it reflective of a growing skepticism about the continuing role of information and communications technologies (ICT) in driving economic growth?

While numerous theories about the causes and the longer-term effect were debated, the experience also gave cause for reflection on the content of undergraduate courses and the relevance of the experiential process to which students are subjected. Clearly, student perceptions of programme relevance to future career needs had changed. Was there a correlation between the perceptions of undergraduates and those of graduates who had been practicing in industry for several years? Perhaps the requirements of the industry had changed? Did the conventional view of the discipline need to be updated in the face of this new reality?

Generally speaking, students' efforts are focused not only on achieving a degree or diploma, but also on the acquisition of marketable skills useful to them when they pursue their future career. One imagines they come into their first year of study with a vision of what their capabilities will be at the end of the educational process. Their vision may not be finely crafted, but it will involve some understanding of the sort of knowledge and skills to be acquired in the educational process. That understanding will partly be determined by the curriculum set by the school in which the student has chosen to study.

If academic institutions are to be responsive to changing student and industry requirements, they need to continually match their academic offerings with both market and student requirements. Of course, these may be divergent, with student perceptions being different from those of employers. At the same time, authoritative educational institutions need to ensure that their offerings are competitive with other similar institutions regionally and internationally, and, built on a substantial theoretical base. Accordingly, many institutions have advisory committees made up of representatives of local industry employers, and possibly also, representatives of undergraduate students and recent graduates.

This chapter will discuss the current state of the information systems discipline from an academic perspective as drawn from existing literature as well as empirical studies to try and understand the skills acquisition process of information systems students.

Defining the Discipline

In a recent article, Benbasat and Zmud (2003, p. 184) maintain that:

IS scholars research and teach a set of diverse topics associated with information technologies, IT infrastructures and IT-enabled business solutions (i.e., information systems), and the immediate *antecedents and consequences of these information systems (e.g., managing, planning, designing, building, modifying, implementing, supporting, and/or assessing* IT-based systems *that serve directly or indirectly, practical purposes.*

They go on to argue "…that a dominant design for the IS discipline has yet to be realized" and that "the core phenomena being explored through IS scholarship…remains amorphous," and finally, that "topical diversity can, *and has*, become problematic *in the absence of a set of core properties*, or central character, that connotes in a distinctive manner, the essence of the IS discipline" (Benbasat & Zmud, 2003, p. 185).

On the other hand, Lee, Koh, Yen, and Tang (2002) record that:

Many researchers report persistent gaps (from a moderate to a very serious level) between knowledge skills that are taught in academia and those that are demanded by the IS industry. (Lee, Koh, Yen, & Tang, 2002, p. 51)

In addition to these expressions of concern about the essence of the IS discipline, Lee et al. (2002) quoting a range of researchers over a period from 1972 to 1996, maintain that:

Many researchers report persistent gaps (from a moderate to a very serious level) between knowledge skills that are taught in academia and those that are demanded by the IS industry. (Lee et al., 2002, p. 51)

They go on to state that "there is no generally accepted classification of IS knowledge/skills nor is there consensus on which knowledge/skills are the critical ones and some are more important than others in the IS profession" (Lee et al., 2002, p. 52). Continuing debate about the core elements of the discipline is symptomatic of growth and dynamism—and entirely desirable where technological change is so rapid and so pervasive.

Changes in technology and perceptions towards IS over the last few decades have resulted in rapid changes in skills requirements for IS workers (Kakabadse & Kakabadse, 2000; Maier, Clark, & Remington, 1998; Todd, McKeen, & Gallupe, 1995). The importance of having IS staff with the most appropriate and relevant skills has been considered to be a critical success factors for IS organisations (Byrd & Turner, 2001; Mata, Fuerst, & Barney, 1995; Witt & Burke, 2002). With universities being the major contributor of qualified workers to the IS industry (Desplaces, Beauvis, & Peckham, 2003) alignment with the skills requirements of industry is critical. In addition, universities need to ensure that their IS curricular content conforms to, but remains competitive with, those other academic institutions with which they compete for students. Their concerns are therefore divided between the need to be responsive to local industry needs, regional and national academic competitiveness and accreditation, as well as maintaining an eye on their international academic acceptability.

It is hardly surprising therefore, that perception gaps emerge between what the universities are teaching and what industry might require. Several investigations have reported perception gaps between industry and universities, most notably in the areas of technical skills (Tang, Lee, & Koh, 2001; Weber, McIntyre, & Schmidt, 2001). As mentioned above, in addition to university degrees, a range of industry qualifications exist (Adelman, 2001) that could be an economic alternative for many prospective students (Brookshire, 2000). Unlike universities, these certifying bodies are not obliged to provide information on their course content, or the number of people awarded their qualifications (Adelman, 2001).

An Agreed Body of Knowledge

Attempts have been made to create IS/IT curricula with the assistance of the industry (Couger et al., 1995; Ehie, 2002; Gonzenbach, 1998; Gorgone et al.,

2002). Important as these initiatives are, the rapidly changing technologies on which they are based, leave them in constant need of revision every two or three years. In the same way, new IS skill areas such as m-commerce and IT security can manifest a demand in the job marketplace long before universities can equip themselves to respond. Some studies have examined job advertisements in newspapers (Liu, Lui, Lu, & Koong, 2003; Maier et al., 1998) but they fail to adequately examine the reasons for the changes in demand for the relevant skills.

It would be surprising if this confusion amongst academics and practitioners did not have an influence on student perceptions of the discipline and of the importance of the skills they have acquired during the course of their undergraduate studies. The importance of obtaining some agreement on the core properties of the IS discipline, and of what needs to be included in any undergraduate curriculum, remains central to the design of any survey instrument that can be quickly and universally administered.

Due to the wide range of skills and technologies involved, combined with rapid changes in related emerging technologies, agreement on topics for information systems curricula is elusive. To some extent the dedicated work done by the Association of Information Technology Professionals (AITP, 1997), Couger et al. (1995), Ehie (2002), Gonzenbach (1998) and Gorgone et al. (2002) in developing a model curriculum has helped shape a set of standards that create international comparability of Information Systems programmes and educational outcomes. Nevertheless there appears to be no agreement on the "essence of the IS discipline" (Benbasat & Zmud, 2003), nor "an accepted classification of IS knowledge/skills" nor "consensus on which knowledge/skills are the critical ones" (Lee et al., 2002).

"Soft Skills" and "Hard Skills"

Several authors have provided different ways of categorising IT skills for research purposes (Lee, Trauth, & Farwell, 1995; Leitheiser, 1992; Liu et al., 2003; Tang et al., 2001; P. Todd et al., 1995). They all share a common differentiation—they can be broken down into two basic categories: soft and hard skills (Byrd & Turner, 2001).

Soft skills cover the non-technical aspects of IS/IT work. They include the following:

- Interpersonal communication skills
- Personal traits

- Technology management knowledge
- Business functional knowledge
- Management skills
- Ethics

Hard skills, on the other hand, are best described as those that require specific technical knowledge as described by Lee et al. (1995) and Leitheiser (1992). However, other authors (Liu et al., 2003; Tang et al., 2001) have provided a more recent list of skills requirements within industry.

- Analysis and design
- Programming languages
- Web development
- Database management
- Networking
- Operating systems

Setting the Parameters of What to Survey

Benbasat and Zmud (2003) argue that "the set of core properties of the IS discipline" includes:

- "The managerial, methodological, and technological capabilities as well as the managerial, methodological, and operational practices involved in planning, designing, constructing, and implementing IT artifacts;
- The human behaviors reflected within, and induced through both the (1) planning, designing, constructing and implementing, and (2) direct and indirect usage of these artifacts;
- The managerial, methodological, and operational practices for directing and facilitating IT artifact usage and evolution;
- As a consequence of use, the impacts (direct and indirect, intended, and unintended) of these artifacts on the humans who directly (and indirectly) interact with them, structures and contexts within which they are embed-

ded, and associated collectives (groups, work units, organizations)." (Benbasat & Zmud, 2003, p. 186)

Quoting several authors' attempts to classify IS knowledge, Lee et al. (2002, p. 53) developed a tabulation of the items of core IS knowledge/skills derived from an analysis of the writings of those authors justifying each skill or knowledge item in each category. (See Table 1.)

A comparative examination of Table 1 with the "core properties" identified by Benbasat and Zmud (2003) above reveals a considerable commonality between with those of the other writers studied by Lee et al. As they stated "the lack of a common classification taxonomy and terminology made the job of constructing our survey instrument difficult and the authors had to rely on sampling question items from several sources as well as on the authors' own knowledge" (Lee et al., 2002, p. 53). However, this argument is considered, it would appear that as long as the survey instrument contains the elements of categories and items identified in Table 1, and as long as the instrument is applied consistently between the variables identified (academics and practitioners in the case of Lee et al.) then a comparison of the findings could be considered acceptably indicative.

In a study at the University of Cape Town (UCT), Hildebrand, Schefter, and Van Assche (2002) derived an instrument to establish a comparison between the skills taught at UCT and to compare them internationally (Hildebrand et al., 2002, p. 11). In developing their instrument, they constructed the following tabulation of skill categories (Hildebrand et al., 2002, p. 5).

Table 1. Items of core IS knowledge/skills (Lee et al., 2002, p. 53)

Category	Items
IS core knowledge	**IS management:** visions about IS/IT competitive advantage and knowledge of IS technological trends **IS technology and development:** hardware, software (packaged products, operating systems, networking/communication software, and programming languages), and systems development and maintenance (systems analysis/design/development methodologies/approaches)
Organization and society	Specific function areas, specific organizations, specific industries, and general environment.
Interpersonal	Interpersonal behaviour, interpersonal communication, international communication ability, teaching and training skills
Personal traits	Personal motivation and ability to work independently, creative thinking, critical thinking.

Skills Acquisition and Industry Requirements

In the early '90s, the IS/IT function of the organisation was seen as being highly technical. Consequently IS/IT staff were often not perceived to be capable of holding management positions (Kakabadse & Kakabadse, 2000). Many organisations compensated for this by handing out higher salaries and exaggerated titles rather than more control and power (Hsu, Chen, Jiang, & Klein, 2003). Hsu et al. (2003) found that developing soft skills at an early stage in an IS/IT workers career was found to be the best way to advance their careers past the invisible barrier that obstructs many IS/IT workers.

Global industry trends have also had an impact on the skill requirements for IS/IT workers. In the 1970s IT did not hold the same level of importance as it does in today's organisations (Byrd & Turner, 2001). The capabilities of IS/IT have provided competitive advantage by significantly improving the organisational output (Kudbya & Diwan, 2002). However many organisations were finding that despite increased investment in IS/IT they were not receiving the returns that they had been expecting. Several authors argue that while IS/IT workers were highly capable in terms of their technical skills their softer skills were relatively poor (Byrd & Turner, 2001; Clark, Cavanaugh, Brown, & Sambamurthy, 1997; Harkness, Kettinger, & Segars, 1996; Mata, Fuerst, & Barney, 1995). While technical skills are important to the IS/IT function, additional softer skills enable IS/IT employees to maximise their effectiveness to the organisation. In many organisations training courses are provided free of charge to enable IS/IT workers to enhance their skills. While it is widely acknowledged that experience is a major requirement when organisations are recruiting staff, qualifications demonstrating skills acquisition are also seen as being important (Desplaces, Beauvis, & Peckham, 2003). The literature suggests that industry certifications and university degrees both play equally important roles within the IS/IT industry (Brookshire, 2000).

Industry certifications were developed to assist in the standardisation of many new information systems and communications technologies (Adelman, 2001). These certifications were designed for post-secondary level students and involved more hard skills learning and development. By the year 2000 there were over 300 different certifications being offered in the IS/IT and telecommunications industry (Adelman, 2001). The most well known of these industry certifications are the Microsoft Certified Systems Engineer (MCSE) and Novell's Certified Network Engineer (CNE). Many of these certifications are offered by large multi national organisations that are referred to as the certifying vendors. Microsoft, Cisco, Novell, Oracle, SAP, and Sun Microsystems all provide qualifications in their specialised fields. Since the certificates are provided by a central authority, the qualification is recognised equally, regardless of what country it was earned in. This also allows for changes in the certification to be made with little time lag—unlike in universities.

One major difference between many industry certifications and university degrees is that certifications can be upgraded based on changes in technology within the industry. For example Microsoft requires individuals who hold MCSE qualifications in Windows 2000 to sit another set of exams to be able to bring their qualification up to date after the release of Windows Server 2003 (Microsoft, 2003). Examining agents located in over 140 countries award certifications. They usually take less than a year to complete including studying and examinations, and can be earned at various levels, with each level signifying greater ability and competence. From an organisation perspective, making sure that their staffs IS/IT qualifications are important as it demonstrates their technical capabilities to their clients.

The IS/IT industry therefore has a vested interest in the courses offered both by universities and other qualifications providers. Accordingly some companies have taken an active role in assisting tertiary institutions to provide the most relevant and up to date curricula for their students such as the ACM (Association for Computing Machinery) initiatives (Chang et al., 2000; Couger et al., 1995; Ehie, 2002; Gorgone et al., 2002; Tang et al., 2001). Todd et al. (1995) suggested that the true IS/IT skills requirements of the organisation are not being properly reflected in the recruitment process giving the impression of new recruits with inadequate skill sets. Therefore it is crucial that senior managers who have a holistic view of the organisation to be involved in the recruitment process as much as possible.

Previous Studies in IS/IT Skills Requirements

Using both qualitative and quantitative methods, studies have been conducted on industry perception of skills requirements. The majority have been conducted using mail surveys aimed at either various subsets of the IS/IT industry or the IS/IT industry as a whole (Byrd & Turner, 2001; Desplaces et al., 2003; Gonzenbach, 1998; Leitheiser, 1992; Witt & Burke, 2002). Longitudinal quantitative studies have also been carried out by looking at job advertisements in newspapers (Maier et al., 1998) or job sites on the Internet (Liu et al., 2003) in which a list of the jobs in terms of their demand within the industry has been compiled. A handful of qualitative studies using interviews (Brookshire et al., 2002; Ehie, 2002) and focus groups (Lee et al., 1995) have also been conducted to assess the IS/IT skills requirements of industry. These studies involved collaboration between academics and industry to develop model curricula to eliminate gaps in perception. (Gorgone et al., 2002).

Studies have been carried out on academics' perceptions of the value of certain types of skills. Brookshire et al. (2002) proposed an e-commerce curriculum with both input from academics and IS/IT industry professionals. Because of the qualitative nature of this study, the authors were able to gain additional insights into the structure and focus of the curriculum in terms of the specific skills that were identified as being important. A study by Gill and Hu (1999) surveyed institutions across the U.S. to examine the structure of IS/IT faculties. The study by Tang et al. (2001) examined specifically what skills the faculty felt were important in an IS/IT curriculum.

Students have been the focus of a handful of studies (Hooper, 2004; Patke, 2004; Weber et al., 2001). The study by Hooper (2004) investigated the perspectives of students at Victoria University of Wellington (VUW) comparing their responses with those of students at the University of Cape Town (UCT). Patke (2004) surveyed the perceptions of graduates from Victoria University of Wellington about the relevance of their undergraduate studies after 3 to 5 years professional practice in industry.

Undergraduate and Graduate Student Perceptions

It can be expected that student perceptions are likely to vary according to the skills emphasis that is implicit in the curriculum design of the programme for which they register. So, what is taught will determine the amount of time students spend on any specific skill development process and this in turn leads on to determine which skills students consider to be important. Curriculum development will also be sensitive to student perceptions of what is importance, creating a cyclical process and therefore the likelihood of a high degree of homogeneity in perceptions within any single cohort of students. In addition, some institutions may have a more technological rather than managerial orientation and their students will see those aspects as being of greater importance. A the same time there may be variation in the emphasis of each institution on "soft" as opposed to "hard" skills and which of these are of more lasting value when considering how to equip students for the demands of industry.

The study by Hooper (2004) showed that, whatever the academic objectives considered as important when the VUW curriculum was first determined, the undergraduate students perceive that their team or group work skills and the communication skills associated were the most developed. What was even more interesting, perhaps, was how little they consider they had developed technical skills in such categories as object-oriented programming, data-access, debugging and error trapping, network communications, systems security and client server architectures. That perception makes a clear statement about "soft" skills development as opposed to the development of the "harder" technical skills that one would associate with a degree in information systems. Part of that statement is the significance attached to business understanding and business analysis skills, possibly gained outside of the IS and electronic commerce courses themselves.

The second analysis in the survey done by Hooper (2004) related to the amount of effort or time that the students perceived themselves to have invested in the development of different categories of skills. Again, with slight changes in ranking, the "softer" skills of teamwork and communications were perceived to have demanded the most effort, with project management, modeling, and systems analysis following closely. Hard skills such as object-oriented programming, data-access, debugging and error-trapping, network communications, systems security, and client server architectures were again ranked much lower. It would appear that these skills had not been developed either because not enough time was spent acquiring them or enough time was allocated to them during the teaching programme.

Similarly, it was expected that skills categories that the students perceived as most important or least important would normally be expected to correlate with those on which most time was spent, or in which the students considered that they had developed the most. While group work and communications skills remain at the top of the table, for VUW students, their ranking was disturbed slightly by the injection of project management and business understanding. Down at the bottom of the table debugging and error trapping, prototyping, systems design, data-access, network communications, object-oriented programming, and client server architectures languish unappreciated. Systems security gained some recognition for being important even though the students perceived themselves as not having significant skills in that area, nor of having spent much time on the topic.

Differences between the VUW perceptions and those of students at UCT were minor. Spearman rank-correlations demonstrated strong associations between the perceptions of the two groups surveyed. Irrespective of the variations in teaching methods and individual course content between the two universities, the end results show that there is significant agreement in the skills the students have acquired by the time they have reached their graduating year. At UCT on the other hand, there was much less emphasis placed on communications skills, especially on the verbal skills. Significantly, UCT recognizes the importance of general programming, whereas VUW students rate that much lower. Clearly, time and effort were allocated to the acquisition of different skills in the two universities—reflective, no doubt, of different curricular structure and emphasis. Similarly, there was an overall correlation between the perceptions of students in both universities about the importance of the topics studied. From this it was concluded that despite their different educational experience there was significant agreement between the students at the two institutions studied on the level of their IS skills acquisition and the importance of those skills.

Patke (2004), in a qualitative survey of IS/IT practitioners in Wellington with 3 to 5 years experience after graduating, found that soft skills—in particular communication skills—and the ability to learn were considered most important. Participants considered that university was the ideal place for students to acquire the basic hard skills on which they can build later in their careers. Changes in university curriculum improved significantly the course offerings, allowing students to build a broad skill set of both hard and soft skills. Participants felt therefore that a university degree offered more flexibility in their careers than would be possible with only industry certifications. Furthermore, by taking a broad range of courses at university students can gain skills and knowledge outside the IS/IT discipline, giving them additional diversity. Management, philosophy, and marketing were considered to be examples of subjects that were mentioned by participants in this connection. There was some difference of opinion on the importance of hard skills between the participants. Some participants felt that hard skills were important especially for graduates as it was the best way to get into most organisations and provides a marketable skill base straight out of university. Other participants felt that it was entirely possible to have a successful career with little technical knowledge as they felt that hard skills were useful only in certain roles but soft skills were more widely applicable in terms of their long term careers.

Conclusion

Generalizing these results in order to draw conclusions that might be broadly applicable is risky. The sample sizes and the narrow focus make specific conclusions untenable. Nevertheless, there do appear to be some interesting features that emerge from these studies.

1.   There appears to be a lack of agreement about the "core competencies" of the IS discipline. This is hardly surprising giving the newness of the discipline and the rapid development of the technology upon which it is

based. It does mean, however, that universities need to relate clearly the content of their teaching programmes to the theoretical underpinnings. It means too, that in any surveys of student perceptions, a clear definition needs to be given of each topic included and the scope of that topic.

2. The propagation of industry certification as a cheaper and quicker alternative to the formal educational structures found in universities and polytechnics may be more likely to guarantee employment. There is no question that they attract people who might otherwise enroll at a university. There is even a temptation for some undergraduate programmes to actively assist their students to acquire industry certificates as an attractive addition to the formal academic education they offer. Also, some industries insist that their graduate employees "forget all they have learned at university" and acquire specific skills required for their own purposes. Such "in-service training" is clearly to the benefit of both employer and employee and should not interfere with academic curriculum development. However, it is interesting to note that the perceptions of graduates seems to indicate that the range of subject choices at university and "the ability to learn" are among the more desirable advantages of enrollment in formal educational programmes.

3. The perception among both final year undergraduate students and recent graduates of Victoria University of Wellington of the importance of the "softer" skills in their study programme. Consistent across both the study by Hooper (2004) and that by Patke (2004) was the perception that the "softer" skills were more important that the "harder" skills. This may be because of the rapid changes in the technology and therefore the "volatility" of such specific knowledge. Or it may be that different industries place a different emphasis on specific technological skills, but can mostly all agree on the value to the business of the "softer" managerial skills, good communication skills, and inter-personal relationship skills that are fundamental to success.

4. The evolution of mid-career taught masters degree programmes to address the interface between those with "industry" qualifications and others with "academic" IS/IT qualifications in a fast developing technological area. Holders of industry certificates in specific technologies are required to upgrade their skills with regular refresher courses as the technology develops. This gives them a choice between remaining in their chosen specialization, and seeking to move into other technologies or into management. Industry certifications provide a very narrow focus compared to the education, and choices, offered by undergraduate programmes at university. It would be interesting to assess the interest of holders of industry certifications in taught masters programmes as a means of mid-career skills upgrading. Certainly, the existence of taught masters programmes in IS/IT

management provides an attractive and viable career alternative to those whose career growth demands management skills. In an era in which undergraduate numbers have declined alarmingly, it is interesting to note that this decline has not had the same impact on taught masters degree programmes.

How does this impact on the management of IT professionals in the Internet Age? Clearly, it is producing a range of skilled professionals with an acceptance of the need for life-long learning and the need to continually upgrade professional skills. Assisting professionals to obtain industry certifications may best achieve this. Alternatively, encouraging mid-career staff to consider enrolling for taught masters programmes could well ensure a flow of people with IT/IS skills into the management arena. In any event, the industry will need to live with a range of professionals who present with a range of qualifications. Only when there is agreement on the "core competencies" of the discipline among academics internationally will we be able to ensure the equivalence of degrees from different institutions in different countries. In the interim, there appears to be some degree of acceptance among students and graduates that university studies in IS/IT are a good preparation for their careers, particularly where the "soft skills" are concerned.

References

Adelman, C. (2001). The medieval guild in cyberclothes: International dimensions of industry certification in information technology. *Tertiary Education and Management, 7*(3), 277-292.

Association of Information Technology Professionals. (AITP). (1997). *Model curriculum and guidelines for undergraduate degree programs in information systems.* Retrieved March 25, 2002, from http://www.IS-97.org/abstract.htm

Benbasat, I., & Zmud, R. W. (2003) The identity crisis within the IS discipline: Defining and communicating the discipline's core properties. *MIS Quarterly, 27*(2), 183-194.

Berthon, P., Pitt, L., Ewing, M., & Carr, C. (2002). Potential research space in MIS: A framework for envisioning and evaluating research replication, extension, and generation. *Information Systems Research, 13*(4), 416-427.

Brookshire, R. (2000). Information technology certification: Is this your mission? *Information Technology, Learning, and Performance Journal, 18*(2), 1-2.

Brookshire, R., Williamson, K., & Wright, N. (2002). An interdisciplinary undergraduate degree program in electronic commerce. *Information Technology, Learning and Performance Journal, 20*(2), 25-30.

Byrd, T., & Turner, D. (2001). An exploratory analysis of the value of the skills of IT personnel: Their relationship to IS infrastructure and competitive advantage. *Decision Sciences, 32*(1), 21-55.

Carr, N. G. (2004) IT doesn't matter. *Harvard Business Review, 81*(5), 41-49.

Chang, C., Denning, P. J., Cross II, J. H., Engel, G., Sloan, R., Carver, D., et al. (2000). *Computing curricula 2001 for computer science.* Retrieved in 2004 from http://www.computer.org/education/cc2001/final/index.htm

Clark, C., Cavanaugh, N., Brown, C., & Sambamurthy, V. (1997). Building change-readiness capabilities in the IS organization: Insights from the Bell Atlantic experience. *MIS Quarterly, 21*(4), 425-454.

Couger, J. D., Davis, G., Dologite, D. G., Feinstein, D., Gorgone, J. T., Jenkins, A. M., et al. (1995). IS'95: Guideline for undergraduate IS curriculum. *MIS Quarterly, 19*(3), 341-359.

Cox, B. G., & Pollock, R. W. (1997). *New Zealand graduates 1990: Follow up survey, 1991 and 1996.* NZ Vice-Chancellors Commitee and Ministry of Research, Science, and Technology.

Creswell, J. W. (2003). *Research design: Qualitative, quantitative, and mixed method approaches* (2nd ed.). Thousand Oaks, CA: Sage Publications.

Desplaces, D., Beauvis, L., & Peckham, J. (2003). What information technology asks of business higher education institutions: The case of Rhode Island. *Journal of Information Systems Education, 14*(2), 193-199.

Du, S., Johnson, R., & Keil, M. (2004). Project management courses in IS graduate programs: What is being taught? *Journal of Information Systems Education, 15*(2), 181-187.

Dube, L., & Pare, G. (2003). Rigor in information systems positivist case research: Current practices, trends, and recommendations. *MIS Quarterly, 27*(4), 597.

Ehie, I. (2002). Developing a management information systems (MIS) curriculum: Perspectives from MIS practitioners. *Journal of Education for Business, 10*(2), 115-123.

Gill, T. G., & Hu, Q. (1999). The evolving undergraduate information systems education: A survey of U.S institutions. *Journal of Education for Business, 74*(5), 289-295.

Gonzenbach, N. (1998). Developing an information systems curriculum with input from business and industry. *Information Technology, Learning and Performance Journal, 16*(1), 9-14.

Gorgone, J. T., Davis, G. B., Valacich, J. S., Topi, H., Feinstein, D. L., & Longnecker, H. E. (2002). *IS 2002 model curriculum and guidelines for undergraduate degree programs in information systems.* Retrieved from http://www.acm.org/education/curricula.html

Harkness, W., Kettinger, W., & Segars, A. (1996). Sustaining process improvement and innovation in the information services function: Lessons learned at the Bose corporation. *MIS Quarterly, 20*(3), 349-368.

Hildebrand, D., Schefter, N. & Van Assche, A. (2002) *How do systems development skills in Information Systems students at the University of Cape Town compare with those from similar local and international institutions...?* South Africa: University of Cape Town, Department of Information Systems.

Hooper, A. (2004, December 1-3). *Student peceptions of skill acquisition during undergraduate Information Systems studies—Report of work in progress.* Paper presented at the Australasian Conference on Information Systems, Hobart, Tasmania.

Hsu, M. K., Chen, H. G., Jiang, J. J., & Klein, G. (2003). Career satisfaction for managerial and technical anchored IS personnel in later career stages. *The DATA BASE for Advances in Information Systems, 34*(4), 64-72.

Johnston, D. (2003). Personal email communication about undergraduate student registrations in the School of Information Management. Victoria University of Wellington.

Kakabadse, A., & Kakabadse, N. (2000). Future role of IS/IT professionals. *Journal of Management Development, 19*(2), 97-154.

Kudbya, S., & Diwan, R. (2002). Research report: Increasing returns to information technology. *Information Systems Research, 13*(1), 104-112.

Lee, D., Trauth, E., & Farwell, D. (1995). Critical skills and knowledge requirements of IS professionals: A joint academic/industry investigation. *MIS Quarterly, 19*(3), 313-340.

Lee, S., Koh, S., Yen, D., & Tang, H. (2002). Perception gaps between IS academics and IS practitioners: An exploratory study. *Information & management, 40*, 51-61.

Lee, T. W. (1999). Specific techniques for focus groups, case study research, and conversational interviews. In T. W. Lee (Ed.), *Using qualitative methods in organisational research* (vol. 4, pp. 67-94). Thousand Oaks, CA: Sage.

Leitheiser, R. L. (1992). MIS Skills for the 1990s: A survey of MIS managers' perceptions. *Journal of Management Information Systems, 9*(1), 69-91.

Liu, X., Lui, L., Lu, J., & Koong, K. (2003). An examination of job skills posted on internet databases: Implications for information systems degree programs. *Journal of Education for Business, 78*(4), 191-196.

Maier, J., Clark, W., & Remington, W. (1998). A longitudinal study of the management information systems (MIS) job market. *The Journal of Computer Information Systems, 39*(1), 37-42.

Mata, F., Fuerst, W., & Barney, J. (1995). Information technology and sustained competitive advantage: A resource-based analysis. *MIS Quarterly, 19*(4), 487-505.

Microsoft. (2003). *2004.* Retrieved from http://www.microsoft.com/learning/mcp/mcse/faq.asp

Miles, M., & Huberman, A. (1994). Early steps in analysis. In M. Miles & A. Huberman (Eds.), *Qualitative data analysis* (vol. 4, 2nd ed., pp. 50-88). Thousand Oaks, CA: Sage.

Mingers, J. (2001). Combining IS research methods: Towards a pluralist methodology. *Information Systems Research, 12*(3), 240-259.

Neiderman, F., & Moore, J. E. (2000). *Computer personnel research: What have we learned in this decade?* Paper presented at the Special Interest Group on Computer Personnel Research, Evanston, Illinois, USA.

Patke, A. (2004). *Skills requirements of the IS/IT industry: A graduate's perspective.* Paper presented at the School of Information Mangement, Victoria University of Wellington, Wellington, New Zealand.

Rusli, A., & Marshall, P. (1995). Using an interpretivist inquiry methodology in IS research: An ethnographic experience in an Indonesian organisation. Paper presented at the *Proceedings of the 6th Australasian Conference on Information Systems*, Curtin University, Western Australia.

Scott, E. (2003) Personal email communication about undergraduate student registrations in the Department of Information Systems at the University of Cape Town.

Tan, X., Yen, D., & Fang, X. (2002). Internet integrated customer relationship management: A key success factor for companies in the e-commerce arena. *The Journal of Computer Information Systems, 42*(3), 77-86.

Tang, H., Lee, S., & Koh, S. (2001). Educational gaps as perceived by IS educators: A survey of knowledge and skills requirements. *The Journal of Computer Information Systems, 41*(2), 76-84.

Tanyel, F., Mitchell, M., & McAlum, H. (1999). The skill set for success of new business graduates. *Journal of Education for Business, 75*(1), 33-37.

Todd, K., Verbick, T., & Miller, M. (2001). *Ethics education in the microchip millenium.* Paper presented at the ACM Special Interest Group on University and College Computing Services on User Services, Portland, Oregon.

Todd, P. A., McKeen, J. D., & Gallupe, R. B. (1995). The evolution of IS job skills: A content analysis of IS job advertisements from 1970 to 1990. *MIS Quarterly, 19*(1), 1-27.

Weber, J., McIntyre, V., & Schmidt, M. (2001). Explaining IS student and IS industry differences in perceptions of skill importance. *The Journal of Computer Information Systems, 41*(4), 79-84.

Witt, L., & Burke, A. (2002). Selecting high-performing information technology professionals. *Journal of Organizational and End User Computing, 14*(4), 37-51.

Section III:

Management of IT Professionals

Chapter VIII

Managing
IT Professionals:
Human Resource
Considerations

Jeffy Luftman, Stevens Institute of Technology, USA

Rajkumar Kempaiah, Stevens Institute of Technology, USA

Abstract

Attracting and retaining top IT talent is a major concern for most organizations. In the early part of this decade when the dotcom boom turned to a bust, Y2K was over and the recession hit, everything came to a dramatic halt. Today the economy is improving and the hiring of IT staff is on the rebound. Today new skills are required to compete in a global economy where organizations have new alternatives to choose from. Finding IT professionals with specific skills is no easy feat these days. Today's job skills require strong technical skills and also excellent business, industry, communication, marketing and negotiating abilities. This chapter will focus on the results of recent research and their implications to IT human resource considerations. It also discusses what IT professionals are seeking in a position, the retention of IT talent, stress in workplace, and IT career development.

Introduction

The market for IT professionals is still the fastest growing sector in the United States economy with 68% output growth rate projected between 2002 and 2012. The IT market in the United States is predicted to add 632,000 jobs between 2001 and 2012 (USBL, 2005). In Australia IT jobs are up 60.4% in May 2005 compared to May 2004 (Foreshew, 2005). These IT job prospects are expected to be good as the demand for computer related positions increases due to advancement in technology, priority for information security, government regulation, and new opportunities for application development. In September 2005, Jerry Luftman presented at the SIM*posium* CIO Executive Summit (over 1,000 IT Executives) the results of his recent survey on key issues for IT executives (Luftman, 2005, 2005a). Among the insights presented was the top 10 IT management concerns (Figure 1) surveyed by the CIOs of SIM (Society for Information Management) companies. Retaining IT professionals was the second largest concern for the second year in a row, ranked among IT executives; only the perennial IT-business alignment received higher scores. This shows that IT executives are recognizing the need to invest in their professional staff. With the recent recession coming to an end, concern that staff will leave for other opportunities, and offshore outsourcing being the most discussed topic from the computer room to the board room, it is no wonder that

Figure 1. Top 10 IT management concerns

1. IT And Business Alignment
2. Security and Privacy
2. Attracting, Developing & Retaining IT Professionals
4. IT Strategic Planning
5. Business Process Reengineering
6. Introducing Rapid Business Solutions
7. True Return on IT Investment
7. Measuring The Value of IT Investment
9. Complexity Reduction
10. IT Governance
10. Project Management Capability

IT executives have raised the need to focus more on HR considerations. Several years ago, IT HR considerations never made the top ten lists of concerns. The colors in Figure 1 represent whether the element has moved closer to number one (numbers top 2, 5-9, and botton 10), stayed in the same position as last year (numbers 1, bottom 2, and 4), or moved further away from number one (top 10).

New skills are needed to manage the global work force and ensure that the current workforce is prepared and motivated (Luftman & McLean, 2004). "Retaining IT professionals" has taken a new meaning-and new sense of urgency. Important considerations include:

- How to retain current employees that have just experienced the end of one of the slowest periods in recent years for IT careers and salary increases;
- How to prepare for the inevitable growth of offshore outsourcing; and
- How to ensure current and future staffs have the appropriate skills (business, management, and technical) to succeed.

The *IOMA (Institute of Management and Administration) report on salary survey* for 2004 (Figure 2) (Anonymous, 2005a) presents the average salaries for various IT positions organized by geographic location (United States). The Hayes Personnel Services report on salary survey for 2004 (Figure 2a) (Heap, 2004) presents the average salaries for various IT positions by seven locations across Australia and New Zealand.

The IT job categories command excellent salaries from entry level to CIO. According to Meta Group, IT executives can expect to see up to 15% salary increases over the next three years. In fact, in a January 2005 survey conducted by CIO magazine, 76% of the respondents described that their organizations are inadequately staffed, and 49% said that they are currently hiring or will hire within the first quarter of 2005. In February 2005, the Meta Group reported, "IT hiring is on the rebound as previously shelved projects are brought back online. Combine the two and the result is an employment environment ripe for the exodus of top IT talent to greener pastures" (Egizi, 2005). The number of Americans employed in IT approached 3.38 million in the first quarter of 2005. IT employment levels haven't been this high in three years. Employment in the last quarter for IT professionals increased by about 39,000 from the end of the previous quarter and about 57,000 from a year earlier (Chabrow, 2005). In the United States, Gartner Group projects an aggregate demand for IT workers of 21 million new jobs by 2012, of which 4 million positions will go unfilled due to a lack of qualified workers; this is referred to as the "gap" in IT workers" (McCall, 2005). In Australia, the employment outlook across all industry sectors is positive for the December 2005 quarter. According to the Hudson Report the

Figure 2. Total IT compensation by region (U.S. dollars)

Total IT Compensation (salary plus bonuses) by region							
	New England	Middle Atlantic	South Atlantic	North Central	South Central	Mountain	Pacific
CIO/Vice President of IT	$172,010	$188,801	$157,398	$154,739	$161,943	$122,680	$163,523
Director of IT/IS	$99,307	$121,691	$103,892	$91,331	$85,543	$88,518	$117,039
Help desk/technical support manager	$75,626	$85,018	$74,947	$66,677	$66,227	$69,760	$74,929
Programming/application development manager	$117,150	$106,440	$103,490	$90,823	$94,127	$87,810	$103,298
Project manager	$99,624	$100,813	$98,361	$90,900	$93,250	$87,195	$91,242
Database administrator	$80,299	$86,930	$81,334	$78,602	$86,449	$73,506	$93,198
Help desk/technical support specialist	$50,429	$48,959	$45,987	$44,552	$42,941	$41,202	$51,036
IT/IS technology business systems analyst	$81,613	$75,812	$73,941	$67,479	$62,470	$58,940	$78,641
Network administrator	$51,479	$54,990	$57,591	$51,904	$48,547	$52,977	$58,357
Network engineer	$76,776	$72,499	$70,324	$72,888	$71,420	$67,515	$72,836
Programmer analyst	$62,966	$71,213	$67,470	$62,437	$65,172	$70,467	$70,361
Project leader	$90,844	$98,287	$89,645	$80,481	$82,820	$80,665	$95,345
Software developer	$85,050	$79,866	$80,557	$73,253	$79,746	$68,600	$91,275
Software engineer	$89,030	$77,271	$86,214	$76,785	$81,548	$82,612	$90,594
Systems administrator	$71,487	$66,085	$69,127	$63,155	$62,122	$68,274	$68,426
Systems analyst	$75,599	$61,323	$65,330	$60,294	$59,100	$59,174	$69,104
Systems architect	$130,446	$105,557	$102,642	$95,241	$98,817	$118,181	$114,365

Figure 2a. Total IT compensation by seven locations across Australia and New Zealand

Total IT Compensation (salary plus bonuses) by region						
	Sydney	Melbourne	Brisbane	Adelaide	Canberra	Perth	New Zealand
CIO	$190,000	$180,000	$160,000	$125,000	$170,000	$120,000	$120,000
CTO	$170,000	$160,000	$150,000	$125,000	$150,000	$120,000	$110,000
IT manager	$120,000	$100,000	$100,000	$80,000	$95,000	$70,000	$85,000
Network manager	$120,000	$110,000	$80,000	$80,000	$95,000	$50,000	$80,000
Helpdesk manager	$80,000	$75,000	$68,000	$55,000	$80,000	$80,000	$75,000
Database administrator	$90,000	$80,000	$72,000	$70,000	$80,000	$70,000	$75,000
Helpdesk Support (Level1)	$45,000	$40,000	$36,000	$34,000	$35,000	$35,000	$36,000
Helpdesk Support (Level2)	$55,000	$50,000	$38,000	$40,000	$45,000	$40,000	$42,000
Network engineer	$95,000	$90,000	$85,000	$80,000	$80,000	$65,000	$85,000
Technical architect	$110,000	$110,000	$100,000	$90,000	$95,000	$80,000	$95,000
Programmer analyst	$70,000	$60,000	$70,000	$60,000	$80,000	$55,000	$65,000
Project manager	$95,000	$90,000	$95,000	$85,000	$90,000	$80,000	$90,000
Software developer	$70,000	$60,000	$55,000	$45,000	$70,000	$40,000	$47,000
Systems administrator	$80,000	$75,000	$75,000	$68,000	$75,000	$55,000	$75,000
Systems analyst	$95,000	$90,000	$90,000	$80,000	$90,000	$75,000	$80,000
Systems architect	$120,000	$120,000	$100,000	$120,000	$110,000	$90,000	$110,000

resources sector is at its highest level of optimism on record with nearly 43.4% of employers planning to increase its headcount in professional services industry (Gardner & Knowles, 2005).

After the dot-com bust, the economy went spiraling downwards, presenting a challenge to all businesses that demanded cuts in many areas, including IT. More than 100,000 Americans dropped out of the IT labor market between mid-2002 and late 2004. Most of the American universities reported a decline in enrollments in information management and computer science programs as the Internet bubble burst discouraged students considering IT careers. However, the critical role technology plays in business helps to maintain the need for IT skills even in the face of an economic slowdown; albeit the specific skills required a change. We all need to ensure that young people are appropriately counseled regarding the future career opportunities in IT.

For example, the expanding integration of Internet technologies and rapid growth in electronic commerce has created a demand for programmers who can develop Web applications. As companies explore new technologies such as wireless or RFID, the IT field will once again advance, increasing the need for skills in these new technologies, and how to upgrade existing systems and infrastructure. One of the most significant challenges for IT management is retaining the critical talent and understanding the mix of skills that are needed as the business strategy evolves. No matter what happens with the economy or the technology, managing the IT human resource remains an important issue for every organization.

What Do IT Professionals Say They Are Looking For?

The 2004 Information Week Compensation Survey (McCarthy, 2004) looks in detail at what IT professionals seek in their working environments. The overall results of the survey indicate that respondents were generally not satisfied and that their level of satisfaction has decreased compared with one year ago. Looking at the specifics, there are some very troubling areas:

1.   More than 55% of the IT staff and more than 65% of IT managers believe that their job and responsibilities are not challenging. This suggests that while they are dissatisfied with their jobs, more than half of the IT professionals believe they must change employers to advance their careers. Organizations face losing a large number of IT professionals just because their job responsibility is not challenging. This churn rate saddles

the average firm with burdensome recruiting and termination costs. The cost of replacing an experienced IT professional has been estimated to average around $20,000 (Essex, 2000).

2.   About 41% of the respondents believe that they are not fairly compensated and 12% of the respondents believe that they got fewer bonuses in 2004 than they got in 2003. Sixty-three percent of the respondents said that higher compensation is the prime reason that they are interested in changing jobs. Research indicates that job satisfaction is more important than bonus and compensation, but this statistic shows how dissatisfied IT professionals are with their salaries. Coupled with the first issue, this compounds the pressure on IT employees to change employers to remedy the bonus and compensation issues.

3.   Fifty percent of the IT staff and 40% of IT managers appreciate flexible work schedules (Figure 3). As the technology improves to allow effective job performance from any location, the pressure increases for organizations to enable telecommuting. Clearly, IT professionals will be aware of the enabling characteristics of the technology long before the general

Figure 3. What is important to IT professionals

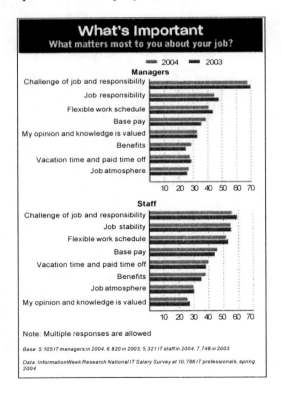

Figure 4. Reasons for leaving

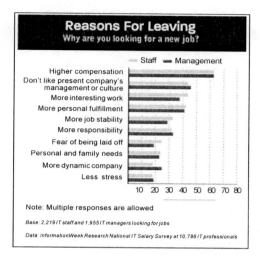

Note: Multiple responses are allowed

Base: 2,219 IT staff and 1,955 IT managers looking for jobs

Data: InformationWeek Research National IT Salary Survey at 10,786 IT professionals

population. They will seek the alternative work style and become disenchanted if the organization denies flexible hours.

4.   More than 40% are dissatisfied with their company's management or culture (Figure 4). Culture emerges through behavioral responses to challenges and problems. The likely scenario here is that IT management, traditionally low on the people skill scale, has not opened up the communication lines to make their staff comfortable to discuss career issues. Most IT managers have not been trained to help foster their staff's careers. Give them a technology problem to tackle and they are off and running; but bring

Figure 5. Job security

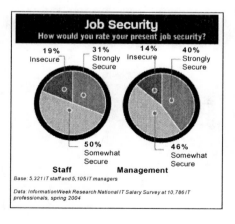

Base: 5,321 IT staff and 5,105 IT managers

Data: InformationWeek Research National IT Salary Survey at 10,786 IT professionals, spring 2004

up a personnel issue and many IT managers are ill-prepared to manage their employees' needs.

5. Nearly 50% of IT professionals believe they do not have job security (Figure 5). Since the dotcom bust, IT, like other areas in the firm, has been downsizing. This trend has resulted in all employees feeling insecure about their jobs. Organizations are treating IT workers as disposable parts; IT staffs are intelligent and skilled, and they always think about solving problems, and they should not be thinking about job security. If they start thinking about job security, the IT manager will have an escalating problem to manage.

6. Eighty-eight percent report their jobs are stressful, up from 82% last year. Budget cuts and increased workloads are the biggest cause of stress (Collett, 2004). Putting all five of the previous concerns together, one can easily surmise that the stress of the environment in IT has increased. There is more work, less time for upgrading skills, less opportunity for advancement, a sense of not being valued and the need to resign in order to improve the situation.

IT Budgets on the Rise

IT budgets took a downward spiral after the dotcom bust in the year 2000 with a lot of job cuts, maintenance being deferred, and projects being cancelled. With economic recovery in sight, IT budgets are on the rise after flat budgets for more than three years. In the CIO survey conducted by Luftman (2005a) regarding IT budgets, the charts (Figure 6 and Figure 7) illustrate that IT budgets are on rise. Sixty-three percent of the respondents said that 2005 budgets were higher than

Figure 6. 2005 IT budget in comparison to 2004 budget

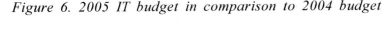

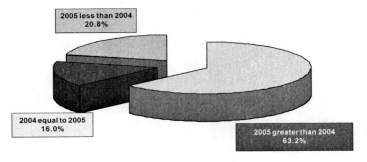

Figure 7. 2006 IT budget in comparison to 2005 budget (projected)

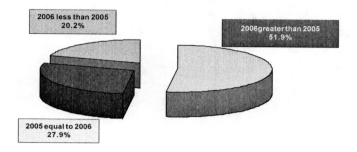

in 2004, and 51% of the respondents said that 2006 budgets will be higher than in 2005. Meta group forecasts that IT budgets will increase in 2005/06 at 3-4% overall, and after 2006 they expect IT budgets to increase 4-6% on average per annum (Passori, 2005). In a similar study by InfoWorld, 52% of the respondents said that the pay raises for IT professionals were put on hold because of the freeze on IT budgets. When IT budgets are constrained IT professionals usually worry about job security. The increase in IT budgets plays an important role in attracting, developing, and retaining staff because 40% of these budgets are allocated toward staffing (Figures 8 and 9).

Forrester research projects that IT spending will grow by 7% in 2005 based on a survey responded by more than 1,300 IT decision makers in the U.S. (Swoyer, 2005) Figure 8 and Figure 9 show the percent of budget allocated for IT staffing. Even though these are relative numbers, budgeted percentages for staffing are decreasing, as can be seen by comparing 2005 with 2006. The pie is larger because budgets have increased overall; so although the relative percent has decreased, the actual amount has risen.

Figure 8. 2005 IT budget allocation

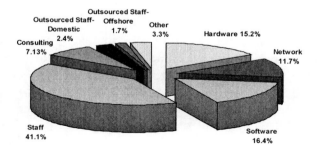

Figure 9. 2006 IT budget allocation

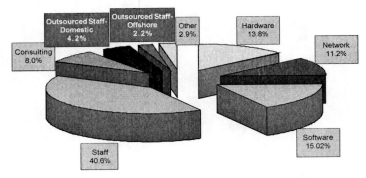

Figure 10. IT head count in comparison to 2004

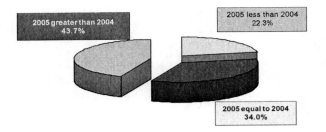

It appears that the IT economy has turned the corner, and the IT job market is improving. The budget increases, along with the higher ranking of attracting, developing, and retaining IT professionals, is encouraging. They show that IT executives appear to be taking the longer-term view of investing in their professional staff.

Also, some companies may be concerned that neglecting their employees during the downturn in the early part of this decade may cause large-scale defections as the economy further improves. It might be too late to be proactive, but these numbers suggest that IT executives are investing more in IT human resource areas.

The U.S. economy is picking up and so is the employment headcount for IT professionals. Figure 10 from Luftman's SIM data (Luftman, 2005a) clearly shows that head count for IT professionals is on the rise, as 44% of the respondents said that IT headcount in 2005 is greater than in 2004. IDC reports that IT professionals' headcount worldwide will grow at a compounded growth rate of 9.8% between 2003 and 2008, reaching 14.9 million IT professionals by

2008 (Hendrick, Byron, & Emberley, 2005). Microsoft expects to hire 6,000 to 7,000 IT professionals in 2005 with more than half to be hired in United States alone. Google has hundreds of job listings on its Web site but has not released its headcount projections for 2005. In 2004, Google almost doubled its IT headcount to 3,000. Priceline.com, the e-commerce Web site has plans to increase its headcount by 20% in 2005 (Kerstetter, 2005).

Outsourcing Done Offshore

IT outsourcing is poised to grow substantially. The year 2005 will see a significant growth in outsourcing. Gartner group projects that outsourcing worldwide will grow from $112.9 billion in 2003 to $176.1 billion in 2008, at a compound annual growth rate of 9.3% (Casale, 2005). Cost savings from outsourcing cannot be ignored. IT is global. Figure 11 from Luftman's SIM data (Luftman, 2005a) show that 65% of the respondents are not using offshore outsourcing but the remaining 35% of the respondents are using offshore outsourcing. Figure 12 shows that in spite of jobs moving offshore, the United States will have a shortage of more than 6 million jobs by 2015. Managing IT work performed all around the world requires new skills, which are extremely scarce. Thus, "attracting, developing, and retaining IT professionals" has taken on new meaning—and new urgency. IT executives appear to be responding to the need to prepare their staff with the new skill of "vendor/outsourcing management." Again, the higher ranking of this issue indicates that IT executives have recognized the need to retool their IT organization for this evolving environment.

Figure 11. Percent outsourcing done offshore

% OF RESPONDENTS

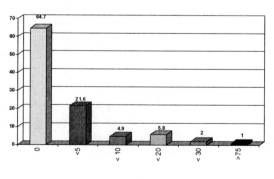

PERCENT OUTSOURCING ⟶

Figure 12. Total number of jobs moving offshore relative to labor shortage (2000-2015)

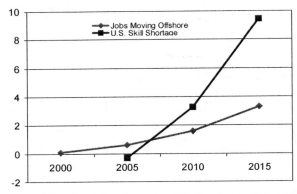

Source: Forester Research, Inc. and development policy foundation. Tabulation of Bureau of Labor statistics and Census Bureau data

Characteristics of the Environment Contribute to the Complexity of Human Resource Management

Characteristics of the IT environment contribute to the complexity of this issue. Continuous learning is critical to be competitive and IT professionals have to deal with the constant change that technology brings. IT professionals must constantly master new technology, business, and management skills to be the stewards of their own careers. Advancement in hardware and software are bringing rapid changes to the market. Software vendors push expanded and improved versions of their products resulting in releases that introduce huge disruptions in service and integration complexities. At the same time, organizations have significant legacy systems requiring traditional IT skills and knowledge, and a commitment to long-term maintenance and support. Constant change in IT weakens the business value of legacy systems, being developed with huge costs and over a period of time. Even though cost effective technologies are available, nearly 80% of the IT systems are running on legacy platforms (Zoufaly, 2002). Within an IT organization, the need for constant learning of new technologies and the need for maintaining the legacy systems can create two

Figure 13. 2004 IT workforce: Job category as a percentage of total IT workforce

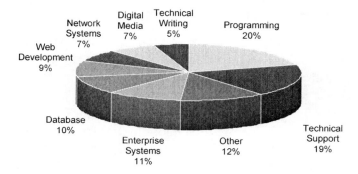

Source: ITAA "Adding Value...Growing Careers" Annual Workforce Development Survey (2004)

groups of IT staff. CIOs are faced with the challenge of keeping two groups of IT staff motivated and productive.

The pie chart in Figure 13 shows that in 2004 there are more than 2 million programmers out of the 10.5 million total IT professionals (ITAA, 2004a; ITAA, 2004b). Technical support is the second largest category followed by enterprise systems and database development. Programming includes a broad range of responsibilities including designing, development, coding, and testing. As organizations upgrade their existing infrastructures and modernize their business functions, programming will be the most important job category in the IT workforce. Some of the IT job responsibilities such as network systems and infrastructure support saw an increase of 5% in jobs from a year ago. As the economy improves, companies are growing and need more IT professionals to handle the workload.

In addition to having technical knowledge IT professionals need to have business knowledge to play an effective role. These days organizations look for "soft skills" such as the ability to work with others, change directions quickly and understand and communicate with the business (Coy, 2004). Business knowledge comes from working with the business units within the firm, some from in-house training or the IT professionals seeking formal education through graduate management degrees. Fifty-two percent of the respondents rated "interpersonal skills" as the highest non-technology skill required by IT professionals (ITAA, 2004). IT professionals are recognizing that in addition to the technical knowledge they need to have business knowledge to have a successful IT career.

Is There a Future Working in Information Technology?

Reports from the U.S. Bureau of Labor Statistics along with those from private research organizations all list IT positions as the fastest growing occupations. Figure 14 illustrates the projections by the Bureau of Labor Statistics, that in the United States nearly 2.5 million IT professionals are needed between the year 2000 and 2010.

Of the 20 fastest growing professional jobs in the U.S. identified by the Bureau of Labor Statistics, seven are in the IT field (Figure 15). Organizations will go after IT professionals with strong programming, systems analysis, and business skills. As the economy improves, organizations will integrate new technologies to maximize the efficiency of their existing computer systems and in doing so the employment for IT professionals will increase.

Technology and business are evolving so rapidly that new growth avenues will continue to arise out of it. We are seeing a rapid increase in the number of internet users. Additionally, wireless internet has created a demand for new ideas and products. As we depend more on notebooks and wireless technologies, it

Figure 14. Projections for professional-level IT occupations continued rapid growth projected: 2.5 million new it workers needed between 2000 and 2010

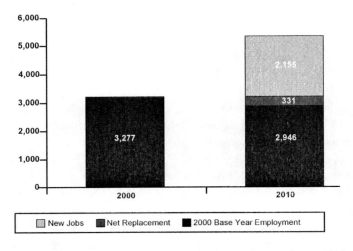

Source: U.S. Department of Commerce, Office of Technology Policy analysis of U.S. Department of Labor, Bureau of Labor Statistics Occupational Employment Projections, 2000-2010

Figure 15. Twenty fastest-growing professional jobs

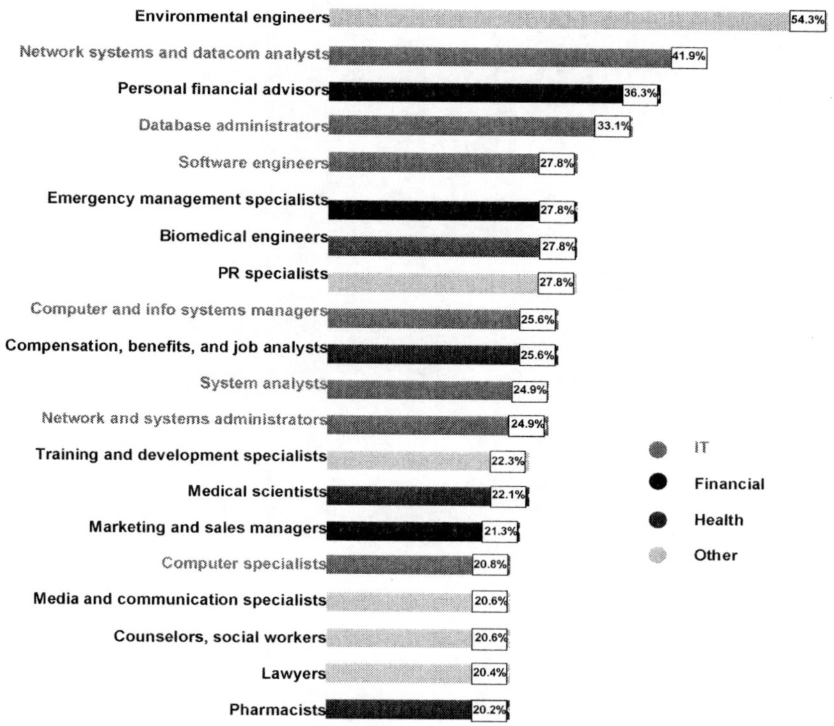

Source: Bureau of Labor Statistics

becomes increasingly important for organizations to integrate the mobile technology with the existing computer systems. In doing so, information security, let alone new government regulations, has risen in importance. All these expansions will demand IT professionals to develop, integrate, run, and maintain these new applications.

Figure 16 shows that the average annual growth rate for IT projected by the Bureau of Labor statistics stands at an average of 9%. It shows that IT professionals will have more job opportunities compared to the growth in other industries. Figure 17 shows projected new jobs by occupational category and there is 11% projected growth in new jobs for IT professionals.

Further analyses from the U.S. Bureau of Labor statistics, predicts that from 2000 to 2010, the top five jobs in percentage of growth are all IT professions:

Figure 16. Detailed industries with faster than average employment growth, ranked by average annual output growth rates projected 2002-12

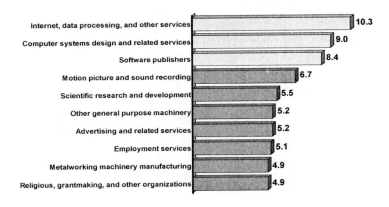

Source: Bureau of Labor Statistics

Figure 17. Projected new jobs by occupational category 2012

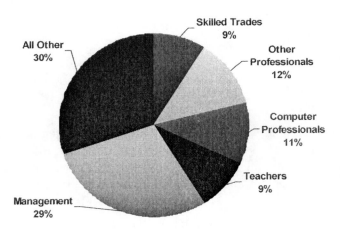

Source: Employment Policy Foundation analysis and projections: Census/BLS and BEA data; Walk & Associates, Inc.

- Computer engineer – 100%
- Computer support specialist – 96%
- Systems analyst – 89%
- Database administrator – 66%
- Desktop publishing specialist – 65%

The reputation of IT as a good career choice presents the IT executive with a dilemma. On the plus side, the good reputation means that there should be a steady stream of talent from which to choose IT staff; on the negative side, the good reputation means that the challenge of retaining quality IT staff continues as companies compete for the best skills. Additional effects of this situation are that there will be a large pool of educated and talented, but inexperienced staff that will continue to require new skills (e.g., business, industry, communications, and vendor management).

Recruiting and Retention of IT Talent

The demand for IT personnel is extremely high, and IT personnel have historically displayed high turnover rates. Turnover of skilled IT personnel is very expensive and disruptive to organizations. Whenever talented personnel leave an organization, costs are incurred with hiring and training of employees, let alone the cost of loosing the employees knowledge about the firm. The hiring costs of skilled IT personnel vary depending on the type of job and the specific skills required. The estimates vary, but all describe considerable value loss:

- 25%-100% of personnel annual salary according to Forrester research (Surmacz, 2004)
- 25% of annual salary plus benefits according to Saratoga Institute (Hauenstein, 2000)
- According to Sibson & Co., turnover directly costs the IT industry $44 billion on an annual basis (Essex, 2000)

The cost of turnover has two components: hiring costs and vacancy costs. Hiring costs are the direct costs associated with recruiting new IT personnel (e.g., advertising fees, and costs for screening, interviewing and processing personnel); the vacancy costs include costs for replacing the former IT personnel (e.g., compensation for interim replacement, overtime costs by current personnel, productivity losses and loss of knowledge).

Recruiting

Recruiting, even when the economy is not good, is not cheap. Gartner group estimates that it costs up to 2.5 times the annual salary of the IT professional leaving the organization. It includes the cost of advertising, recruiter's cost, traveling costs, interview and training times, and also the lost productivity with the learning curve of the new IT professionals being hired. Studies show that 78% of IT professionals leave their organizations before their fifth anniversary (Del Monte, 2004).

Recruiting strategies differ from organization to organization. Figure 18 shows how IT talent is recruited. 89% of the IT talent is recruited by newspaper ads, executive search firms, word of mouth, or internal job listings. Newspaper ads are expensive and organizations have to spend a lot of time screening the applicants and doing background checks. Most IT organizations find newspaper ads generate a high percentage of unqualified applicants. Another problem with newspaper ads is that IT professionals probably will not spend much of their time reading them (Hamilton & Kern, 2001).

Organizations around the world are realizing that more than 421 million people worldwide are online (Snell, 2003). iLogos research found that an organization's Web site is now a key component of recruiting in 88% of global 500 companies (Snell, 2003). Online recruiting has revolutionized the way that recruiting takes

Figure 18. How IT talent is recruited

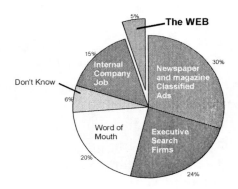

Source: Lee Hecht Harrison Inc., New York

place. Many agree it saves time and cuts costs. Many IT professionals turn to the internet to research salary range to get an understanding of the current job market, positions that are open and salaries being offered. A number of Web sites such as www.computerworld.com, www.dice.com, www.information week.com carry the results and surveys on their Web sites. Organizations that are hiring have to make use of the available internet resources for advertising, searching resumes and for prescreening IT professionals.

Many organizations encourage internal referrals through employee referral programs by providing bonus for referring IT professionals. The cash incentive provided is much less compared to what the executive search firms charge.

Executive search firms provide excellent sources of IT professionals. They are expensive but they offer IT professionals a vehicle for prescreening and doing background checks. Executive search firms usually charge 10%-33% of the IT professional's salary (Southgate, 2002).

Retention

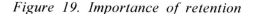

After the downturn of the early 2000s a lot of IT professionals were downsized as budgets were reduced. Now, as the economy is improving, organizations are faced with the challenge of keeping the IT professionals from being lured away by competitors. Organizations that have not made retention a top priority or had underestimated the impact will have a tough time managing the migration of IT professionals. In a survey conducted by Robert Half Technology, 33% of the respondents (Figure 19) said that retention is somewhat important, while 25% said that retention is very important.

Figure 19. Importance of retention

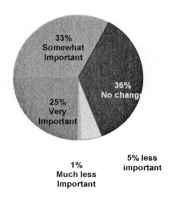

Source: Robert Half Technology

Figure 20. It isn't the money

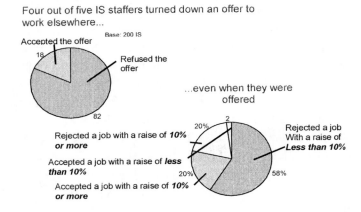

Source: SIM

It is not only the money that IT professionals are looking for. In a survey conducted by the Society of Information Management (SIM), four out of five IT professionals turned down an offer to work at another organization. As Figure 20 shows, 82% refused the offer, and more interestingly even when they were offered more money, 20% rejected with a raise of 10% or more. This clearly shows that money is not the only factor for IT professionals. Money is important but so are the other factors such as leadership, the ability to use new technologies, job security, faith in financial security of the organization, challenging assignments, location, retirement plans and bonus plans. An environment has to be created where IT professionals feel that they are the key contributors to the organization.

Motivating IT professionals to increase productivity and reduce turnover involves a number of factors that IT managers need to manage. The following are the seven key factors that IT managers should consider in any motivational program to increase productivity and help reduce IT staff turnover (Zawacki, 2004):

1.   Provide strong leadership during periods of rapid and random change

2.   Provide employees with a personal development plan; give them a clearly defined career path

3.   Allow people to learn new technologies as they emerge; allow people to attend technology conferences

Figure 21. Top retention skills

1.	GOOD WORKER - SUPERVISOR RELATIONSHIP
2.	CHALLENGING WORK EXPERIENCE
3.	OPEN AND HONEST COMMUNICATION
4.	OUTSTANDING TRAINING AND EDUCATION OPPORTUNITIES
5.	PAY FOR INCREASED CONTRIBUTION AND TO SHARE IN FIRM'S SUCCESS
6.	WORK/LIFE BALANCE
7.	MEDICAL, DISABILITY, LIFE AND LONG-TERM-CARE INSURANCE
8.	LATEST TECHNOLOGY
9.	A DIVERSE WORKFORCE
10.	TOP-OF-THE-LINE RETIREMENT PROGRAM
11.	THE AVAILABILITY OF "LIFE PLANNING" TOOLS (E.g., FINANCIAL PLANNING)
12.	HIGHEST PAYING EMPLOYER

Source: Human Resource Institute, Eckerd College, St. Petersburg, FL, USA

4.   Give people the resources they need to do their jobs well

5.   Be competitive in terms of salary and benefits; consider annual salary surveys to keep abreast of salary levels

6.   Make certain people perceive that what they do on the job is meaningful work

7.   Ask employees what they desire; do not wait for an exit interview

Figure 21 shows the top retention skills identified by Human Resource Institute, Eckerd College, St. Petersburg, Florida. The best antidote for turnover is to develop a strategic retention plan. The number one reason that IT professionals leave an organization is because they do not have a good relationship with their immediate supervisors. The top priorities should be in creating a challenging work environment for IT professionals while opening the communication lines so that they can have positive interactions with their supervisors. Of course, offering an effective education and training program is also important.

One of the most important aspects of retaining IT employees is making sure they understand their career path. Figure 22 illustrates the results of a survey done by an HR consulting firm, Personnel Decisions Inc.; 96% of the respondents indicated that understanding the career path is the most important reason for staying in their positions.

Figure 22. Career path choices

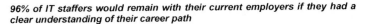

96% of IT staffers would remain with their current employers if they had a
clear understanding of their career path

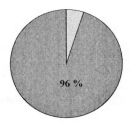

Source: Personnel Decisions Inc., a human resources consulting firm in Minneapolis, MN, USA

Stress in the Workplace

Stress among IT professionals is an important factor affecting productivity and turnover. In a survey conducted in 28 nations among IT professionals, the productivity of U.S. programmers per year was found to be on average 7,700 lines of code compared to 16,700 lines of code for non-U.S. programmers; the main reason cited was the job stress (Hoffman, 1999; Sethi, King, & Campbell, 2004). Moore (2000) demonstrated that job stress and burnout were leading causes of turnover among IT professionals.

On average IT professionals put in more than 50 hours per week; almost half of IT professionals work an average of 6 hours on weekends; and about 70% have worked even when they are sick (King, 1995). Seveny-two percent of the respondents in the 2004 CIO survey said that their IT professionals were suffering from high or very high levels of stress (Blodgett, 2004). The chart in Figure 23 shows that 55% of the CIOs said that "increasing workloads" is the greatest factor causing stress among IT professionals, followed by "office politics" (24%), and "issues of work/life balance" (12%) (Robert, 2000). Other research on stress and productivity shows that working incredibly long hours without proper breaks affects both health and productivity (Mortleman, 2004).

Having to do more with fewer IT staff and keeping up-to-date with the latest technology and business changes are all adding to stress. Figure 24 shows the contributors to IT job stress are lack of job security (43%), having to do more with less (20%), few opportunities for growth or promotion (15%), being underpaid (13%), and learning new skills (9%). IT managers should recognize all of the stress related factors and how to manage them. Some considerations include:

Figure 23. Greatest source of work place stress for IT professionals

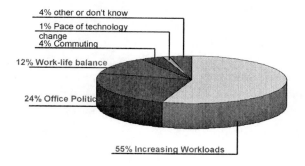

Data: RHI Consulting Survey of 1,400 CIOs (2000, May)

Figure 24. Greatest contributor to IT job stress

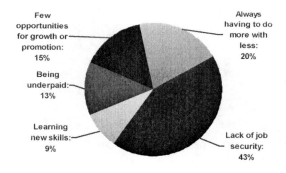

Data: IDC
Source: Survey by Korn/Ferry International

1. Hire IT consultants to reduce the workload of IT staff. By hiring an external IT consultant in addition to temporarily addressing the workload problem, your organization will have access to the wide range of skills the consultant brings. The workload can also be outsourced, but outsourcing must be carefully managed and must not be seen as threatening by the current IT professionals within the organization; this will only increase the stress.

2. Office politics can be diffused by opening the lines of communication and by encouraging team building and cross training. Sixty-five percent of the

CIOs in the 2004 Mid-Year IT staffing update reported using cross training (Blodgett, 2004). When IT professionals do not understand what is happening in their job area, their tendency is to assume the alternatives which might be the worst alternative. IT managers should not allow this to happen. The best way is to promote communication in a clear and understanding approach, and create a culture that makes relationships at work more fruitful. An important aspect of communication for the IT managers is to listen to each IT professional's complaints and ideas. Failing to listen will demotivate the IT professional.

3.   IT managers should involve IT professionals in handling the workload. IT managers should tell them that they value their contributions. Sometimes they can come up with innovative solutions which otherwise can never be solicited. Once IT professionals feel comfortable and feel that they are a part of the team they might come up with creative solutions for solving the workload problems, as well as trust the solution the firm is taking.

4.   Plan and promote office social events to break up the monotonous work routine and give the employees the opportunity to get to know each other better and to have fun. Introducing other activities such as providing membership to gyms and team sports will also help.

The successful IT manager is one who sees these challenges and works to solve them. By doing so the IT manager will be able to increase the productivity of the IT professionals and thereby the success of the department, while helping to retain valuable employees.

There are techniques that can de-stress IT professionals. The following techniques adapted from stress management and counseling centers suggest steps that IT professionals can take to de-stress themselves. Everyone needs to be concerned about avoiding the stress issues that result in lower productivity, poor work performance, lost work time, or loss of a valued IT professional.

- Update your supervisor and co-workers regularly on the status of your projects
- Make sure you know what's expected of you and when it's due
- Prioritize your projects with feedback from your supervisors and co-workers
- Try to make your deadlines
- Take a break every hour and stretch, especially the back, neck and shoulders

- Set aside time to familiarize yourself with the latest developments in your field

- Have regular massages

- Eat a well balanced diet

- Exercise at least three times a week

- Work with a "stress buddy" who can encourage you to keep up your stress-reducing practices

- Keep a "stress diary" to help identify ways to reduce high-stress situations

- Take time off if you're stressed, whether a walk around the block or an extended vacation

- Ask for help when you need it.

- Make sure your work area includes ergonomic equipment, proper lighting, and good ventilation

- If all else fails, find a new job

IT Career Development

To get a high paying job, education is a must. In fact, for 49 out of the 50 highest paying jobs in the United States, a college degree or higher is the most significant source of education or training (USBL, 2003)

With the IT slowdown of the early 2000s, universities in the United States saw a steep decline in the enrollments for IS majors. Statistics released by the National Science Foundation (NSF) reveals that the United States awards fewer degrees in mathematics, sciences, and engineering when compared to other countries. Students in Asia and Europe earn 25% more science and engineering degrees than students in United States (Huisman, 2005). Microsoft research highlights the fact Russia graduates 180,000 students a year with IT skills; India generates 60,000; and China sits third with 50,000. The United States is nowhere close to producing this level of IT graduates (Robb, 2005). Around the world, competition is rising to perform the IT work. The United States needs to provide a high quality of education and training to keep the IT workers competitive and on the leading edge of innovation and technology; especially knowing the demand for IT professionals is on the rise.

Figure 25 shows that the 70 million projected new jobs by 2012 will require college degrees, compared to 50 million jobs in year 2002 requiring college degrees. Figure 26 shows that the United States will be short by over seven million college degrees by 2013. This shortage of educated talent is more

Figure 25. New jobs will require more education

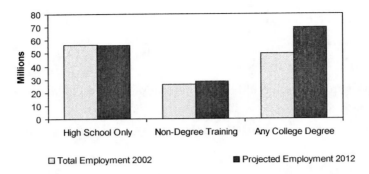

Source: Employment Policy Foundation projections based on Current Population Survey data (1992-2002)

Figure 26. Over seven million college degrees short, degree holders needed to fill new and replacement jobs, 2003-2013 compared to current graduation rate

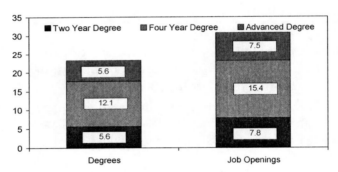

Source: Employment Policy Foundation projections

pronounced in Figure 27, where the number of engineering and science degrees awarded in the United States is much lower than the degrees awarded in life sciences. The United States is slipping its dominance in science and innovation and is facing a critical shortage of science and engineering students. The United States is very much dependent on science and engineering graduates and it is time that all academic and business leaders make students getting these degrees a top priority because public is not aware of the importance and the implications it will create on future job creation in the United States. The IT trend of

Figure 27. Science and engineering bachelor's degrees

Science & Engineering Bachelor's Degrees

Life Sciences Up...
...Engineering, Physical Sciences, and Math Down

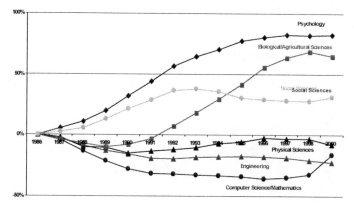

Source: Employment Policy Foundation projections

"outsourcing" is not the only cause of the decrease in enrollment of IS programs–it is one of the many factors that have contributed.

Part of the problem is that many believe that IT jobs are being outsourced offshore. What is likely to happen is a self-fulfilling prophecy, where the demand will be there, as previously discussed, but the skills will not; so the U.S. will be forced to go offshore where the talent lies.

College graduates with background in information systems and computer science have promising job opportunities in 2005 according to the National Association of Colleges and Employers (NACE). According to NACE's job outlook 2005 survey, a degree in information systems is one among the top 10 majors that organizations will plan/need to hire (Anonymous, 2005b). The survey also reports that the employers expect to increase college hiring in 2005 by 13.1% over 2004. Even at the master's level and doctorate level, IT majors are most important to employers. Figure 28 shows that 87.5% of IT professionals who hold bachelors or higher degree have earned degrees in science, mathematics, or engineering.

Some of the attributes that employers look for in graduating students:

Figure 28. Educational background of professional-level IT workers

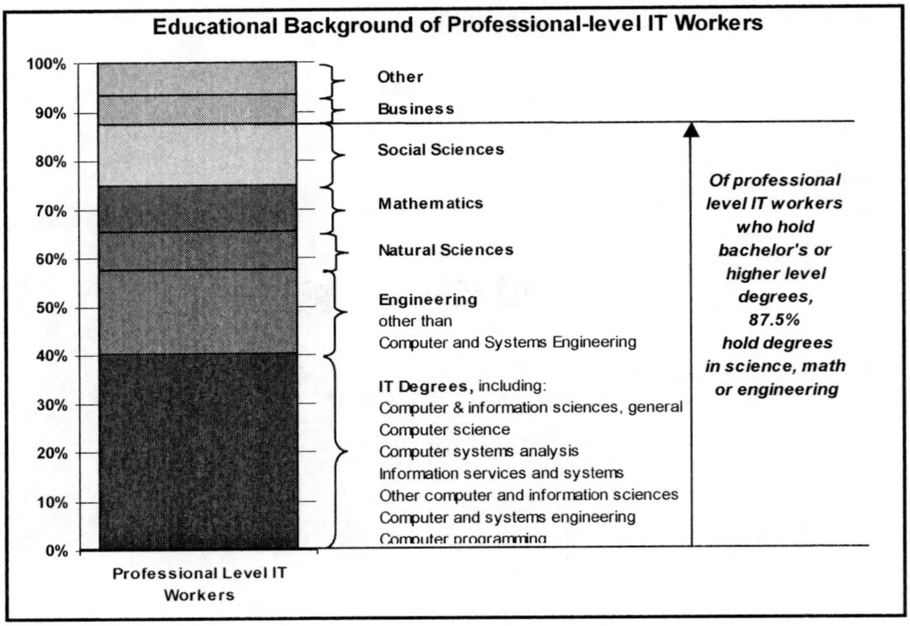

Source: Tabulated by National Science Foundation/Division of science resources statistics

1. **GPA:** A good GPA is very important for employers to select among the talented pool of graduates. Sixty-nine percent of the employers reported that they select graduates based on their GPA.

2. **Communication skills:** Another important attribute that employers look for is communication skills (verbal and written). Employers often complain that graduates lack good grammar and writing skills, and some even complain that graduates have trouble in getting the ideas communicated without saying words "like" and "you know." Graduates are expected to communicate with co-workers (IT and business) and customers. Communications is considered a key part of your growing portfolio. Taking more writing and communication classes are an important consideration for the future. Included here are effective marketing and negotiating skills.

3. **Interpersonal skills:** Employers prefer to hire graduates, who are honest, have teamwork skills, good interpersonal skills, and are really motivated with a strong work ethic. Even if you are not a designated leader, you always being assessed to see you how work within in the team. Getting leadership experience when fresh out of college is an important way to

prepare for the future. Also, being able to negotiate, propose, market, and influence will be critical to your performance as well for the team. Included here is how effectively candidates can work in a team environment.

4. **Corporate culture:** Every organization has its own unique culture and behavior. New employees are expected to conform. Many employers say that new graduates lack experience in the corporate environment and are not familiar with good work ethics. Some add that graduates lack confidence, focus, and goals that are expected in a corporate environment. Before being hired looking at the job expectations will prepare the candidate for their entry into the corporate environment.

All of these skills should be key elements for any university and training program.

Epilogue

So, is there a looming shortfall of IT talent or are will there be an overabundance of IT trained employees? Should people be encouraged to pursue a career in IT? Is it okay that enrollment is decreasing in the United States in IT related areas? We all need to ensure that young people are appropriately counseled regarding the future career opportunities in IT. This chapter has discussed the elements for managing human resources in the IT organization. The particular challenges associated with this environment and the demands of IT professionals have been highlighted. It seems likely that the future of IT is strong! The chapter also discussed how organizations can prepare for this great opportunity. Continuous enhancement of technical, business, and management skills is fundamental to a successful IT career.

References

Anonymous. (2005a). *IOMA's report on salary surveys*. Retrieved March 2005, from http://www.ioma.com

Anonymous. (2005b). *Outlook is good for certain college graduates*. Retrieved March 2005, from http://ioma.com.

Blodgett, M. (2004). *The few and the stressed.* Retrieved April 2005, from http://www.cio.com/archive/110104/survey.html

Casale, F. J. (2005, Spring). Outsourcing essentials. *Outsourcing.com, 3*(1). Retrieved from http://www.outsourcing.com/content.asp?page=01b/other/oe/q105/default.html&nonav=false

Chabrow, E. (2005). IT employment on upswing. *Information Week.* Retrieved March 2005, from http://www.informationweek.com/shared/printable ArticleSrc.jhtml?articleID=160403526

Collett, S. (2004). Salary Survey: Near the boiling point. *Computerworld.* Retrieved January 2005, from http://www.computerworld.com/action/article.do?command=viewArticleBasic&articleId=96850

Coy, P. (2004). The future of work. *Business Week Online.* Retrieved February 2005, from http://www.businessweek.com/magazine/content/04_12/b3875615.htm

Del Monte, J. (2004). *Cost of hiring/turnover (COH).* JDA Professional Services, Inc. Retrieved February 2005, from http://www.jdapsi.com/Client/Articles/Default.php?Article=coh

Egizi, C. (2005). *It's cheaper to keep 'em.* Retrieved April 2005, from http://www.cioupdate.com/career/article.php/3482646

Essex, D. (2000). *Employee turnover: The costs are staggering.* Retrieved March 2005, from http://www.itworld.com/Career/1993/ITW2491/pfindex.html

Foreshew, J. (2005). Strong growth in tech jobs: IT rebounds. *James Cook University.* Retrieved July 2005, from http://www.it.jcu.edu.au/general-info/ITtoday07june2005.shtml

Gardner, J., & Knowles, K. (2005). Australian employment optimism softens, first time since Q2 2003. *Hudson Report.* Retrieved July 2005, from www.Hudson.com

Hamilton, M., & Kern, H. (2001). *Recruiting the best talent.* Retrieved March 2005, from http://www.harriskern.com/index.php?m=p&pid=377&authorid=14&aid=31

Hauenstein, P. (2000). *Understanding turnover, advantage hiring.* Retrieved April 2005, from www.advantagehiring.com/newsletter/n99q4_1.htm

Heap, N. (2004). *Australia and New Zealand salary survey 2004.* Hayes Personnel Services. Retrieved June 2005, from http://www.hays.com.au/salary/pdfs04/InformationTechnology.pdf

Hendrick, S., Byron, D., & Emberley, D. (2005). *Professional software developers to number 14.9 million worldwide in 2008, IDC.* Retrieved March 2005, from http://www.tekrati.com/T2/Analyst_research AnnouncementsDetails.asp?Newsid=4878

Hoffman, T. (1999). Are U.S. programmers slackers? *Computerworld*. Retrieved April 2005, from http://www.cnn.com/TECH/computing/9904/15/slacker.idg/

Huisman, S. (2005). *Student loan relief to be provided for math and science majors*. Retrieved April 20 2005, from http://www.collegiatetimes.com/newsadmin/printable.php?ID=5761

ITAA (2004a). Adding value... growing careers. Annual workforce development survey. *ITAA*. Retrieved April 2005, from www.itaa.org/workforce/studies/04wfstudy.pdf

ITAA (2004b). The employment outlook in today's increasingly competitive job market. *ITAA*. Retrieved April 2005, from http://www.itaa.org

Kerstetter, J. (2005). The shape of tech this year. *Business Week online*. Retrieved January,2005, from http://businessweek.com/technology/contents/jan2005

King, J. (1995). Stress rattles 'help!' desks. *Computerworld*. Retrieved 1995 from http://static.highbeam.com/c/computerworld/march131995/stressrattleshelpdesk/index.html

Luftman, J. (2005). Key issues for IT executives 2004. *MIS Quarterly Executive, 4*(2), 269-286.

Luftman, J. (2005a). *SIMposium 2005*. SIMPosium CIO Executive Summit, Boston.

Luftman, J., & McLean, A. (2004). Key issues for IT executives. *MIS Quarterly Executive, 3*(2).

McCall, T. (2005). *Gartner people 3 says organizations must implement a workforce planning process to address looming IT workforce shortage*. Retrieved April 2005, from www.gartner.com/press_releases/asset_119845_11.html

McCarthy, J. (2004, June). 2004 Info world compensation survey: What are you worth? *Info World*. Retrieved April 2005, from http://www.infoworld.com/article/04/06/11/24FEcompsurv_1.html

Moore, J. E. (2000). One road to turnover: An examination of work exhaustion in technology professionals. *MIS Quarterly, 24*(1), 141-148.

Mortleman, J. (2004). *IT staff skip holidays because of work pressure*. Retrieved March 2005, from http://www.vnunet.com/print/it/1156681

Passori, A. (2005). Some see sunny forecast for 2005. *META Group Research*. Retrieved February 2005, from http://www.metagroup.com/us/displayArticle.do?oid=51446

Robb, D. (2005). *Will fewer computer students hurt U.S. IT market?* Retrieved March 2005, from http://itmangement.earthweb.com/career/print.php/3488816

Robert, H. (2000). Is it Friday yet? *Robert Half Technology.* Retrieved April 2005, from http://www.roberthalftechnology.com/PressRoom? LOB Name=RHIC&releaseid=113

Sethi, V., King, R., & Campbell, J (2004). What causes stress in Information system professionals? *Communications of ACM, 47.*

Snell, A. (2003). *Website research is going global.* Retrieved March 2005, from http://www.ilogos.com/en/expertviews/articles/careers/20010703_AS.html

Southgate, D. (2002). *Four ways to find IT talent—and the costs.* Retrieved March 2005, from http://www.davidsouthgate.com/020501.shtml

Surmacz, J. (2004). *Turnover is expensive.* Retrieved March 2005, from http://www.cio.com/archive/061504/tl_numbers.html

Swoyer, S. (2005). Careers: IT salaries fell, IT budgets rebounded in 2004. *Enterprise Systems.* Retrieved March 2005, from http://www.esj.com/news/print.aspx?editorialsId=1244

USBL (2003). Education and training, US Bureau of Labor Statistics. Retrieved March 2005, from http://www.bls.gov/oco/oco2003.htm

USBL (2005). Career Guide to Industries 2004-05, US Bureau of labor statistics. Retrieved March 2005, from http://www.bls.gov/

Zawacki, R. (2004). Zawacki and Associates, Colorado Springs.

Zoufaly, F. (2002). *Issues and challenges facing legacy systems.* Retrieved April 2005, from http://www.developer.com/mgmt/article.php/1492531

Chapter IX

Increasing the Effectiveness of IT Management through Psychological Awareness

Eugene Kaluzniacky, University of Winnipeg, Canada

Abstract

Largely because of the potential for Internet connectivity, the area of electronic commerce has been proliferating since the start of the century. In this context, IT professionals are being counted on to provide central and impactful systems with a capacity for competitive advantage. In other areas of intense IT usage, we have also seen increasing emphasis on systems with critical impact. There is a need to be original and creative, yet precise and timely. The more IT workers produce, the more is demanded of them. A number of sources are highlighting the reality of impending and widespread IT burnout. Thus, IT management is faced with the imperative of eliciting high-quality work from an overburdened workforce. To aid in this endeavor, it is here suggested that development of multi-dimensional psychological awareness among those managing and those managed be given serious consideration.

This chapter outlines three main areas of psychological awareness: (1) personality type, (2) cognitive style, and (3) the deep inner self (leading to "emotional intelligence"). It points out how such awareness could contribute positively and significantly to IT management.

Involvement of Psychological Factors

"Efficiency" and "effectiveness," common management terms, are becoming undeniable imperatives in the work of an IT professional in the 21st century. At times, such imperatives are mandated by IT management seemingly "at any cost." This brute-force approach may lead to short-term gain, but will inevitably result in considerable, perhaps largely unanticipated long-term pain for all involved. Is there another way to motivate and to succeed?

Albert Einstein is credited with asserting that a problem cannot be solved effectively at the same level of awareness at which the problem was created. Growth in awareness is necessary. What might this mean to the overburdened IT worker and his impatient, and often perplexed manager?

Over twenty years ago, U.S. researchers Couger and Zawacki (1980) reported that, while IS professionals (systems analysts and programmers) had the lowest needs for social interaction on the job, they reported much higher "growth needs" than the other professionals surveyed. While, at the time, growth needs were largely understood as greater development of professional competencies, might the IT profession now be ready for a more holistic approach to growth?

Just as an Olympic athlete might assimilate useful insights from nutrition, biochemistry, kinesiology, psychology, and philosophy to deliver an optimum performance, so might the modern IT professional examine the possible impact of different dimensions of psychological awareness on his or her daily work. Recent IT textbooks have confirmed the view that IT (and IS development in particular) is a *socio-technical* field and have promoted the development of "soft skills." Yet the profession as a whole, as well as its academic MIS counterpart, has, at best, "scratched the surface" of applying psychological awareness comprehensively and purposefully in the course of IT work.

At best (with notable exceptions), one or two personality type workshops have typically been arranged by IT management for their subordinates, leaving the participants to "sort it out for themselves" as to if and how they would use the gained insight in the course of their daily work. Little concerted effort has expended on relating, for example, specific personality and cognition dimensions to *specific tasks* in system development (e.g., data modeling, GUI design).

Moreover, hardly any such observations have been systematically journalized for widespread distribution.

It is hypothesized here that as an IT professional becomes more explicitly aware of his own inner psychological dynamisms and of those of the persons with / for whom he works, he will be able to harness his inner, intellectual/psychological work resources much more effectively resulting in the mandated efficiency and effectiveness and in a significant decrease in work stress.

While not many IT managers would perhaps argue vociferously with the above hypothesis, it is, at this point in IT's development, quite likely that not many would "dive in" immediately and initiate a large-scale program of comprehensive psychological awareness among their staff. Widespread, convincing, "bottom-line" results are not yet available to catalyze such initiatives on a broad basis. Thus, at this point in the history of MIS, the situation lends itself to more concerted interdisciplinary research as to specific benefits of involving psychological factors.

To this end, the chapter outlines several psychological dimensions that may be worthy of consideration for MIS, presents highlights of existing studies and applications and suggests areas for further research, whether by an "objective" academic or a motivated practitioner engaged in action research. Psychological dimensions addressed in this context include a personality system, cognitive style considerations and the emerging promotion of the "deepest inner self" as the foundation for "emotional intelligence."

Personality Awareness: Myers-Briggs

Personality can be defined as "a complex set of relatively stable behavioral and emotional characteristics" of a person (Hohmann, 1997). It refers to, essentially, how a person functions in life. Most of us, even without any training in this area, will recognize that the world consists of people of different types. We notice that people of different types will often react differently to the same situation. But, is this an issue that is closely connected to IT work? It depends on the factors of which the work consists. For example, most would agree that personality relates to communication, learning style and to what one finds stressful.

The Myers-Briggs personality type approach to classifying personalities has been widely accepted an applied in a diversity of fields such as social work, counseling, career planning and management (Keirsey & Bates, 1978). It assesses four different dimensions of a person:

1.   **Introversion/extraversion:** Relates to *how a person is oriented*, where he/she focuses more easily; within oneself or on other people and the surrounding environment. This dimension is coded I or E respectively.

2.   **Intuition/sensing:** Relates to two different *ways of perceiving*, of taking in information. An intuitive person focuses on new possibilities, hidden meanings, and perceived patterns. A sensing person focuses on the real, tangible, and factual aspects. Thus a sensing person can be described as being more practical, whereas an intuitive is more imaginary. This dimension is coded N for intuitive and S for sensing.

3.   **Thinking/feeling:** Relates to *how a person comes to conclusions*, how a person normally prefers to make judgments. A thinking person employs logical analysis, using objective and impersonal criteria to make decisions. A feeling person, on the other hand, uses person-centered values and motives to make decisions. This dimension is coded T for thinking and F for feeling.

4.   **Judging/perceiving:** Relates to two essential *attitudes of dealing with one's environment*. A judging person prefers to make judgments, or come to conclusions about what one encounters in one's outer environment. A perceiving person prefers to notice one's outer environment while not coming to conclusions or judgments about it. This dimension is coded J for judging and P for perceiving.

Thus, we see how the Myers-Briggs personality classification system identifies personality according to four dimensions. Since there are two possibilities for each dimension, there are sixteen different Myers-Briggs personality types. Elaborating on the four dimensions, Extraversion/introversion refers to where a person gets most psychological energy. Sensing/intuition points out to what a person pays most attention. Thinking/feeling shows how a person prefers to make decisions, and Judging/perceiving relates to a preferred attitude to life.

There is considerable documentation outlining general work characteristics of each Myers-Briggs dimension. Many of these modes of operation can have significant relevance to system development work. Some highlights from this area are now presented.

Myers-Briggs in IT

The Myers-Briggs type indicator (MBTI) had made its way into IT over 15 years ago. In "The DP Psyche" (Datamation, 1985), Michael Lyons reports on an international survey of personalities of over 1000 professionals employed by over

100 different companies. About one-third of those surveyed were employed as programmers or analysts, and about 20% were in IS management. Table 1 shows the breakdown along the four MBTI dimensions. We notice twice as many introverts as extraverts, slightly more intuitives than sensing people, a very high percentage (80-90%) of thinking types and a two-to-one ratio of judging to perceiving types.

We now examine the main characteristics of each of the four dimensions as they could relate to IT work.

Extraversion/Introversion (E/I)

While there clearly is room for both extraverts and introverts in systems development, it is not surprising to see a 2:1 ratio of introverts: extraverts. Tasks such as detailed data modeling, coding, quality assurance testing and network design can lend themselves quite well to preferred introversion. However, extraverts can feel especially at home in requirements determination, joint application development, presentation to users/senior management, user training, and help desk activities, for example.

Sensing/Intuition (S/N)

The clear distinction here is "reality thinking" vs. "possibility thinking." A considerable amount of system development activity definitely fits with and appeals to the practical, details-and-facts-oriented sensing mentality. Much of actual technology is practical and activities such as system installation, detailed telecommunication design, physical data modeling, as well as programming, testing, activity scheduling, and detailed documentation would appeal to and energize the sensing person.

However, there are certainly more conceptual aspects to system development, some more structured and others more open-ended. Activities such as system

Table 1. Breakdown by personality dimension of 1229 system development professionals (Lyons' Datamation Study)

Introverts:	67%	Intuitives:	54%
Extraverts:	33%	Sensors:	46%
Thinkers:	81%	Judgers:	66%
Feelers:	19%	Perceivers:	34%

planning, high-level business and data modeling, object modeling, and political "positioning," would be much more in the realm of intuitive types. Since there is considerable opportunity for both sensors and intuitives to find IT work appealing, in Lyons' survey we find the most balance along sensing/intuitive lines (46% S to 54% N).

Thinking/Feeling (T/F)

We recall that while both types certainly think and feel, the thinking types prefer to decide with logical analysis while feelers tend to base decisions on personal values and feelings. Considerable IS development activity, no doubt, involves the thinking function, whether it be practical thinking (as in telecommunication design or testing) or conceptual thinking (object modeling, system planning). Often, the thinking must be structured and yield specific deliverables that can execute on specific machines. But, how can feeling types find a home in IT work?

Since they place considerable focus on harmony, feelers can be particularly sought after as group/team leaders, high-level business modelers, or analysts, where considerable effective interaction with non-IT staff is essential. Feelers may become prominent IS "politicians" who can forge effective relationships with others in organizations. They can also contribute innovatively and effectively in development of training materials and in the training process itself. As systems move towards integration of a variety of communication modes through multimedia and Internet access, the contribution of artistically minded feelers will be increasingly desirable. It is worth pointing out that an "F" is a person who *prefers* to decide from personal values, but he or she may be more capable or less so in exercising the logical thinking function when it is called for. Most Fs in IT however, would need to possess a well-developed capacity for thinking. Lyons' study showed an overwhelming proportion (80.9%) of thinking types. Later, we will see evidence that such significant dominance may slowly be changing.

Judging/Perceiving (J/P)

This dimension relates to the need for order, structure, and closure in one's life and work. Computing itself is largely structured with emphasis on precision. Thus procedural language programming, for example, would be ideal for a Judging orientation as would be detailed telecommunication design. Yet, there certainly are activities in the development and maintenance of systems where too much structure and predictability would not be desirable. System planning and brainstorming, for example, thrive on flexibility and spontaneity. Business and data modeling for a new system also mandate adaptability and flexibility. Maintenance and help-desk work is often unpredictable and varied. Lyons' study shows an almost 2:1 ratio of judging to perceiving types. This reflects a large reliance on structure but admits open-endedness as a preference in one-third of the sample.

We thus see that each part of each Myers-Briggs dimension has a role to play in system development work. In this field, it is beneficial if the individual is flexible, and has developed considerable strength in the areas which are not his/her preference. Also, it is very desirable to have a variety of personalities in various facets of system development.

Research on MBTI in IS

Lyons' research, introduced earlier, has brought out several noteworthy points:

- R&D organizations and firms that do a lot of state-of-the-art development attract and hire more Ns than Ss
- A great many of the communication difficulties experienced on the job are based on the S-N difference
- A difference in J-P attitude is second only to an S-N difference in causing communication problems
- Feeling is an especially appropriate judging process when dealing with people and it can be very helpful in supervisory and management positions
- It is almost always good to have some diversity on the team in terms of psychological types

A second research effort is that of Thomsett (1990). His focus is more directly on effective IS project teams. He reports figures for 656 IS professionals in Australia, where 63% of them are of types STJ. His research team had applied MBTI along with two other instruments, the Job Diagnostic Model and the Belbin Team Role Model in an IS team context within an organization with over 200 computer and related specialists. *Immediate productivity increases of 200% have been reported by the senior management of the computing group.* Such results cannot be ignored!

More involved academic research involving MBTI and information systems had been carried out by Kathy Brittain White. In one study (1984), White compared two IS project teams that were given the same assignment involving the same user. One team was composed of all thinkers while the other contained 50%

feelers. The all-thinker team did not produce a successful system. The system that this team produced did not meet the needs of the users. Also, communication with the users during system development was lacking. The developers spoke in overly technical language. With the 50% feeler team, the users expressed satisfaction both with the developed system and with the development process itself. They felt that this team was indeed concerned with their needs. Such an experience is consistent with type theory.

In another study (1984), White's results indicated that the MB types of team members and task structure both impact team effectiveness. White found that heterogeneity of types is best for solving unstructured tasks, but such diversity of types could be counter-productive in solving structured tasks. Her findings also indicated that one team might not be appropriate for all the stages of a project. In yet another study, White contends that "personnel awareness training can enhance change management and increase productivity."

Another noteworthy research effort is that of Kaiser and Bostrom (1982). The researchers note that personality characteristics of individuals involved in systems development impact the way these developers perceive the organization, organizational members, and the function of information systems. They also suggest that *system design reflects the design team's personality styles*. In addition, they comment that feelers were often missing from teams that were involved in project failure.

Joy Teague of Deaken University in Australia (1998) has hypothesized which personality types would be best suited to each of analysis, design, and programming. She proposed NTs (intuitive thinkers) and NFs (intuitive feelers) for analysis, NTs for early design stages and SJs for latter design stages with ISTJs for programming.

She then presented statistics from a survey of 38 computer professionals who were MB-typed and asked to rank their preference for analysis, design, and programming. Proposed personality characteristics were then compared with observed results. Eighty-five percent of the people who preferred analysis were NTs or NFs. For design, 50% were NTs 17% were SJs and 17% SPs, with 17% NFs; Among programmers, 42% were SJs, 17% SPs, 17% NFs, and 25% NTs. Although the sample was rather small, the study did address an important question: *the issue of different types being suited to different tasks.*

Noted IT consultant and educator Edward Youndon (1993) has also referred to MBTI in IT. He quotes a seminar participant "simply *knowing* the roles and the personality types makes everyone much more sensitive and aware of the team's strengths and weaknesses" and then asserts, "The world-class software organizations are, at the very least, *aware* of these team-role and performance management issues (e.g., personality awareness). The aggressive ones are providing training to their professional staff in these areas, and the very best have added professional experts—for example, industrial psychologists—to their staff of consultants and advisors."

The previous references to IT research involving MBTI are by no means exhaustive. However, they do indicate a level of acceptability for this personality system within the IT area. As well, the research has produced noteworthy results, which can have a significant influence on system development work.

Four Temperaments

Psychologist David Keirsey (1978) identified four *temperaments* which can be derived from the 16 MBTI types: Promethean (Rational) – NT; Apollonian (Idealist) – NF; Epimethean (Guardian) – SJ; and Dionysian (Artisan) – SP. Thus, each of the 16 types belongs to one and only one temperament. There are specific life attitudes particular to each temperament and, of course, these attitudes are carried into the work environment.

The Guardian comprises about 38% of the U.S. population. A person of this type longs for duty and exists primarily *to be useful* to society. The SJ must belong and this belonging has to be earned. He has a belief in and a desire for hierarchy. The SJ is "the foundation, cornerstone, flywheel and stabilizer of society." This is the conservative traditionalist. As we have seen earlier, SJs make up the largest fraction of IT professionals.

The Rational is found in about 12% of the U.S. population. The NT values competence and loves intelligence. He wants to be able to understand, control, predict, and explore realities. He often seeks to study the sciences, mathematics and engineering—what is complicated and exacting. NTs tend to live in their work and to focus on the future, having a gift for the abstract. They have the capacity to think strategically and to develop visions of the future. They work on ideas with ingenuity and logic. They can be self-critical, perfectionistic and can become tense and compulsive when under too much stress.

The Artisan is found in about 38% of the U.S. population. She is impulsive, living for the moment, wishing to be free, not tied down or confined. She has a hunger for action in the here and now. SPs are spontaneous, optimistic, and cheerful. They thrive on variety, and can be easily bored with the status quo. They also have a remarkable ability to survive setbacks.

The Idealist is found in about 12% of the U.S. population. She is the deepest feeling person of all types and values deep meaning in life. The main need of this type is authenticity to one's deepest self. NFs speak and write fluently, often with poetic flair. They seek interaction and relationships. They enjoy bringing out the best in other people. NFs work towards a vision of perfection and can be unreasonably demanding on themselves and others.

In certain situations, 16 MBTI types may be considered too many. The four derived temperaments, each consisting of four MBTI types, thus offer a more aggregated approach, which nonetheless highlights key differences among people.

As we consider the key strengths of each temperament: NT – vision, competence, abstraction; SJ – detail, practicality, facts, organization; SP – spontaneity, practicality and NF – authenticity, relatedness, we see readily that each of these strengths is very welcome in the systems profession. Information systems development comprises a variety of activities and tasks, and the strengths of the different temperaments are instrumental in these different tasks.

Temperaments in IS Work

Table 2 shows temperament frequencies in the three surveys: the ones by Lyons and Thomsett, mentioned earlier, as well as a survey of my own undergraduate business computing students at the University of Winnipeg. In two of the surveys, the SJ-Guardian temperament is overwhelmingly the most frequent, with the NT-Rational in second place. In the other survey (by Lyons) the NT slightly outnumbers the SJ. In all three surveys, the frequency of SPs and NFs together was under 22%.

Once we consider the issue of the task-temperament match in more depth, we begin to appreciate that literacy in this area can indeed have an impact on the workers' energy and productivity. Detailed work in *attempting to link specific system development tasks with temperaments* have been done by Patricia Ferdinandi of Strategic Business Divisions in the U.S. or challenge this information.

Table 3 is reproduced from her insightful article (*Software Development*, 1994).

Although the identified connections are hypothesized by the author, they are made with an extensive awareness of both task and type. It is a call to MIS researchers to corroborate or challenge this information.

Table 2. Temperaments in three surveys

	Lyons	Thomsett	Kaluzniacky
NT	40.7%	14.8%	21.1%
NF	12.1	8.7	6.0
SJ	36.9	73.1	64.5
SP	10.3	3.3	7.5

Table 3. Matching task to type (From Ferdinandi)

Task or Function	Preference/Temperament
Identify the scope of the project	Intuitive, Thinking/Rational
Define the current process	Sensing/Guardian
Facilitation/JAD session leaders	Intuitive, Thinking/Idealist, Rational
Planning and architecture	Intuitive/Rational
Project-planning tracking	Sensing, Thinking, Judging/Guardian
Establishing business policy	Intuitive, Thinking, Judging/Rational
Essential business model	Intuitive/Rational, Idealist
Technology model	Sensing/Guardian, Artisan
Programming, testing, problem solving	Sensing, Perceiving/Artisan
Installation	Sensing/Artisan, Guardian
Organization and motivation	Feeling/Idealist
Network and communication design	Sensing/Artisan, Guardian
Entitity Relationship model	Intuitive/Rational, Idealist
Logical data model	Intuitive/Idealist, Rational
Physical data model	Sensing/Guardian, Artisan
Data repository management	Sensing, Judging/Guardian
Brainstorming	Intuitive, Perceiving/Idealist, Rational
Structure diagram or charts	Sensing, Judging/Guardian
State transition diagrams	Sensing/Artisan, Guardian
User acceptance criteria	Sensing, Feeling/Guardian
Procedure manual	Sensing, Judging/Guardian
Training manual	Intuitive, Feeling/Idealist
Mini specifications	Sensing, Judging/Guardian
Scribe	Sensing, Judging/Guardian
Identifying objects or entities	Intuitive/Idealist, Rational
Identifying methods or processes	Intuitive/Rational, Idealist

Applications in IT Practice

MBTI has been widely accepted in the area of general management. Thus, many organizations have been bringing in consultants for a half-day or one-day workshop. In some cases, a follow-up workshop may be held some time later. IT professionals have, in many cases, been included in such workshops and have thus been introduced to personality type concepts. However, often there has been little follow-up to an initial workshop and the typical IT worker may have benefited only marginally from initial exposure.

However, there are indeed situations in IT where MBTI was accepted more seriously with impactful results. At Corning, Inc., MBTI has been used more extensively, particularly in relation to teams. After initial introduction to MB type, the IT staff go through four-hour training sessions that have participants play roles, solve hypothetical problems, and listen to one another.

For example, they may gather all NFs in one group and SJs in another and have the two groups solve the same system development problem. Then each group shares with the other how it solved the problem (i.e., what steps it took). These steps are then related to MB concepts. *This is a prime example of psychological awareness education in the IT area.* Such heightened awareness has increased trust among Corning's team members, since they are aware of each other's perceptual differences and are not as likely to be intimidated by them.

Another significant application of MBTI occurred more recently at IBM, as part of their Team Pac program, used to train teams. MBTI was chosen as the personality component of the program because it had (1) acceptable validity studies and documentation, (2) books and conferences where people could learn more about type, (3) a self-scoring version for easy administration, (4) considerable acceptance in the business world.

There were 26 topics selected for Team Pac and of those, three topics related well with MBTI—the three related to group work stages. Thus, IBM created three separate modules, each about four hours long.

The first module introduces type differences and gives participants exercises to understand each of the four dimensions. Then, the members respond to a series of teamwork dilemmas. This module ends with formation of a plan of action as to how this team will work with its differences.

The second module looks at the function pairs ST, SF, NT, NF, since these are seen as influencing communication the most. People examine their communication styles and each person practices communicating with someone of another type. Then the participants are shown how famous business decisions were made and which of the function pairs were used in making them.

The third module examines leadership and learning styles based on the four Kersey temperaments. Team members' leadership preferences are related to the leader's temperament.

IBM finds that having three modules is effective, since people have time to absorb basic information and only then get into more depth: In just over three years, more than 30,000 booklets of the Team Pac materials for the MBTI modules have been used.

Such an extensive and focused application of MBTI is encouraging. The use of MB in the IT area may, at some point, need to be assessed through a maturity stages model. Many organizations have yet to introduce it, some have introduced it, but have left any follow-up to the individuals themselves, and a few, like IBM, have taken MBTI involvement to another level of maturity. It is likely, though, that unless type awareness is an ongoing effort in the IT environment, it will not realize its true potential.

Yet another noteworthy application has occurred at Hewlett-Packard in California. A team was created to implement SAP enterprise resource software. Considerable time was spent at the start examining communication and personality dynamics on the team. At first, team members were skeptical about investing such a significant amount of time on "touchy, feely stuff." But, as the group gelled, the people realized that they did not lose days, but actually gained weeks. *One HP manager commented that, for them, Myers-Briggs was a turning point*! Team members realized that "diversity and differences are what made the team successful in the first place."

The two most highlighted uses of MBTI in systems development relate to *teams* and *tasks*. In teamwork, it is important to be conscious of the reality that what energizes one person actually drains another, decreasing the person's effectiveness, productivity, and motivation. As a concrete example, two analysts at a finance company, one an ISTJ and the other an ISTP, were asked what stresses them most in the course of their daily work. The ISTJ replied that she was really stressed when she had a number of different projects to work on simultaneously. She would have much preferred to complete one item of work, put it away, and then start on another. The ISTP, on the other hand, indicated that she felt very much stressed when she was working on one thing too long. She actually needed to be working on several items at once and likely switching from one to the other spontaneously.

The above story is very significant not only because it is true and agrees with type theory but it is noteworthy above all because it shows *how the work energy of the different types, if not harnessed properly by psychologically aware IT management, will largely be wasted.*

In teamwork, therefore, assigning tasks to people naturally suited for them is a primary issue. Following this is the need to balance teams such that each member's energy is utilized as functionally as possible. Such an orientation requires considerable awareness on the part of team members and managers as well as deepened trust, in order for team members to be open enough to discuss genuinely their strengths, weakness, and occasions of drained energy.

The Myers-Briggs personality system and its derived Keirsey temperaments is a psychological factor that has already entered the IT field. Promising research results and initial but impactful applications seem to be reason enough to promote further consideration and in both research and practice.

Cognition Awareness

While personality relates to one's behaviour as a whole, *cognitive function* relates more explicitly to mental information processing. Since the majority of system development work and IT work in general involves intellectual functioning, it is not difficult to see that how a person performs "mind work" is a relevant psychological factor in IT work. In fact, it is in the area of cognition that a majority of psychological research in computing/information systems has been carried out.

According to Hayes and Allinson (1998), cognitive style is "a person's preferred way of gathering, processing, and evaluating information." Streufert and Nogami (1989) identify cognitive style as a pervasive personality variable. It influences what information in one's environment a person focuses on and how he/she interprets this information.

One main way of dichotomizing cognitive functioning is the *analytic, sequential* vs. *intuitive, holistic* functioning. Some psychologists have referred to the former as "left-brain thinking" and the latter "right-brain thinking" (although other scholars may consider this an oversimplification). The former focuses on "trees" and the latter sees the "forest" in solving problems and coming to conclusions. There are suggestions that link MBTI temperaments with the two predominant cognitive styles. Huitt (1992) identifies NTs and SJs as more linear and serial, and NFs and SPs as more holistic and intuitive.

We have all likely seen classic examples of each style, either at work or elsewhere. The analytical person abstracts, analyzes structures, organizes, and plans systematically. He can articulate clearly and may focus on details. However, he can miss "intangible clues" such as facial expressions or other "body language." He may also be criticized for being bureaucratic with limited imagination.

The intuitive person integrates many perspectives, finds problems and discovers opportunities and generates new visions. She is sensitive to both logical and emotional issues, viewing them as one. However, she may overlook important details, may not communicate precisely enough, and may put off decisions.

The analytic is like a tax lawyer, the intuitive, like a criminal lawyer; the analytic like an accountant or chemist, the intuitive like an athlete or artist; the analytic prides himself on intellectual rigor, the intuitive on imagination. As with personalities, most people may not fall exactly into two opposing "boxes"; however, there appears to be a definite preference in one direction.

The Adaptor-Innovator

One of the main theories on cognitive styles, along with an instrument to evaluate the style is the Kirton adaptation/innovation theory. This theory of cognitive strategy relates to the amount of structure that a person feels appropriate within which to solve a problem or to embark on creativity.

The Adaptor (left-brained) prefers to work within current paradigms; focussing on *doing things better* while the Innovator (right-brained) prefers to "colour outside the lines," constructing new paradigms, focussing on *doing things differently*. According to psychologist/consultant Michael Kirton (1989), the Adaptor favors precision, reliability, efficiency, prudence, discipline, and conformity. He seeks solutions in "tried and true" ways, seeks improvement and efficiency and rarely challenges rules. He is seen as sound, dependable, safe, and conforming and is an authority within given structure.

The Innovator, on the other hand, cuts across and often invents new paradigms. He is more interdisciplinary, approaches tasks from unsuspected angles, and often treats accepted means with little regard. He tends to take control in unstructured situations, but is usually capable of detailed routine work for only short bursts of time. While an Adaptor has higher self-doubt and is vulnerable to social pressure and authority, an Innovator does not need consensus to maintain confidence in face of opposition.

To distinguish Adaptors from Innovators, Kirton developed the Kirton adaptation/innovation inventory (KAI), a questionnaire consisting of 32 items, each scored from 1 to 5. KAI scores thus range from 32 for a pure Adaptor to 160 for a pure Innovator The stability of the KAI has been observed over time and culture; it may be measured adequately even early in a person's life. KAI distributions for general population samples from six countries conformed almost exactly to the normal curve with a mean of just above 94 (where the theoretical mean would be 96) (Kirton, 1989). KAI scores did not correlate significantly with IQ, achievement, or creativity tests. This emphasizes that KAI is a measure of cognitive/creativity *style* rather than *capacity*.

Cognitive Style in IT

It is not difficult to realize that there will be both Adaptors and Innovators in the IT profession. It is also easy to see that each style, if properly harnessed and managed, will provide significant contributions to the development and implementation of information systems, particularly Web-based multimedia applications.

The late researcher Dan Couger (1996) applied KAI to a representative sample of IS professionals and found that most were inclined to the Adaptive rather than the Innovative style. This would agree with the preponderance of SJ temperaments in IS. In this situation, however, many IT organizations will develop Adaptor managers who prefer the Adaptor (analytic) style. Valuable contributions from talented Innovators may be ignored or discouraged. This may indeed be dangerous in an area where paradigm changes are paramount.

In Kirton's book, we see a consulting case where an international oil company was experiencing a conflict between two department managers and their senior analyst. The managers required that the analyst's work tie in directly to the business plan and not deviate from the established "business climate"; he had to establish credibility with other managers. The analyst accused the managers of being shortsighted and not perceiving the future patterns of business nor preparing adequately for this. When the three took the KAI, the managers averaged 86 and the analyst 117. Eventually, the analyst decided to seek employment elsewhere (Kirton, 1989). Anecdotal reports suggest that the difference of more than one standard deviation in KAI scores may cause significant problems in employee communication. Again, for the IT professional, the key is awareness.

In IS development, there are tasks that require applying established technologies to new situations (adapting) and others that benefit from entirely new approaches. The latter can usually enhance competitive advantage. However, according to MIS researcher Michael Epstein, "the need to integrate the mechanistic logic of computers with the ambiguous nature of living human systems remain fundamental to the successful design and implementation of computer-based information systems" (1996). Thus, the mature IS developer will increasingly need to combine both views consciously and effectively. Moreover, it is not only a matter of "system" issues requiring an analytic approach and "people" issues requiring the integrative, holistic perspective. "Right-brain" contribution can indeed be significant in specific areas of analysis, design, and development. Design of user interface and Web pages, as well as multimedia components, clarifying and improving upon user-identified system requirements, process re-engineering for ERP implementation and identification of domain objects can all benefit significantly from a thinking process that is intuitive and innovative. It remains for interdisciplinary IT research to identify more specifically *how* such "right-brained" efforts complement the traditionally accepted analytic approaches to IS development.

To gain practical insight into the issue of thinking style in IT, one can consider some significant developments in applied computing and hypothesize which style may have contributed most in each case. For example, the concepts of CASE tools or ERP systems may well have resulted from a more traditional, analytic style. CASE mainly automates and integrates existing approaches to system development; thus, the CASE concept is an extension of an existing paradigm. Similarly, Enterprise Resource Planning systems are a large-scale adaptation of previously existing smaller integrated business applications.

However, the OO paradigm is likely the result of the innovative, intuitive thinking style—it models data and related processes in an entirely new way. Such an intuitive style may also be responsible for innovative ways in assisting system users, for example the recording by an EIS of which screens an executive uses most often. Also, considering that system development efforts are often initiated by problems and opportunities, it is quite possible that while "left-brain" thinking can address existing problems adequately, it is the "right-brain" approach that can capitalize on new opportunities from an IT perspective.

With the scope of information systems continually and rapidly expanding, the many problems to be solved and decisions to be made will no doubt benefit from a functional, conscious synergy among workers with differing styles. Huitt (1992) stated a researcher's opinion that "the problem solving techniques…are most powerful when combined to activate both the logical/rational and intuitive/creative parts of the brain." Agor (1991) stated emphatically that "it is of great concern today that organizations often thwart, block, or drive out intuitive talent," and also "organizations typically know their personnel by formal job title, responsibility, or years of experience—seldom do they know which brain skills are possessed that can be applied to difficult problems." Undoubtedly, the latter comment applies quite directly to most IT organizations.

Noteworthy Research

The issue of cognitive style in IT has been one of the more researched psychological factors. Regarding information processing in general, Churchman and Schainblatt (1965) and then Huysmans (1970) suggested that individuals may ignore information presented in a format that does not fit their cognitive style. Applying this insight to IT, Mason and Mitroff (1973) emphasized the importance for IS developers to consider the user's cognitive style. They advised, "with some imagination and creativity, designers should be able to give each manager the kind of information systems he or she is psychologically attuned to and will use most effectively."

Bariff and Lusk (1977) also advised that "the successful development and implementation of an information system should explicitly involve consideration of the psychological disposition of the system's user." They recommended that designers "match report content, format, and presentation mode with the user's psychological structure." They suggested that the use of psychological tests with recognized validity and reliability to evaluate user cognition represents a step toward a more systematic basis of MIS design.

A strong scholarly contribution during the initial years of connecting cognitive style to IS design was made by Benbasat and Taylor (1978). They stated emphatically "the human decision-maker must be included in any complete analysis of MIS design since he is the user of the information or output of the system." However, they added "cognitive styles represent only some of the characteristics of information system users which may influence MIS design. Characteristics such as intellectual ability, attitudes, demographics (age, education, etc.) and cultural background would also be expected to figure prominently in MIS design." They present Witkin's definition of cognitive styles as "... characteristic modes of functioning that we show throughout our perceptive and intellectual activities in a highly consistent and pervasive way," and consider such styles as "promising variables" which "appear central to MIS design."

Benbasat and Taylor further commented on the lack of a uniform measure or classification for cognitive style. In addition to the analytic-intuitive classification, they present those of cognitive complexity and field dependence-independence. The authors point out that cognitive complexity deals with differentiation, the number of dimensions extracted from the data, articulation—fineness of discrimination and integration—complexity of the rules used to combine data. This approach to assessing cognitive style relates to both the amount of information decision makers tend to use and the degree of focusing in the use of data they exhibit.

A cognitive style that measures field dependence-independence has been developed by Witkin (1971) and can be assessed by the *Witkin Embedded Figures Test*. The central characteristic here is the ability to overcome the influence of an embedding context. The field-dependent does not easily separate parts from their context, he looks at the totality of the situation (e.g., not separating a person's words from her facial expression). The field-independent can separate parts from their context (e.g., may consider words but not body language). The former style parallels with the intuitive and the latter with the analytic.

Looking at cognitive style based on an analytic vs. heuristic (intuitive) approach, the researchers referred to other studies that showed analytic decision makers preferring reports that have formulas embedded in the text and are quantitative. They then identified a challenge for the MIS designer—to find some kind of decision aid to help the problem-solving task of the heuristic decision maker. They also pointed out that heuristic decision makers need to have more data search capabilities prior to reaching decisions. Since they rely on trial and error, a system capability that can show trends and period-by-period comparisons would suit such individuals.

Finally, Benbasat and Taylor suggested that the systems analyst broaden his perspectives to better satisfy the psychological needs of the user-managers. They also proposed that the analysts *develop cognitive style profiles of their system users*, either by informal interviews or by using established psychological tests.

An important question that arises here in the mind of the reader of this chapter is how would one accommodate different cognitive styles of users of the same system. Options would need to be presented to users. But, how many options, and at what points in the system? Nonetheless, the work above certainly legitimized concerns regarding cognitive style in MIS research.

Davis and Elnicki (1984), in their paper "User cognitive types for decision support systems" emphasized that a decision support system needs to communicate information to a decision maker in a style that is congruent with the decision maker's decision process. They conducted exploratory research experiments on 96 MBA students regarding the use of a system to support production management decisions. They used the Myers-Briggs indicator to identify four cognitive types: NT (intuitive thinker), NF (intuitive feeler), ST (sensing thinker) and SF (sensing feeler). They found that ST managers would improve performance with graphical, raw data reports; SF managers would appreciate tabular raw or tabular summarized data, NT managers would synergize with tabular raw data while NFs would relate most to graphical, raw data reports. In their experiments, the authors identified three performance measures: time taken to make the decision since receiving the report, user confidence in this decision, as self-reported on a scale of 1-10, and cost incurred as result of each of the production decisions.

Although their work did show a connection between cognitive style of the user-manager and the type of information best suited for effective semi-structured decisions, the authors categorized their research as "exploratory." They also stated that "no methodology presently exists for implementing system design with cognitive type." Furthermore, in discussing prior research, the authors indicated that "experimental results on the effects of report format and level of data summarization have not been consistent." They point out, for example, that Amador (1977) and also Lusk and Kersnick (1979) had found that users with a tabular report format performed significantly better than those with a graphical report. However, Benbasat and Schroeder (1977) found the opposite effect on performance.

A damper on the enthusiasm for cognitive style research was provided by the "sobering" article by Huber (1983), "Cognitive style as basis for MIS/DSS design—Much ado about nothing?" Noting inconclusive research results, Huber questioned the need for the analyst to concern himself explicitly with users' cognitive styles. One could introduce enough reporting/usage flexibility in information and decision support systems that users would select preferred ways of using the system without either analyst or user being explicitly aware of cognitive style.

Huber also cautioned that fitting DSS to user styles may actually reinforce cognitive bias in the decision makers. This, however, begs the question "do not all decision makers possess some type of cognitive bias?" As well, Huber observed that "the currently available literature on cognitive styles is an unsatisfactory basis for deriving operational guidelines for MIS and DSS designs." At that point, research had been done, but there was little that could appreciably influence the daily work of an IS professional.

While most of the literature cited above applies cognitive style exclusively to the user of information systems, Robey's article (1983) provided additional perspective. While he acknowledged the validity of Huber's concerns, he used those concerns as a catalyst for new insight. Firstly, he addressed the issue of the flexibility of DSS functioning and reporting options. Huber suggested that if DSS were to be made flexible enough, users would adapt this to their preferred way of use without explicit consideration of cognitive style on the part of the user or designer. However, Robey pointed out that in deciding on *possible alternatives* for the flexibility of a system, cognitive considerations could indeed contribute. Responding to Huber's concern of reinforcement of cognitive bias, Robey raised the possibility of using a DSS to *complement* the users preferred style, if the user could overcome a threshold resistance to using a system to which he is not accustomed. He suggested that managers, perhaps aided by personnel specialists, should conduct an ongoing study of their styles for a more complete awareness of how they make decisions.

In addition, Robey presented one very significant insight: cognitive style considerations will become more central as *we study the system design process itself* and the styles of not only the users but also the designers. In developing today's multifaceted, Internet-based business systems, might it not be indeed advantageous to use cognitive style consciousness among developers to enhance synergy and effectiveness on development teams? After Huber, Robey and others, a question of interest in the late '80s related to seeing whether, in a highly customizable system as to both interfaces and output, user cognitive style needs to be an explicit factor when designing such a system.

Tan and Lo (1991) presented empirical evidence from studying 160 senior administrators and their secretaries in an educational institution. They investigated whether after users' customizing an adaptable office automation system interface, user cognitive style was a factor in system success as perceived by the user.

The study did not find evidence that the cognitive styles of the users had any significant impact on the success of an OA system that had its user interfaces customized to the user's requirements. Thus, the researchers concluded that, if the interface to an OA system can be customized, then system designers do not need to consider users' cognitive styles explicitly when they are designing the system. This is analogous to saying that, if enough food groups were placed on a banquet table, one would not specifically need to canvas the diet preferences of the attendees. However, is it possible that cognitive considerations may indeed assist designers in determining the types of options available for customization?

With somewhat inconclusive and possibly conflicting research results by the beginning of the '90s, we witness yet a new research slant in 1997 in the work of Spence and Tsai (1997). These researchers wondered whether a particular system user's cognitive style will remain the same over a variety of tasks and in a variety of environments (e.g., would the same person exhibit the same style in the task of assessing a room's suitability for a movie scene and assessing the room's need for a restructuring by carpentry, plastering, and painting). Thus, Spence and Tsai focus their attention on cognitive *processes* rather than on cognitive *style*. A cognitive process relates to the approaches used in sensing, concept formation, comprehension, problem solving, decision-making, research, composition and oral discourse (Marzano et al., 1988). A cognitive process, according to the authors, involves using a sequence of cognitive skills to process information. Thus, the *pattern* of skills characterizes the cognitive processes. The Marzano source identifies 21 cognitive skills, aggregated into the following categories: focusing, information gathering, remembering, organizing, analyzing, generating, integrating, and evaluating. For information processing and decision making, the higher the complexity, the more sub-tasks the decision maker must complete.

Using experiments with 101 volunteers, the researchers proposed that cognitive *style* has no impact on the cognitive *process* used during a decision making task whether the task be quantitative, qualitative, or if high or low complexity. Cognitive styles were considered as "analytic" for Myers-Briggs thinking types and as "non-analytic" for feeling types.

Results did not support the impact of cognitive *style* on an individual decision making *process*. Results suggested that "subjects with a particular cognitive style do not always use the same approach to solve problems." In the experiments, subjects changed their decision-making processes across four experimental tasks. Thus, it seems that the task influenced the processes rather than the cognitive style. Thus, the authors concluded "since cognitive style only indicates general traits of information-processing behaviour, cognitive style is neither appropriate nor useful in providing operational guidelines for IS design characteristics which are task based."

Clearly, more research along this line appears warranted, with experiments involving different tasks (planning, controlling, scheduling, etc.) and different information systems in various settings. Definitive conclusions certainly appear premature.

Most of the research outlined so far has concerned itself with cognitive style involved in using system output for decision-making. The output is usually that from traditional "reporting systems," although it may be presented in different forms and in different degrees of aggregation.

However, the scope of IS is broadening significantly with the availability of enabling technologies. In this context, new questions are being raised regarding cognitive style. Palmquist and Kim (2000) explored cognitive style related to efficient use of the Web. Their exploratory study aimed to investigate the effect of cognitive style and online database search experience on the World Wide Web search performance of 48 undergraduate college students. Cognitive style was classified as field-dependent or field-independent (we recall that the former, intuitive, takes in information while considering the context while the latter, analytic is more adept in abstracting the information from its context, for example, words may be assimilated without absorbing the body language). Earlier studies, for example, by Korthauer and Koubek (1994) and Ellis, Ford, and Wood (1993) had applied the FD/FI cognitive construct satisfactorily to hypermedia contexts. Web search performance was defined by (1) time required for retrieving required information and (2) the number of nodes transversed for retrieving what was required.

Research results showed that FD/FI cognitive style significantly influenced the search performance of *novice* searchers. Field dependents needed to spend a longer time and to visit more nodes than did the field independents. However, the influence of cognitive style was greatly reduced in those searchers who had online database search experience. The researchers suggest that online search experience may help the FDs to overcome the spatial complexities of hypermedia information architecture. They then provide preliminary suggestions for Web based interface designers: "it seems that the FDs, especially those with little or no experience with online databases, might need special attention from the interface designers or those who train Web users. Interface designers may want to incorporate devices that can help the FDs become better oriented and less likely to get lost. Providing a graphical map of their search progress would be an example."

British researcher Nigel Ford, in his recent (2000) article, "Cognitive styles and virtual environments," points out that "virtual" environments "enable a given information space to be transversed in different ways by different individuals, using different routes and navigation tools. He identifies two main categories of learners, "serialists" who examine one thing at a time, with the overall picture emerging much later, and "holists" who examine interrelationships early, concentrate first on building a broad overview and subsequently fill in the details. Ford presents a variety of research results on cognition, learning and thinking and then outlines applications to hypertext navigation and database searching (e.g., CD-ROM). He then calls for more research in order to assess the extent to which awareness of global (holist) and analytic (serialist) styles of information processing may be useful in the development of virtual environments. He notes evidence that "when information is presented in a way that matches or mismatches individuals' preferred holist or serialist biases, learning is significantly enhanced or disrupted respectively."

Ford then promotes "intelligent, adaptive" systems in a virtual environment. "Such systems could: (a) identify particular learning strategies being used by individual users (b) classify them in terms of a provisional model of learning, (c) offer individualized strategic support based on the model and (d) use feedback data progressively to improve the model." He finally states "the capability of virtual environments to integrate, and allow the explicit manipulation of global and analytic aspects of a given body of information would seem to map well onto learning requirements suggested by research into cognitive styles."

Cognitive style is likely the most prominent psychological factor applied to IS, at least from a research perspective. Now may be the time to concentrate not just on *research* in this area but also on *development*, so as to develop applied tools for IT management to use in applying effectively conclusive and potentially impactful research results.

Core Awareness:
The Deepest Inner Self

Psychological factors examined until now have dealt largely with how we behave and function and also how we think and work. But, are we simply "rational animals" with an intellect, feelings, and a body? Is there, from a conceptual as well as experiential point of view, yet another component to the human person? If so, how can explicit awareness of this component contribute to the work effectiveness of an IT worker?

This section assumes that, indeed, the deepest inner self (inner core, center, being), does exist in and can be consciously accessible to a well-adjusted, aware human person. Furthermore, this central core can truly provide rejuvenated psychological energy in times of stress and change and it can also provide stability and impetus to significantly creative efforts. Thus, although specific research in this area as applied to IT has not yet been popularized, it is proposed here that conscious awareness of one's deepest self can indeed add a very important dimension to the work of an IT professional, particularly one whose work involves human interaction. As well, it is pointed out that connection to one's inner self provides the theoretical and empirical basis for the notion of "emotional intelligence."

A Two-Tier Model of Human Consciousness

For a majority of people, at least in today's Western world, their self-awareness is largely limited to a one-tiered view as shown in Figure 1. Here the mind (intellect), feelings (emotions) and the body (with its senses) are identified. The will is the force, which channels one's consciousness to the various parts in various proportions during the day.

A person at this level of awareness has the three components available for use. However, each of these three parts can be at different levels of positivity or negativity at any point in time. For example, the mind can be thinking clearly or be confused, feelings can be elated, peaceful, or angry, the body can be healthy or sick. Indeed, these very "human" imperfect components cannot be counted on to come through for us "in top form" in situations of definite need (e.g., dealing with a system crash the day before installation).

However, a variety of personal growth programs and literature, some of which have received notable acceptance from professional circles, propose the *two-tiered model* of the human person, shown in Figure 2. Here the three human

Figure 1. One tier model of the human person

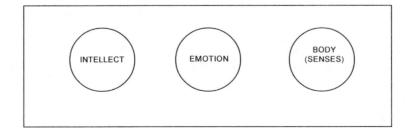

Figure 2. Two-tier model of the human person

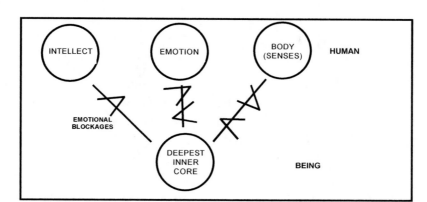

dimensions are receiving energy/direction from the deepest self/core energy/ inner being, which operates on a separate, deeper level. Moreover, the substance of this core energy is *only positive*—there is nothing negative and nothing missing (for deep psychological wellness) in the inner being. The difficulty, though, lies in establishing and maintaining a strong enough connection between the *human* and the *being* parts.

Dr. Bernie Siegel, well-known health counselor and former Yale University surgeon, points out that "*most of us are in touch with the inner self only intermittently, if at all... It's not located in the conscious mind...this perfect core self seems to fit in with neuropeptide theories...I first got to know this perfect core self through meditation.... However you get there, you'll know you've arrived—it's like coming home, and home is where the healing can begin...within your true, unique, and authentic self*" (Siegel, 1989).

We can usually switch our attention, our concentration, willingly from the mind to the body or to the feelings—the use of will is more direct here. However, *it is not possible to will oneself into the deepest self.* One can, at best, willfully relinquish control of the mind, body, or feelings and try to focus on one's "felt truths"; the core energy simply surfaces to consciousness.

Also, in the two-tiered model, note the "wedges" between the human parts and the inner core energy. These are the reasons why most of us are not often in touch with our "true, authentic self." According to a number of personal growth perspectives, there are *five basic inner needs* that we have when we are developing psychologically:

1.   To be SEEN for what we are experiencing deep within us;

2.   To be HEARD attentively when we try to communicate something of deep importance to us;

3.   To be TRUSTED in our innate ability to develop "for the good" without "micromanaging";

4.   To be RECOGNIZED and addressed as a unique person who has infinite value much beyond behavior and performance; and

5.   To be SAFE to open deeply inner experiences, awareness, struggles and discoveries without being judged.

Significant frustration of the above five needs, by deprivation and/or negative (perhaps, but not necessarily abusive) impact creates emotional blockages, many of which are initially subconscious. These are largely the reasons why many people, IT professionals included, are not sufficiently aware of, or connected to their most positive inner asset. Personal growth programs, such as PRH International (1997) and Hoffman's quadrinity process (as outlined in Hoffman, 1988) aim at recognizing, identifying, and removing these debilitating and limiting blockages. The reality of the pure, deep inner core energy has shown to have significant potential for psychological empowerment in personal and professional life. Can IT professionals afford to ignore such a potential?

IT workers, more of whom are TJ types in MBTI , are accustomed to structure and precisely, logically definable realities. For some, perhaps many, such realities have exclusively formed their life view. In such a view, being in control, understanding and "scientifically predicting" are counted on to provide inner security, self-worth and motivation. However, the rapid change in technology and in IT paradigms (such as OO) coupled with increased expectation in the Internet era of mega-connectivity are eroding, at times significantly, "security from control." Consequently, many IT workers may, knowingly or not, be in or heading for a major crisis, not only due to overwork and frustration, but most importantly due to *significant experiential threats to their source of inner security and identity* on which most (perhaps all) of their life rests.

The IT profession seems to be recognizing the threat of impending "mass burnout." In a recent issue of the *Cutter* IT journal, dedicated to IT burnout, Edward Yourdon states "Burnout is still a topic that most senior managers would rather not confront, but it has become so prevalent and severe that some IT organizations have become almost completely dysfunctional" (December, 2002).

However break*down* can lead to break*through*. To minimize the damage of prolonged stress in IT, a new vision is first of all needed, a *holistic model of a "functional IT worker,"* a model that can have its roots in the two-tier perspective outlined earlier.... From this vision, effective assistance measures could be provided.

A major contribution to such a "new vision" that can apply to IT professionals can be seen in the work of Gary Zukav (author of the bestseller *The Seat of the Soul* (1990)) and Linda Francis. In their collaborative book, *The Heart of the Soul* (2001), Zukav and Francis declare:

... spiritual growth {awareness of the deep self} is now replacing survival as the central objective of the human experience ...

.. and the old species explored the physical world and it created security by manipulating and controlling what it discovered. The new species creates security by looking inward to find the causes of insecurity and healing them... This is the path to authentic power.

Authentic power is the alignment of your personality with your soul {i.e., deepest core energy}

For these authors, and numerous others, a deep, inner self-awareness is capable of providing a complementary psychological empowerment that awareness of personality factors and cognitive concerns cannot, by themselves, offer. With this in mind, the two-tier model can thus form a basis for a strategic vision of a "functional information resource facilitator" of the 21st century. However, strategy must lead to tactics. There must be available prescriptions as to how one can develop a "deep inner connection" as well as a clarification of the relationship of such an experienced connection to the increasingly popular concept of "emotional intelligence."

An Underlying Foundation for Emotional Intelligence

When one is working, albeit perhaps not explicitly, with a one-tier model of the human (intellect, emotions, body and its sensations), an intelligence not of the intellect per se and not specifically bodily-kinesthetic can be easily labeled "emotional." *There is no other component in this model to which to appeal.*

However the term "emotional intelligence" may appear vague and confusing. IT professionals in particular (where many are thinking and structured (judging) types) may be uncomfortable in knowing *how* to make their emotions "intelligent." Understandably, considerable confusion and ambiguity could abound in, say, trying to make an IT department "emotionally intelligent" when working from a one-tier model of the human person.

However, if we *consider the two-tier model* introduced in this chapter, where the intellect, emotions and body serve and receive the all-positive deep psychological core energy from the deepest inner self / being, *then the entire concept of "emotional intelligence" is immediately clarified.* The intelligence comes from the gratuitous innermost zone, the second tier. It then illuminates the intellect, the emotions, and the body, which, having access to this reservoir of wisdom, can thus display all the features that Daniel Goleman (1995, 1998) and others identify with "emotional intelligence." Both the mind *and* emotions become the servant of the inner being.

Thus, in this view, the way to develop emotional intelligence is to work at removing (evacuating) the blockages between the intellect-emotions-body and the deepest inner self, and then to allow one's thoughts and feelings to be guided by the now accessible inner energy where all the necessary awareness should ultimately be found.

Possible Benefits of Increased Core Awareness to IT

Is it likely that increased inner consciousness and the resulting empowerment can yield important benefits to the IT workers, their employers and to the user community?

The main benefit to IT of growth into and work from the deepest inner self would be *psychological robustness*, capacity for psychological resilience in the face of overwhelming challenges. Change management consultant Diana Larsen, in *Embracing Change* (2003) notes: "Change agents and those involved with change who have the personal and social skills of emotional intelligence will show more resilience in the face of a shifting environment." Personal growth programs that help one to access one's deepest self could, thus, be a very impactful resource for IT workers.

Ordinarily, when reacting to stressful, unfamiliar circumstances, unfavorable emotions such as anger, frustration, fear of failure etc. can take over the psyche and largely disempower the intellect. However, the revitalizing psychological energy of the inner being is present deep within, at the level more foundational than the intellect, emotions, or body. It indeed provides the empowering psychological energies that accrue when one has grown sufficiently to be able to "drop oneself into" one's deepest core energy in the face of external storms in the course of IT work. Availability of such an empowering inner resource depends on maturity in growth. This affects significantly one's essential, emotional orientation to the required efforts of one's daily work.

Thus, an IT manager may begin to wonder while GUI design, code testing, or data modeling are going on among her subordinates, *what is likely happening for each of them at an inner level?* What are they feeling, how are they reacting emotionally to the tasks and challenges at hand? More importantly, she may wish to assess which persons are capable of being very involved, yet not attached in dependency (not addicted to their work). This is emotional intelligence in action!

With a two-tier consciousness in IT workers, *teamwork and user communication* will unquestionably become more effective, by a "quantum leap." With a one-tier consciousness, much communication is hampered by emotional "self-protection"—one does not want to show one's professional and/or personal insecurity; one may be threatened by approaches or styles different from one's own. With a growth-induced two-tier awareness, such defense mechanisms are unnecessary and would not even be considered. With such an awareness, one knows that one can dissipate self-consciousness with consciousness of the pure, all encompassing energy emanating freely from the deepest inner part. With an awareness of the deepest self and connection to it, it is very easy to admit, fully and truthfully, as appropriate, one's shortcomings and limitations, because one is simultaneously aware of one's indisputable value, goodness and worthiness which come from deep within.

With an expanded consciousness and self-concept and, thus, a transformed identity (from techie to a multidimensional "information resource facilitator"), one could believe that the new IT worker can indeed be effective in the current system development climate. Through his/her now natural capacities for cooperation, respect, listening, flexibility of viewpoints, fairness, optimism and emotional resilience, coupled with an awareness of other psychological factors as outlined earlier, such an IT worker would become truly emotionally intelligent.

In *teamwork*, he would gladly listen to and assess opposing viewpoints, and would be secure enough at the deepest level to welcome constructive criticism. Out of a profound sense of self-respect, the sense that comes freely from deep within, a developed IT worker could indeed make users feel valued and have their needs and reservations respected and addressed adequately. A project manager with considerable growth in the inner self could be sensitive to the unique talents and psychological needs of subordinates. She could truthfully express firmness or disapproval of a person's behavior without anger or fear and without having the person feel undesirable. Through her openness and genuine humanity, she could invite openness among subordinates, generating considerable *trust*.

If a manager addresses a subordinate from the intellect (alone), the subordinate's reaction will also likely come from the intellect. If the manager communicates with emotion (perhaps superficial), the subordinate will respond likewise. However, if the manager connects from her own deepest inner, authentic self, this will prompt a response from the same deep level, especially if the subordinates have been undergoing their own process of inner unblocking and deeper connecting. As an example of such a phenomenon, we can relate the eloquent words of Jim McCarthy, from his book, *Dynamics of Software Development* (1995):

...a leader's empathic perception of the psychological state of his or her team is the beginning of what we call vision. If the leader can then resonate with the team's complex emotional state—identify with it, articulate it, and give the whole constellation of feeling and thought a visible, concrete reality in his or her own personal voice or gesture—the boundaries among individual team members and the leader will collapse.... Empathy will be established: the leader and the team will feel and know as one, giving voice and identity to what was an incoherent psychological community substrate. And it will feel good to the team to be understood and to understand.... Without empathy, vision is hollow, an ersatz vision that might fulfill a requirement that some words appear on a slide, but won't provide the visceral motivation that inspires a team to greatness.

As well, Kent Beck, the originator of the extreme programming (XP) paradigm dismisses the idea that IT work is "some Vulcanic world of pure rationality" and declares that "*To be successful, we must learn and grow our whole selves*" (2000). Without doubt, truly "being-centered, 'whole-self' IT Teams" of the future will indeed be a sight to behold and a model for work in the post-modern era.

Conflicts with a team or with users can be much easier to resolve from an inner center consciousness. There will never be attacks on a person or his dignity out of a sense of bruised ego, since inner-centered persons do not rely on ego for security and strength. The deep, freely available inner strength will allow for considerable flexibility in generating new approaches which parties in conflict will be able to accept—people will not need to "defend their turf" so rigidly as if their life, self-worth and meaning depended on it. Furthermore, such an orientation to conflict management, made possible by a two-tier operational self-awareness, could be developed not only among working IT professionals, but among IS university students. Hignite, Margavio, and Chin studied conflict resolution profiles of emerging IS professionals (2002) and isolated factors that were shown to influence conflict resolution style. Could a two-tier consciousness significantly influence, or perhaps even alter a specific style and could it make the style more effective?

In the course of IT work, frustration, anger, and disillusionment, which are humanly natural, will not disappear from people who are considerably integrated. However, the negative effect of these *stress-inducing emotions* on the thinking capacity, motivation and physical health will be considerable lessened, since these emotions will not need to be inappropriately expressed or unhealthily repressed, but will be offset and largely "melted" by access to a more centered, profound, powerful, peaceful and energizing inner force. As well, such emotions will not be as likely to perpetrate dysfunctional work decisions among IT workers. For example, in "XP and Emotional Intelligence" (2002), Kay Pentecost relates an incident where her development team, wishing to please its manager, took on a dubious goal of trying to improve a working demo for an executive in a very short period of time, and failed to have even the basic demo working on time. In hindsight, she acknowledged that the desire to please their manager clouded the team's judgment as to the feasibility of his request. She pointed out that "In this group of supposedly logical developers was a lot of negative emotion: blame, fear, anger, frustration and some amount of despair." Then, some time later, a similar situation arose, with an inappropriate request for an "express enhancement" to a working demo. The author, tapping into her inner strength and wisdom, truthfully told the supervisor that the team could not do it, in spite of angry reactions. The original demo was promoted to the VP, without desired enhancements—the VP was impressed.

The issue of *control* is often central for many IT workers. With many system developers having come from third-generation language programming background, structure was paramount and control over one's program was very possible. Now with realities such as unrealistic deadlines, ongoing changes in requirements and development approaches and frequent organizational restructuring, a sense of control over one's work tasks, one's competency level and one's career path is often eroded. For many structured personalities who may have relied on such control for most of their essential personal security, such an erosion can indeed be traumatic, causing what is termed as "image violation". Recently, Niederman and Sumner (2003), in a study of turnover among IT professionals, propose that forward-thinking companies develop "management programs to head-off declining job satisfaction associated with image violation." In time, such programs may well address the reality of the deepest inner self and present methods of how to access this stabilizing psychological reality.

With an active connection to one's deep inner self, which feeds one's consciousness with all the deep essential security one needs or wants, one can be emotionally *interdependent* with work structure and control rather than being emotionally *dependent* on it. One can be close to structure, work with it, maintain it, yet be simultaneously emotionally free of it. Then, a disruption in structure and loss of control, while it may generate discomfort at one level, will never disrupt one's inner sense of deep security, one's conviction of being "ok." Thus, considerably less energy is being drained, leaving the energy for productive responses to the IT work reality.

Related to loss of control are the needs within IT (among both developers and users) for coping with *ongoing change* and the need for constant, substantial learning. With a two-tier connection, one can be emotionally *close and free* to one's work efforts. Considerable distress in change results from needing to let go emotionally of what has become comfortable, fulfilling, and even affirming. However, an emotional "letting go" is significantly easier if one is deeply inwardly connected. In recent research, Shen and Gallivan (2004) showed that negative consequences of the need to deal with change are moderated by the autonomy that IT users experience in their work. Yet in the two-tier model, there is, besides *external autonomy* (in the workplace environment) an *internal autonomy* (lack of emotional "clinging" enabled by a connection to the deepest self). The role of the latter will certainly be worth exploring, as IT workers and their managers collectively begin to accept the reality of the psychological inner core.

Rootedness in one's deep authentic self provides positive energy to the emotions and intellect. One then can, by his authentic presence, *motivate* others genuinely. One can also be inwardly free enough to attempt new, creative approaches to established work tasks. As well, deeper inner consciousness has positive effects on the *planning of one's IT career*. Following one's deep authentic self, one is motivated basically by truth (as seen by the "inner eyes") and not by image or external goals. Such an IT worker will seek to know, truthfully, his natural talents and shortcomings, he will be content to work at his current level until genuinely motivated, in all parts of him, to seek another level. He will avoid career management through restlessness, drivenness to constant progress or addiction to "mental highs" in order to drown out a basic inner malaise. Sumner and Yager (2004) identified "managerial competence" as a career anchor of IT personnel. In time, IT workers *may look for managerial support of two-tier self-awareness* as a component of such competence.

A rooted IT worker living mostly with her intellect, emotions, and body at the service of the deepest inner core energy will indeed become emotionally intelligent at work. She will have the courage and ability to access and understand her feelings, and to intuit about the feelings and attitudes of others. Moreover, the inner wisdom of the being will serve as a valuable guide in specific situations. She will "just know" what words to use to diffuse a client's anger, she will "know" how to handle an apprehensive user and she will "know" how to correct a subordinate without bruising his ego. Considerable IT literature calls for development of "soft skills." Such a development is best addressed by comprehensive integration, by connecting an informed intellect, aware feelings, and a healthy body to the deep core energy—by promoting "personal wholeness" within IT work.

Applications in Research and Practice

Explicit, empirical research on applying "two-tier" psychological consciousness to IT work specifically has not yet arisen. However, in 1988, U.S. management scientist and academic Robert Thierauf in his book *New Directions in MIS Management*, in a chapter on "Motivating MIS Personnel" describes self-actualization as "realizing one's ambition," that is, self-fulfilment. He then questions whether "I do my thing" is the final goal, the farthest one can go in personal/professional development. He answers "No," and proposes further stages of *mutual actualization*, where "two or more individuals enrich one another and in doing so, they grow both as individuals and as a group," and then *self-donation*, when one has an attained a level of expertise and satisfaction and now offers assistance to a junior person in her growth. Thierauf also declares that "change and growth are not necessarily pleasant processes. Sometimes there is sadness, sometimes "raw" pain. But what happens to us is real. It deserves our full attention." This may well be seen as a precursor to the growth in being promoted in this chapter.

Several IT industry newspapers have carried relevant columns. In 1996, *Computerworld* called for "emotional literacy" among IT personal. Articles on emotional intelligence have appeared in *Computing Canada*. In one such article, a president of a Toronto firm specializing in increasing human performance says, "Promoting emotional intelligence can be the key element in assisting IT employees in developing interpersonal skills." He believes that it is the emotional relationships and connections workers have with their peers and supervisors that make the difference in their productivity and loyalty to the company. In another article, entitled "Info tech workers emotionally weak," a psychologist defines EI as a "measurement of how people cope with life." He administered an EQ (emotional quotient) test to a number of different professionals and found IT workers had a slightly lower score than most other groups. He had used the Bar-On EQ-i test, developed by Israeli psychologist Dr. Reuven Bar-On, to gauge the coping abilities of 150 IT professionals. It would be interesting to apply such a test one time and then again, 5 years later to a test group of IT workers who would seriously undertake a growth program such as PRH for at least 4 years.

Meditation, an attempt to "still the intellect" so that the deep inner core energy can surface to one's consciousness, can be a helpful aid on the road to inner growth. In the article "The use of meditation-relaxation techniques for the management of stress in a working population" (*Journal of Occupational Medicine*, 1980), researchers Carrington et al. report, where telephone company employees practiced meditation twice daily for six months, effective reduction in symptoms of stress, such as depression, somatization and anxiety.

Also, from participants' spontaneous comments, the most frequent benefit was "improvement in cognitive functioning." Other comments have included "my reasoning process is clearer," "I think, remember, and organize better," "increased interpersonal awareness," and "do not feel so defensive in my relationships with other people." These effects may indeed be interpreted as resulting from having the mind at the service of the deep inner core self.

In a 1998 weekend edition of the Boston Globe, an advertisement for IT jobs in an insurance company contains the following: "Sometimes you have to listen carefully, to hear the loudest voice. It's the voice inside. Stop ignoring that voice—it's coming from your soul." Such a direct reference to the deepest inner core can now be more clearly appreciated in the light of Zukav and Francis' contention that authentic power comes from "alignment of your personality with your soul." Such an orientation can induce human resource recruiters and IT managers to try to assess not only whether a candidate/employee is highly motivated but whether such motivation is largely resulting from an insatiable, addictive drivenness of unbridled ambition or whether the motivation comes from the deepest authentic self. It may be a challenge for researchers to develop and validate a questionnaire, which may try to assess such an important factor.

The other pioneering comment comes at the start of the popular IT text, *Introduction to Information Systems: Essentials for the Internetworked Enterprise* (1998). Author James O'Brien tells his readers, "May you love the Light within you, And in everyone you meet, And in everything you experience". A clear reference to the deepest inner self in such a context is indeed enlightening. It can certainly be understood as a call to a deeper inner awareness while developing an IS orientation. Might it happen in the near future that self-awareness and inner-core-led empowerment, within appropriate case studies, may become part of IS management curricula?

In 1994, a computer consultant in Louisville, Kentucky, published over 40 articles on the "human system" in a computer newspaper. He was also involved in giving "human system" seminars to help people to live more satisfying personal and work lives. In one article, he points out how "our spirit controls our mind, and, in turn, our mind controls our body" and encourages reader to "control your mind with your spirit {deep inner core energy}." This same person has been promoting the slogan "we are spirits having a human experience," as opposed to humans having a spiritual experience (he had even been selling t-shirts with such a motto at an IT convention). He provides feedback received from his listeners (e.g., "It gave me a whole new understanding of myself.")

A 1998 article in *Time* magazine titled "Get thee to a monastery" identifies a developing trend for overworked professionals to retire to rural monasteries for relaxation and inner refocusing. There, nature, simplicity, pervasive silence as well as the attentive presence and rhythmic chants of monks disciplined in living a deeply rooted and authentic life offer "the most refreshing vacation going." The article describes a 45-year-old computer specialist who considers herself "spiritual, not religious," who has decided to come back to an upstate New York monastery each year for her only vacation away from her job. Then, she finds inner peace and can "sit, think, and pray." It is also interesting to note that in the book *Using SAP R/3* (Que, 1997) in the chapter on "The Human Side of SAP Implementation," meditation and religion are identified explicitly as avenues for managing stress.

As the IT field itself recognizes a new era in IT management, it is searching for innovative approaches. Considerable work efforts on the dimensions of personality, cognition and emotional intelligence both within the IT field and generally can provide IT with a viable avenue to enhance its management effectiveness. However, such a perspective will have to be accepted more broadly by IS researchers and practitioners in the near future.

Possible Future Efforts

This section, thus, provides suggestions and challenges as to studies and projects that would facilitate MB type application to IT at a deeper and more comprehensive level.

There are a number of research questions that could be addressed further by motivated academics, often working hand-in-hand with cooperating IT management:

1. Does the distribution of types in IT ("in IT" would need to be defined) vary across organizations, industries, and countries?

2. Do hypothesized connections between type/temperament and system development tasks prove accurate?

3. Exactly *how* does each temperament tend to carry out main IT tasks. Is the way of working consistent with type theory? How is the "order of preference" evident in carrying out IT tasks?

4. To what degree is MBTI used in IT organizations? What impact has it had?

5. What notable drawbacks (if any) have been observed in application of MBTI?

6. What appears to be the actual impact of MBTI use on productivity, effectiveness, and employee morale?

7. What activities/tasks are being emphasized by development of systems supporting e-commerce that were not evident in basic reporting systems? Is more personality type variety desirable in e-commerce project teams?

8.   What are the identifiable stages of application of MBTI in IT in an
     organization?. Does the stage of MB application correlate with degree of
     "IT maturity?"

Apart from academic *research*, there is also a call for specific *development*
efforts that would help to motivate more directly the application of MBTI to
information technology work. Firstly, there already exists a booklet, published by
Consulting Psychologists Press called *Introduction to Type in Organizations*
by Hirsh and Kummerow (1990). For each of the 16 types, it contains information
on contributions to the organization, leadership style, preferred learning style,
problem-solving approach, preferred work environments, potential pitfalls and
suggestions for development.

Such information is more directly useful to organizational management since it
applies type theory to specific, relevant issues. Could not a similar booklet
oriented solely to IT work, titled perhaps *MB Type in the Context of IT Work*
be produced? Based on experienced MIS research and extensive anecdotal
evidence (perhaps largely made known through the Web), strengths, weaknesses, preferred ways of addressing major IT tasks and strategies for being
managed can be explicitly outlined for each type. Such a resource would be a
necessity for MB personality awareness to develop to a truly impactful level in
many IT environments.

Another proposed development could be even more ambitious. This would
involve *development of a personality indicator parallel to the MBTI*, but
using questions only from an IT work setting. This could take the form of a
"sorter," similar to the Kersey temperament sorter. A main psychometric
challenge would be to show that the estimated "types" from such a sorter
correlate adequately with the true MBT indicator. Availability of such an
exclusively IT-oriented instrument could eliminate concerns (on the part of
individuals or even labor groups) as to the ethics of asking questions irrelevant
to the work environment.

For MB type orientation in IT to really become commonplace, more training and
clarification material will need to become available. Videos, perhaps downloadable
through the Internet, could point out explicitly how types and their order of
preference "attack" specific issues across the system development stages.
Exercises could be provided and discussed, synthesizing both research results
and practical observations.

Regarding cognitive style, Epstein (1996) stated unquestioningly "the need to
integrate the mechanistic logic of computers with the ambiguous nature of living
human systems remains fundamental to the successful design and implementation of computer-based information systems." He further cautioned that "design

strategies which over-value either perspective at the expense of the other are likely to be less powerful and more highly at risk than those which incorporate both," and advocated "cultivating conscious awareness of the designer's ... predisposing characteristics" within IT.

It is quite probable that the IT profession and system development in particular is ready to begin such "conscious awareness." However, an individual system developer needs to be sufficiently motivated and sufficiently supported to achieve this goal. Specific training materials, video clips, etc. can be developed competently and creatively to address cognitive style considerations across the life cycle stages (e.g., in planning, requirements determination, modelling, design, prototyping and user support). Cognitive style, along with personality type awareness can indeed become more than a passing conversation topic in IT, especially once many incidents (although initially anecdotal) of improved performance, decreased cost and increased morale are credibly reported.

Regarding the deepest inner self, it could be an interesting and useful research question in IT management to explore what events and experiences might tend to block IT workers from accessing their deepest selves. What events in IT work give rise to specific emotions? Are there classes of IT workers that will tend to react with similar emotions in given work difficulties? Are such reactions related to personality type? What (subconscious) belief systems might initiate these reactions? Are such reactions "contagious" and what psychological conditions make certain IT workers more resistant to epidemics of negativity, blame, and resulting dysfunction? What are the symptoms of a "dysfunctional IT organization" and can a specific "recovery program" be developed for such situations? Perhaps a new field of IT management, called *psycho-informatics* may emerge.

As well, an orientation to connectedness to one's deepest core energy can induce human resource recruiters and IT managers to try to assess not only whether a candidate/employee is highly motivated but whether such motivation is largely resulting from an insatiable, addictive drivenness of unbridled ambition or whether the motivation comes from the deepest authentic self. It may be a challenge for researchers to develop and validate a questionnaire, which may try to assess such an important factor.

As mentioned earlier, a systematic, effective, well-established program to guide persons into their deepest inner self is the Hoffman quadrinity process, offered worldwide by the Hoffman Institute. Michael Ray, Professor *Emeritus* of Creativity, Innovation, and Marketing at the Stanford University Graduate School of Business says, "*Everything changed after the Hoffman Quadrinity Process, because I then understood the obstacles to my full potential... It presents a powerful combination of practical approaches that have been honed to a package of **incredible power that stays with you**.... Any accom-*

plishments that someone might list after my name came largely because of this experience."

It would be fitting for a number of adventurous IT executives who would like to explore this dimension of inner growth and stress management to be sponsored for the Hoffman quadrinity process. It is quite possible that many such executives, after two years or so, would become significantly empowered from a totally new inner dimension. Then, testimonies of practical IT work-related results could indeed initiate more widespread interest and eventually acceptability of deep inner growth within the IT profession.

Conclusion

In highlighting three separate dimensions of psychological awareness, we have seen research results showing relevance and impact on the IT profession. A more concerted research effort in this area might result in even more impactful insights. With recognition of information systems as a socio-technical field and with widespread publicizing of noteworthy research results, greater awareness of specific psychological dynamisms within and among IT professionals can become a specific goal at this point in the profession's evolution. Judging by research results as well as guarded intuition, one could reasonably hypothesize that properly harnessing such awareness could result in more efficient and effective IT work effort and in significantly decreased stress for IT workers. However, it will be up to motivated, interdisciplinary researchers to corroborate this hypothesis and up to courageous, collaborative IT management to cooperate in the research efforts and to apply notable findings.

Even with concerted efforts, the psychological maturing of the IT profession will not happen overnight. Hypothesized growth stages towards such maturity, as proposed in Kaluzniacky (2004), could well take over 15 years to implement. But, at this point, the stage appears set for starting. With individual IT workers, employing IT departments, professional associations, university academics and the user community each doing their part, the IT work world of the future could respond to its challenges with wisdom and fruitful innovation.

References

Agor, W. H. (1991). The logic of intuition: How top executives make important decisions. In J. Henry (Ed.), *Creative management* (pp. 163-77). London: Sage.

Amador, J. A. (1977). *Information formats and decision performance: An experimental investigation.* PhD dissertation, University of Florida.

ASAP World Consultancy. (1997). *Using SAP R/3.* Indianapolis, IN: Que Corporation.

Bariff, M., & Lusk, E., (1977). Cognitive and personality tests for the design of management information systems. *Management Science, 23*(8), 820-829.

Beck, K. (2000). *Extreme programming explained: Embrace change.* Reading, MA: Addison-Wesley.

Benbasat, I., & Schroeder, R. (1977). An experimental investigation of some MIS design variables. *MIS Quarterly, 1*(1), 37-49.

Benbasat, I., & Taylor, R. N. (1978). The impact of cognitive styles on information system design. *MIS Quarterly, 2*(2), 43-54.

Carrington, P., et al. (1980). The use of meditation/relaxation techniques for the management of stress in a working population. *Journal of Occupational Medicine, 22*(4), 221-231.

Churchman, C. W., & Schainblatt, A. H. (1965). The researcher and the manager: A dialectic of implementation. *Management Science, 11*(4), B69-B87.

Couger, J. D. (1996). *Creativity and innovation in information systems organizations.* Danvers, MA: Boyd & Fraser.

Couger, J. D., & Zawacki, R. (1980). *Motivating and managing computer personnel.* John Wiley & Sons.

Davis, D., & Elnicki, R. (1984). User cognitive types for decision support systems. *Omega - International Journal of Management Science, 12*(6), 601-614.

Ellis, D., Ford, N., & Wood, F. (1993). Hypertext and learning styles. *The Electronic Library, 11*(1), 13-18.

Epstein, M. (1996). *The role and worldview of systems designers: a multimethod study of information systems practitioners in the public sector.* College of Commerce, University of Saskatchewan.

Ferdinandi, P. (1994, July). Re-engineering with the right types. *Software Development.*

Ford, N. (2000). Cognitive styles and virtual environments. *Journal of the American Society for Information Science, 51*(6), 543-557.

Goleman, D. (1995). *Emotional intelligence.* London: Bloomsbury.

Goleman, D. (1998). *Working with emotional intelligence.* London: Bloomsbury.

Hayes, J., & Allinson, C. W. (1998). Cognitive style and the theory and practice of individual and collective learning in organizations. *Human Relations, 51*(7), 847-871

Hignite, Mi., Margavio, T., & Chin, J., (2002). Assessing conflict resolution profiles of emerging information systems professionals. *Journal of Information Systems Education, 13*(4), 315-324.

Hirsh, S. K., & Kummerow, J. M. (1990). *Introduction to type in organizations.* Palo Alto, CA: Consulting Psychologists Press.

Hoffman, B. (1988). *No one is to blame.* Oakland, CA: Recycling Books.

Hohmann, L. (1997). *Journey of the software professional.* Englewood Cliffs, NJ: Prentice-Hall.

Huber, G. P. (1983). Cognitive style as a basis for MIS and DSS designs: Much ado about nothing? *Management Science, 29*(5), 567-579.

Huitt, W. (1992). Problem solving and decision making: Consideration of individual differences using the Myers-Briggs Type Indicator. *Journal of Psychological Type, 24*, 33-44.

Huysmans, J. (1970). The effectiveness of the cognitive style constraint in implementing operations research proposals. *Management Science, 17*(1), 92-104.

Kaiser, K., & Bostrom, R. (1982, December). Personality characteristics of MIS project teams: An empirical study and action-research design. *MIS Quarterly, 6*(4), 43-60.

Kaluzniacky, E. (2004) *Managing psychological aspects of information systems work: An orientation to emotional intelligence.* Hershey, PA: Idea Group Publishing.

Keirsey, D., & Bates, M. (1978). *Please understand me.* Del Mar, CA: Prometheus Nemesis.

Kirton, M. J. (1989). *Adaptors and innovators: Styles of creativity and problem solving.* London: Routledge.

Korthauer, R. D., & Koubek, R. J.,(1994). An empirical investigation of knowledge, cognitive style, and structure upon the performance of hypertext task. *International Journal of Human-Computer Interaction, 6*(4), 373-390.

Larsen, D. (2003). Embracing change: A retrospective. *Cutter IT Journal,* *16*(2), 39-46.

Lusk, E., & Kersnick, M. (1979). The effect of cognitive style and report format on task performance. *Management Science, 29,* 797-798.

Lyons, M. (1985, August 15). The DP Psyche. *Datmation.*

McCarthy, J. (1995). *Dynamics of software development.* New York: Microsoft Press.

Marzano, R., Brandt, R., Hughes, C., Jones, B., Presseisen, B. Z., Rankin, B. S., et al. (n.d.). *Dimensions in thinking: A framework for curriculum and instruction.* Alexandria, VA: Association of Supervision and Curriculum Development.

Mason, R. O., & Mitroff, I. I. (1973). A program for research on MIS. *Management Science, 19*(5), 475-487.

Niederman, F., & Sumner, M. (2003). Decision paths affecting turnover among information technology professionals. In *Proceedings of the ACM SIGMIS Conference* (pp. 133-143).

O'Brien, J. (1998). *Introduction to information systems: Essentials for the internetworked enterprise.* New York: McGraw-Hill.

Palmquist, R., & Kim, K. (2000). Cognitive style and online database search experience as predictors of Web search performance. *Journal of the American Society for Information Science, 51*(6), 558-566.

Pentecost, K. (2003). XP and emotional intelligence. *Cutter IT Journal, 16*(2) 5-11.

PRH-International. (1997). *Persons and their growth.*

Robey, D. (1983). Cognitive style and DSS design: A comment on Huber's paper. *Management Science, 29*(5), 580-582

Shen, Y., & Gallivan, M. (2004). An empirical test of the job demand/control model among it users. In *Proceedings of the ACM SIGMIS Conference* (pp. 39-47).

Siegel, B. (1989). *Peace, love, and healing.* New York: Harper & Row.

Spence, J. W., & Tsai, R. J. (1997). On human cognition and the design of information systems. *Information & Management, 32,* 65-73.

Streufert, S., & Nogami, G. Y. (1989). Cognitive style and complexity: Implications for I/O psychology. *International Review of Industrial and Organizational Psychology,* Chichester, UK: Wiley.

Sumner, M., & Yager, S. (2004). Career orientation of IT personnel. *Proceedings of the ACM SIGMIS* (pp. 92-96).

Tan, B., & Lo, T. (1991). The impact of interface customization on the effect of cognitive style on information system success. *Behaviour & Information Technology, 10*(4), 297-310.

Teague, J. (1998). Personality type, career preferences, and implications for computer science recruitment and teaching. The *3rd Australasian Conference on Computer Science Education* (pp. 155-163). Association for Computing Machinery.

Thierauf, R. (1988). *New directions in MIS management: A guide for the 1990s.* New York: Quorum Books.

Thomsett, R. (1990, July-August). Effective project teams. *American Programmer, 3*(7-8).

White, K. B. (1984). A preliminary investigation of information systems team structures. *Information & Management, 7*(6), 331-335.

White, K. B. (1984). MIS project teams: An investigation of cognitive style implications. *MIS Quarterly, 8*(2), 95-103.

Witkin, H. A., et al. (1971). *A manual for the embedded figures tests.* Consulting Psychologists Press.

Yourdon, E. (1993). *Decline and fall of the American programmer.* Upper Saddle River, NJ: Prentice-Hall.

Yourdon, E. (2002). *Cutter IT Journal* (December).

Zukav, G. (1990). *The seat of the soul.* West Albany, NY: Fireside.

Zukav, G., & Francis, L. (2001). *The heart of the soul.* New York: Simon & Schuster.

Chapter X

The Impact of Agile Methods on Managing IT Professionals

Mark Toleman, University of Southern Queensland, Australia

Fiona Darroch, University of Southern Queensland, Australia

Mustafa Ally, University of Southern Queensland, Australia

Abstract

This chapter examines the potential for agile methods to provide mechanisms to deal with the software development environment that has evolved in response to the inadequacies of traditional, heavyweight development approaches. A framework is proposed which identifies three major areas of organizational impact that require management attention when undertaking system development in the new environment. This is followed by a detailed examination of the constructs within those three main areas, and assesses the potential for agile methods to address those issues. The current literature and empirical research into agile methods (and eXtreme Programming in particular) underpins the proposals for dealing with contemporary software development challenges. The authors hope that understanding the environment from the perspective of the framework will assist managers in their perception of the challenges of contemporary software development, and provide them with a firm basis on which to consider the adoption of agile methods.

Introduction

Globalization, the pressure to lower development costs and the requirement to deliver software in "Internet time" demand new approaches to management of system development. Agile methods have evolved in recognition of the short-comings of the more traditional, heavyweight software development methods. This chapter explores the ways in which the increasing adoption of agile methods has changed the role of the software developer and how agile methods impact on the management of personnel involved in the software development process.

A range of issues within the tenets, principles and core practices of the agile methodologies impact directly and indirectly on the management of software development. For example, three of the four tenets espoused in the agile manifesto (www.agilemanifesto.org), namely, those that emphasize "individuals over processes," "customer collaboration over contract negotiation" and being able to "respond to changes instead of following a plan," place new demands on software developers and their managers. Likewise, several of their principles suggest that managing agile teams will bring significant challenges for manage-ment. The principles of agile software, developed in conjunction with the agile manifesto, encourage trust in individuals to "get the job done," "promote sustainable development," assume emergence of "self-organizing teams" and assume teams will "reflect" on their effectiveness, and work directly with their customers to satisfy their needs for systems that give a "competitive advantage." Such requirements will test managers, developers, and customers from a range of perspectives but particularly the management of staff.

There are a range of methods that fall under the agile label. The most well known include eXtreme Programming (XP), SCRUM, Crystal and Feature Driven Development (FDD). These methods embody principles and practices that require particular management consideration for their successful implementa-tion. In all these approaches, the changing role of the developer has resulted in a major paradigm shift that needs to be addressed by management in order to make the software developers effective members of an agile team. Some developers may find the transition extremely challenging. To successfully introduce an agile methodology, organizations will need to manage, harness, and direct the skills and talents of these developers in an environment where they focus less on task and more on organizational concerns such as communication, team-work, customer focus and quality.

This chapter presents professionals and academics alike with current research and empirical evidence of the impact of agile approaches on the practice of managing IT personnel in an environment where the Internet and approaches relevant to development of Internet applications is the norm.

Background

According to Fitzgerald (1998), practitioners have been reluctant to adopt software/system development methodologies, with more than 60% of them abstaining. Furthermore, he noted that nearly 80% of the non-adopters intended to stay that way. Fitzgerald (1998) identified a number of "arguments" from practitioners against the use of methodologies, and "pressures" preventing their adoption. Fitzgerald (2000) postulated eight "canons" for systems development all of which could be answered with agile practices. It has been argued elsewhere that agile methodologies do provide a solution from a technological view (Highsmith & Cockburn, 2001) but perhaps more importantly from a people perspective (Turner & Boehm, 2003). Both aspects are explored here and the discussions are relevant to users and non-users of traditional methodologies.

eXtreme Programming (XP) (Beck, 1999) is perhaps the most well known agile methodology (Fowler & Highsmith, 2001) currently receiving much attention, particularly by practicing software developers. There are now at least two major international conferences annually (XP, 2005, XP Agile Universe, 2005) and there have been several special issues of journals on the topic (for example *IEEE Software*, November/December 2001, *Journal of Defense Software Engineering*, October 2002, *IEEE Computer*, June 2003, *Journal of Database Management*, April 2004). The Giga Information Group predicted that by 2004, agile processes will be incorporated in two-thirds of corporate IT departments (Barnett, 2002). Also, with software development luminaries such as Tom DeMarco (cited in Beck & Fowler, 2001) making statements such as:

XP is the most important movement in our field today. I predict that it will be as essential to the present generation as the SEI and its Capability Maturity Model were to the last.

There can be little doubt this is no passing fad, but in fact a topic worthy of serious research from information systems and human resources researchers, and the software development community.

XP was originally centred on 12 core practices (Beck, 1999), also known now as *Xp Xtudes*, which guide the software development process (Table 1). An updated version of XP is available (Beck & Andres, 2005) that is less restrictive in terms of defining practices but the essential features and practices are still relevant. These practices reflect the sentiment/intent of the twelve principles underpinning the agile manifesto. Most of these practices are not new but the way they are presented as a package in XP represents to many software

Table 1. XP core practices (P: people-related practice, T: Technical practice)

XP CORE PRACTICES	DESCRIPTION
The Planning Game (P)	The customer decides on the functionality (called stories) to be implemented while the developers estimate the time required, and through negotiation, workloads for the next cycle (project-dependent but perhaps week) are planned.
Small Releases (T)	Production software is released to customers regularly, usually weekly, but potentially daily.
System Metaphor (T)	The team has an overarching view or model of the system being developed. At the very least, a common vocabulary is required.
Simple Design (T)	Developers avoid unnecessary complication with respect to software architecture and coding, staying with the stories agreed with the customer each cycle.
Test Driven Development (T)	Tests are written prior to code development.
Design Improvement (T) (was Refactoring)	There is a process of continual improvement of the code as the developer's understanding of the system grows. Functionality is not altered so all tests should still operate effectively.
Pair Programming (P)	Two programmers collaborate on the same program code. Every code fragment is developed by a team of two programmers sitting together working at the same workstation. There are two roles, namely, a driver controlling the mouse, keyboard or other input device to write the code and unit tests, and a navigator, observing and quality assuring the code, asking questions, considering alternative approaches, identifying defects, and thinking strategically. The partners are considered equals and will regularly swap roles and partners.
Collective Code Ownership (P)	Developers were free to work on all code. Any code may be changed provided it is done by pairs of developers, complying with coding standards and subject to a satisfactory run of all tests.
Continuous Integration (T)	This involves the integration of new code into the project with consequential system building and testing.
Sustainable Pace (P) (was 40-Hour Work Week)	Developers are restricted to about 40 hours of work per week.
Whole Team (P) (was On-site Customer)	Customer availability in project gives developers continuous access thereby lessening the need for extensive requirements documents. They can ask the customer about functionality, test cases, interfaces, etc, at any time.
Coding Standards (T)	Coding standards are developed for each project. Since code may be worked on by any programmer at any time, coding standards are essential and must be rigorous.

developers how they really develop software systems (Sleve, 2002) or, in some cases, desire to develop software for clients. Some of the practices are primarily people-related relying heavily on interactions between people while others are principally technical involving the individual skills of software developers.

XP has been successfully applied in many projects. A range of experience reports have been published that demonstrate the wide variety of situations considered suitable to trial agile methods. These reports fall into several categories including academic teaching (Lappo, 2002; Mugridge, MacDonald, Roop, & Tempero, 2003,), tertiary student projects (Karlstrom, 2002), small-scale industry developments (Bossi & Cirillo 2001, Toleman, Darroch, & Ally 2005), and large-scale industry developments (Elssamadisy, 2001; Grenning, 2001; Pedroso, Visoli, & Antunes, 2002; Schuh, 2001; C3 Team, 1998). These are examples of a growing literature about agile methods and XP but there has been little attempt to grapple with the factors affecting the adoption of this new methodology or the human resource implications (except for some specific practices such as pair programming in, for example Ally, Darroch, and Toleman (2005)). Toleman, Ally, and Darroch (2004) contributed by examining the extent to which agile methodologies might address the shortfalls in methodology uptake of a relatively new methodology in a specific environment. However, the extent to which organizations have addressed the changing role of developers applying or resisting agile methodologies and their practices has not been examined. The impact of agile methods on recruitment and management strategies has also received little attention.

Figure 1. Organizational impacts of an agile approach

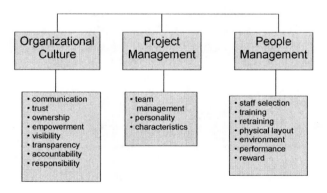

A Framework for Understanding the Organizational Impact of Agile Methods

In this chapter, we discuss three personnel-oriented areas we believe significantly impact the changing role of the software developer and their management in an agile software development environment: organizational culture, people management, and project management. Some of the evidence for the importance and relevance of the areas and associated concepts is derived from analysis of the tenets and principles of agile methods, and the practices of perhaps the most common implementation of agile, XP. Evidence is also drawn from the literature where it is available including our own studies. Figure 1 represents our current framework. This framework is one possible representation or combination of concepts and others will exist. The concepts within are inextricably linked and interrelated as well.

Today's business environment dictates speed, flexibility, and a people-centred focus. The pressure to lower costs and provide products, including software and Internet applications quickly, implies that traditional approaches with their long timeframes until working systems are available are no longer appropriate. Many of the new and emerging agile approaches accomplish these goals by calling for communication, collaboration and team skills at all levels of the development process and by including all stakeholders. This is a major paradigm shift for personnel, including project managers, developers and customers, and indeed the organization; cultural change is inevitable and change management guidance is required.

The following sections further expand on the important concepts within each of the three areas impacted by the changed development environment. In doing so, there is an examination of the potential for mechanisms within the agile approaches to assist in dealing with the issues. Specifically, the effects of XP practices on these concepts or how the practices provide solutions are considered, firstly for the primarily people-related and then for more technical XP practices.

Organizational Culture

An organization's culture is a shared understanding of the important characteristics of the organization that helps distinguish it from another organization. The actual characteristics will be argued about by various authors but for the purposes here include issues such as communication, trust, ownership, empowerment, visibility, transparency, accountability, and responsibility.

Communication

Good communication between team members, project managers and with customers is critical to development of quality software products. XP's practices and agile methods encourage high levels of quality communication between the different technical areas. Having a clear concept of the final product early can speed progress and facilitate communication between all stakeholders. The team should have an overarching view or model of the system being developed. At the very least, a common vocabulary is required to facilitate the communication process and ensure shared meaning.

Communication is clearly important for the primarily people-related practices of XP. The planning game relies heavily on verbal communication, as often there is only minimal documentation produced. Meetings and other face-to-face communication are the main mechanisms for ensuring the effective operation of the planning game. Project source code provides an important communication channel between developers and development teams. By implementing concepts such as collective code ownership where developers are able to read and alter the code generated by their colleagues, project teams engender implicit and explicit communication between the project team members, that is, the individual IT professionals. With pair programming, the interaction between the individual pairs and regular swapping between the pairs ensures an environment in which there is a continuous exchange of knowledge, ideas, and information. This also has the effect of spreading specialist knowledge with nearly everyone on the project team. Ensuring that the pace of development is sustained and sustainable relies on effective communication among team members to ensure that it is understood, accepted, and complied with.

Communication is at least implicit in the more technical practices of XP. Simple designs, either in their original form or refactored (design improved), are more easily communicated to other developers and to customers than complex ones. Small releases will require more effective and frequent communication between team members to ensure that the timeframes are met. Test-driven development ensures that the communicated requirements are actually delivered as working software. Requiring a system metaphor to be developed provides a key focus for developers and the customer. Coding standards are an obvious syntax requirement to ensure developers communicate with the same vocabulary. For effective and continuous integration, there is a need for ongoing communication between members of the development team particularly when there is a need to merge code with that of other pairs. In an environment where continuous integration is in practice this happens regularly during a day's effort. In this environment, the skill set for IT professionals generally, and programmers in particular, is expanded from one largely focussed on coding to a greater emphasis on communication with customers, colleagues and various levels of management.

Trust

Agile methods require close working relationships often for months at a time and with a diversity of personnel involved. IT professionals need to trust each other to perform the tasks required, to undertake all appropriate tests and to respect the work of others in any rebuilding or refactoring.

The planning game is typically a highly democratic process, where tasks are allocated on a volunteer basis, so there are naturally high levels of trust generated/involved. If programmers are to be allowed to read and alter each other's code then it is important for them to trust and respect the abilities of their team members.

The originators of the code need to build the appropriate unit tests so that their code can be shown to work and those who are further enhancing the code (refactoring or improving the design of) must respect the work of their colleagues and make certain all tests are completed and verified. Developers are sometimes prone to "running their own show" and working on things in an order driven by their own interests and priorities. With small releases, there must be a commitment to work on what has been prioritized by the customer. The tight timeframes of small releases have less slack time to hide unauthorized work that can throw out the whole project release cycle. The confidence derived from knowing that a test passes each time it runs, coupled with the knowledge that it is unlikely for the code to be "broken" further down the development track without being easily detected, instills a great deal of trust in the overall process. Agile methods stress the unforgiving honesty of working code, and by avoiding and detecting compatibility problems early, continuous integration has the added effect of engendering trust in the system being developed by all of the players concerned.

A relationship of trust can be built within the project team through the transparent nature of the process. Direct exposure to the efforts, competencies, and integrity of partners has the potential to influence trusting beliefs. Building an open relationship between team members can engender a sense of comradeship and trust in one another and in the systems that they build together. On the other hand, programmers who have been accustomed to working alone could find this direct exposure to the team of their code and coding skills both intimidating and intrusive. The effective handling of such resistance poses some of the more challenging issues to be dealt with in this new development environment.

Ownership

Traditional approaches do not encourage ownership of an entire system since the deliverables are split into requirements documents, specifications, design models, code and test suites all typically developed by different individual IT personnel. In contrast, the principles and practices of agile methods require broad ownership as a fundamental attribute of projects.

The planning game facilitates high levels of ownership for all stakeholders. Since the process is highly democratic, where all parties have a say in the selection and process of work allocation, there is a strong sense of ownership of project deliverables. Allowing any developer to work on any code opens the problem of someone discovering another developer's coding deficiencies. However, if combined with pair programming this situation should be mitigated against. On the positive side knowing others are so closely reviewing development might encourage extra effort to get things right. In developing code together in alternating pairs, programmers can assume a greater share of collective code ownership and find less of a need to protect their work as personal intellectual property. Because customers are part of the development team, ownership of the final product is much clearer for them also.

Small releases encourage commitment to and ownership of their work as there are very clear-cut responsibilities when the jobs are volunteered for and/or handed out. The concept of collective code ownership is enhanced through a test-driven development environment where the need to be protective over one's effort, for fear of it being made to malfunction by someone else, is largely allayed. Some programmers will find it difficult to "give up" their solution for an alternative. Of course, they may not be involved in refactoring their own code; others will. Metaphors encourage a more meaningful understanding of the project by the whole of team, and increased understanding translates to increased sense of shared ownership. Ownership is relevant to the team overall and is most evident in the practice of continuous integration where modules are checked in and integrated into the system so the code becomes the domain of the whole team. For today's IT professional this entails a paradigm shift from traditionally viewing software production as an individual effort and responsibility to one where collaborative coding, collective ownership and working for the common good are the order of the day.

Empowerment

In a traditional development environment, customers and developers are typically shielded from each other, with business and system analysts playing the intervening roles. Agile approaches, on the other hand, encourage a new more communicative role for IT professionals generally and developers in particular.

All stakeholders have a say in the planning, scheduling and allocation of tasks within a project. Since all code developers have access to all code, novices as well as experts within the team have equal access and rights. The nature of pair programming fosters a development environment that enables programmers of varying skill levels to work cooperatively and develop a sense of confidence and self-esteem that would otherwise not have been the case through working in isolation. Customers are empowered as they have a constant input to development and acceptance testing while the project is proceeding.

By allowing refactoring to occur, developers are empowered to better their own code design or that of others. All team members may contribute to the development of the metaphor and will certainly be aware of the metaphor in use. A system that integrates successfully on a regular basis can generate a feeling of confidence among the developers as they observe the success of their efforts.

Visibility/Transparency

Agile methods lead to increased levels of visibility and transparency within the organization. Several of XP's practices demonstrate this.

The planning and allocation of tasks and responsibilities is clear, specific and detailed at the individual story level for a development cycle that lasts only weeks. This results in a highly visible project plan. The planning game engenders a spirit of egalitarianism into organizational culture. This is due to the high levels of personal interaction, the involvement of all levels of staff and the sense of shared destiny it brings. Since all code is available to all developers, every aspect of the system under development is visible. Traditionally peer reviews have been undertaken through walkthroughs and code inspections, but these were largely considered in a negative light by developers. In agile methodologies pair programming may more effectively facilitate this process of peer review. However, pair programming is one of the more controversial practices of several agile methods and does raise many management and personnel challenges. Pairs watch each other and with rotations watch the entire team, so all effort is highly visible. Sustainable pace ensures that team velocity is not artificially inflated, and therefore makes project schedules very transparent, and difficult to manipulate. Since the customer is working with the developers, all development activity is visible to the customer which results in improved (if not ideal) transparency of process and outcomes.

In contrast to traditional software development methods which tend to focus on delivering larger chunks of functionality much later in the development schedule, agile methods suggest the release of production software to customers regularly, usually weekly, but potentially daily. Small releases encourage transparency as the user stories for each release are clearly and publicly agreed and allocated at the start of each release. From a management perspective, this is considered advantageous because it facilitates early identification of project schedule problems. Agile methods also emphasize keeping the design simple. In this way, the team takes a minimalist approach to the addition of functionality and ensures the customer receives essential features in the order of priority requested. Agile methods encourage a high quality assurance culture through practices such as test driven development and pair programming. A test driven development environment places additional requirements on developers to implement these tests, customers to undertake acceptance tests, and management to encourage testing within the organization as a whole. Until now, there has been an assumption on the part of business managers that testing was going on, when at most companies this was not the case. Now, with test-driven development there is a higher visibility with regard to testing and the role of testers. Customers can demand proof and evidence of quality. If organizations make testing part of the culture of the production team then the increased level of accountability engendered creates a heightened sense of trust inside the development team, between teams and especially with customers. Since tests are written for all code and all tests must run at code integration time and after refactoring, any issues or irregularities are noticed immediately. Metaphors offer a highly visible means of promoting a clear understanding by all team members, and thus contribute to a more transparent understanding of the project. Test-driven development is an approach to software development that will be new to many developers. Greater exposure during all stages of the development process places particular demands on the IT professional since deliverables are subject to increased scrutiny throughout, and sooner rather than later as would have been the case in traditional environments.

Accountability/Responsibility

The need for shared responsibility, in an environment where all the stakeholders partake in the development and decision-making processes, is essential when managing complex and volatile Internet-based systems development. Agile methods promote shared responsibilities through approaches such as XP's "whole-of-team-approach" and "collective code ownership." In traditional methodologies, design architecture is usually predefined, which does not offer the same flexible approach. However, an agile approach can result in significant additional pressure on individual IT professionals and development team members to be more accountable, to focus on the agreed tasks and report their progress accurately.

With ownership, comes responsibility and accountability. Responsibilities are clearly defined, for example, customers are responsible for developing the stories and allocating the development priority. If pair programming is implemented, there is also a shared responsibility here. By having to explain and justify actions throughout the coding process, pair programmers inevitably become more accountable for their work. All those who would alter the code in any way either via enhancements or refactoring have a responsibility to not break any working component.

Technical staff are responsible for estimating development time and providing advice on technical considerations. All developers are accountable for their code and the tests within. Companies are making testing part of the culture of the production team. Any refactoring needs to recognise that the code already in place satisfies the requirements and has been tested and possibly accepted by the customer. If refactoring is to take place then the new design should be simpler and or contribute significantly to improved performance. Programmers checking in their code and integrating it into the existing code base are responsible for ensuring that every test in the system runs including all currently running acceptance tests. When a build fails any existing test that fails must be fixed by the pair responsible for the integration before finishing the check in. The impact of collective code and design ownership on the individual IT professional is the need to take on responsibility for the whole system per se, rather than only on pre-designated aspects of it.

People Management

All organizations, large and small, have staff whose tasks include handling resource servicing and advice as well as undertaking a range of operational activities. Some organizations will have dedicated staff for various aspects related to financial and human resources and others will include the roles within those of the managers. However, all organizations will have to deal with selection of staff, training and re-training, provision of resources to enable work completion and mechanisms to reward staff for normal and extra duties.

Staff Selection

In selecting developers, it would be useful to consider their prior education, experience and training as well as their personality traits in terms of the specific requirements of an agile software development environment.

Selection processes for developers should include criteria requiring respect for the work of others. Selection of developer staff, where collective code ownership is in operation, must take account of developers who prefer to work alone and who are guarded of their output. The fact that pair programming is one of the more controversial agile practices is in no small part due to the resistance traditional IT professionals and programmers feel about working with and alongside others during the coding stage. Ensuring that software developers fit the personality profiles of those who are able and/or willing to work in an agile environment will establish a solid foundation for this practice to gain acceptance and succeed. Potential staff need to be made aware of the requirement to work at a sustained pace and not to under or over perform in this regard. Where there is evidence that the potential employee prefers to work excessive hours care should be exercised in their recruitment. Selecting appropriate staff to act as on-site customers will require careful screening since they will need to understand the functionality required as well as to be empathetic with developers in recognizing the issues relevant to the development process.

Staff selection processes may need to be realigned to enable potential employees to demonstrate how they would transform complex problems into ones more simply solved and explained (coded). Skills in refactoring and test-driven development are required as the techniques are not the norm for traditional development environments.

Training/Re-Training

Training and re-training are expensive exercises. Over and above basic programming skills the agile developer will be required to demonstrate an ability to reduce code complexity to simple design; incorporate a test driven development regime; program in pairs; and be able to work at a sustainable pace. While selection processes can alleviate some of the costs by ensuring new staff brought to the organization and projects have the requisite skills and attributes, existing staff need to be trained and possibly given assistance with coping with changing requirements.

Members of the planning game team will need training in their rights and responsibilities since these will be clearly defined and might not always be their preferred role. For example, the role of the on-site customer is to set priorities, and the role of technical staff is to make estimates. If collective code ownership is implemented then this culture will need to be tempered and indeed changed so that egoless development is allowed. Such retraining will not be trivial. It may require gradual build-up via small projects. Most tertiary students are educated in an environment where collaboration of this type is not encouraged and indeed penalised. Curriculum design for courses such that students are required to work with and from the code of others is one solution. Clearly it would be unwise for all courses but some could implement this concept in a relatively controlled way. Working in pairs does not come naturally to all programmers initially and not all of the aspects of the pair programming process are clearly understood. The issues and challenges of team dynamics and the development of people skills and people management need to be continually re-enforced through ongoing training and education. One of the most entrenched characteristics of programmers has been their tendency to overcommit themselves in terms of the amount of work they take on. Consequently, they work long, often non-standard hours, which often makes them burn out and not be available for customer contact. Hence it is important to (re)train them in the concept of sustainable pace. On-site customers will need training in areas such as team and group dynamics, and user acceptance testing including script writing if they are to be effective and respected members of the development team.

Traditional development environments build a culture of egocentric programming where ownership of code and systems is important to the developers. Where developers are used to developing complex solutions they will need retraining to become developers of simple designs. How to introduce test-driven development and the skills associated with it into the local programming culture, where generally the technical complexities and political pressures of real-world development pose their own challenges, is a key issue. There is a need to create an environment supported by a coach/mentor. Refactoring and redesigning the code of others is not necessarily a "natural" developer skill. Many current maintenance coders will need retraining to more critical thinking skills so that the current code is not necessarily considered adequate but requires constant re-thought. All staff (whole of team) should be trained in what the system metaphor means and how it may be developed. Use of coding standards may require some training. The process of continuous integration in an agile environment demands a fundamental shift to the traditional development pattern. The need for and benefits of continuous integration as well as the techniques and tools in use should be inculcated through training and education programs.

Physical Layout/Environment/Tools

The physical layout plays a significant role in an agile environment more so where pair programming is implemented. Various options concerning the layout of the desks and computer equipment should be considered conducive to pair programming. Careful thought should also be given to the need for constant conversation, interaction and swapping between pairs and how this might impact neighbouring developers. Developers also need their own space for email, telephone, staff development, and so forth. Since the customer is on-site the workspace layout will need to accommodate them. It is likely that on-site customers will not be full-time members of development teams so this layout will require consideration for their other roles and responsibilities. Software tools are required which allow developers to share code without compromising each others' efforts. Tired programmers make more mistakes. A key requirement for effective software development is for developers to work in an environment in which they can operate at a sustainable pace, that is, one in which "burn out" can be avoided. XP enables this through one of its core practices that stipulates a standard working week. This improves the quality of the work performed, and improves the team's morale but has obvious implications for human resources and management of personnel.

Automated tools for unit testing and acceptance testing are now readily available but training will be required in some cases. Software tools are required if refactoring is to be effective and safe to the current code-base. The processes involved in continuous integration can largely be automated and monitored through available software tools.

Performance Appraisal/Reward Mechanisms

A critical issue for management of IT staff is their remuneration. Obviously management wishes to reward good developers but in a project with collective code ownership some of the traditional measures or metrics of performance will be hidden. Intellectual property (IP) rights may be an issue in certain projects also. Employment contracts that allow payment and bonus allocation, and reduce IP disputes will be necessary for these projects. Metrics will need to be constructed to encourage and reward simple designing and refactoring that simplifies designs and/or provides more efficient processing. The resultant code arising out of a pair programming effort is designed and authored by both members. With programmers developing code cooperatively the ability to determine individual effort and worth can become a significant problem when it comes to reward and remuneration. New mechanisms and metrics will have to be developed to reward value creation rather than number of lines of code written or the number of hours worked or defects per thousand lines of code. Many agile methodologists are openly critical of such metrics-gathering initiatives and are averse to accepting them as reflective of the true value of the work being done. In an agile development environment IT professionals will be faced with being assessed on a number of different levels and on different criteria, over and above the quantity and quality of their code.

Project Management

Most IT artefacts are developed within projects. Traditional development methods typically use formal project management approaches but such approaches will be challenged with agile methods where change is "welcomed" and the focus from the earliest of stages is the production of working software.

Most agile methods have a mechanism to determine the system functionality to be developed during a particular time period. In XP this is known as "the planning game" where the customer decides on the functionality to be implemented while the developers estimate the time required, and through negotiation and prioritization, workloads for the next cycle are planned. This is in stark contrast to traditional software development methods where requirements gathering, specification and design of entire systems precede any implementation. In an agile environment the short life cycles, the need for collaboration throughout the process and the specific characteristics of the project itself raise various issues and tensions that have to be understood and managed effectively.

Team Management

Team-based work is becoming more common in recognition of its suitability for Internet style, short-turnaround projects. Agile teams address many problems from past development efforts by bringing all stakeholders together and thereby overcoming the "them-and-us" divide which has been the cause of much expensive re-work.

Team management is influenced by the democratic, egalitarian nature of project management and the high levels of personal communication involved. The challenges and problems of working in and managing larger teams are often magnified in a pair programming environment where the close proximity of the members and the concentrated nature of the task pose unique problems to management (Ally et al., 2005). Team management is very important in ensuring that developers adhere to the standard work week. Sustainable pace is very important to project management, since the basic premise of team velocity is centred on how much work can be done by the team in standard hours. Because of the level of autonomy it may be difficult for project managers to be fully aware of the activities of customers and developers and thus development may "go off" at tangents to that expected. It can be difficult for managers to observe how effective or productive developers are. Since code is collectively owned it is difficult for managers to apportion blame when things go wrong. If tests are not written correctly or do not test the code adequately then faults are likely to occur.

IT professionals will find themselves working to standard hours, in an environment with new working conditions and new challenges, placing greater demands on their ability to work in teams.

Personality

Issues of personality need consideration within projects as well as for people management. They are considered here since it is within projects is where problematic behaviours relevant to certain personality types are most important.

The planning game assumes open and "team like" communication and relies on people who are committed to making the project and the approach work. One of the reasons many workers enter the IT field is that they prefer working by themselves; they tend to be introverted. Some IT professionals build an aura of complexity around their tasks and do not let others get to know their work or get inside their projects. Some programmers may not want to give up their complex designs. The personality traits, habits, attitudes, and preferences of individuals who are now required to work in pairs need to be understood and handled appropriately. Developers have a reputation for being "lone wolf" types who enjoy working in isolation, and thus naturally adopt non-standard work habits. As this counters the agile spirit of team-based development and communication, these personality types may find the new demands being placed on them challenging and/or frustrating. The on-site customer will need a personality suited to being a member of a diverse team, responding to short deadlines (not typical of traditional approaches), and working within open plan workspaces in close proximity to others.

Project Characteristics

The size, type, and complexity of a project will impact how the planning game proceeds. The larger and more complex a project the greater the level of formal documentation needed both in terms of project management and in specification of requirements. Larger projects will require multiple pairs of programmers who will need to swap regularly. Whether this can be done effectively is questionable. In large projects, several on-site customers are likely to be needed raising challenges of coordinating and integrating the varied and diverse requirements within the context of a single planning game process.

For some project types promoting the notion of collective code ownership can pose practical problems. In large projects, such as enterprise systems (ERP systems) where it is possible that developers deal only with certain aspects of a system it would be impractical to allow free reign across all code for all developers. Equally in some safety critical systems or high security systems it may be inappropriate to permit complete access and there may be levels of security access applicable. The implications for agile approaches and individual IT professionals are unclear in some of these situations and more research is needed to understand them. Indeed for some projects an agile approach may be unsuitable or difficult to implement, and in organizations where agile methods have been adopted, reverting to another methodology may be confronting.

Future Trends

It is well-documented that many of the techniques used in agile methods were selectively drawn from existing practices. Software tools, such as those for testing, integration, collaboration, refactoring and version control, used for facilitating the different stages were developed separately and largely independently of each other. The newer integrated development environments (IDEs) entering the market appear to address the need for a single "one-stop-shop" where all of these tools are made readily available to the programmer. These environments encourage particular patterns of work that are consistent with agile approaches so management will need to adapt its practices and styles to suit. On the other hand, programmers using such IDEs but not engaging in a formal adoption of any of the agile practices will find it increasingly difficult to ignore the presence of these embedded features.

There are at least two aspects of agile approaches with implications for future adoption that have been hotly debated. The first relates to the manner in which agile methods are to be adopted. For example, many purists claim that all XP practices must be implemented, and in the prescribed manner. However, many organizations are either adopting all the practices incrementally, or implementing only a subset of the practices. Such decisions are based on the management perception of which practices will best suit and benefit a particular context or environment, as well as being cognizant of catering for organizational change issues.

Another contentious aspect of agile methods that is influencing the shape of future agile adoptions, and that is particularly relevant to individual IT professionals, is pair programming. There has been much debate in the literature about variations to the prescribed approach to implement and manage pairs. The variations proposed cover areas such as: using pairs on an as needs basis rather than all the time; identifying particular types of tasks best suited for pair work; matching pairs on skill and personality rather than randomly; and variation to the period of rotation and time spent pairing. Many of these variations will be driven by management perception of the effective use of resources, as well as concern for productive harmony within the teams.

Conclusion

Any change is problematic and changing IT development from traditional to agile approaches is no different. Whether it be the IT professionals, the project managers or the customers, all will need to learn new skills and change their attitudes if such a transition is to work for even simple small projects. How quickly should such changes take place? Which practices should be adopted and in what order? What if there is resistance from the various stakeholders? These are just some of the questions that need to be addressed from the outset. Particular attention must therefore be given to implementing effective change management during the introduction of each stage of the process. Human resource services will need to develop strategies to minimize and reconcile staff tensions arising out of adopting agile practices and build a culture of trust, respect, and collaboration. Appropriate human resource processes should be put in place to support and facilitate this software development reform. Consideration of the areas described here and the concepts within will go some way to enabling a better understanding of these types of problems and possible solutions.

References

Ally, M., Darroch, F., & Toleman, M. (2005, June 18-23). A framework for understanding the factors influencing pair programming success. In H. Baumesiter (Ed.), The *6th International Conference on Extreme Programming and Agile Processes in Software Engineering—XP 2005* (pp. 82-91). Lecture Notes in Computer Science LNCS 3556. Sheffield, UK: Springer-Verlag, Berlin.

Barnett, L. (2002). *IT trends 2003: Application development methodologies and processes*. IdeaByte. September. Retrieved November 11, 2004, from http://www.forrester.com/Cart?addDocs=28123

Beck, K. (1999). *Extreme programming explained: Embrace change*. Boston: Addison Wesley.

Beck, K., & Andres, C. (2005). *Extreme programming explained: Embrace change* (2nd ed.). Boston: Pearson Publishing.

Beck, K., & Fowler, M. (2001). *Planning extreme programming*. Boston: Addison Wesley.

Bossi, P., & Cirillo, F. (2001, May). Repo margining system: Applying XP in the financial industry. *Proceedings of the 2nd International Conference on eXtreme Processing and Agile Processing Software Engineering (XP 2001)*, Villasimius, Italy. Retrieved January 7, 2005, from http://www.xp2003.org/conference/papers/Chapter35-Bossi+alii.pdf

C3 Team. (1998, October). Case study: Chrysler goes to "extremes." *Distributed Computing*. Retrieved January 7, 2005, from http://www.xprogramming.com/publications/dc9810cs.pdf

Elssamadisy, A. (2001, July). XP on a large project—A developer's view. *Proceedings of the XP Universe Conference*, Raleigh, NC. Retrieved January 7, 2005, from http://www.xpuniverse.com/2001/pdfs/EP202.pdf

Fitzgerald, B. (1998). An empirical investigation into the adoption of systems development methodologies. *Information and Management, 34*(6), 317-328.

Fitzgerald, B. (2000). Systems development methodologies: The problem of tenses. *Information Technology and People, 13*(3), 174-185.

Fowler, M., & Highsmith, J. (2001, August). *The agile manifesto*. Software Development. Retrieved November 1, 2004, from http://www.sdmagazine.com/documents/s=844/sdm0108a/0108a.htm

Highsmith, J., & Cockburn, A. (2001, September). Agile software development: The business of innovation. *Computer, 34*(9), 120-122.

Grenning, J. (2001). Launching extreme programming at a process-intensive company. *IEEE Software, 18*(6), 27-33.

Karlström, D. (2002). Introducing extreme programming—An experience report. *Proceedings of the 3rd International Conference on eXtreme Processing and Agile Processing Software Engineering (XP2002)*, Alghero, Italy. Retrieved January 7, 2005, from http://www.xp2003.org/xp2002/atti/DanielKarlstrom—IntroducingExtremeProgramming.pdf

Lappo, P. (2002). No pain, No XP: Observations on teaching and mentoring extreme programming to university students. *Agile Alliance*. Retrieved January 7, 2005, from http://www.agilealliance.org/articles/articles/PeterLappo—ObservationsonTeachingandMentoringXP.pdf

Mugridge, R., MacDonald, B., Roop, P., & Tempero, E. (2003). Five challenges in teaching XP. *Proceedings of the 4th International Conference on eXtreme Processing and Agile Processing Software Engineering*

(XP2003) (pp. 406-409). Genova, Italy. Retrieved January 7, 2005, from http://www.cs.auckland.ac.nz/~rick/5ChallengesTeachingXP.pdf

Pedroso Jr., M., Visoli, M. C., & Antunes, J. F. G. (2002). Extreme programming by example. *Proceedings of the 3ʳᵈ International Conference on eXtreme Processing and Agile Processing Software Engineering (XP2002)*, Alghero, Italy. Retrieved January 7, 2005, from http://www.xp2003.org/xp2002/atti/Pedroso-Marcos—ExtremeProgrammingby Example.pdf

Schuh, P. (2001). Recovery, redemption, and extreme programming. *IEEE Software, 18*(6), 34-41.

Sleve, G. (2002). Agile before agile was cool. *The Journal of Defense Software Engineering, 15*(10), 28-29.

Toleman, M., Ally, M. A., & Darroch, F. (2004, July 8-11). Aligning adoption theory with Agile system development methodologies. *Proceedings of the 8ᵗʰ Pacific-Asia Conference on Information Systems - PACIS 2004* (pp. 458-471). Shanghai, China.

Toleman, M., Darroch, F., & Ally, M. (2005, May 8-11). Web publishing—an eXtreme, Agile experience. In R. L. Baskerville, L. Mathiassen, J. Pries-Heje, & J. I. DeGross (Eds.), *Business agility and information technology diffusion* (pp. 245-256). New York: Springer.

Turner, R., & Boehm, B. (2003). People factors in software management: Lessons for comparing agile and plan-driven methods. *Journal of Defense Software Engineering, 12*(03), 1-9. Retrieved January 7, 2005, from http://www.stsc.hill.af.mil/crosstalk/2003/12/0312Turner.pdf

Chapter XI

Cultural Diversity Challenges:
Issues for Managing Globally Distributed Knowledge Workers in Software Development

Haiyan Huang, The Pennsylvania State University, USA

Eileen M. Trauth, The Pennsylvania State University, USA

Abstract

This chapter discusses cultural diversity challenges in globally distributed software development and the implications for educating and managing the future global information technology workforce. It argues that the work practices of global software development are facing a variety of challenges associated with cultural diversity, which are manifested in and can be analyzed from three dimensions: the work environment of global software development, the globally distributed knowledge workers, and the global software development work. It further articulates how cultural diversity is manifested in these three dimensions. Furthermore, it highlights the importance of developing cultural awareness and cultural diversity understanding as important skills for the future information technology workforce.

Introduction

In this chapter, we explore the cultural diversity challenges of managing globally distributed knowledge workers who engage in global software development work practices. This topic is important to information technology personnel management and knowledge management for three reasons. First, there has been a significant increase in global software development work practices in recent years. Such work practices not only adopt the conventional characteristics of knowledge intensive work, but also generate a set of distinct features, which call special attention to managerial researchers and practitioners. Second, in global software development, the information technology (IT) professionals are globally distributed in the forms of global virtual teams and represent a wide range of nationalities and, thus cultures. Therefore, we should not only acknowledge the existence of cultural diversity of globally distributed knowledge workers, but also explore how such cultural diversity may affect global software development work, and how to explore, assess, and manage this cultural diversity. Third, although cross-cultural issues have been one of the major concerns of the global information systems discipline, there are still on-going debates about how to assess culture and cultural diversity. As a result, different views of culture and cultural diversity will have impacts on the related human resource strategies used in managing global IT personnel. Consequently, evaluation and reflection on those issues in global software development work environments are very important.

As knowledge work is increasingly outsourced globally, we would like to take the opportunity in this book chapter to consider the cultural diversity challenges of managing globally distributed knowledge workers. The objectives of this book chapter are: (1) to propose a framework to address the cross-cultural aspects of managing IT personnel in globally distributed software development work; and (2) to discuss some managerial implications that are derived from this framework. We believe both professionals and academics working in the field of global information technology and information systems (IS) management will benefit from these discussions.

The organization of the book chapter proceeds as follows. In the Background section, we introduce the concepts of global software development and virtual teamwork. Then we present our research framework, which focuses on articulating how cultural diversity is manifested in global software development workplaces, workers, and work practices. In the following section on recommendations, we discuss how we may address the cultural diversity challenges in managing globally distributed knowledge workers who are engaged in global software development activities, particularly from the perspectives of IS/IT education and organizational human resource management.

Background

Global Software Development

Global software development as one type of information technology offshore outsourcing activities (Lacity & Willocks, 2001), has become an established practice for software and information systems development (Carmel & Agarwal, 2002; Herbsleb & Moitra, 2001). Global software development can be defined as software and information systems development practices that are knowledge intensive and involve the work arrangements between two or more organizations across the national boundaries.

Software and information systems development has been widely conceived as knowledge-intensive work (Henninger, 1997; Swart & Kinnie, 2003) with three characteristics. First, knowledge as intellectual capital is an important input to a software development project, and an important output as well (Swart & Kinnie, 2003; van Solingena, Berghoutb, Kustersc, & Trienekensc, 2000). Second, Waterson, Clegg, and Axtell (1997) pointed out that software development work is "knowledge intensive" in the sense that building a complex software system demands selecting and coordinating multiple sources of knowledge (Shukla & Sethi, 2004). Drucker (2004) argued that the specialized knowledge in knowledge work indicates that knowledge workers need to access the organization—the collective that brings together a diversity of specialized knowledge workers to achieve a common goal. For example, a software development project may involve a variety of IT personnel such as designer, analyst, programmer, tester, implementer, and manager. Therefore, collaborations of team work are necessary and critical for software development projects. Third, knowledge associated with software development is rapidly changing as the complexity and diversity of the application domain is increasing (Henninger, 1997). Therefore, software development knowledge is not static but, rather, is evolving with the changing needs of the customers and business environments (Henninger, 1997). Drucker (2004) pointed out that knowledge workers not only need formal education to enable them to engage in knowledge work in the first place, but also need continuous learning opportunities through the work practice to keep the knowledge up-to-date. These three characteristics of software development work usually refer to the work practices within a single organizational domain. As software and information systems development work is increasingly outsourced globally, how to manage the knowledge workers to facilitate effective software development work practice in the cross-cultural context has become a great challenge.

Since the 1990s, software development and IT services have become dominant in global sourcing, which includes application packages, contract programming, and system integration (Lee, Huynh, Kwok, & Pi, 2002). And the global IT outsourcing market is continuously growing (Sahay, Nicholson, & Krishna, 2003; Trauth, Huang, Morgan, Quesenberry, & Yeo, 2006). It was projected that the IT outsourcing revenue would reach $159.6 billion by 2005 (Laplante, Costello, Singh, Bindiganaville, & Landon, 2004). The U.S. is the primary user of the global software and systems development market, followed by Western European countries such as the UK and Germany (Sahay et al., 2003). Countries such as India, Ireland, and Israel, have dominated the offshore outsourcing supplier market (Gopal, Mukhopadhyay, & Krishnan, 2002). A news release (*InformationWeek*, June 3, 2004) indicated that India's revenues from exports of software and back-office services is at $12.5 billion in the latest fiscal year and with growth of 30% compared with $9.6 billion in the previous year. Another news release (Friedman, 2005) reported that 7 out of 10 top software designers have operations in Ireland.

When compared to the traditional characteristics of software development work, globally distributed software development knowledge work has three additional characteristics. First, it is mainly conducted through a virtual environment that is supported to a great extent by networking technologies. Such virtual space is global by nature and transcends national and organizational boundaries. Second, it is situated within different complex, multi-leveled socio-cultural contexts. Walsham (2000, 2001) argued that the distinct cultures of different local contexts are critical factors in mediating the globalization process in the specific contexts. Therefore, the globally distributed workplace has a global-local duality. Third, the work practices of global software development are facing a variety of challenges associated with the difficulties of temporal and spatial distance, and cultural diversity.

Global Virtual Team

The globally distributed virtual team is the basic unit engaged in software development work. A global virtual team can be defined as a collection of individuals who are organizationally and globally dispersed, and culturally diverse, and who communicate and coordinate work activity asynchronously or in real time primarily through information and communication technologies (ICTs) (DeSanctis & Poole, 1997; Jarvenpaa & Leidner, 1999).

A variety of strategic and catalytic factors have contributed to the increasing trend of using globally distributed virtual teams for software and information systems development (Carmel, 1999; Herbsleb & Moitra, 2001). These include: 24/7 around-the-clock development activities, the desire to reduce development costs and have access to a global resource pool, and the proximity to the customer. In addition, some authors have further emphasized the contribution of diversity of heterogeneous teams to work performance brought about by globally dispersed team members (Adair, 1986; Harrison, McKinnon, Wu, & Chow, 2000; Hartenian, 2000; Maugain, 2003; Trauth et al., 2006). For example, Maugain (2003) argued that the different thinking modes and dissimilar problem solving methods brought in by diverse team members in multicultural R&D (Research & Design) teams will stimulate novel ideas and creativity. Hartenian (2000) pointed out that diverse groups have a tendency to make higher quality decisions, to be more creatively motivated, and have a higher productivity potential than less diverse groups.

However, research also shows that the absence of regular face-to-face interactions and the breakdown of traditional communication and coordination mechanisms are negatively associated with the effectiveness of globally distributed software development teams (Cameral, 1999; Herbsleb & Mockus, 2003). Systems development tasks, particularly front-end activities, require formal and informal communication and coordination (Audy, Evaristo, & Watson-Manheim, 2004) to facilitate knowledge exchange and learning (Curtis, Krasner, & Iscoe, 1988). According to Herbsleb and Mockus (2003), the change of communication patterns and the lack of effective communication channels (formal or informal) in globally distributed software development teams can lead to delays in global software development projects. The study by Cramton and Webber (2005) shows a negative relationship between geographic dispersion and perceived team performance with respect to complex and interdependent tasks.

The cultural difference may further exacerbate the communication problems (Herbsleb & Moitra, 2001). Carmel (1999) pointed out that the barriers of time, space, and cultural distances may be detrimental to building trust and achieving team cohesiveness in global virtual teams. Nicholson and Sahay (2004) argued that the barriers of knowledge sharing among knowledge workers in offshore software development are related to the embeddedness of knowledge in the local cultural context, and should be investigated at the interconnected societal, organizational, and individual levels of analysis.

While cultural factors may influence global virtual teams engaged in a variety of activities in general, they are particularly important to software development work for three reasons. First, compared to other activities such as new product developments in manufacturing sectors, the processes of software development are more complexly interdependent and iterative, the products of software development are less tangible, and knowledge perspectives involved in software development are more tacit and fast changing in nature (Sahay et al., 2003). Second, a number of studies have shown that culture is a critical influential factor in global software development work and has impacts on a variety of issues. While some issues are general issues faced by global virtual teams engaged in other activities in general (e.g., managing conflicts—Damian & Zowghi, 2003), building trust (Zolin, Hinds, Fruchter, & Levitt, 2004), some issues are specific to software development, such as managing IT outsourcing relationships (Krishna, Sahay, & Walsham, 2004; Nicholson & Sahay, 2001; Sahay et al., 2003), preference of software development methods (Borchers, 2003; Hanisch, Thanasankit, & Corbitt, 2001), preference of computer supported collaborative technologies (Massey, Hung, Montoya-Weiss, & Ramesh, 2001), knowledge transfer and management related to software development (Baba, Gluesing, Rantner, & Wagner, 2004; Nicholson & Sahay, 2004; Sarker, 2003), and the process and performance of globally distributed software development teams (Carmel, 1999; Olson & Olson, 2003). Third, as more and more countries are now entering the IT outsourcing market, global software development work practices are facing more cultural diversity (Sahay et al., 2003; Trauth et al., 2006). Companies in Japan and Korea join those of the U.S., Canada and other western European nations in outsourcing their software or information system development and services activities to other countries. Besides the current leading outsourced countries such as India, Ireland, and Israel, Russia and China are now establishing their capabilities as outsourcing providers (Sahay et al., 2003).

Globally distributed software development efforts, thus, must deal with trade-offs between taking advantage of the global resource pool and cultural diversity while managing the cultural and distance barriers to effective communication and coordination in a geographically dispersed environment. How to make sense of cultural diversity and its impact on managing globally distributed knowledge workers who are engaged in global software development work activities are becoming the primary concerns of global IT personnel management and knowledge management.

In the research framework (Figure 1), we propose that cultural diversity is situated and manifested in three interrelated dimensions of global software development activities: the virtual workplace, the workers, and the work (Trauth, 2000). These three main constructs reflect what dimensions of global software development may be affected by cultural diversity. And the bullets under each main construct further indicate how cultural diversity is manifested in each of these dimensions. Trauth (2000) studied the information economy development in Ireland and pointed out that culture is one of the major influential factors. More specifically, she addressed the cultural influences from three perspectives: multinational workplaces, knowledge workers, and knowledge work. These three perspectives are interrelated and serve as our analytical lenses to study how the cultural factors influence IT work, and in this chapter, how cultural diversity is manifested in and affects global software development.

The virtual workplace of global software development is situated within a multi-leveled socio-cultural context with the global-local duality characteristic, which

Figure 1. Research framework: Situating cultural diversity in global software development

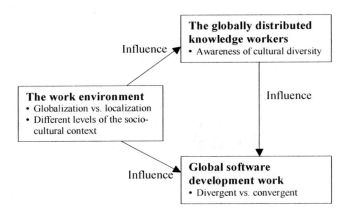

constitutes a unique work environment. Being engaged in global software development activities within such a work environment, globally distributed knowledge workers should be aware of the complexity and dynamics of cultural diversity, and constantly make sense of and negotiate meanings of such diversity. Global software development work, which includes both divergent and convergent perspectives is affected by the effectiveness of the sense-making processes and the management of cultural diversity. This framework adopts a situated approach and emphasizes the importance of studying globally distributed knowledge work as socially negotiated work practices by situating it within the both the global and local contexts (Avgerou, 2002; Trauth, 2000; Weisinger & Trauth, 2002, 2003). In the following sections, we discuss in detail how cultural diversity is manifested in each dimension of the framework, respectively.

The Work Environment

Globalization vs. Localization

Globally distributed software development work can be seen as a result of the globalization process—the IT industry is becoming more and more globally interconnected. According to Castells (1996), the globalization process involves the flows of capital, commodities, technology, cultural influences, and human resources across national boundaries, thereby creating a networked society. One stream of sociological and cultural research considers processes of globalization and flows of cultural elements across frontiers as a global "cultural homogenization" (Kellner, 2002; Schuerkens, 2003). Schuerkens (2003) criticized such "cultural homogenization" arguments of globalization by pointing out that they usually ignore the existence and active role of local cultural perspectives. Castells (1996) also pointed out that the globalization process is selective and segmented with many imbalances, and the networked society is both centralized and decentralized, which shows heterogeneous and global-local duality characteristics.

Sahay et al. (2003) argued against the "cultural homogenization" assumption of globalization and proposed that global software development work relationships can be seen as "models of" globalization process and "models for" globalization as well (p. 27). They emphasized the dynamic reciprocal relationships between the local cultural contexts and the globalization processes. Similarly, Walsham (2001) used Giddens' structuration theory (1990) and Castells' network society theory (1996) to study global IT development and stressed that the existing socio-cultural context of a country is a critical factor in mediating the globalization process in the specific context and, in turn, will have an impact on the complexity of globalization. They both acknowledge the uniqueness and importance of local contexts to globally distributed software development.

To illustrate the continuous interactions of local cultural elements and global cultural influences, Schuerkens (2003) cited Long's (1996) discussion: "Local situations are transformed by becoming part of wider global arenas and processes, while global dimensions are made meaningful in relation to specific local conditions and through the understandings and strategies of local actors" (p. 217).

Therefore, the local cultural context is neither a passive recipient of globalization and external cultural influences as indicated by the "global homogenization" argument, nor is it a static and deterministic factor that remains unchanged during the globalization process. The local cultural forms and meanings are constantly reconstructed (Schuerkens, 2003; Walsham, 2001).

We believe that such continuous interactions of globalization and localization processes have three implications for conceptualizing the cultural diversity of global software development work environments. First, global software development work is situated within a complex and dynamic global-local societal context. Second, cultural diversity is inherent in global software development and is a critical influential factor affecting global software development work practices. Third, the emergent nature of both the local cultural context and the globalization process indicates that we should focus on the appropriation and transformation of local cultural elements to address the dynamic perspectives of cultural diversity of the global software development work environment.

Different Levels of the Socio-Cultural Context

Another important feature of the cultural diversity of the virtual workplace of global software development is the multi-levels of analysis ranging from societal (national) to regional, organizational, professional, and team. Different cultural factors at different levels coexist, interact with each other, and together produce different work environments of globally distributed software development work practices. However, the influence of different cultural factors at different levels is not equal and varies across work environments. Some cultural factors may be more visible than others and some may seem trivial compared to the predominant factors depending on different cases.

For example, Robey, Gupta, and Rodriguez-Diaz (1988) studied one multinational company's efforts to implement an account system in its subsidiaries in two Latin American countries: Chile and Panama. Their findings showed that cultural and political differences between Chile and Panama could not explain the significant differences in the implementation outcomes. They believed that those differences were due to the organizational cultural differences of the two subsidiaries. This case is an example of the dominance of organizational cultural influences while national and organizational cultural differences coexist. Barrett and Walsham (1995) studied the global software development relationships between a Jamaican insurance company and an Indian software company. They pointed out that although the Indian and Jamaican team members of this joint venture development shared a similar professional culture, there were major differences between the local work culture at the Indian software company and the Jamaican insurance company. This case demonstrates the dominance of national and organizational cultural influences. The case study by Kaiser and Hawk (2004) on a long-term alliance outsourcing relationship between a U.S. company and an Indian company showed that the mutual understanding of ethnic and corporate cultures was an important factor to build stable and trust relationships.

In global IT outsourcing research, the focus tends to be on the national level of analysis. Therefore in most cultural studies of global software development, the national culture is predominant while other factors such as regional, organizational, and team cultures are in the background. This is probably due to the high visibility of cross-national cultural differences. Another reason may be that the cultural elements at different levels interact with each other and somehow diffuse into some inseparable influential factors.

Some studies (Cougar, Adelsberger, Borovits, Zviran, & Motiwalla, 1990; Constantine, 1995) pointed out that while the national culture may show divergent characteristics across national boundaries, the professionalism of the knowledge workers will share certain common cultural elements that constitute the professional culture. As a result, the team culture of the global virtual team may show a different pattern from either the national culture or the organizational or the professional culture. Earley and Gibson (2002) pointed out that through communications and interactions, the highly heterogeneous global team may appear to develop a common identity over the course of a long-term project, which they referred to as the team culture.

The contemporary work environment of global software development is situated within a complex multi-leveled socio-cultural context in which culture and its influences are emergent as the work practices evolve. The emergent perspective of cultural diversity indicates that it cannot be reduced to a set of variables and treated as unchanging inherited properties. In a sense, globally distributed knowledge workers are not passively embedded in their local context. Instead, they continuously and actively engage and negotiate with their work environment in everyday work practices.

The Globally Distributed Knowledge Workers

Brannen, Gómez, Peterson, Romani, Sagiv, and Wu (2004) pointed out that the concept of culture is by no means free of controversy. According to Worsley (1984), there are four ways of conceptualizing culture: the elitist view – culture implies superior power; the holistic view–culture implies the whole way of life; the hegemonic view – culture is a set of behaviors imposed by the majority; the relativist view – culture is localized and may bear different behaviors in different regions or communities from the same society.

There are two general doctrines of conceptualizing culture—the functionalist view and the interpretivist view (Schultz & Hatch, 1996). The functionalist view assumes that culture can be studied from several generalized dimensions and those dimensions are universal. As a result, the functionalist studies focus on categorizing cultural dimensions and predicting their influences. Hofstede's (1984) framework of five major national cultural dimensions is one example of the functionalist doctrine. The interpretivist doctrine, on the other hand, argues that culture may be ambiguous and unstable and should be studied within a specific local context instead of using general frames.

Schultz and Hatch (1996) studied the difference between the functionalist and interpretivist paradigms of cultural research. They proposed that these two paradigms can somehow interact to address the different perspectives of culture. To some extent, the mainstream of each of these doctrines can be integrated to a "multiparadigm" approach. They suggested that for example, to study national cultural patterns, the functionalist view uses predefined categories to provide a clear, generalizable and stable pattern, while the interpretivist view uses interpretation and symbolic representation to describe the ambiguous, situated and instable perspectives of culture. However, this approach may still be problematic since it assumes that there is a line between the stable and unstable elements of culture. In reality, the line itself may be ambiguous and dynamically changing.

The anthropological view of culture is a constructivist view which rejects the idea of culture as having hard and fast boundaries (Avison & Myers, 1995). On the contrary, culture is seen as contestable, temporal, and emergent, and is constantly interpreted and re-interpreted in social relations (Carrithers, 1992). Therefore, the anthropological cultural view rejects the notion of culture as a set of predefined variables peculiar to a certain society. In the information systems discipline, Walsham's notion of culture mediating the global process in specific local contexts (Walsham, 1993, 2000, 2001), Avegerou's proposal on relativism (2002), and the situated culture perspective suggested by Weisinger and Trauth (2002, 2003) are three approaches to studying culture through exploration, interpretation, and sense making, which reflect the anthropological perspective of conceptualizing culture.

We argue that when managing global software development practice, the functionalist approach may provide general guidance if cautiously adopted. However, it is lacking the capability to provide an in-depth understanding of cultural dynamics. Therefore, we take the following statement as a working definition of culture:

Culture is the sense making of different social structures and relations such as beliefs, values, and norms, attitudes, hierarchies by a group of people within a particular social context.

In this definition, we view culture as the "sense making" which actively strives for interpretation and re-interpretation of the relationships between the self-identity and the surrounding contexts. We believe that viewing culture as dynamic and emergent instead of static and predefined will provide the corresponding cross-cultural management the capability of accounting for the evolving and diversified nature of global software development phenomena.

Child (2002a, b) pointed out that the globalization trend and subsequent interconnectivity of networking technologies have pushed the traditional boundaries between nations and organizations to become somehow "borderless." At the same time, they enhance the people's awareness of their own identity and cultural distinctiveness as they have more and more opportunities to interact with a variety of cultural groups during the processes. In a sense, they interpret and reinterpret self-identity and the relationships between the self-identity and the surrounding contexts.

We argue that cultural awareness of globally distributed knowledge workers should have two levels—the self-awareness of their own identity and the mutual awareness of the existence of the cultural diversity and differences in others. Baba et al. (2004) pointed out that in order for team members of a globally distributed team to bring together and integrate the divergent knowledge, they should first develop the mutual awareness and shared cognition of the divergences. They further stressed (Baba et al., 2004) that the mutual awareness is not simply exchanging declarative or procedural knowledge—it requires: "…suspending our own judgment as we learn the cultural logic and rationality of others' divergent beliefs and values, while also allowing those others to call our own beliefs and values into question as they learn about us…" (p. 583).

The Global Software Development Work

Studies have shown that while cultural diversity may lead to advantages with respect to the divergent processes of knowledge work, it may also cause problems for the convergent processes (Miroshnik, 2002). Divergent knowledge work processes in software development refer to processes of generating and articulating different viewpoints by different team members, as well as challenging the existing assumptions in requirement analyses and systems designs, which are important for surfacing and exploring alternatives, thus promoting creativity and innovation in software development (Kryssanov, Tamaki, & Kitamura, 2001; Nickerson, 1999). Convergent knowledge work processes refer to processes of developing shared understanding and building common ground among team members with respect to different perspectives of software development, which are important to decision-making and effectiveness of teamwork (Potts & Catledge, 1996).

Knowledge intensive work, such as design and development of new software and information systems is usually characterized as highly ambiguous, uncertain, equivocal, and interdependent (Curtis et al., 1988; Herbsleb & Grinter, 1999; Hoegl & Proserpio, 2004). The analysis of systems requirements, which is a critical task at the front-end of software and information systems development, is highly dynamic, complex, fluctuating, and evolutionary in nature (Audy et al., 2004; Curtis et al., 1988; Mathiassen & Stage, 1990). Cultural diversity may provide benefit to the front-end of software development work by providing different perspectives, ideas, and approaches. Dafoulas and Macaulay (2001) pointed out that cultural diversity may be beneficial to team performance, especially on tasks for which differing perspectives might increase team performance (Trauth et al., 2006). Miroshnik (2002) also argued that cultural diversity can be used as a resource to enhance creativity, flexibility and problem solving skills, all of which are important for knowledge-intensive work.

On the other hand, to bring the divergent perspectives into a convergent development practice, cultural diversity may become a barrier to knowledge sharing and transference since knowledge is contextually dependent and culturally contingent (Nicholson & Sahay, 2004). To a great extent, the convergent processes require both formal and informal communication and coordination mechanisms to exchange diverse knowledge perspectives and facilitate learning (Curtis et al., 1988), to surface conflicts and negotiate differences (Audy et al., 2004; Briggs & Gruenbacher, 2002; Curtis et al., 1988), and to build shared understandings and common ground regarding various issues such as how to represent the system requirements and which system development methodologies are more appropriate (Cramton & Webber, 2005; Damian & Zowghi, 2003). During these convergent processes, cultural diversity may create cultural distance and barriers to knowledge sharing and transference. Herbsleb and Moitra (2001) pointed out that while cultural diversity can be seen as an enriching factor by bringing together divergent bodies of knowledge, it can also lead to serious and chronic misunderstandings.

For example, in the case study of distributed software development between England and India, Nicholson and Sahay (2004) identified cultural difference in perceptions of time between India and England. In England, a 9 AM to 5 PM working routine and the separation of working life from personal life are encouraged. In India, the boundaries between working life and home life are less defined (Nicholson & Sahay, 2004). Thus, Indian employees may respond to personal or home needs during regular working hours and may spend extra time working later hours or on weekends (Nicholson & Sahay, 2004). Such cultural differences are implicitly embedded in each local cultural context. Without building corresponding mutual knowledge and awareness about these differences, team members from one site may have misconceptions about the availability of team members from the other site. Saunders, van Slyke, and Vogel (2004) argued that different global virtual team members may have different time visions, which may influence the management and performances of global virtual teams.

The interchange of benefits of cultural diversity and hindrance of cultural distance put forward special challenges of teaching cultural diversity to future IS/IT workforce and managing globally distributed knowledge workers. On one hand, we need to address issues related to bridging cultural distance to encourage knowledge sharing and transference across different cultures. On the other hand, we need to study how to cultivate and integrate cultural diversity in order to develop new organizational capabilities (Baba et al., 2004).

Recommendations for Practice

As suggested by our research framework, it is very challenging to manage such a diverse workforce for global software development for three reasons. First, the culture of the virtual work environment is complex and dynamic. Second, the cultural diversity of globally distributed knowledge workers has the potential for both great accomplishments and great conflicts. Third, the cultural diversity of such a global workforce needs to be proactively managed, and cultivated in order to facilitate both the divergent and convergent perspectives of software development work activities.

To address these challenges, we recommend the following. First, treat cultural awareness and cultural diversity understanding as important and necessary skills for the future IS/IT workforce, provide IS/IT students opportunities to experience cultural diversity, and help them explore and develop a proper mind-set towards diversity. Second, adopt the sense-making approach in human resource practices to motivate and facilitate globally distributed knowledge workers' articulation of their self-identities and the identities of others during the social interactions of teamwork processes. Third, balance the tensions between the values and the conflicts of cultural diversity by encouraging contested, diverse thinking while building the trust and shared understanding among globally distributed team members. Finally, value cultural diversity knowledge as an important part of the organization's intellectual capital and strategic resources for competing in the global market.

IS/IT Education

The gap of critical skills and knowledge required for information technology professionals between academe and industry has been a major concern for IS/IT education (Lee, Trauth, & Farwell, 1995; Miller & Donna, 2002; Swanson, Phillips, & Head, 2003; Trauth, Farwell, & Lee, 1993). Academics and practitioners have called for assessing and expanding IT, IS, and MIS curricula to adapt to the needs of future global IS/IT workforces (Miller & Donna, 2002; Swanson et al., 2003). For example, Swanson, et al. (2003), and Noll and Wilkins (2004) discussed the growing needs for soft skills such as communication skills and teamwork skills in information technology professionals. Larsen and McInerney (2002) simulated the inter-organization virtual teamwork environment in course design to teach students certain skill sets needed in virtual work.

However, only a few of these programs specifically target the global IT environment and conceptualize diversity as one of the core elements in the global IT environment. One of those few examples is the online "IT Landscape in

Nations" repository initiated by Carmel and Mann (2003) to facilitate students conducting comparative analyses of different nations and developing greater awareness of the global IT environment. Therefore, there is a great gap between current IS/IT education and the increasing demands of the global IS/IT workforce. Educators should focus on designing and implementing corresponding curricula, renovating and expanding current pedagogical approaches to bridge such a gap.

IS/IT Human Resource Management

Along with the focus shifting from capital resources to knowledge resources in modern economic development, the role of knowledge has been fundamentally changed (Drucker, 1994). As a result, the role of human resource management has become more and more important because *"people are the only sustainable asset in modern business"* (Schwarzkopf, Saunders, Jasperson, & Croes, 2004, p. 28). The strategies and implementations of human resource practices directly affect how knowledge workers will be continuously motivated and trained to perform their value creation tasks (Hill & Jones, 1998; Pfeffer, 1994). Trauth et al. (2006) pointed out that it is critical that researchers and practitioners take an active role in creating HR solutions and it is important to understand diversity issues in the global IT environment.

Kakabadse and Kakabadse (2000) pointed out that organizational outsourcing initiatives have both negative and positive effects on their employees. As more and more IT jobs shift offshore, it may hamper the employment relationship of belonging and dedication when employees feel unsafe with respect to job security (Kakabadse & Kakabadse, 2000). The cultural diversity and the lack of trust and cohesiveness of global virtual teams may influence team members' working experiences (Carmel, 1999). It is also argued that outsourcing and global software development arrangements may provide career enhancement and learning opportunities for employees and organizations provided that special expertise and skills can be acquired and knowledge can be mutually shared and transferred across borders (Baba et al., 2004; Carmel, 1999; Kakabadse & Kakabadse, 2000). Therefore, one of the primary concerns of human resource management in global software development practices is how to mitigate the negative impacts and enhance the positive effects.

Given the complexity and dynamics of cultural diversity and its criticality in global software development work practices, it is important to emphasize the sense-making perspective in cultural training and provide employees proper and continuous cross-cultural training. When knowledge workers are involved in different virtual work environments, the stereotypically and culturally specific approach may fail to help them make sense of different cultural nuances from different cultural contexts (Goodall, 2002; Osland & Bird, 2004). Therefore, cross-cultural training should focus on how to develop and improve the cultural sense-making skills of employees.

Foster (2000) studied the cultural training for expatriates of multi-national companies and pointed out that most of those training programs focus on pre-departure training and fail to provide continuous training during the work processes. Krishna et al. (2004) pointed out that systematic cross-cultural training is less common than informal experience sharing in their case studies of global software development activities. And if in place, that cultural training is usually in one direction: for the outsourced companies to learn the culture of the outsourcing companies (Krishna et al., 2004). Osland and Bird (2004) advocated the sense-making approach for cultural training and stressed that there should be both formal and informal mechanisms for sharing cultural knowledge.

We believe that organizational human resource management together with knowledge management practices should value cultural diversity knowledge as an important part of the organizational intellectual capital and strategic resources for competing in the global IT market in the future. Cross-cultural sense making, understanding, and knowledge sharing are critical to develop flexible, competitive, and yet sustainable learning organizations (Garvin, 1998). In cross-cultural training and learning practices, we should allow distributed knowledge workers to have opportunities to continuously reflect on their cultural experiences in the course of accomplishing working processes and encourage them to take such reflections as learning opportunities.

Conclusion

To address the cultural diversity challenges of managing globally distributed knowledge workers in global software development, we proposed a research framework to articulate how cultural diversity is manifested in global virtual work environments and how the cultural diversity of distributed knowledge workers may influence global software development work practices. The main objective of the chapter is to promote the awareness of cultural diversity challenges to managing information technology professionals in the increasingly globalized IT environment. Our analyses show that we should critically examine the global-local context of the cross-cultural issues to overcome the obstacles of cultural diversity in convergent tasks of software development work and maximize its values in divergent tasks of the work activities.

As researchers and educators in academic settings, we believe that cultural awareness and cultural diversity understanding should be viewed as important skills for the future IS/IT workforce. We also believe that organizational human resource practices should adopt the sense-making approach for cross-cultural training and knowledge sharing. In order for organizations to compete in the global market in the future, cultural diversity knowledge should become an important part of the organization's intellectual capital and strategic resources.

References

Adair, J. (1986). *Effective teambuilding: How to make a winning team.* London: Pan.

Avgerou, C. (2002). *Information systems and global diversity.* Oxford; New York: Oxford University Press.

Avison, D. E., & Myers, M. D. (1995). Information systems and anthropology: An anthropological perspective on IT and organizational culture. *Information Technology & People, 8*(3), 43-56.

Audy, J., Evaristo, R., & Watson-Manheim, M. B. (2004). Distributed analysis: The last frontier? *Proceedings of the 37th Hawaii International Conference on System Sciences.* IEEE.

Baba, M. L., Gluesing, J., Rantner, H., & Wagner, K. H. (2004). The contexts of knowing: Nature history of a globally distributed team. *Journal of Organizational Behavior, 25*(5), 547-587.

Barrett, M., & Walsham, G. (1995). Managing IT for business innovation: Issues of culture, learning, and leadership in a Jamaican insurance company. *Journal of Global Information Management, 3*(3), 25-33.

Borchers, G. (2003). The software engineering impacts of cultural factors on multi-cultural software development teams. *Proceedings of 25th International Conference on Software Engineering* (pp. 540-545).

Brannen, M. Y., Gómez, G., Peterson, M. F., Romani, L., Sagiv, L., & Wu, P. C. (2004). People in global organizations: Culture, personality, and social dynamics. In H. W. Lane, M. L., Maznevski, M. E., Mendenhall, & J. McNett (Eds.), *The Blackwell handbook of global management: A guide to managing complexity* (pp. 26-54). Malden, MA: Blackwell Publishing.

Briggs, R. O., & Gruenbacher, P. (2002). Easy winwin: Managing complexity in requirements negotiation with GSS. *Proceedings of 35th Annual Hawaii International Conference on Systems Science.* IEEE.

Carmel, E. (1999). *Global software teams: Collaborating across borders and time zones.* Upper Saddle River, NJ: Prentice Hall PTR.

Carmel, E., & Agarwal, R. (2002). The maturation of offshore sourcing of information technology work. *MIS Quarterly Executives, 1*(2), 65-77.

Carmel, E., & Mann, J. (2003). Teaching about information technology in nations: Building and using the "landscape of it" repository. *Journal of Information Technology Education, 2*, 91-105.

Carrithers, M. (1992). *Why human have cultures.* Oxford: Oxford University Press.

Castells, M. (1996). *The rise of the network society.* Oxford: Blackwell.

Child, J. (2002a). Theorizing about organization cross-nationally: Part 1 – An introduction. In M. Warner & P. Joynt (Eds.), *Managing across cultures: Issues and perspectives* (2nd ed., pp. 26-39). London: Thomson Learning.

Child, J. (2002b). Theorizing about organization cross-nationally: Part 2 – Towards a synthesis. In M., Warner & P. Joynt (Eds.), *Managing across cultures: Issues and perspectives* (2nd ed., pp. 40-56). London: Thomson Learning.

Constantine, L. (1995). *Constantine on Peopleware.* Englewood Cliffs, NJ: Yourdon Press.

Cougar, J. D., Adelsberger, H., Borovits, I., Zviran, M., & Motiwalla, J. (1990). Commonalities in motivating environments for programmer/analysts in Austria, Israel, Singapore, and the USA. *Information and Management, 18*(1), 41-46.

Cramton, C. D., & Webber, S. S. (2005). Relationships among geographic dispersion, team processes, and effectiveness in software development work teams. *Journal of Business Research, 58*(6), 758-765.

Curtis, B., Krasner, H., & Iscoe, N. (1988). A field study of the software design process for large systems. *Communications of the ACM, 31*(11), 1268-1287.

Dafoulas, G., & Macaulay, L. (2001). Investigating cultural differences in virtual software teams. *The Electronic Journal on Information Systems in Developing Countries, 7*(4), 1-14.

Damian, D. E., & Zowghi, D. (2003). An insight into the interplay between culture, conflict, and distance in globally distributed requirements negotiations. *Proceedings of the 36th Hawaii International Conference on System Sciences.* IEEE.

DeSanctis, G., & Poole, M. S. (1997). Transitions in teamwork in new organizational forms. In B. Markovsky (Ed.), *Advances in group processes* (Vol. 14, pp. 157-176). Greenwich, CT: JAI Press.

Drucker, P. F. (1994). The age of social transformation. *The Atlantic Monthly, 274*(5), 53-80.

Drucker, P. (2004). *The next workforce*. Retrieved on February 17, 2005, from http://207.36.242.12/data/html/pop/article3print.htm

Earley, P. C., & Gibson, C. B. (2002). *Multinational work teams: A new perspective*. Mahwah, NJ: Lawrence Erlbaum Associates Publishers.

Foster, N. (2000). Expatriates and the impact of cross-cultural training. *Human Resource Management Journal, 10*(3), 63-78.

Friedman, T. L. (2005, June 29). The end of the rainbow. *New York Times.* Retrieved January 26, 2006, from http://www.nytimes.com/2005/06/29friedman.html ?ex=127769700&en=a3f1a208e2617871&ei=5088&partner=rssnyt&emc=rrs

Garvin, D. A. (1998). Building a learning organization. In *Harvard Business Review on Knowledge Management* (pp. 47-80). Boston: Harvard Business School Publishing.

Giddens, A. (1990). *The consequences of modernity*. Cambridge: Polity Press.

Goodall, K. (2002). Managing to learn: From cross-cultural theory to management education practice. In M. Warner & P. Joynt (Eds.), *Managing across cultures: Issues and perspectives* (2nd ed., pp. 256-268). London: Thomson Learning.

Gopal, A., Mukhopadhyay, T., & Krishnan, M. S. (2002). The role of software process and communication in offshore software development. *Communications of the ACM, 45*(4), 193-200.

Hanisch, J., Thanasankit, T., & Corbitt, B. (2001, June 27-29). Understanding the cultural and social impacts on requirements engineering processes– Identifying some problems challenging virtual team integration with clients. *Proceedings of the 9th European Conference on Information Systems* (pp. 11-22). Bled, Slovenia.

Harrison, G., McKinnon, J., Wu, A., & Chow, C. (2000). Cultural influences on adaptation to fluid workgroups and teams. *Journal of International Business Studies, 31*(3), 489-505.

Hartenian, L. (2000, December). Cultural diversity in small business: Implications for firm performance. *Journal of Developmental Entrepreneurship*, 209-219.

Henninger, S. (1997). Case-based knowledge management tools for software development. *Automated Software Engineering, 4*(3), 319-340.

Herbsleb, J. D., & Grinter, R. E. (1999). Splitting the organization and integrating the code: Conway's law revisited. *Proceedings of the 21st International Conference on Software Engineering* (pp. 85-95). Los Alamitos, CA.

Herbsleb, J., & Mockus, A. (2003). An empirical study of speed and communication in globally distributed software development. *IEEE Transactions on Software Engineering, 29*(6), 481-494.

Herbsleb, J. D., & Moitra, D. (2001). Global software development. *IEEE Software, 18*(2), 16-20.

Hill, C. W. L., & Jones, G. R. (1998). *Strategic management: An integrated approach* (4th ed.). New York: Houghton Mifflin.

Hoegl, M., & Proserpio, L. (2004). Team member proximity and teamwork in innovative projects. *Research Policy, 33*(8), 1153-1165.

Hofstede, G. (1984). *Culture's consequences: International differences in work-related values*. Beverly Hills, CA: Sage.

InformationWeek (2004, June 3). India's software exports reach $12.5 billion. Retrieved on December 10, 2005, from http://www.informationweek.com/story/showArticle.jhtml?articleID=21401198.

Jarvenpaa, S., & Leidner, D. (1999). Communication and trust in global virtual teams. *Organization Science, 10*(6), 791-815.

Kaiser, K. M., & Hawk, J. (2004). Evolution of offshore software development: From outsourcing to cosourcing. *MIS Quarterly Executive, 3*(2), 69-81.

Kakabadse, N., & Kakabadse, A. (2000). Critical review – Outsourcing: A paradigm shift. *Journal of Management Development, 19*(8), 670-728.

Kellner, D. (2002). Theorizing globalization. *Sociological Theory, 20*(3), 285-305.

Krishna, S., Sahay, S., & Walsham, G. (2004). Managing cross-cultural issues in global software development. *Communications of the ACM, 47*(4), 62-66.

Kryssanov, V. V., Tamaki, H., & Kitamura, S. (2001). Understanding design fundamentals: how synthesis and analysis drive creativity, resulting in emergence. *Artificial Intelligence in Engineering, 15*(4), 329-342.

Lacity, M., & Willcocks, L. (2001). *Global information technology outsourcing: Search for business advantage*. Chichester, UK: John Wiley & Sons.

Laplante, P. A., Costello, T., Singh, P., Bindiganaville, S., & Landon, M. (2004). The who, what, why, where, and when of IT outsourcing. *IT Professional, 6*(1), 19-23.

Larsen, K. R., & McInerney, C. R. (2002). Preparing to work in the virtual organization. *Information & Management, 29*, 445-456.

Lee, D. M., Trauth, E. M., & Farwell, D. (1995). Critical skills and knowledge requirements of IS professionals: A joint academic/industry investigation. *MIS Quarterly, 19*(3), 313-340.

Lee, J., Huynh, M., Kwok, R., & Pi, S. (2002). Current and future directions of IS outsourcing. In R. Hirschheim, A., Heinzl, & J. Dibbern (Eds.), *Information systems outsourcing: enduring themes, emergent patterns, and future directions* (pp. 195-220). Berlin, Germany: Springer-Verlag.

Massey, A. P., Hung, Y. T. C., Montoya-Weiss, M., & Ramesh, V. (2001). Cultural perceptions of task-technology fit. *Communications of the ACM, 44*(12), 83-84.

Mathiassen, L., & Stage, J. (1990). Complexity and uncertainty in software design. *Proceedings of the 1990 IEEE Conference on Computer Systems and Software Engineering* (pp. 482-489). Los Alamitos, CA: IEEE.

Maugain, O. (2003). *Managing multicultural R&D teams: An in-depth case study of a research project at CERN.* PhD thesis. Retrieved on January 26, 2006, from http://www.unisg.ch/www/edis.nsf/wwwDisplayIdentifier/2820/$FILE/dis2820.pdf

Miller, R. A., & Donna, D. W. (2002). Advancing the IS curricula: The identification of important communication skills needed by is staff during systems development. *Journal of Information Technology Education, 1*(3), 143-156.

Miroshnik, V. (2002). Culture and international, management: A review. *Journal of Management Development, 21*(7/8), 521-544.

Nicholson, B., & Sahay, S. (2004). Embedded knowledge and offshore software development. *Information and Organization, 14*(4), 329-365.

Nickerson, R. S. (1999). Enhancing creativity. In R. E. Sternberg (Ed.), *Handbook of creativity* (pp. 392-430). Cambridge: Cambridge University Press.

Noll, C. L., & Wilkins, M. (2004). Critical skills of IS professionals: A model for curriculum development. *Journal of Information Technology Education, 3*, 117-131.

Olson, J. S., & Olson, G. M. (2003). Culture surprises in remote software development teams. *QUEUE, 1*(9), 52-59.

Osland, J. S., & Bird, A. (2004). Beyond sophisticated stereotyping: Cultural sensemaking in contex. In S. M. Puffer (Ed.), *International management: Insights from friction and practice* (pp. 56-66). Armonk, NY: M.E. Sharpe.

Pfeffer, J. (1994). *Competitive advantage through people: Unleashing the power of the work force.* Boston: Harvard Business School Press.

Potts, C., & Catledge, L. (1996). Collaborative conceptual design: A large software project case study. *Computer Supported Cooperative Work, 5*(4), 415-445.

Robey, D., Gupta, S. K., & Rodriguez-Diaz, A. (1988). Implementing information systems in developing countries: organizational and cultural considerations. In S. C. Bhatnagar & N. BjØrn-Andersen (Eds.), *Information technology in developing countries* (pp. 41-50). New York: Elsevier Science Publishers.

Sahay, S., Nicholson, B., & Krishna, S. (2003). *Global IT outsourcing: Software development across borders.* Cambridge, UK: Cambridge University Press.

Sarker, S. (2003). Knowledge transfer in virtual information systems development teams: An empirical examination of key enables. *Proceedings of the 36th Annual Hawaii International Conference on System Sciences* (pp. 119-128).

Saunders, C., van Slyke, C., & Vogel, D. R. (2004). My time or yours? Managing time visions in global virtual teams. *Academy of Management Executive, 18*(1), 19-31.

Schuerkens, U. (2003). The sociological and anthropological study of globalization and localization. *Current Sociology, 51*(3/4), 209-222.

Schultz, M., & Hatch, M. J. (1996). Living with multiple paradigms: The case of paradigm interplay in organizational culture studies. *The Academy of Management Review, 21*(2), 529-557.

Schwarzkopf, A. B., Saunders, C., Jasperson, J., & Croes, H. (2004). Strategies for managing IS personnel: IT skills staffing. In M. Igbaria & C. Shayo (Eds.), *Strategies for managing IS/IT personnel* (pp. 37-63). Hershey, PA: Idea Group Publishing.

Shukla, M., & Sethi, V. (2004). An approach of studying knowledge worker's competencies in software development team. *Journal of Advancing Information and Management Studies, 1*(1), 49-62.

Swanson, D. A., Phillips, J., & Head, N. W. (2003, June 8-12). Developing growing need for soft-skills in IT professionals. *Proceedings of the 2003 ASCUE Conference* (pp. 263-269). Myrtle Beach, SC.

Swart, J., & Kinnie, N. (2003). Sharing knowledge in knowledge-intensive firms. *Human Resource Management Journal, 13*(2), 60-75.

Trauth, E. M. (2000). *The culture of an information economy: Influences and impacts in the Republic of Ireland.* Dordrecht, The Netherlands: Kluwer Academic Publishers.

Trauth, E. M., Farwell, D., & Lee, D. (1993). The IS expectation gap: Industry expectations versus academic preparation. *MIS Quarterly, 17*(3), 293-307.

Trauth, E. M., Huang, H., Morgan, A., Quesenberry, J., & Yeo, B. J. K. (2006). Investigating diversity in the global IT workforce: An analytical framework. In F. Niederman & T. Ferratt (Eds.), *Human resource management of IT professionals.* Hershey, PA: Idea Group Publishing.

van Solingena, R., Berghoutb, E., Kustersc, R., & Trienekensc, J. (2000). From process improvement to people improvement: Enabling learning in software development. *Information and Software Technology, 42*(14), 965-971.

Walsham, G. (1993). *Interpreting information systems in organizations.* New York: John Wiley & Sons.

Walsham, G. (2000). IT, globalization and cultural diversity. In C. Avgerous & G. Walshem (Eds.), *Information technology in context: Studies from perspective of developing countries* (pp. 291-303). Aldershot, UK: Shgate Publishing.

Walsham, G. (2001). *Making a world of difference: IT in a global context.* Chichester, UK: John Wiley & Son.

Waterson, P. E., Clegg, C. W., & Axtell, A. M. (1997). The dynamics of work organization, knowledge, and technology during software development. *International Journal of Human-Computer Studies, 46*(1), 79-101.

Weisinger, J. Y., & Trauth, E. M. (2002). Situating culture in the global information sector. *Information Technology and People, 15*(4), 306-320.

Weisinger, J. Y., & Trauth, E. M. (2003). The importance of situating culture in cross-cultural IT management. *IEEE Transactions on Engineering Management, 50*(1), 26-30.

Worsley, P. (1984). *The three worlds.* Chicago: The University of Chicago Press.

Zolin, R., Hinds, P. J., Fruchter, R., & Levitt, R. E. (2004). Interpersonal trust in cross-functional, geographically distributed work: a longitudinal study. *Information and Organization, 14*(1), 1-26.

Chapter XII

The Journey to New Lands:
Utilizing the Global IT Workforce through Offshore-Insourcing

Subrata Chakrabarty, Texas A&M University, USA

Abstract

This chapter introduces a prescriptive conceptual framework from the practitioner's perspective for the "offshore-insourcing" journey. In the decision phase of offshore-insourcing, we answer the questions "Why to insource from offshore?" "What to insource from offshore?," and "Where to offshore?" In the implementation phase we answer the question "How to insource from offshore?" and describe the importance of evaluating outcomes. In the process of answering these questions, we discuss insourcing vs. outsourcing and the possible need for offshoring. We think of ways to select the IT functions that can be insourced from offshore, and also look at the popular offshore destinations. We discuss process of managing change, setting up the offshore center, recruiting IT professionals at offshore, and managing the IT professionals at onshore and offshore within the ambit of the global delivery model. Throughout the decision and implementation phases of offshore-insourcing, the focus is on the challenges related to managing IT personnel.

Introduction

The pressure to lower information technology (IT) costs is high on companies worldwide. The cost of IT, *a major component of which is the cost of IT professionals,* is sometimes a stumbling block in the decision to upgrade to newer and better technology alternatives. The internet provides new opportunities for offshoring of IT or IT enabled work. When a service is made available on-line, all the user knows is what they see on the screen. If they type in an internet address and access a service, they do not need to know about the nationality or race of the IT professionals that have actually developed the Web site. Companies in advanced economies are being driven to look across the horizon by the lure of low costs of IT professionals in other countries and the desire for high software quality. Dibbern, Goles, Hirschheim, and Jayatilaka (2004) note the following:

*Even the popular press (*Business Week*, 2003;* USA Today*, 2003) have reported on this issue noting that as much as 50% of IT jobs will be offshored to India and other off- and near-shore destinations in the next 10 years. Such change it is argued is nothing more than the natural progression of first moving blue-collar work (manufacturing, textile production, etc.) overseas followed by white-collar work.*

By *offshore-insourcing* of IT work, a company sets up its own IT department or subsidiary in another country (that is, it *insources* IT work from its own IT department or subsidiary located in an *offshore* country). However, there are also some concerns regarding the larger impacts of *offshoring* by a nation on its job market and its knowledge centric competitiveness. Process and operations knowledge may get leaked to local entrepreneurs and competing companies at *offshore* locations (Karamouzis et al., 2004). The other major concern that is often highlighted by the popular media is that of job losses. *Offshoring* is sometimes regarded as a reason for the slackness in growth of employment opportunities in developed economies. However, Karamouzis et al. (2004) of Gartner Research interestingly note the following about job losses:

According to U.S. labor statistics and several academic studies, less than 5% of jobs lost in the United States are attributed to offshoring IT services. A study commissioned by the Information Technology Association of America and developed by Global Insight put the estimate at 2.8%. U.S. government statistics for the last 15 years show that most job losses have occurred due to automation, changes in industry dynamics and process re-engineering.

Many proponents of the above logic face criticism that job growth at onshore may be slower due to offshoring of new projects. Karamouzis et al. (2004) however state that *"new job creation has decelerated in the past three years, perhaps due to greater efficiencies, automation, the economic downturn or pressure on companies to improve productivity without new hires."* Karamouzis et al. (2004) go on to state that concern should not be the number of jobs displaced which is a cyclical trend, but rather the *"potential loss of critical competencies and knowledge-centric roles."* Hence, *offshore-insourcing* is an option to gain access to low-cost & high-quality skills of offshore IT professionals, and also to retain critical competencies and knowledge centric roles within the company, but not necessarily within a nation.

This chapter will explore the *offshore-insourcing* process by asking the questions "Why?," "What?," "Where?," and "How?" in a prescriptive conceptual framework. It will analyze the forces that are driving offshoring in the internet age, and how various organizations can respond to this demand. The process of implementing a decision to insource from offshore is studied by discussing the process of recruiting IT professionals at offshore, understanding the need for change management, and discussing the management of IT professionals at onshore and offshore within the ambit of the *global delivery model*.

The Terminologies

Before we delve deep into this chapter, a quick brush up on the basic terminologies will help. We broadly define a *"client"* as anyone in need of services. The terms *"client"* *"customer,"* and *"buyer"* imply a firm (or even an individual) that is seeking services, from either *internal service providers* (like the client's own internal IT department, or its subsidiary) or from *external service providers* (a vendor/supplier). The term *"client-entity"* implies any entity that is owned by the client, such as the client's internal IT department or its subsidiary. In the same vein, the terms *"vendor,"* *"supplier,"* *"third party,"* and external *"consultant"* imply an *"external service provider"* or a *"non-client entity"* whose business is to provide services to the client.

The two *cross-organizational* terminologies that deal with transfer of work within or across organizations are *"insourcing"* and *"outsourcing."* A company *"insources"* work from its own IT personnel and *"outsources"* work to the IT personnel in an external company (vendor). In other words, *insourcing* implies that the service providers are client employees (who work for its subsidiary or internal IT department); whereas *outsourcing* implies that the service providers are external IT personnel (such as employees of vendor/supplier firms or external consultants).

Figure 1. (In/out) sourcing from (on/off) shore

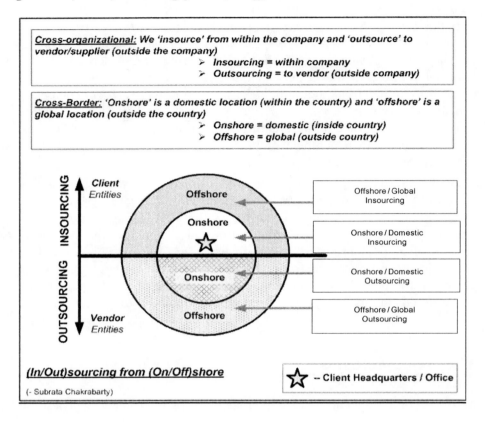

The two *cross-border* terminologies that deal with transfer of work within or across countries (or geographical borders) are "*onshoring*" and "*offshoring*." A company "*onshores*" work to IT personnel residing in its own country, and "*offshores*" work to IT personnel some other country. In other words, *onshoring* implies that the service providers are IT personnel located in the same country as the client; this is also known as *domestic-sourcing* or *onshore-sourcing*. On the other hand, *offshoring* implies that the service providers are IT personnel located in a country, which is different from the client's country; this is also known as *global-sourcing* or *offshore-sourcing*. For example, both China and India may be considered as "offshore" countries with respect to the United Kingdom or USA.

As shown in Figure 1, these basic cross organizational and cross border terminologies can lead to four combinations: (1) *onshore-insourcing* (or *domestic-insourcing*) implies that both the client and its internal IT department (or subsidiary) that provides IT services is located in the same country, (2) *offshore-insourcing* (or *global-insourcing*) implies that the its IT department (or subsidiary) that provides IT services is located in a country that is different from the client's country, (3) *onshore-outsourcing* (or *domestic-outsourcing*) implies that both the client and the vendor personnel are located in the same country, and (4) *offshore-outsourcing* (or *global-outsourcing*) implies that the vendor personnel are located in a country that is different from the client's country. In this chapter, we will be discussing about *offshore-insourcing* or (*global-insourcing*).

The Conceptual Framework/Model for Offshore-Insourcing

Figure 2 gives the proposed conceptual framework/model for offshore-insourcing that will be used in this chapter. Simon (1960, as cited in Dibbern et al., 2004, pp. 14-17) had proposed a four-stage model for decision making that comprised of the stages (1) intelligence, (2) design, (3) choice, and (4) implementation. Dibbern et al. (2004) had adapted Simon's model in their literature survey of information systems *outsourcing*. Similarly, Simon's model is adapted here for *offshore-insourcing,* by modifying Simon's intelligence, design and choice stages into the *why, what,* and *where* stages respectively and clubbing these three stages into the *decision phase*. Furthermore, we break down the final *implementation* phase into the two stages of "*how*" and "*outcomes.*"

Hence, the offshore-insourcing process has been assumed to have two distinct phases, namely the *decision phase* and the *implementation phase*. In the *decision phase* a company asks the following three questions:

- *Why* to insource from offshore
- *What* to insource from offshore
- *Where* to offshore

These three decision-phase questions (or stages) can be combined into the single decision question, that is: "*'Why' to insource 'what' from 'where' in off-shore?*" Furthermore, the *implementation* phase comprises of two stages that asks the "how" question and finally evaluates the outcomes:

- *How* to insource from offshore
- Evaluate *outcomes*

In the "*Why to insource from offshore?*" stage we ask the question of whether a company needs to *insource* from within or *outsource* to a vendor, and whether the company needs to go *offshore* to another country? If the company does decide go *offshore* to another country, then, should it look at an offshore-based vendor (for *offshore-outsourcing*) or should it set up its own offshore subsidiary (for *offshore-insourcing*)? Moreover, given that there are so many concerns about offshoring in the media and in the public, how should the company filter out the realities from the myths and make a knowledgeable decision?

In the "*What to insource from offshore?*" stage we ask the question on how a company can select the IT functions that it should *insource* from *offshore*? In the "*Where to offshore?*" stage we look at the criteria for choosing an offshore destination, and also survey some of the popular offshore countries and cities (see Appendix I of this chapter).

Figure 2. Conceptual framework/model for offshore-insourcing

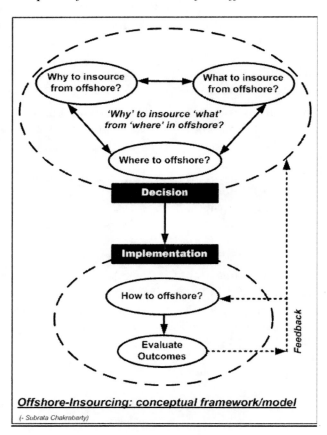

In the *"How to insource from offshore?"* stage we discuss and prescribe the processes for creating the team that will be implementing the decision to offshore, managing change, getting the offshore office ready, analyzing options for recruiting at offshore, and the setting up onshore-offshore coordination for recruitment and induction training. We also discuss the *global delivery model* and the management of the IT professionals at onshore and offshore. Finally, we *evaluate the outcome* of the entire offshore-insourcing process, and use the feedback to further improve the decision making and implementation phases.

Decision:
Why to Insource from Offshore?

The decision question "why to insource from offshore?" can be broken down into the questions "why to insource?" and "why to offshore?"

Why to Insource?

Hirschheim and Lacity (2000) conducted fourteen case studies that assess the experiences of companies with outsourcing. They provide evidence that companies need not necessarily turn to outsourcing to improve IT performance, and

Table 1. Insourcing vs. outsourcing

Insourcing	Outsourcing
✓ More suitable when it is difficult to define requirements (**uncertainty**)	✓ Enables organization's personnel to focus on its **core business**, by outsourcing the non-core activities
✓ More **control** over strategic **assets, resources** and IT **personnel**	✓ Assists in major **reorganizations** by making transitions smoother & quicker
✓ In the **absence of** competent **vendor** personnel in the market, insourcing is the only option	✓ **Frees up** in-house resources and IT personnel for **new and innovative** business/technology development, by turning over legacy systems to vendors
✓ Lower risk of intellectual property rights violation by internal IT personnel (in comparison to difficulty in negotiating **IP rights** with external vendors)	✓ **Quality** and service improvements from established service providers
	✓ Access to technical **expertise of external IT personnel**, when the same is not available internally.
✓ Better when a very high degree of firm specific **business knowledge** is required by IT personnel (since knowledge transfer to external vendor personnel would be difficult)	✓ Financial advantages: o **Cost** reduction (possible reduction in IT personnel costs) o **Costs are predictable** (determined while negotiating outsourcing deal) o Reduction in **Capital expenditure** (for IT infrastructure)
✓ No threat of **opportunistic behavior** by external vendor personnel	✓ **Flexibility** and control in increase/decrease of IT manpower as needed

believe that IT managers can often times replicate a vendor's cost reduction tactics, provided they get the much needed support from their upper management. In many of the case studies it was found that large scale outsourcing, often led to lower than expected flexibility and lower than expected service levels from the vendor's IT personnel. Furthermore, a number of contracts are either being renegotiated or being terminated; and some companies are considering pulling their IT functions back in-house once an outsourcing contract is terminated.

Outsourcing is not the panacea for all ills. At shown in Table 1, both insourcing and outsourcing have their pros and cons (Ang & Straub, 1998; Aubert, Rivard, & Patry, 1996; Currie & Willcocks, 1998; Earl, 1996; Jurison, 1995; Loh & Venkatraman, 1992, 1995; Nam, Rajagopalan, Rao, & Chaudhury, 1996; Nelson, Richmond, & Seidmann, 1996; Poppo & Zenger, 1998).

Why to Offshore?

Why is there such great excitement about offshoring work to IT personnel in the other countries? Is offshoring sustainable over the long-term or is it just a passing fancy? Literature suggests that offshoring of IT work will continue to grow for the following reasons:

- **Access to large markets with high growth potential:** The favorite locations for offshoring like China and India (see Appendix I) are also large and growing markets. It is strategically important to establish an early presence in such developing countries which have a higher growth potential than the relatively mature developed countries (Apte & Mason, 1995, p. 1252).

- **Cost savings:** The offshoring option offers lower cost advantages (primarily due to lower salary levels of offshore IT personnel) and is probably biggest driver behind the offshoring trend (Apte & Mason, 1995, p. 1252; Carmel & Agarwal, 2002; Sinha & Terdiman, 2002; Sobol & Apte, 1995).

- **Fastest time to market by working round the clock:** Potentially all 24 hours of the day can be devoted to any task by globally distributing the work to IT personnel across multiple time zones. This for example can lead to a faster cycle time for software production (Apte & Mason, 1995, p. 1252; Sinha & Terdiman, 2002), and allow continuous 24x7 operations and monitoring of critical IT functions and infrastructure by IT personnel (needed for customer service, network management, production support, etc.).

- **Latest technologies and the Internet:** The latest technologies allow collaboration among globally distributed IT professionals (Carmel & Agarwal,

2002, p. 66). The internet has greatly helped the phenomenon of IT sourcing by allowing personnel across the work to easily share information. Communication technologies such as e-mailing, teleconferencing, videoconferencing, and instant-messaging allow for better coordination in spite of the geographic distances.

- **Modular design of IT tasks:** Certain IT tasks (for e.g., in IT production or support) can be designed in a modular fashion (i.e., they can be broken down into smaller and relatively independent modules) that makes it easier to distribute the work globally among IT personnel with reduced transactions costs (cost of coordinating work activities among the personnel), and allows for easier synchronization, communication, supervision, and feedback mechanisms among the IT personnel (Carmel & Agarwal, 2002, p. 66).

- **Skilled pool of IT professionals:** There is large supply of qualified IT professionals in many offshore destinations like India (Apte & Mason, 1995, p. 1252; Carmel & Agarwal, 2002; Sinha & Terdiman, 2002).

- **Scalability and bench-strength:** The sizable supplies of qualified low-cost IT personnel at offshore allows companies to have a certain number of IT personnel in the "waiting mode" i.e. waiting to be assigned to projects, and are used to quickly ramp-up projects with IT personnel when the need arises. Having a small number of low-cost but highly skilled personnel in the "*waiting mode*" for being assigned to projects is also known as "*bench strength*," and allows the firm to respond rapidly to sudden requirements. Alternatively, companies can also hire IT personnel rapidly from the job market, thanks to the huge availability of qualified low-cost IT professionals in many of the offshore destinations (like China and India).

Concerns About Offshoring

However there are some valid concerns about offshoring work to IT personnel in other countries, which include: (1) problems of communication and coordination, (2) cultural differences, (3) lack of trust, (4) difficulties in arranging visas/work-permits, (5) offshore unit's lack of company/industry specific domain knowledge (both business & technical), (6) lack of control over quality and schedule, (7) possible violation of intellectual property rights, (8) unclear government attitude towards cross border data flow and trade-in services, (7) unsatisfactory infrastructure in the offshore destination, (8) possibility of an unstable economic, political, or social environment, (9) security of physical assets and intellectual capital, and privacy, (10) knowledge transfer, and (11) managing uncertainty in IT requirements and unanticipated changes in scope of offshored work (Apte & Mason, 1995, pp. 1252-1253; Carmel & Agarwal, 2002, p. 68; Sinha & Terdiman, 2002; Sobol & Apte, 1995, p. 271).

Some of the reasons that motivate companies to insource their IT needs from their offshore subsidiary (or offshore IT department) rather than to outsource them to an offshore (external) vendor are: (1) greater information & data security, and intellectual property (IP) protection, (2) absence of some specific expertise in the offshore vendors, and (3) possibility of gaining greater low-cost benefits by running one's own subsidiary, rather than pay high margins to vendors (Karamouzis et al., 2004). However, some of these offshore subsidiaries may be short-lived due to several factors that make it challenging to sustain it as a competitive option. We categorize the contributing factors as follows:

- **Difficulty in achieving economies of scale:** "Economies of scale" will be difficult to achieve since a company has a finite limit to its internal needs. An alternative is to convert the internal IT department (or subsidiary) to a "spin-off." A *spin-off* is a company, which was originally an internal IT department (or subsidiary) of its parent company, but is now independently selling its services to the market. This would help in expanding the spin-off's revenue base and number of IT personnel, and thereby achieve greater *economies of scale,* but this will also involve additional investments/costs. (Karamouzis et al., 2004; Willcocks and Lacity, 1998, p. 26, pp. 31-32)

- **Costs of technology infrastructure and human resource management:** The recurring investment costs required for staying updated with the latest technology and infrastructure can cause the offshore subsidiaries to be less cost-efficient. Also, costs for recruiting and managing IT personnel in a new and increasingly competitive labor market can grow. Additionally, management time and effort spent to manage one's own offshore subsidiary or IT department would be higher than when the IT work is outsourced to vendor personnel (Karamouzis et al., 2004)

Decision:
What to Insource from Offshore?

A two step approach might be helpful to answer the question "What to insource from offshore?" The first step would be to "*look inside*" and select the IT functions can be insourced from offshore IT personnel, starting with the "easiest first". The second step would be to "*look outside*" and find out about the skills of the IT personnel available at offshore.

Step 1: Look Inside – Select the IT Functions that can be Insourced from Offshore, Starting with the "Easiest First"

How does a company decide what IT functions are suitable for insourcing from offshore? IT functions are easiest to offshore when a company is confident about the following (Apte et al., 1997; Hotle & Iyengar, 2003; Iyengar & Terdiman, 2003; Sobol & Apte, 1995):

1. **Maturity** of associated **processes** is high; processes are well defined and documented

    o   For example, a company with a higher CMM rating will be better at insourcing of software development from offshore, since its processes are of the higher quality and its IT personnel are educated about the best quality processes

2. **Project management skills** of IT managers and professionals are good at both and onshore and offshore

3. Requires lesser **degree of interaction (communication and coordination)** with onshore management or onshore users, and face-to-face interaction between onshore and offshore IT personnel is not necessary

    o   Activities that require higher degree of user interaction should not be carried out at offshore. The extent of user interaction is inversely proportional to possibility of carrying out an activity remotely. Hence, initial requirements gathering, analysis and design phases are generally conducted at onshore by IT professionals

4. High **availability of offshore IT professionals** who have high levels of skills required for the IT function

5. **Ease of knowledge transfer** of both business domain knowledge and special technology skills to IT personnel at offshore

6. **Requirements** can be well defined and documented by IT personnel, and there is less uncertainty

    o   **Documentation & prioritization:** Requirements-gathering and management is best handled face-to-face. The gathered requirements must be well documented and prioritized by IT personnel at onshore, before sending them to offshore IT personnel

    o   **Requirements change management:** Often users of IT systems don't know what they want, or are unable to define them satisfactorily. Hence changes to requirements over time are common. If the frequency of these changes can be controlled, and brought down then the IT function can be more comfortably offshored

Based on the above considerations suitable IT functions should be chosen for insourcing from offshore IT personnel.

Step 2: Look Outside – Find Out About the Skills Available at Offshore

A suitable investigation would be required to find out more about the skills of IT professionals at the prospective offshore destination. But how does one find out the skills of the IT professionals in a prospective offshore destination? One option may be to survey *"what services the offshore based software service providers (vendors) have to offer?"* For example, if India is a prospective offshore destination, and if some large India based software service providers can provide certain IT services for certain industries, then, there is a good probability that skilled IT professionals are available in India for those IT functions (Marriott & Wiggins, 2002). *Though a company that is attempting offshore-insourcing of IT will not actually outsource to any of these vendors, these kinds of surveys can provide valuable information about the skills available in the offshore destination.* As an example, we have listed the services offered and the industries targeted by a large India based software services provider named "Infosys" (http://www.infosys.com) in Appendix II at the end of this chapter, which would give an idea about the capabilities of the IT personnel at the respective offshore location (Infosys, 2005b, 2005c).

Decision: Where to Offshore?

Kempf, Scholl, and Sinha (2001) reported the evaluation of competitiveness of various countries as preferred destinations of offshoring, based on studying factors like infrastructure, IT personnel availability, capital and entrepreneurship. The characteristic of the labor pool of IT professionals was used to filter an initial list of 33 countries to a short list of 17 countries, namely: *China, India, South Korea, Malaysia, Philippines, the three Baltic States, the Czech Republic, Hungary, Poland, Russia, South Africa, Argentina, Brazil, Chile,* and *Mexico.* For further short listing, infrastructure, capital, and risk ratings of countries were then used by Kempf et al. (2001) to identify the following key regions for offshoring:

- **Brazil** is possibly the best suited for cross-border collaboration opportunities among the four countries short-listed from the Americas (Argentina, Brazil, Chile and Mexico). Though currently below a lot of radar screens, Brazil displays some strong fundamental characteristics that make it a potentially attractive country to consider. One of Brazil's key attributes is the level of telecommunication and Internet infrastructure deployed.

- **China** has created an environment supportive of cross-border collaboration. The labor force appears to be strong in high technology and data from other industry sources indicate that China offers very competitive charge rates in the IT sector. Measures of China's infrastructure are also positive, though, like India, China does not seem to be spending as much on investments in telecommunications. In fact between 1995 and 1999, China spent a total of $5.9 billion—only slightly more than the Philippines' $5.1 billion.

- The **Baltic states of Estonia, Latvia and Lithuania** offer some interesting opportunities for cross-border collaboration. While data on wages for these three countries is unavailable, each of these countries has some of the highest numbers of scientists and engineers in research and development per million people of all the countries studied.

- **India** continues to be the predominant offshore player with software and services. India has a large, technologically advanced labor pool. In fact, the U.S. Immigration and Naturalization Service (INS) reports that Indian nationals received 42.6% of the H1-B temporary skilled worker visas issued between October 1999 and February 2000. Also, government support of its tertiary education systems and private IT training institutions, along with a low-wage-rate environment, continues to make India attractive as a source of skilled technologists. However, the economic data collected in our research reflects a dichotomy between the growth of demand for IT services and the development of telecommunication and information technology infrastructure that may cause concern in the future.

Going by reports in the media and various other sources, as of now China and India are among the topmost players in offshore-insourcing arena (Cohen, 2005; Karamouzis & Young, 2004; Kempf et al., 2001; Wiggins, Datar, & Liu, 2002a; Wiggins, Datar, Leskela, & Kumar, 2002b). The offshore-insourcing scenarios of these two countries have been discussed in Appendix I of this chapter. However, it is important to note that these are not necessarily the only countries that can successfully offer the advantages of offshore-insourcing. Though China and India seem to be among most "popular" destinations at present, this can change in the future. The countries that offer the optimum balance in terms of cost, infrastructure, accessibility, skilled IT personnel, political climate and social acceptability would be "right" destinations in the future, depending on the needs of relevant company. The following factors need to be considered while considering an offshoring location (Iyengar, 2005; Karamouzis & Young, 2004):

1. **Cost of IT personnel:** Salaries for IT personnel vary from location to location

2. **Infrastructure:** Telecommunications, roads, real estate, water, and power

3. **Access:** International access and quality accommodation

4. **Talent pool/skills:** Availability and diversity of skilled IT personnel, and academic institutions that can continuously generate such skilled IT personnel with diverse skills

5. **Cost of living**

6. **Political climate and support:** National and state/local governments, political ideology, and religious tolerance

7. **Quality of life:** Housing rates, cosmopolitan feel, religious tolerance, transportation, crime rate, climate and public infrastructure

8. **Expatriate friendliness:** A job posting at the chosen location should not be considered a hardship assignment by the expatriates

9. **Service-line capabilities:** Some locations may be specialized hubs for particular types of industries and services

Implementation: How to Insource from Offshore?

Various issues related to offshore-insourcing were discussed in the earlier sections (i.e., decision making phase), namely "why to insource from offshore?," "what to insource from offshore?", and "where to offshore?" We find that there is a scarcity of literature on "how" to insource from offshore. Therefore, a conceptual approach is adopted in this section where the author utilizes his experience of working in the Indian software industry to come up with a possible conceptual framework that attempts to answer the "how" question[1].

How to Create the Offshore Implementation Team?

An "*Offshore Implementation Team*," which is the "core" team with the responsibility of overseeing the implementation of the offshoring operation, can be created. This core team may comprise of the company's onshore employees and/or external consultants. The *offshore implementation team* can use the assistance of the onshore company's high-level management and various external entities such as legal consultants, HR consultants, telecommunications/ network consultants and facilities/infrastructure consultants. Visas/permits will need to be processed and issued for all offshore implementation team members and other people that will be traveling to offshore.

For example as shown in Figure 3, the offshore implementation team may consist of a project manager, human resource coordinators, technology and infrastructure coordinators, and an offshore-insourcing process coordinator.

Figure 3. Creating an offshore implementation team

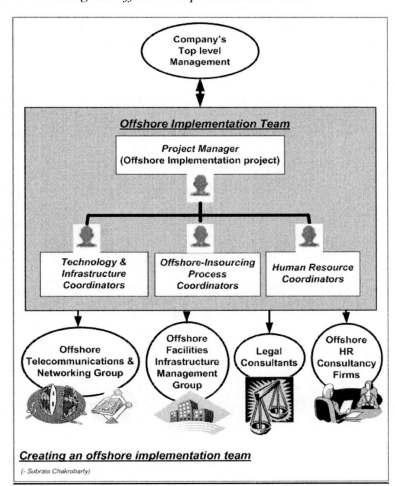

Creating an offshore implementation team
(- Subrata Chakrabarty)

The "*project manager*" (of this offshore implementation project) will have general managerial responsibilities towards setting the offshore facility, will interact with the company's top level management, and will have the various coordinators reporting to him or her. The "*HR coordinators*" will take up responsibilities of organizing training, staffing and related scheduling and management activities. The "*technology and infrastructure coordinators*" will take up the responsibility of network/system infrastructure management, which involves procurement and setting up of equipment for the offshore facility, and related scheduling and management activities. The "*offshore-insourcing process coordinators*" should ideally be people with prior experience in setting up such offshore facilities, in advising and coordinating the offshoring process, in change management, in addressing challenges of the offshoring process, and in related risk mitigation activities.

The *offshore implementation team* will interact with various other groups like the company's top level management, the offshore telecommunications and networking group, the offshore facilities infrastructure management group, the legal consultants, and the offshore HR consultancy firms.

The *company's top level management* will have the responsibilities of sanctioning funds for the offshore implementation project, monitoring the business value of the offshore implementation exercise, getting the go-ahead from the firm's shareholders, championing change management, reviewing the status at identified milestones, and making relevant decisions and approvals for future phases (Kobyashi-Hillary, 2004, pp. 231-248).

The *offshore telecommunications and networking group* will be responsible for designing the core network that will be required to set up offshore operations, shipping/installing/configuring of the core network infrastructure in the new offshore office, setting up connectivity (wide area network or WAN) among the onshore and offshore offices for secure data communication, and setting up of telecommunication networks such as phone lines and internet service (CMIS, 2004).

The *offshore facilities infrastructure management group* can help, for example, in either setting up the offshore office in a previously established IT Park which houses other international companies, or actually hiring contractors to build a new offshore facility building. The facilities should include office furniture, power systems, cooling systems, and network cabling (CMIS, 2004).

The *legal consultants* would provide counseling on labor laws, offshore telecom regulations, data privacy and cross-border information transfer, offshore intellectual property laws, taxation, software copyright and license laws, etc.... (Kobyashi-Hillary, 2004, pp. 177-190)

The *HR consultancy firms* will be responsible for advertising, creating brand awareness in the offshore labor market, and assisting the offshore implementation team's HR coordinators with staffing activities like executive search, recruitment, training and temporary staffing (Cerebrus Consultants, n.d.; Ma Foi, n.d.).

By *benchmarking* against companies that have successfully set up offshore-insourcing operations (see Appendix I), the *offshore implementation team* must plan and then compare its offshore implementation performance. Appendix-I, which addresses the question "Where to offshore?" provides a list of the 15 biggest InfoTech companies in the world, most of which have an offshore presence in China or India. These companies may be used as benchmarks of successful offshore-insourcing.

How to Manage Change Among Onshore IT Personnel?

Iyengar and Morello (2004) suggest that the questions listed in Table 2 are asked by the onshore business unit staff and onshore IT professionals whenever they hear the dreaded "offshore" word in their organization. IT professionals at onshore share the concerns of the business unit, and also have additional concerns since they are the primary individuals affected by any offshoring decision. Staff members in the business/administrative units are primarily concerned about changes in work procedures, loss of expertise, personal benefits, and risks and the need for a cautious approach. IT professionals are additionally concerned about the possibility of loss of their own jobs and those of their friends, their perpetually uncertain future, and their own capabilities to handle such a change. Companies may face non-cooperation and lack of initiative from unmotivated employees while offshoring.

Table 2. Business unit and IT staff concerns on offshoring (Compiled from Gartner Research, Iyengar and Morello (2004))

Business Unit Staff concerns on offshoring	IT Staff concerns on offshoring (in addition to concerns shared by Business staff)
<ul><li>"How will my business unit get the work done now?"</li><li>"Won't we lose our subject matter expertise?"</li><li>"Why should I support this effort? What's in it for me?"</li><li>"Isn't this initiative risky?"</li><li>"Shouldn't we take things slowly--one step at a time?"</li></ul>	<ul><li>"Will I lose my job?"</li><li>"Will my friends lose their jobs?"</li><li>"Even if I make it through the first round of layoffs, what happens next?"</li><li>"They're only keeping me through the transition, so why should I help out?"</li><li>"How can I possibly perform in my new role--one that I don't like and am not trained to handle"</li><li>"Will I need to work additional hours or shifts so that I will be able to communicate with my offshore counterparts?"</li></ul>

Table 3. Change management challenges (Compiled from Gartner Research, Iyengar and Morello (2004))

Emotional challenges	Communications challenges	Execution challenges
▪ **Emotions:** disbelief, anxiety, fear, denial, shock, resentment, anger, stress, resistance, disengagement and a desire to leave the organization. As a result, productivity falls ▪ **Fear:** employees wonder if they will lose their jobs next	▪ **Information accuracy:** Delays, second-hand information, distortion ▪ **The Media:** Misinformation from media stories causing panic and resentment ▪ **Management communication:** Conflicting information from managers	▪ **Tolerance:** Lower initial tolerance for offshoring by normal employees ▪ **Processes:** IT process need to be redesigned for more complex global delivery ▪ **Knowledge Transfer:** Business & IT knowledge transfer to offshore ▪ **Control:** Power & control of onshore management/staff over offshore ▪ **Transition:** Long transition time and employee attrition during this time

Iyengar and Morello (2004) further suggest three kinds of challenges that companies encounter in early stages of offshoring, namely: emotional, communications and execution challenges, which are explained in Table 3. Emotional challenges are often triggered by emotion rather than reason; communication challenges involve misinformation and distortion; and execution challenges represent practical concerns in performing successful offshoring.

Hence, a *communication strategy* should be created to introduce the concept of an offshore IT team and to address the fears of the existing onshore IT professionals about *offshoring*. Communication can be affected through periodic staff briefings, weekly newsletters, increased notice board activity, etc. The company moving offshore might want to undertake *awareness training* sessions for the company's onshore employees to familiarize them with their proposed *offshoring plans and processes*, and hence lead to better mutual understanding. Managers should communicate offshoring plans with maximum details and honesty to the onshore IT personnel. Failure to do so effectively might result in a backlash and lower productivity from onshore IT personnel, and can adversely affect the employer's image in the job market (Morello & Terdiman, 2004). The communication strategy can include the following rules (Morello & Terdiman, 2004):

1.   Make a communication plan for onshore IT personnel, and communicate transparently all that is known and not known

2.   Convey the truth to onshore IT personnel about the intentions and reasons for offshore sourcing

3.   Analyze the strengths, weaknesses, opportunities, and threats for the departments/projects and IT personnel most closely affected

4.   Clearly state the jobs to be retained at onshore, and state if the affected IT professionals would be retrained for other roles by identifying new opportunities, career options and transition periods for the affected IT professionals

How to Get the Offshore Office Ready for IT Personnel?

The offshore implementation team will need to get certain important things in place (Kobyashi-Hillary, 2004, pp. 123-248) before staffing the offshore office:

- Getting the *Facilities Infrastructure* ready
- Getting the *Technical Infrastructure* ready
- *Other tasks* would include:
    o   Establishing a banking relationship
    o   Selecting legal representation
    o   Setting up an accounting system
    o   Obtaining required licenses/permits
    o   Obtaining insurance and establishing a security plan

One of the major tasks for a company moving offshore is to get the *Facilities Infrastructure* ready (CMIS, 2004). The offshore office can be located in a previously established offshore development park with other international companies, or can be purchased or built in a suitable location. In case the facility is leased, general maintenance and janitorial services need to be included in the lease agreement. The facilities should feature all of the basic elements for establishing a working office for IT professionals that includes office furniture, power, cooling, initial telecomm, and network cabling. Appropriate power and cooling will need to be provided for any technical equipment required.

Another major task would be to get the *Technical Infrastructure* ready (CMIS, 2004). The offshore office will need to be highly self-sufficient, and yet remain connected with the onshore corporate location for productive collaboration between IT professionals at offshore and onshore. The technical infrastructure that would be needed by offshore IT personnel include e-mail servers, file servers, Web servers, application servers, database servers, personal computers, printers, software and also the network infrastructure. Licenses for the software should allow its usage in the offshore location. A *network operation team* has to design the core network required to support the IT personnel's offshore operations. Time should be allocated to ship, install, and configure the core network infrastructure in the new offshore office. For example, a private MPLS (Multi-protocol Label Switching) wide area network (WAN) between the offshore office and the onshore facilities may be set up for secure, inter-corporate data communication. Telecommunications networking (phones, PBX (private branch exchange) equipment, Telco, ISP (Internet service provider) setup) will also need to be done.

How to Plan Staffing at Offshore?

An organization chart, staffing projection, and staffing budget will have to be made (CMIS, 2004):

- An *organization chart* for the offshore staff and IT personnel should be developed. It should also explain how the offshore office should report into the onshore office.

- An offshore *staffing projection* describing the skill set of each staff member and IT professional, complete with approximate salary bands appropriate for the offshore region will be needed.

- A *staffing budget* will need to be prepared, and this will include costs for legal procedures, consultants, training, travel, communication, accommodation and various infrastructure facilities.

How to Make Use of the Recruiting Options at Offshore?

The options for recruiting at offshore possibly include (1) direct/permanent hiring, (2) contract hiring, and (3) contract-to-permanent hiring (Moses Associates, n.d.; Schweyer, n.d). The pros and cons for each option should be studied. Also, the labor laws of the offshore region need to be studied in great detail (Kobyashi-Hillary, 2004, pp. 177-190).

Permanent hiring is highly recommended if the position requires the IT professional to have access to highly critical information systems, have security rights/privileges, or if the position requires a managerial role. If a company can groom and retain its offshore managerial and IT talent, then there is greater knowledge retention within the company, and there is a lesser threat of leakage of the company's proprietary or sensitive information. Since there is a greater dependence on the knowledge possessed by the permanent IT personnel on key processes/tools/functions, if a key skilled employee quits, it is harder to find a replacement that can be equally knowledgeable and productive (however, strict emphasis on documentation of processes/tools/functions across the organization can help new hires to learn quickly). Permanent IT personnel also increase the companies' benefits costs, they may become lackadaisical and may take their job for granted, and during business slumps it is expensive and difficult to manage the surplus manpower.

Contract hiring involves hiring IT personnel temporarily on projects (such as for project work involving programming or engineering services) and the contracted IT personnel may be released by the company at any point. Contract hires can be more responsive to their responsibilities since they don't take their job for granted. They try to stay updated with the latest technology and retrain on their skills. This is a more cost-effective approach because during business slow-downs the contracted IT personnel can be easily released. However, contract employees have very low job-security and this may lead to high attrition; also there is significant knowledge loss when the contract hire is released (there is scope for intellectual capital theft, and sensitive data may leave the company). When the economy is booming, it is difficult to find quality IT personnel in the competitive job market and getting good employees as contract hires will be a tough call.

In *Contract-to-permanent hiring*, the IT professional is hired on a contract basis for a fixed period of time, beyond which there is an expectation that they could be converted into permanent employees based on performance. The company can groom, and test the technical knowledge and team skills of the IT professionals before deciding to retain them full-time. This ensures quality staffing. If business declines during the "term-of-contract," the IT professional can be easily released.

Offshore managers must be ideally hired on a permanent basis, because continually changing managers will significantly effect and slowdown the effective execution of IT and administrative functions. Moreover, managerial skills are rather hard to come by, and managers need to build a long-term rapport with their counterparts at onshore to better coordinate the operations of the two offices and develop a good working atmosphere in the offshore facility. *Non-managerial staff at offshore can* be hired on a contract-to-permanent basis, that is they will be on a contract basis for a limited period (say a year), beyond which they will either be made permanent or released (based on their perfor-mance). This allows the management to observe their work before making a permanent hiring decision.

It is necessary to groom and build managerial and IT talent at offshore. To reduce the effects of attrition, there needs to be a strict enforcement of documentation of key processes, tools and functions, which in turn leads to better knowledge management. During temporary labor spikes, the company can step up the *hiring of contract personnel* on a project to project basis and release the temporary hires when demand declines. This will help the offshore company to be flexible and agile in terms of meeting business and staffing needs while keeping costs down.

How to Use Expatriates for Offshore?

Companies can bridge the gap of time zones, interaction styles and flawed communications by using the talents of individuals with multicultural fluency that is often found in expatriates who have been immersed in the customs, language and workplace rhythms that are essential in the diffusion of new offshoring processes with the overall enterprise (Bittinger, 2003). Some personnel from onshore may be deputed at offshore, and some personnel from offshore may be deputed at onshore, to bridge the onshore-offshore divide. Bittinger (2003) reports from a study by Hilary Harris (Cranfield School of Management, Cranfield University, UK) that organizations are using four types of international work assignments:

- **Long-term:** The expatriate and his or her family move to the host country for more than one year
- **Short-term:** Assignments are less than a year, and may involve family accompaniment
- **International commuter:** The employee commutes on a regular basis, while the family remains at home
- **Frequent flyer:** The employee takes frequent trips abroad, but does not relocate

Candidates selected for expatriate roles should preferably have work experience abroad for better cultural sensitivity and adaptability, language/communication/interpersonal skills, leadership skills, ability to work and collaborate from remote locations, understanding of parent companies mission, vision and culture, and most importantly the person's and the person's family's willingness to travel (Bittinger, 2003). Bittinger (2003) states that the biggest reason why the expatriate strategy sometimes fail is due to soft family related issues like resistance from spouse due to various personal and career related reasons, inability to adapt to foreign culture, or plain homesickness.

How to Carry Out the Recruitment and Induction Training Process?

Will a company's current structure be able to support the offshore recruitment process or will the company need to employ the services of a local HR consultant at offshore? The task of selecting the right staff and IT professionals and creating the right organization structure may require localized experience. A company moving offshore might want to maintain authority over the entire advertising, hiring and training process to gain greater control over the skill level and service quality of new employees. Figure 4 shows a possible example of how the recruitment and induction training may be conducted.

Recruitment

Hiring of staff and IT professionals at offshore will involve many tasks (see Figure 4). *Brand awareness* should be created by advertising the recruitment program in the media (such as leading newspapers) and ensure that the job postings and advertisements have been posted on the company Web site and others job-search Web sites.

Most HR consultants provide two types of selection services: *database selection* and *advertised recruitment* (Ma Foi, n.d.). *Database selection* uses an automated Web enabled database that allows for speedy matching of candidate profiles with recruiting company's needs. *Advertised recruitment* can be used for tasks like "head-hunting" to attract specific segments of personnel such as senior managers, and also for skill specific recruitment.

Interviews with short listed candidates need to be arranged. Interviews at offshore may be conducted by managers at onshore through videoconferencing; and in such a scenario, the difference in time-zones between onshore and offshore need to be taken into account. Access to facilities such as rooms, computers, internet-connectivity, projectors, printers, teleconferencing, videoconferencing, etc... should be available at interview sites.

Induction Training

The newly hired managers from offshore may need to travel to the onshore offices to acquaint themselves with the company's business, work culture, policies, practices, and people (see Figure 4). During this time, managers from offshore can study the onshore company's business and IT work. Information gathered at onshore needs to be clearly documented so that the entire organization, including new employees, may benefit from it.

Figure 4. Staffing at offshore (A possible recruitment and induction training process)

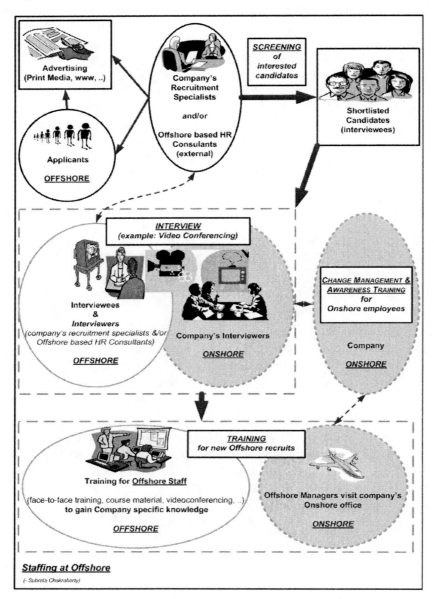

Figure 5. Global delivery in offshore-insourcing of custom software development

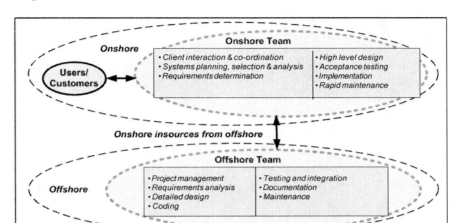

All the other offshore hires can be trained on the same matters by their offshore managers (when the managers return to offshore from onshore after their training), or by the onshore managers (by videoconferencing, or they can fly down from onshore to offshore). The knowledge transfer process for the new employees who haven't traveled onshore may be limited by a lack of face-to-face contact. Though it might be advisable to send several of the offshore employees to onshore for training, this may involve a huge cost burden (temporary relocation, compensation, and travel needs).

How to Manage the IT Personnel at Onshore and Offshore?

How does a company overcome issues of communication, coordination, culture, language, trust, distance, time-zones, and knowledge transfer among IT professionals at onshore and offshore? These issues can be managed with the effective and intelligent implementation of the *global delivery model*.

The *global delivery model* has been used by offshore based vendors like TCS (http://www.tcs.com), Infosys (http://www.infosys.com), and Wipro (http://www.wipro.com) to successfully provide services to its onshore clients. The same global delivery model can be adopted when a company decides to *insource* it's IT needs from its own offshore subsidiary. In *global delivery*, a company's offshore delivery centers are located worldwide and are comprehensively networked with collaborative systems and technologies that allow the seamless integration of projects being delivered from multiple locations, and thereby provide economies of scale & scope (Tata Consultancy Services, n.d.).

The "*global delivery model*" is an offshoring model that takes advantage of the global talent pool to give the best value to a company in terms of cost and quality. As illustrated in Figure 5, the work is broken down into logical components, which are then distributed to suitable global locations such that the company gets access to the global talents (of IT professionals from various countries) and also creates maximum value in terms of cost and quality (Infosys, 2005a). The procedure of narrowing down on the IT functions that can be insourced from offshore has been explained in the earlier section "What to insource from offshore?" In the example shown in Figure 5 where *custom development of software* is selectively offshored, the onshore IT professionals can be involved in user/customer interaction & coordination, systems planning & selection, systems analysis, requirements determination, high level design, acceptance testing, implementation, and rapid maintenance support; while the offshore IT professionals can be involved in project management, requirements analysis, detailed design, coding, testing and integration, documentation, and maintenance.

The global delivery model (GDM) allows a company to make best use of low-cost and skilled IT professionals from across the world. This geographical and psychological distance between onshore and offshore IT personnel creates unique challenges that need to be managed. Bell (2003) proposes five steps to succeed in the implementing the GDM: *(1) integrate levels of leadership, (2) focus on processes, (3) invest in cross-team training, (4) deploy collaborative tools, and (5) track success to team goals.*

How to Integrate Levels of Management at Onshore and Offshore to Build a Relationship?

In the first step, leadership at both onshore and offshore must flow from "functional" managers (and not just the CIO/senior IT leadership), which is inclusive of various IT professionals such as application developers, infrastructure managers and project managers (Bell, 2003). The goal should be to develop a *sense of team purpose* and an understanding of the overall mission and vision of the onshore-offshore relationship.

As discussed earlier, IT managers need not turn to *offshore-outsourcing* of work to external vendors for gaining access to low cost skills. Hirschheim and Lacity (2000) believe that with the support of upper management, IT managers can take the lead in replicating a vendor's cost reduction strategies even with *insourcing*. The *offshore-insourcing* option offers lower cost advantages (primarily due to lower salary levels of offshore IT personnel) and this low cost advantage is probably biggest driver behind the offshoring trend (Apte & Mason, 1995; Carmel & Agarwal, 2002; Sobol & Apte, 1995). However, for achieving the kind of *efficiency* that established offshore vendors have attained, the IT managers should strive to integrate its own onshore and offshore units towards a common goal and purpose.

A culture of *collaboration, transparency, and accountability* among the IT professionals, coupled with clearly delineated roles and responsibilities would enhance cooperation and communication between onshore and offshore (Bell, 2003; Murphy, 2003). Personal relationships should be developed between the onshore and offshore IT professionals by encouraging regular videoconferencing and by actually visiting each other's countries to better understand the cultural and social aspects of their counterparts.

How to Focus on Processes to Coordinate Activities of Onshore and Offshore IT Professionals?

In the second step, IT managers must clearly define the *work processes* such as workflows and *scheduling*. Offshoring can lead to problems of communication, coordination, and lack of control over schedule and quality (Apte & Mason, 1995, pp. 1252-1253; Carmel & Agarwal, 2002, p. 68; Sobol & Apte, 1995, p. 271).

Protocols should be established for coordinating across time zones, efficiently using resources, reporting expenses, resolving open issues, and managing risk (Bell, 2003).

IT tasks can be designed in a *modular* fashion (by breaking down the larger tasks into smaller and relatively independent modules), which makes it easier to distribute the work globally. This also reduces transaction costs (the cost of coordinating work activities between onshore and offshore), improves synchronization, and simplifies the supervision and feedback processes (Carmel & Agarwal, 2002, p. 66).

Processes should be established to coordinate activities between IT professionals at offshore and onshore. 24x7 operations (needed for faster cycle time for software production, customer service, network management, production support, etc...) can be potentially achieved by globally distributing the work across time zones, and this would need effective *coordination processes* among the onshore and offshore IT professionals (Apte & Mason, 1995, p. 1252; Sinha & Terdiman, 2002).

The transition of IT processes *from old to new state should be managed by* creating a new onshore-offshore model of IT management, and establishing the new procedures and relationships with the cooperation of both onshore and offshore IT professionals. A variation of the *Lewin's* "unfreeze-change-refreeze" change-management model may be used:

- **Unfreeze:** Prepare for change by unfreezing processes that are affected by offshoring
- **Change:** Implement the change by introducing new procedures and processes for effective offshoring
- **Refreeze:** Strive to regain stability by practicing and documenting the new procedures and processes. Proactively improve the onshore-offshore coordination, communication, and management processes for successful offshoring

How to Invest in Training and Relationship Building to Overcome Diversity Between Onshore and Offshore IT Professionals?

In the third step, the firm should invest in an ongoing onshore-offshore training programs, where the main challenges to overcome are: *distance, issues of trust, cultural and language differences. Training sessions* should focus on *improved team collaboration, planning, interpersonal skills, negotiation skills, dispute resolution skills, work processes, and knowledge transfer*; all of which may be done through online self paced trainings, virtual classrooms (Web-casts, videoconferencing), or even traveling of onshore and offshore IT professionals to each other's locations for face-to-face training (Bell, 2003). This can help in overcoming the barriers like cultural differences, lack of trust, distance, and language (Apte & Mason, 1995; Carmel & Agarwal, 2002; Sinha & Terdiman, 2002; Sobol & Apte, 1995).

Also, the earlier section in this chapter titled *"How to manage change among onshore IT personnel?"* gave a detailed account on managing change and addressing such issues at onshore early on; and the earlier section *"how to use expatriates for offshore?"* elaborated on how expatriates may be used to bridge the onshore-offshore divide.

How to Deploy Collaborative Tools to Manage Projects Across Distance and Time-Zones?

In the fourth step, challenges of communication between onshore and offshore IT professionals, and time-zones should be continually mitigated using the best of collaboration technologies. Deployment of software applications/tools for online collaboration and synchronous meetings (audio/video), e-mail, calendar functions, scheduling, assigning tasks, time accounting, process and workflow management should be considered (Bell, 2003). Effective execution of the globally distributed work across time zones would need the latest collaboration tools and technologies, which can lead to successful 24x7 operations for faster cycle time for software production (Apte & Mason, 1995, p. 1252; Sinha & Terdiman, 2002), for continuous monitoring of critical IT functions and infrastructure, and for 24x7 customer service.

The internet and the latest communication technologies such as e-mailing, teleconferencing, videoconferencing and instant-messaging allow collaboration among globally distributed teams in spite of the geographic distances (Carmel & Agarwal, 2002, p. 66). Pauleen and Yoong (2001) suggest that some electronic communication channels are more effective than others in building relationships. At the same time, Compeau, Higgins, and Huff (1999) state that self-efficacy with respect to information technology use is a factor in our choices about what technologies to adopt, how to use them (if we have a choice), and how much to persist in the face of obstacles to successful use of such technologies. Pauleen and Yoong (2001) suggest that while *e-mail* is a basic communication channel between distant teams, it is more suitable for communicating information and coordinating projects than for building relationships. The *telephone* on the on other hand is regarded as a reliable means for building relationships. Furthermore, desktop *videoconferencing* is seen to be an affordable alternative to face-to-face meetings, which can enhance relationships by putting face to a name; however internet based videoconferencing is taking time to catch on as it requires access to greater bandwidth. Also, *Chat* programs were found to set up opportunities for informal and spontaneous communication that facilitates socialization and allow participation of activities happening "backstage" where feelings and emotions can be exchanged. This seems to be in line with the findings of Compeau et al. (1999), from the perspective of an IT professional's capacity or power to produce the desired effect (self-efficacy) of building better relationships.

How to Track Individual and Team Successes of Onshore and Offshore IT Professionals?

In the fifth and final step, using effective measures/metrics and periodic appraisals, individual and group performance should be tracked based on an established set of achievement criteria. The links between company and project goals, team behavior, onshore-offshore collaboration, and individual contributions should be continually reinforced (Bell, 2003).

Implementation: Evaluating Outcomes

While evaluating outcomes, the company should examine the open issues and develop risk mitigation strategies to continually improve its chances of success in the future (Currie & Willcocks, 1998). Some of the possible frustrating experiences are: (1) lower than expected service quality of the offshored work, (2) the communication/coordination/collaboration issues between the onshore and offshore IT professionals, and (3) hidden costs that were not estimated earlier. On the other hand there may be many positive outcomes too, like: (1) satisfaction with skills and quality of work by offshore IT professionals, (2) the significant cost savings, (3) faster time to market and 24x7 hour support from IT professionals worldwide, and (4) the possibility of new business at the emerging offshore markets.

To evaluate the outcomes, some of the key considerations are (Murphy, 2003):

- **Onshore-offshore rapport:** Do the onshore and offshore IT professionals share good rapport?

- **Allocation of roles and responsibilities:** Are the roles and responsibilities understood and agreed? Is there confidence that each party will live up to its promises and is trustworthy in its actions?

- **Measurement of employee performance:** Is there a process for measuring success achieved by offshore and onshore IT teams and professionals? Do processes exist for providing performance based feedback?

- **Measurement of work quality and financial performance:** Can satisfaction with quality and costs be accurately assessed relative to estimated expectations from offshore IT work?

- **Business process risks:** Is the business at onshore and offshore being managed right? What changes in process and governance are required to improve the success rate?

- **Technology/Infrastructure risks:** Have the right technology, infrastructure and collaborative tools been deployed?

- **Financial/Economic risks:** Are the financials as per expectation? Are we realizing the expected economic benefits of offshoring?

Once outcomes have been evaluated, the next step is documenting the best practices and risk mitigation plans. These "lessons learned" should be analyzed in depth and the resultant feedback should be used to further improve the procedures in the *decision* and *implementation* phases of offshore-insourcing.

Future Trends

Is the trend of sourcing IT work from offshore sustainable? Or is it just a fancy paradigm that is over-hyped? Karamouzis et al. (2004) of Gartner Research list the following predictions:

- Gartner estimates that less than 3% of companies' global IT services spending ($606 billion) will be on globally sourced services in 2004. By 2007, Gartner forecasts that the globally sourced component (external labor as billed to the client) of IT services spending will be about $50 billion, or about 7% of the $728 billion total. India will continue to dominate as a supplier of globally sourced services.
- By 2006, infrastructure services delivered in a global delivery model from India to U.S. companies will surpass $1 billion (0.8 probability).
- Gartner estimates that the BPO market will grow to $173 billion by 2007; of which, 14 % of labor costs will be delivered by offshore resources, with India accounting for more than half of that activity.
- By 2005, security and privacy concerns will replace human capital issues (such as job loss and displacement) as the No. 1 offshore-related backlash issue (0.7 probability).
- By 2008, labor rates for application-related services in India will rise by 40 to 60 %age points over 2004 rates (0.7 probability).

The previous predictions by Gartner Research point out that offshoring will continue to rise phenomenally, but the rise will be tempered by possible increase in labor rates, and security and privacy concerns. Iyengar and Terdiman (2003) interestingly note how strict immigration policies by certain governments can actually have the unintended of effect of encouraging offshoring:

Some countries are tightening immigration rules and policies to limit the temporary or permanent migration of overseas staff into a country. This may have the unintended consequence of causing more work to be moved offshore. This is particularly the case in countries such as the United States, where business decisions are strongly driven by the need to deliver good returns to shareholders.

Hence, the trend of offshoring would continue. Companies worldwide are realizing the benefits of offshore-insourcing, and at the same time managing various challenges that come with such bold initiatives (especially with regard to setting up the offshore facility for IT professionals, and thereafter managing the IT professionals).

Conclusion

This chapter introduced a prescriptive conceptual framework for the *offshore-insourcing* journey. The question *"Why to insource from offshore?"* was answered by discussing how a company should decide whether it needs to insource or outsource, and whether it needs to go offshore. Furthermore, the relevant challenges and issues were discussed, so that a company can make knowledgeable decisions towards making the best use of IT professionals worldwide. The question *"What to insource from offshore?"* was addressed by describing how a company can select the IT functions that it should insource from the offshore IT personnel. The question *"Where to offshore?"* was answered stage by looking at the criteria for choosing an offshore destination and by surveying some popular offshore countries.

The question *"How to insource from offshore?"* was addressed by describing the process of creating the team that will implement the decision to offshore, process of managing change at onshore, getting the offshore office ready, and the process of recruitment and induction training. We discussed the management of the IT professionals at the offshore center using the global delivery model. Finally, we stated the importance of continuously *evaluating the outcomes* of the entire offshore-insourcing process, and of using the feedback to further improve the decision making and implementation phases.

The prescriptive conceptual framework for decision making and implementation of offshore-insourcing presented in this chapter will hopefully serve as a guide to those who are curious about the journey of IT companies to new lands.

Note

The author may be contacted at schakrabarty@tamu.edu or chakrabartys @yahoo.com.

References

Ang, S., & Straub, D. W. (1998). Production and transaction economies and IS outsourcing: A study of the U.S. banking industry. *MIS Quarterly*, *22*(4), 535-552.

Apte, U. M., & Mason, R. O. (1995). Global disaggregation of information-intensive services. *Management Science*, *41*(7), 1250-1262.

Apte, U. M., Sobol, M. G., Hanaoka, S., Shimada, T., Saarinen, T., Salmela, T., & Vepsalainen, A. P. J. (1997). IS outsourcing practices in the USA, Japan, and Finland: A comparative study. *Journal of Information Technology*, *12*(4), 289-304.

Aubert, B. A., Rivard, S., & Patry, M. (1996). A transaction cost approach to outsourcing behavior: Some empirical evidence. *Information & Management*, *30*(2), 51-64.

Bell, M. A. (2003). Virtual teams tackle the global sourcing challenge. *Gartner Research Note (Publication Date: 30 September 2003, ID Number: TG-21-0414)*. Retrieved July 4, 2005, from http://www.gartner.com/

Bittinger, S. (2003). Expatriates help reduce risks in offshore outsourcing. *Gartner Research Note (Publication Date: 23 October 2003, ID Number: TU-21-2151)*. Retrieved July 4, 2005, from http://www.gartner.com/

BusinessWeek. (2004, June 21). The InfoTech 100 (pp. 63-101). Retrieved March 14, 2005, from http://www.businessweek.com/pdfs/2004/0425_it100.pdf

Carmel, E., & Agarwal, R. (2002). The maturation of offshore sourcing of information technology work. *MIS Quarterly Executive*, *1*(2), 65-78.

Cerebrus Consultants. (n.d.). *Services*. Retrieved March 14, 2005, from http://www.cerebrus-consultants.com/

Chakrabarty, S. (2006a). Making sense of the sourcing and shoring maze—The various outsourcing & offshoring alternatives. In H. S. Kehal & V. P. Singh (Eds.), *Outsourcing & offshoring in the 21st century: A socio economic perspective*. Hershey, PA: Idea Group Publishing.

Chakrabarty, S. (2006b). Real life case studies of offshore outsourced is projects: Analysis of issues and socio-economic paradigms. In H. S. Kehal & V. P. Singh (Eds.), *Outsourcing & offshoring in the 21st century: A socio economic perspective*. Hershey, PA: Idea Group Publishing.

CMIS. (2004). *Apollo chemicals offshore development center—request for proposal*. Retrieved March 14, 2005, from http://cmis.tamu.edu/web/case-web/case2004.doc, http://cmis.tamu.edu/web/case-web/caserules.asp

Cohen, D. (2005, February 19). *India special: The silicon subcontinent.* NewScientist. Retrieved February 20, 2005, from http://www.newscientist.com/special/india/

Compeau, D., Higgins, C. A., & Huff, S. (1999). Social cognitive theory and individual reactions to computing technology: A longitudinal study. *MIS Quarterly, 23*(2), 145-158.

Currie, W. L., & Willcocks, L. P. (1998). Analyzing four types of it sourcing decisions in the context of scale, client/supplier interdependency, and risk mitigation. *Information Systems Journal, 8*(2), 119-143.

Dibbern, J., Goles, T., Hirschheim, R., & Jayatilaka, B. (2004). Information systems outsourcing: A survey and analysis of the literature. *ACM SIGMIS Database, 35*(4), 6-102.

Earl, M. J. (1996). The risks of outsourcing IT. *Sloan Management Review, 37*(3), 26-32.

Hayward, B. M., Iyengar, P., Karamouzis, F., Marriott, I., Terdiman, R., Young, A., et al. (2004). The myths and realities of offshore services. *Gartner Research Note (Publication Date: 24 June 2004, ID Number: G00121546).* Retrieved July 4, 2005, from http://www.gartner.com/

Hirschheim, R. A., & Lacity, M. C. (2000). The myths and realities of information technology insourcing. *Communications of the ACM, 43*(2), 99-107.

Hotle, M., & Iyengar, P. (2003). Offshore application sourcing and the CMM. *Gartner Research Note (Publication Date: 28 January 2003 ID Number: TG-18-9789).* Retrieved July 4, 2005, from http://www.gartner.com/

Infosys. (2005a). *Global delivery model.* Retrieved January 27, 2005, from http://www.infosys.com/gdm/default.asp

Infosys. (2005b). *Service offerings.* Retrieved March 13, 2005, from http://www.infosys.com/bpo/services.asp

Infosys. (2005c). *Services listing.* Retrieved March 13, 2005, from http://www.infosys.com/services/default.asp

Iyengar, P. (2005). How to assess cities in India for your IT outsourcing needs. *Gartner Research Note (Publication Date: 11 March 2005, ID Number: G00126067).* Retrieved July 4, 2005, from http://www.gartner.com/

Iyengar, P., & Morello, D. (2004). Ease global sourcing stress with a change management program. *Gartner Research Note (Publication Date: 22 September 2004, ID Number: G00123099).* Retrieved July 4, 2005, from http://www.gartner.com/

Iyengar, P., & Terdiman, R. (2003). Decide where to do application work with global delivery. *Gartner Research Note (Publication Date: 28 January 2003, ID Number: DF-18-9786)*. Retrieved July 4, 2005, from http://www.gartner.com/

Jurison, J. (1995). The role of risk and return in information technology outsourcing decisions. *Journal of Information Technology, 10*(4), 239-247.

Karamouzis, F., & Young, A. (2004). India maintains its offshore leadership position. *Gartner Research Note (Publication Date: 30 June 2004, ID Number: G00121630)*. Retrieved July 4, 2005, from http://www.gartner.com/

Karamouzis, F., Young, A., Iyengar, P., Terdiman, R., Marriott, I., & Brown, R. H. (2004). Gartner's global offshore sourcing predictions. *Gartner Research Note (Publication Date: 28 June 2004, ID Number: COM-22-9634)*. Retrieved July 4, 2005, from http://www.gartner.com/

Kempf, T., Scholl, R. S., & Sinha, D. (2001). Cross-border collaboration: a service aggregator model for offshore IT services (Executive Summary). *Gartner Research Note (Publication Date: 5 October 2001, ID Number: ITSV-WW-EX-0037)*. Retrieved July 4, 2005, from http://www.gartner.com/

Kobyashi-Hillary, M. (2004). *Outsourcing to India: The offshore advantage*. Berlin, Germany: Springer-Verlag.

Loh, L., & Venkatraman, N. (1992). Diffusion of information technology outsourcing: Influence sources and the kodak effect. *Information Systems Research, 3*(4), 334-358.

Loh, L., & Venkatraman, N. (1995). An empirical study of information technology outsourcing: Benefits, risks, and performance implications. *Proceedings of the 16th International Conference on Information Systems* (pp. 277-288). Amsterdam, The Netherlands.

Ma Foi. (n.d.). *Staffing solutions*. Retrieved July 04, 2005, from http://www.mafoi.com/

Marriott, I., & Wiggins, D. (2002). Factors in choosing a Chinese or Indian software company. *Gartner Research Note (Publication Date: 7 June 2002, ID Number: SPA-16-6344)*. Retrieved July 4, 2005, from http://www.gartner.com/

Morello, D., & Terdiman, R. (2004). Seven rules for effective communication when going offshore. *Gartner Research Note (Publication Date: 20 July 2004 ID Number: DF-23-2873)*. Retrieved July 4, 2005, from http://www.gartner.com/

Moses Associates. (n.d.). *Solutions and services*. Retrieved July 4, 2005, from http://www.mosesassociates.com/solutions.htm

Murphy, J. (2003). Management update: Evaluating and mitigating outsourcing risk. *Gartner Research Note (Publication Date: 6 August 2003, ID Number: IGG-08062003-02)*. Retrieved July 4, 2005, from http://www.gartner.com/

Nam, K., Rajagopalan, S., Rao, H. R., & Chaudhury, A. (1996). A two-level investigation of information systems outsourcing. *Communications of the ACM, 39*(7), 36-44.

Nelson, P., Richmond, W., & Seidmann, A. (1996). Two dimensions of software acquisition. *Communications of the ACM, 39*(7), 29-35.

Pauleen, D. J., & Yoong, P. (2001). Facilitating virtual team relationships via Internet and conventional communication channels. *Internet Research: Electronic Networking Applications and Policy, 11*(3), 190-202.

Poppo, L., & Zenger, T. (1998). Testing alternative theories of the firm: transaction cost, knowledge-based, and measurement explanations for make-or-buy decisions in information services. *Strategic Management Journal, 19*(9), 853-877.

Schweyer, A. (n.d). *The case for "total workforce management" solutions*. Retrieved July 4, 2005, from http://www.peopleclick.com/knowledge/ind_schweyer1.asp

Sinha, D., & Terdiman, R. (2002). Potential risks in offshore sourcing. *Gartner Research Note (Publication Date: 5 September 2002, ID Number: ITSV-WW-DP-0360)*. Retrieved July 4, 2005, from http://www.gartner.com/

Sobol, M. G., & Apte, U. M. (1995). Domestic and global outsourcing practices of America's most effective IS users. *Journal of Information Technology, 10*(4), 269-280.

Tata Consultancy Services. (n.d.). *Flexible global delivery*. Retrieved March 14, 2005, from http://www.tcs.com/investors/BusinessOverview/FlexibleGlobalDelivery.aspx

Wiggins, D., Datar, R., & Liu, L. (2002a). Comparison: Indian and Chinese software services markets. *Gartner Research Note (Publication Date: 31 May 2002, ID Number: M-16-1762)*. Retrieved July 4, 2005, from http://www.gartner.com/

Wiggins, D., Datar, R., Leskela, L., & Kumar, P. (2002b). Trends for the Indian and Chinese software industries. *Gartner Research Note (Publication Date: 7 June 2002, ID Number: SPA-16-6118)*. Retrieved July 4, 2005, from http://www.gartner.com/

Willcocks, L., & Lacity, M. (1998). *Strategic sourcing of information systems*. Chichester, UK: Wiley.

Endnotes

1   Acknowledgements to Ms. Swetha Rao, and Mr. Vidyaranya M. Devigere (both have graduated from Mays Business School, Texas A&M University, USA, and both have previous work experience in the Indian software services industry) for their valuable suggestions on "how" offshore-insourcing can possibly be carried out.

2   A survey of Web sites of the world's 15 biggest IT companies for their presence in China and India was done by the author and Ms. Jun Wang. Acknowledgements to Ms. Jun Wang, a Chinese graduate student at Mays Business School, Texas A&M University, USA, with previous work experience in the Chinese software industry, for compiling information related to China.

Appendix I:
Surveying the Offshore-Insourcing
in China and India

Let us compare the two big offshore insourcing players, namely China and India (Cohen, 2005; Karamouzis & Young, 2004; Kempf et al., 2001; Wiggins et al., 2002a; Wiggins et al., 2002b). Some of the relevant comparative statistics between India and China are presented in Table 4 (Wiggins et al., 2002a). India seems to have a clear advantage in terms of its software exports and number of IT professionals, while China seems to have an advantage in terms of Internet Bandwidth, number of software companies and marginally lower costs of IT professionals.

Let us consider the case of India in more detail. It is sometimes difficult to speak about information systems "offshoring" without using the word "India." Debates on offshoring often target India, earning it both ire and admiration. Karamouzis and Young (2004) state that India continues to hold the undisputed leadership position as an offshore destination for IT firms in developed countries such as US and Western Europe. They attribute India's competitiveness to abundance of resources, significant cost of labor differential, proven execution capacity, and also its English speaking capabilities, and predict the following:

Table 4. India's and China's IT statistics (Compiled from Wiggins et al., 2002a) (Source: Gartner Research/Gartner Dataquest)

Attribute	India	China
Total Exports	$ 43.75 billion (+5.77%)	$ 265.1 billion (+6.8%)
Software Exports	$ 6.2 billion (+37.78%)	$ 0.85 billion (+112.5%)
Software as a % of Total exports	14.17%	0.37%
IT professional graduating each year	73,218	50, 000
Current IT Professionals	522,000	150,000
Demand for IT Professionals	400,000	350,000
Number of software companies	3000+	6000+
Internet Bandwidth	1.4 Gbps	7.6 Gbps
Hourly rate for Developer (2 years experience)	$24	$12 - $25
Hourly rate for Project Manager	$30 ($50 for top end)	$50
Annual Salary for Entry Level Developer	$2,555 - $4,913	$2,423 - $4,846
Annual Salary for Developer (2 years experience)	$4,913 - $9,212	$4,486 - $6,057
Annual Salary for Project Manager	$9,580 - $26,529	$6,057 - $28,992
Legend: All numbers are for 2001, unless specified. Percentage increase/decrease figures are for a one year period.		

Figure 6. World's 15 biggest info tech companies (Presence in Chinese and Indian cities)

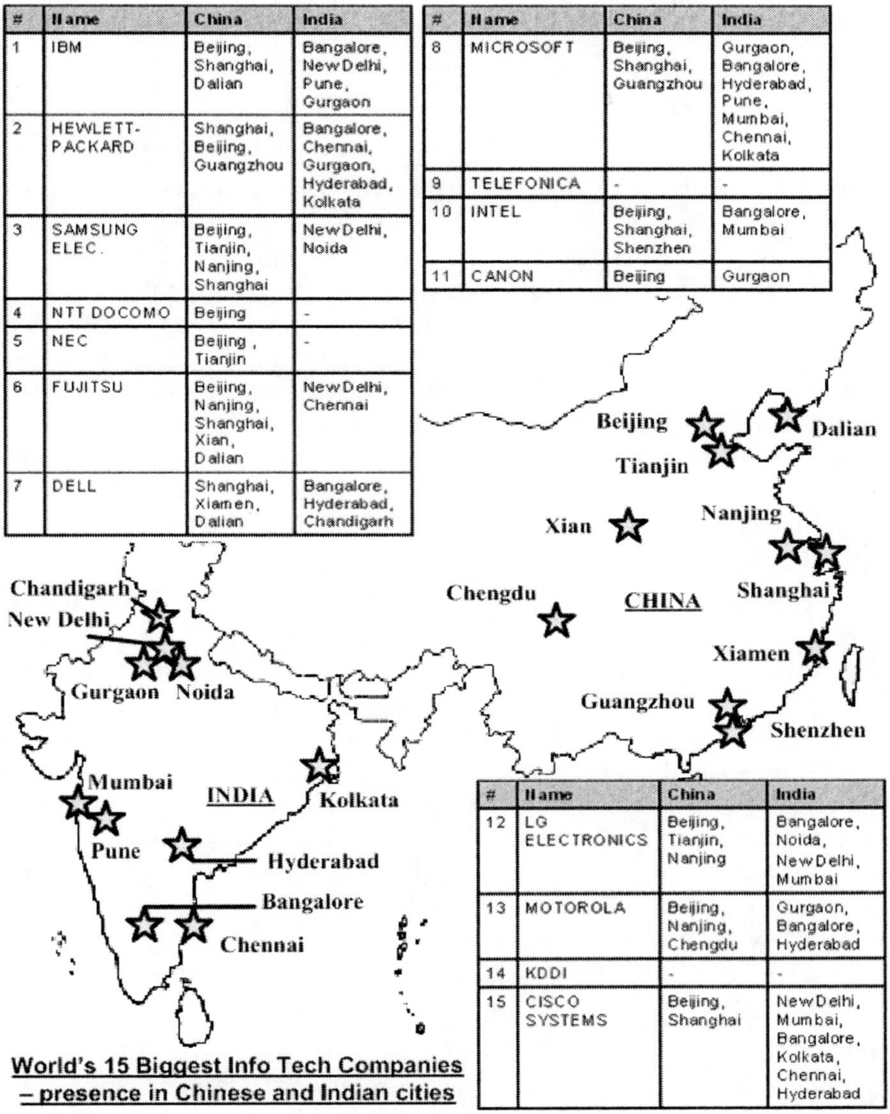

#	Name	China	India
1	IBM	Beijing, Shanghai, Dalian	Bangalore, New Delhi, Pune, Gurgaon
2	HEWLETT-PACKARD	Shanghai, Beijing, Guangzhou	Bangalore, Chennai, Gurgaon, Hyderabad, Kolkata
3	SAMSUNG ELEC.	Beijing, Tianjin, Nanjing, Shanghai	New Delhi, Noida
4	NTT DOCOMO	Beijing	-
5	NEC	Beijing, Tianjin	-
6	FUJITSU	Beijing, Nanjing, Shanghai, Xian, Dalian	New Delhi, Chennai
7	DELL	Shanghai, Xiamen, Dalian	Bangalore, Hyderabad, Chandigarh

#	Name	China	India
8	MICROSOFT	Beijing, Shanghai, Guangzhou	Gurgaon, Bangalore, Hyderabad, Pune, Mumbai, Chennai, Kolkata
9	TELEFONICA	-	-
10	INTEL	Beijing, Shanghai, Shenzhen	Bangalore, Mumbai
11	CANON	Beijing	Gurgaon

#	Name	China	India
12	LG ELECTRONICS	Beijing, Tianjin, Nanjing	Bangalore, Noida, New Delhi, Mumbai
13	MOTOROLA	Beijing, Nanjing, Chengdu	Gurgaon, Bangalore, Hyderabad
14	KDDI	-	-
15	CISCO SYSTEMS	Beijing, Shanghai	New Delhi, Mumbai, Bangalore, Kolkata, Chennai, Hyderabad

World's 15 Biggest Info Tech Companies – presence in Chinese and Indian cities

Through 2008, India will remain the dominant offshore service provider, with no other nation achieving a double-digit share of the global offshore service revenue (0.8 probability).

By 2008, Indian labor rates for application-related services will rise by 40% to 60% beyond 2004 rates (0.7 probability).

India graduates a total of 300,000 to 400,000 engineering and computer/IT majors every year (of which graduating IT majors are more than 73,000 per year, however, many of remaining non-IT majors are already skilled or re-skill themselves on IT); at the same time, hiring and managing growth is challenging in India since it is witnessing unprecedented growth in demand for skilled human resources and the largest India based vendors plan to hire several hundred to thousand employees each month (Karamouzis & Young, 2004; Wiggins et al., 2002a). Furthermore, though there is ample supply of fresh graduates, "middle managers" are currently scarce in India, and the eagerness of expatriates of non-Indian decent to assume these scarce "middle manager" positions are low, thereby increasing effort is focused on tapping Indian repatriates from U.S. or Western Europe, or to build on local talent.

Choosing a nation for offshoring is not an end in itself. Cities within nations have their own advantages and disadvantages. Choosing the right city to match your needs is crucial. To find out the extent to which top IT companies have offshore offices in Chinese and Indian cities, we[2] first short listed the Top 15 Information Technology companies from BusinessWeek's list of 'The InfoTech 100' based on Sales Revenues (BusinessWeek, 2004). We then decided to find out the cities in China and India in which these companies have set up offices by searching their respective Web sites. Attempt has been made to provide only the locations where information systems related work (R&D, software development, support, etc.) is probably performed, and explicit sales offices were omitted. See Figure 6 for each of the top 15 companies' names, country of origin, rank, sales revenues, Chinese cities, Indian cities, and the Web site address.

Most of the top 15 companies have set up offshore bases in China and India, the only exceptions being the Spanish Telefonica and the Japanese KDDI. While searching the Web sites it was found that most of these companies carry out high end R&D activities in China and India, which is contrary to the popular perception that these companies move offshore only for the low-cost advantage. A premier science and technology magazine "*NewScientist*" recently had a cover story titled "India: The next knowledge superpower," and one article named "India special: The silicon subcontinent" (Cohen, 2005) stated:

Some of the biggest names in IT are heading towards Bangalore once more, and this time round it's not cheap labour they are looking for. They are hunting down the brightest, most inventive minds in India to populate a swathe of cutting-edge research facilities. The work being done in these labs rivals any in the U.S. and Europe.

The article lists companies like Microsoft, General Electric, Hewlett-Packard, Texas Instruments, Google, and IBM that have set up *research labs* in India to take advantage of its skilled professionals. This realization of the value of offshore-insourcing is not just for the cities like Bangalore, but this optimism isseen across many emerging offshore-insourcing destinations across the world.

Appendix II:
Surveying for IT Skills
in Offshore Destinations

As an example, we have listed the services offered and the industries targeted by a large India based software services provider named Infosys (http://www.infosys.com) in Table 5 (Infosys, 2005b, 2005c). Such a survey might help a company to decide about the skill set availability of the IT professionals in the respective offshore destination, and hence aid in addressing the decision question "where to offshore?"

Table 5. Services offered and industries targeted by Infosys Technologies Ltd.

Services offered by Infosys (http://www.infosys.com)	Industries targeted
Application and Infrastructure Services: Custom Application Development, Application Maintenance, Application Re-engineering, Infrastructure Management, Independent Testing and Validation, Application Portfolio Management ***Enterprise Services*** (1) ***Packaged Applications:*** Supply Chain Management (SCM), Customer Relationship Management (CRM), Enterprise Application Integration (EAI), Enterprise Resource Planning (ERP) (2) Business Intelligence and Data Warehousing (3) *Systems Integration:* Strategic Technology and Architecture Consulting, Enterprise Content Management, Identity Management, Migration and Deployment, Enterprise Information Portal, Enterprise Mobility (4) Business Continuity (5) Platform Services ***Product R&D Services:*** Product Design & Development, Product Sustenance, Testing & Automation, Offshore Product Development Center, Additional Product Services, Product Consulting & Professional Services ***Consulting Services:*** Corporate Performance Management, Balanced Scorecard ***Business Process Outsourcing*** (1) ***Banking:*** Credit cards, retail lending, mortgage processing, retail banking and account management, cash management, trade services, lease and loan processing, investment banking, (2) *Securities Industry:* Custodians and Fund Administrators, Investment Managers, Investment Banking and Brokerage firms, Market Data and Analytics providers, (3) *Insurance:* Life, non-life, intermediaries, re-insurers, (4) *Finance & Accounting:* Accounts payable, accounts receivable, GL and fixed asset accounting, reporting and regulatory filings, (5) *Telecom:* Operators, OEMs and value service providers	▪ Aerospace and Defense ▪ Automotive ▪ Banking and Capital Markets ▪ Communication Services ▪ Discrete Manufacturing ▪ Energy ▪ Healthcare ▪ High Technology ▪ Insurance ▪ Life Sciences ▪ Media and Entertainment ▪ Resources ▪ Retail & Consumer Packaged Goods ▪ Transportation ▪ Services ▪ Utilities

About the Authors

Pak Yoong is an associate professor of information systems/e-commerce at Victoria University of Wellington, New Zealand. Yoong teaches in the areas of virtual organisation, research methods and IS leadership. Yoong's research, teaching, and consulting experience is in the facilitation of virtual meetings, online communities of practice, online knowledge sharing, mobile collaborations, and human resource development in information technology environments.

Sid Huff is a professor of information systems and the head of the School of Information Management at Victoria University of Wellington, New Zealand. His research addresses electronic commerce, IS strategy, IT governance, and senior management roles in IS. He has published extensively in the leading information systems journals; he has also written more than 50 teaching cases, and is the lead author of *Cases in Electronic Commerce* (Irwin/McGraw-Hill).

* * *

Mustafa Ally (allym@usq.edu.au) is a lecturer in information systems at the University of Southern Queensland (Australia) where he is currently teaching Java and Visual Basic .NET. His research interests are in the field of internet payment systems and he has written several papers in the area of trust and security. Ally has been experimenting with pair programming in the classroom and adapting and extending its particular benefits to enhance his students' learning abilities.

Darrell Bennetts is a PhD candidate enrolled with La Trobe University, Melbourne and works part-time at The Open Polytechnic of New Zealand. His research field is in the history of ideas, which straddles sociology, history, and philosophy, and is focussed upon the circulation of ideas and personnel within colonial policy networks. This is an interest in (19th to mid 20th century) globalisation, before (late 20th century) globalization. In addition to his PhD research, he also has great pleasure teaching social science research methodology and cultural studies for The Open Polytechnic of New Zealand, and contemporary issues in sociology for La Trobe University.

Eugene Cash is an Australian born, New Zealand-educated business consulting professional. Earning his Master of Commerce in information systems from Victoria University of Wellington, he has gone on to work for a variety of private and public organisations: Accenture, Fonterra, The Ministry of Social Development and more recently The New Zealand Food Safety Authority. With a keen interest in the use of technology to "locate" and facilitate collaborative networks, Cash has spent the majority of his career involved in business process redesign, large scale system development and knowledge management projects.

Subrata Chakrabarty has been pursuing his PhD at Mays Business School, Texas A&M University (USA) since 2004. His research and consulting interests include global sourcing of information systems (IS), quality assurance & control, global project management, business processes in the IS industry, and strategic and organizational issues related to offshoring and outsourcing. Before pursuing his PhD, he had more than two years of work experience in the software services industry with Infosys Technologies (India), where he worked with large clients based in the U.S. and UK. He completed his undergraduate degree in India, and received the first rank in his college and was a top rank holder in the university. He is a certified software quality analyst (CSQA) indicating a professional level of competence in the principles and practices of quality assurance in the IT profession. He is willing to take up research and consulting assignments in areas related to his interest. His hobbies include swimming, painting, and cartooning.

Barbara Crump teaches in the Department of Information Systems, Massey University, Wellington, New Zealand. She has long had an interest in reasons for the low participation of women in tertiary computing programmes and their involvement in the IT industry. Her research has included a New Zealand national study of women in the IT workforce and this developed into a cross-national one when she was appointed visiting scholar at the University of Malaya, Kuala Lumpur in 2004. Another area of research interest is the digital divide. Barbara has been involved in evaluating community computing initiatives involving a partnership model.

Fiona Darroch (darroch@usq.edu.au) is a lecturer in information systems at the University of Southern Queensland, Australia. Her computing career has been spent mainly in industry in the areas of project management, business analysis and applications development; with a move to academia three years ago. She is currently undertaking research projects as PhD preparation. Particular areas of research interest include: the academic-practitioner relationship divide and research relevance; extreme project management; agile system development methodologies; analysis and design methods, and online learning environments. Teaching responsibilities include systems analysis and design, project management and database design.

Tony Hooper is director of professional programmes in the School of Information Management of Victoria University of Wellington (New Zealand), administering both the master of information management and the master of library and information studies programmes. He teaches electronic commerce and information systems. His work on student skills development has been based on comparative work done at several universities and at both undergraduate and graduate level.

Xiaorui Hu (hux2@slu.edu) is an assistant professor of management information systems at the John Cook School of Business, Saint Louis University (USA). She received her PhD from the University of Texas at Austin. Her research focuses on trust related issues in electronic markets, risk management, and global aspects of electronic commerce.

Haiyan Huang is a doctoral candidate and research assistant at the School of Information Sciences and Technology (IST) in the Center for the Information Society at The Pennsylvania State University (USA). Her primary research interests include global software and information systems development, global virtual team, cross-cultural management, knowledge management. Other research interests include HCI design, computer supported cooperative work, socio-culture, socio-cognitive, and socio-technical issues in distributed collaborative work and learning.

Eugene Kaluzniacky is an instructor in the Department of Applied Computer Science and Administrative Studies at the University of Winnipeg, Canada. Kaluzniaky has a varied academic and professional background that comprises mathematics, statistics, computer science, management science, accounting, information systems, personality psychology, holistic health, spiritual development, and education. He has carried out research and consulting on applying the Myers-Briggs personality type in IT organizations, on stress in the IT profession, and on IT education. He has also developed a workshop on personal wellness for the IS professional. He is interested in stress management and personal growth in the IT field and has lectured internationally on this topic.

Rajkumar Kempaiah is completing his PhD in information management at Stevens Institute of Technology, Hoboken New Jersey. He teaches systems analysis and design and management information system courses at Stevens Institute of Technology. His current research is in IT business alignment maturity.

Keri A. Logan is a lecturer in the Department of Information Systems, Massey University, Wellington, New Zealand. Her interest in women and information technology arose from the lack of female students enrolling in tertiary IT courses. As a result, she has investigated the perceptions of secondary school students regarding their computing learning environment, as well as those of women in the IT workforce and community computing. One particular focus has been on the distinct male computing culture which is said to exist and which is considered to be a contributing factor to the low participation of females in computing.

Jerry Luftman is the associate dean of graduate information systems programs, and distinguished professor of information systems, at Stevens Institute of Technology, Hoboken, New Jersey (USA). His career includes strategic positions in management (information technology, including being a CIO, and consultant), management consulting, information systems, and executive education. After a notable 22 year career with IBM, and over 10 years at Stevens, Dr. Luftman's experience combines the strengths of practitioner, consultant, and academic. His framework for assessing IT-business alignment maturity is considered key in helping companies around the world understand, define, and scope an appropriate strategic planning direction that leverages IT. Dr. Luftman is the founder and leader of Stevens graduate IS programs. He created and teaches a popular end-of-master's course on managing the IT resource, which explores how to be a successful IT executive. Dr. Luftman's new book *Competing in the Information Age: Align in the Sand* (Oxford University), is expected to surpass the initial bestseller *Competing in the Information Age* which is still selling strong around the globe. His active membership in SIM includes being the VP of chapter relations for the SIM executive board. His advice is frequently requested as an executive mentor.

Fred Niederman serves as the Shaughnessy endowed professor of MIS at Saint Louis University (USA). His primary research areas pertain to global IT; IT personnel; and using IT to support teams and groups. Most recently he has been investigating the role of UML in development project success and management of ecommerce projects. He has published 30 refereed journal articles including *MIS Quarterly*, *Communications of the ACM*, and *Decision Sciences*; has presented at several major conference; and serves as associate editor of the *Journal of Global Information Systems*.

Ani Patke graduated from Victoria University of Wellington (New Zealand) in 2004 with a BCA (Hons) in information systems. After graduation he joined Cap Gemini NZ as a graduate level consultant where he was involved in a large-scale .net project as a junior developer. He is currently employed at Hewlett Packard Business Consulting as a technology services consultant. His interests include the human aspects of IT, in particular how the skill set of IT workers evolve over their careers.

Jeria L. Quesenberry is a doctoral candidate and research assistant at the School of Information Sciences and Technology (IST) in the center for the information society at the The Pennsylvania State University (USA). Her research interests include the study of social and organizational aspects of information technology (IT), with a particular focus on the role of gender and under represented groups in the IT workforce. From 1999 to 2002, she served as a consultant at Accenture, specializing in the implementation of enterprise resource planning (ERP) packages. In 1999, she earned a BS in decision sciences and management information systems from George Mason University.

Helen Richardson is a lecturer at The Open Polytechnic of New Zealand, School of Information and Social Sciences. Her work involves teaching adult students many whom are IT practitioners. She also belongs to an IT family and this has cumulated in her interest in addressing the social and psychological issues that the IT industry affords its workers. She has also worked for Massey University teaching ICT management through a critical lens using sociology and communication theory. Her research interests span from, knowledge management, reengineering, to the management of ICT in creative environments. She also has a strong interest in research methodology, in the qualitative, critical and post modern domains.

Bernd Carsten Stahl is a senior lecturer in the Faculty of Computing Sciences and Engineering and a research associate at the Centre for Computing and Social Responsibility of De Montfort University, Leicester, UK. His interests cover philosophical issues arising from the intersections of business, technology, and information. This includes the ethics of computing and critical approaches to information systems. He is editor-in-chief of the *International Journal of Technology and Human Interaction.*

Mark Toleman (markt@usq.edu.au) is an associate professor of information systems at the University of Southern Queensland (Australia) where he has supervised postgraduate students and taught undergraduate and postgraduate computing subjects to engineers, scientists, and business students for nearly 20 years. He has a PhD in computer science from the University of Queensland and has published over 85 peer-reviewed articles in books, journals, and conference proceedings. He is also deputy chair of the University of Southern Queensland's Academic Board and is a member of the Association for Information Systems, the Computer-Human Interaction Special Interest of the Human Factors and Ergonomics Society of Australia and the International Federation for Information Processing Working Group 13.1.

Eileen M. Trauth is a professor of information sciences and technology and director of the Center for the Information Society at The Pennsylvania State University (USA). Her research is concerned with societal, cultural, and organizational influences on information technology, information technology work and the information technology workforce. Her investigation of socio-cultural influences on the emergence of Ireland's information economy is published in her book, *The Culture of an Information Economy: Influences and Impacts in the Republic of Ireland.* She is currently engaged in a multi-country study of women in the information technology workforce in Australia, New Zealand, Ireland, and the U.S. Dr. Trauth has published nine books and over 100 research papers on her work. She is associate editor of *Information and Organization* and serves on the editorial boards of several international journals. Dr. Trauth received her PhD in information science from the University of Pittsburgh.

Chris Wood is a senior lecturer in the faculty of computing sciences and engineering at De Montfort University, Leicester, UK. His teaching and research interests are focused around the themes of computer related ethics, professionalism, and social responsibility that are represented within the university's internationally acclaimed Centre for Computing and Social Responsibility.

Index